No Ordinary Crown

by the same author

Salute to Greece
Starvation in Greece
The Royal House of Greece
(illustrated monograph)

No Ordinary Crown

A Biography of
King Paul of the Hellenes

Stelio Hourmouzios

Weidenfeld and Nicolson
5 Winsley Street London W1

ISBN 0 297 99408 5

Printed in Great Britain by
Ebenezer Baylis and Son Limited
The Trinity Press, Worcester, and London

To
Constantine II
King of the Hellenes
worthy son of a worthy father
this book
is respectfully dedicated

Contents

List of Illustrations

List of Illustrations

Acknowledgements

I owe a debt of gratitude to a number of people who have helped me with this book. Perhaps it would be invidious to mention each of them by name, but I welcome this opportunity of expressing my sincere thanks to them all, from the humblest to the most exalted.

My special thanks are due to Dawn Cox, who did a vast amount of typing for me.

The letter from Sir Winston Churchill to Queen Frederica on page 267 is reproduced by kind permission of the Controller of Her Majesty's Stationery Office as Custodian of Crown Copyright.

Stelio Hourmouzios
London, July 1971

Preface

When the future historian looks back with the dispassionate eye of
retrospective judgement, it may well be found that the immediate
post-war period marked the most critical time in European history
since the fall of Constantinople. Had Greece succumbed to the
Communist onslaught in 1944 and 1946–9, the Iron Curtain would
now be stretched in an unbroken line from the Baltic to the
Mediterranean, and the world would not be as we know it today.

Greece was able to withstand this aggression thanks to the courage
and determination of her people, reinforced in no small measure by
the fact that during these crucial years the throne was occupied by
King Paul. This was no warrior king like his father but a gentle
giant of a man whose understanding and compassion helped many
who had strayed from the path of patriotism to return to the national
fold.

Unprepared for kingship – he was the youngest of three sons – he
came to the throne at a time when Greece was in the throes of civil
strife. He lived to see his people reunited, and died content.

'I have glorified Thy name on earth; I have finished the work
which Thou gavest me to do' is written on his tomb among the trees
at Tatoi. This book seeks to show how this was accomplished.

Kings of the Hellenes

Part One

❈

1821-1936

❯ I ❮

In 1821, after nearly four centuries of subjugation, the Greek people rose against their Ottoman oppressors. On 25 March of that year at the Monastery of Agia Lavra near the village of Kalavryta in the Peloponnese, the Metropolitan of Patras raised the Standard of revolt – a banner representing the Dormition of the Virgin – and called upon all Greeks to take up arms for the liberation of their country. In savage reprisal the Sultan had the Supreme Head of the Greek Orthodox Church, the Oecumenical Patriarch Gregory V, dragged from the altar of the Cathedral of Agia Sophia in Constantinople where he was celebrating Mass on Easter Day and hanged him in his pontifical robes from the porch of the patriarchal palace, the jewel-encrusted Crown of St Andrew still on his head.*

Thus began the Greek War of Independence in which more than half the Greek nation died before the other half finally succeeded in achieving freedom.

There had been considerable preparation for this war. In their desire to have some sort of administrative authority with which they could negotiate, and with the arrogant indifference which characterized the attitude of the Moslem conquerors towards those of their subject races that were not of the True Faith, the Turks had left the Greek Orthodox Church and its local institutions virtually intact: in the eyes of the Sublime Porte, the Oecumenical Patriarch in Constantinople was not only the spiritual head of all the Christians within the Ottoman Empire but also the obvious and most convenient civic representative of the Greek nation. And if the Church proved helpful to the slothful Turkish rulers in providing them with a ready-made and fairly competent civil service, it was

* Gregory V was canonized on the centenary of his death in 1921.

3

also able through its undiminished authority and the privileged status still accorded to it to keep alive in the enslaved Greek people the Hellenic spirit and the sense of national identity which rightfully belonged to them as heirs of Byzantium and ancient Athens.

With their cultural heritage, their keen intellect and their skill in negotiation, the Greeks had been able even during the most oppressive years of Turkish rule to occupy posts of high civil responsibility in the administration. Key positions in the machinery of State were in Greek hands; the highest offices in the Ottoman Empire, even that of Chief Dragoman or Foreign Minister, became virtually a Greek preserve. The Hospodars and Voivodes of the Danubian principalities of Moldavia and Wallachia – present-day Rumania – were invariably drawn from among the Greek patrician families collectively known as the Phanariotes* – the Ypsilanti and the Mavrogordato and the Soutso, who may have governed these provinces nominally as vassals of the Sultan but who nevertheless enjoyed the status and the privileges of princes, and who chose most of their assistants and subordinates from among their own people.

In the diplomatic field also preparation had not been lacking. In 1814 four Greek merchants in Odessa, where a flourishing Greek trading community had been established for many years, founded the 'Philiki Etaireia' or Society of Friends, an organization which under this innocuous title controlled an underground network of agents throughout the world with high-level contacts in the Chancelleries of Europe.

Turkey's neutrality during the Napoleonic Wars had enabled the ubiquitous Greek merchants to develop a thriving business in the carrying trade. They built themselves splendid houses with fine furniture from abroad – houses that can be seen in Hydra and Spetsai and Andros to this day – but most of their wealth went on fitting out and arming their fast merchantmen, ostensibly as protection against the Levantine pirates that infested the Mediterranean but actually in anticipation of the day when these ships would be converted overnight into men-of-war manned by crews already expert in handling them. It was this fleet, and the

* From the quarter in Constantinople called the 'Phanar' or Lantern where most of them had their residences and where the Oecumenical Patriarchate itself was, and still is, situated.

4

bold and skilful use of improvised fireships, that gave the Greeks superiority over the cumbersome Turkish warships.*

The War of Independence was long and bloody, and was marked by deeds of heroism that have become the folklore of the country, and by quarrels and dissensions over which the Greeks prefer to draw a veil.†

Britain, France and Russia – all Powers with vital interests in the Mediterranean and South-Eastern Europe – manifested their sympathy for the struggling Greeks from the very beginning and eventually intervened physically in their support. On 20 October 1827 an Allied fleet under Admiral Sir Edward Codrington fought and completely destroyed the combined Turkish and Egyptian fleets in the Bay of Navarino, on the west coast of the Peloponnese. Shortly afterwards Greece was recognized as an independent State comprising the Peloponnese, the Cyclades Islands and continental Greece north of the Gulf of Corinth up to a line drawn from the Gulf of Arta in the west to the Gulf of Volos in the east. It was a frontier that did not include Thessaly and Macedonia and the Epirus, Crete, the Ionian Islands and other Greek-inhabited areas, and left the majority of the Greek nation still under Turkish rule.

It had always been the understanding among the Three Protecting Powers that the newly-created State of Greece should be established in the conventional form of a monarchy, and on this point the London Protocol of 3 February 1830 stipulated a 'hereditary Sovereign Prince of Greece' to be chosen from outside their own ruling Houses. The monarchical system of government, constitutional or absolute, was at that time almost universal. The post-Napoleonic settlement, dominated as it was by staunch traditionalists like Metternich and Talleyrand and Castlereagh, had further consolidated the institution of monarchy. As for the Greeks, their innate sense of equality and the rivalries among the leading families, which the War of Independence had if anything intensified,

---

* It also laid the foundations of the present-day phenomenon of a small country of less than ten million people controlling the largest merchant fleet in the world.

† The outstanding military figure of the War of Independence was undoubtedly Theodore Kolokotronis, the doughty Peloponnesian warrior immortalized in Greek legend as 'The Old Man of the Morea'. It says much for the reverence in which the modern Greeks hold their heroes that his name, which literally translated means 'God's-Gift Bullet-in-the-arse', should be spoken by all and sundry to this day without even the suspicion of a snigger. His last direct descendant, General Vladimir Kolokotronis, died on 12 May 1970 when this historic Greek family became extinct.

rendered the idea of one of themselves becoming head of State quite inconceivable: no Greek was ever going to accept another Greek as his sovereign. In any case the 'Philiki Etaireia' had always been in favour of a non-Greek monarch 'so that all division and rivalry for preference should cease among us'. Already, while the war was still going on, the names of several European princes had been canvassed and rejected on grounds of religion, personal unsuitability or dynastic ties with the Protecting Powers. In April 1827 the Third Greek National Assembly, meeting at the ancient site of Troezen, elected Count John Capodistrias to the office of President or Governor of an embattled and still-unrecognized Greece. Although Capodistrias's appointment was for a nominal term of seven years, it was generally regarded as a stop-gap arrangement until such time as a suitable prince could be found to occupy the throne of the Kingdom to be established.

Capodistrias, a nobleman from the island of Corfu, had entered the Russian diplomatic service in 1809 and had played a prominent part at the Congress of Vienna. His obvious talents soon attracted the attention of Czar Alexander I, who eventually appointed him joint Foreign Minister with Nesselrode. The outbreak of the Greek revolt, however, made it an embarrassment for the Czar to have among his principal officers of State someone who was clearly involved with the rebels, so Capodistrias was given 'indefinite leave of absence' and took up residence in Geneva, where he devoted his energies to mustering international support for the Greek cause. He arrived in Greece to take up his appointment a good nine months after his nomination, having first undertaken a goodwill tour of the capitals of Europe, including Russia, where the new Czar Nicholas I gave him his blessing.

Capodistrias's long service in the Russian Court, together with his own aristocratic background and upbringing, had made him something of an autocrat himself. His diplomatic experience and the high office he had held in the service of the Czar of All the Russias had left him with a haughty manner and an air of frigid superiority which he did not trouble to conceal – 'he seems to be working for a world composed of beings as perfect as himself,' Nesselrode said of him in another context – and which created a steadily growing gap between himself and his less sophisticated countrymen. His aloofness and his predilection for foreign mannerisms – when abroad he preferred the Italianate rendering of his name, Capo d'Istria, and in Greece he usually wore Russian Court dress on formal occasions – further alienated him from his compatriots. A rebuff to Petrobey, head of the Mavromichales clan, earned him the enmity of the proud family that had lorded it for centuries over the mountain fastnesses of the Mani in the Southern Peloponnese with a hereditary authority that even the Sultans had found it prudent not to challenge.

The end was predictable: on Sunday, 27 September 1831, while walking to the Church of St Spyridon (the patron saint of his native Corfu) in Nauplia at 6 o'clock in the morning as was his regular habit, Capodistrias was ambushed and shot dead by Constantine and George Mavromichales, who thus wiped out the insult to their kinsman and chief in the time-honoured tradition of the Maniote family feud.*

With the death of Capodistrias, the question of finding a permanent solution to the question of the regime assumed greater urgency. Early in 1830, while Capodistrias was still Governor, the Protecting Powers had sounded Prince Leopold, the forty-year-old son of the Duke of Saxe-Coburg. He had formally accepted the crown but when the territorial limits of the Greek kingdom as envisaged at the time by the Protecting Powers became known, Capodistrias had no difficulty in convincing Leopold that such a State was not viable, and in May of that year Leopold abdicated the throne he had never actually occupied.

In May 1832 the throne was offered to Prince Otto, second son of King Ludwig of Bavaria, who accepted it. This time Turkey was persuaded to agree to a more generous delineation of Greece's northern frontier, and the Protecting Powers also arranged for a substantial international loan to Greece – which was just as well, since the Treasury was found to contain the equivalent of £4·78. The new agreement with Turkey provided for the evacuation of certain districts still occupied by Turkish troops, including the Athens area, so that although Otto actually landed at the provisional capital of Nauplia in the Peloponnese when he disembarked from a British frigate on 6 February 1833, the seat of government was transferred to Athens itself on 1 December 1834.

* Constantine Mavromichales was killed on the spot by Capodistrias's one-armed bodyguard; Petrobey's son George was arrested, sentenced to death by court-martial and executed by firing squad a few days later.

Otto inaugurated his reign by Hellenizing his name to Otho and by adopting Greek national dress. A good-looking, earnest and well-meaning young man, he was not quite eighteen when he set foot on Greek soil and was accompanied by a Council of Regency consisting of three of his own countrymen. When he came of age he promptly assumed the reins of government himself, taking his duties so much to heart that he insisted on presiding at all Cabinet meetings in person, with the inevitable result that criticism which would normally have been directed at his ministers was levelled at him instead. Despite Palmerston's strong hints, he turned a deaf ear to insistent demands for a constitution and a more representative form of government, until a bloodless revolution on 3 September 1843 obliged him to dismiss his Bavarian advisers, appoint a new Ministry composed entirely of Greeks, and summon a National Assembly to draft a constitution – the first that Greece had ever had.

The respite was only temporary. Party factions, financial difficulties, disaffection in the army and national discontent over the country's frontiers again brought matters to a head. Another revolution deposed Otho, who quit Greece with his childless Queen Amalia on 12 October 1862 on board a British warship and returned to his native Bavaria, where he died from measles five years later at the age of fifty-two. At his own request he was buried wearing Greek national dress complete with fustanella.*

With the throne vacant, the problem of finding another Head of State assumed an acute form. A referendum to nominate a new king gave 230,016 votes to Queen Victoria's second son, Prince Alfred, Duke of Edinburgh, as against 2,400 votes for the Russian-sponsored Duke of Leuchtenburg and just 93 votes in favour of a Republic. Victoria withheld her consent, however, on the grounds that the Protocol of 1830 between the Three Protecting Powers specifically excluded members of their own ruling houses, and also because Prince Alfred was at that time only second in line of succession to the throne of England as well as being heir to the

---

* Queen Amalia had asked King Ludwig II of Bavaria if in the fullness of time she might be buried alongside her husband in the Theatinerkirche in Munich but the King, who disliked her, had refused with the excuse that the tomb was too small – a rather ungallant aspersion on the physique of the widowed Queen, who had become somewhat corpulent in her later years. The King's reply so shocked Amalia that she suffered a heart attack and died shortly afterwards in 1875.

Duchy of Saxe-Coburg, to which in fact he succeeded some years later.

After many soundings in various directions a suitable candidate acceptable to all parties was eventually found in the person of Prince William, second son of Prince Christian of Schleswig-Holstein-Sonderburg-Glücksburg.

The young prince, who like Otho was seventeen when he arrived in Greece, was the founder of the present Greek dynasty. King Paul was his grandson. And Queen Frederica is his sister's granddaughter.

⇒ 2 ⇐

At the time of Prince William's birth on 24 December 1845, his father Prince Christian was not even heir to the Danish throne. Christian's wife Louise of Hesse-Cassel was the nearest heir-presumptive to the childless King Frederick VII, but she ceded her rights to her husband – also in line but more remotely – who in 1852 was formally recognized as heir to the throne of Denmark, to which he duly succeeded as King Christian IX in 1863, five months after his son had become King of Greece.

He was to be known during his lifetime as the 'Father of Europe', and with good reason. He had six children: three sons and three daughters. His eldest son succeeded him on his death in 1906 as King Frederick VIII of Denmark; his second son William became King of Greece; and the third, Waldemar, married the daughter of the Duc de Chartres and died in 1939 in his eighties, a bearded patriarchal figure known in his turn as the 'Uncle of Europe'. Of the three daughters the eldest, Alexandra, married the Prince of Wales, later King Edward VII of England; the second, Dagmar or Maria Feodorovna as she was to be known in Russia, became the wife of Czar Alexander III; and the youngest, Thyra, married Ernest Augustus, Duke of Cumberland and Brunswick-Luneburg, *de jure* King of Hanover.

The offer of the Greek throne to Prince William was proposed in the first instance to King Frederick VII as head of the Danish royal House. He gave his consent, but the young Prince himself had certain hesitations. He had recently entered the Naval Academy in Copenhagen and found life as a cadet very much to his liking; Greece, on the other hand, was a distant land inhabited by a people of whose language he did not speak one word and who moreover had just deposed and expelled their previous king. William's father shared these reservations and expressed them to the King, who angrily brushed them aside. William was duly summoned and the decision was left to him. After thinking it over alone for an hour, he accepted.

On 6 June 1863 a Greek deputation, headed by the aged hero of the Greek War of Independence, Admiral Kanaris, was received by King Frederick at the Christiansborg Palace in Copenhagen to announce formally Prince William's election as King of the Hellenes. The change of title from the previous 'King of Greece' was not without significance, and the implication was underlined by Kanaris who concluded his speech with the following words:

Greece, which bases all her hopes upon her young Sovereign and who relies upon the support of the three great Protecting Powers, is firmly convinced that she will one day see the fulfilment of her national aspirations.

In his reply King Frederick accepted the Greek crown on behalf of his young kinsman, and then officially revealed what had in fact been common knowledge for some months:

We have made it a condition of the acceptance of the crown that the Ionian Islands be united to the Kingdom of Greece. It gives us pleasure to be able to express the confident expectation that this union will take place in the near future, as it has been our desire that the young king, when he is received for the first time by his people, may be greeted as the harbinger of the fulfilment of this well-founded and long-cherished wish.

The King then addressed his great-nephew:

Before you leave this place, I will give you some words of advice: Let it always be your endeavour to win and retain the love of your people.... Abide firmly by the constitution of your country, strive constantly to make it respected and see that it is adhered to. Make this your rule, and all will go well with you and your country.

The King also invested the young man with the Order of the Elephant, embraced him fondly, and gave him his blessing.

Later that day the Greek delegation waited on their new King.

Praise be to God [said Kanaris with tears in his eyes] that He has vouchsafed me in my old age to greet Your Majesty as King.... We regard this day as the fairest in our lives, since we are here to affirm the loyalty and love of a nation whose history and sufferings render it worthy of Your Majesty's sympathy.... Greece has placed her whole future and all her hopes in the hands of her Sovereign.... As for myself, having lived to see this day I am able to cry with Simeon, 'Lord, suffer now Thy servant to depart in peace.'

With these words, the white-haired old sea dog kissed the hand of the young King, who, visibly moved by this scene, said:

I feel deeply conscious of the responsibility that has now devolved on me. I have grown up in a country where law and order go hand in hand with constitutional liberty. The lessons I have learned here will go with me and guide me in my new country, and I shall always keep before me the motto: THE LOVE OF MY PEOPLE IS MY STRENGTH.

In the fifty years of his reign, he proved to be as good as his word.

The election of King George I to the throne of Greece was ratified on 13 July 1863 by a Treaty between the three Protecting Powers and Denmark which stipulated, *inter alia*, that his successor should belong to the Greek Orthodox Church – George himself was a Protestant and remained one all his life – and that the crowns of Greece and Denmark should never be united under the same sovereign (although all members of the royal House of Greece are automatically also Princes of Denmark to this day). The Treaty also made some financial provision for the new King, who was to receive a sum of £12,000 per annum relinquished in his favour by the Three Powers from Greece's annual loan repayments, as well as another £10,000 ear-marked for him out of the revenues of the Ionian Islands.

On 29 October 1863* King George arrived in Athens, having previously called on Queen Victoria, Czar Alexander II and Emperor Napoleon III to thank them for their support. On the following day he took the oath to the constitution, swearing 'to defend the Greek religion, to protect and preserve the inviolability and independence of the Greek State, and to rule according to the Law'. At the same time he issued his first Proclamation to the people over whom he had come to reign.

It is neither skill nor experience that I bring to you, as these are qualities you cannot expect from my age. What I bring is confidence and sincere

---

* The same year, almost on the same day, in a small village on the island of Crete, a son was born to the local school teacher. The boy was destined to become the outstanding personality of modern Greece, to guide his country to supreme heights of glory and international prestige, to be voted by the Greek Parliament 'a worthy son of Hellas' in the manner of Pericles, to plunge his country into revolution and civil war, and to end his days in exile in a foreign land. His name was Eleftherios Venizelos.

love, coupled with a deep faith that from now on my destiny is linked with yours. . . . I shall not only respect and observe scrupulously your laws, and above all your Constitution* but I shall also respect and learn your customs, your language and all the things you love yourselves. . . . It is my ambition, so far as it lies within my power, to make Greece the model Kingdom of the East. May the Almighty lead me by the hand in all my endeavours so that I may never forget the promises I publicly made to you today.

In May of the following year he set out on a tour of the country – a good deal of it on muleback – finally boarding the frigate *Hellas* at Calamata for the Ionian Islands. H.M.S. *Revenge*, with the British envoy Mr Horace Rumbold on board, joined *Hellas* in the Bay of Navarino, where the Russian warship *Oleg* and the French *Le Magicien* were already waiting with their respective envoys. The small flotilla then sailed out, *Hellas* leading, *Revenge* and *Le Magicien* astern to port and starboard, and *Oleg* bringing up the rear. At Catacolo they were met by H.M.S. *Duke of Marlborough*, a great wooden three-decker of 130 guns carrying Sir Henry Storks, Lord High Commissioner of the Ionian Islands, and the last remaining battalion of the British Garrison. An Admiral's barge flying the Ionian Standard came over, carrying Sir Henry and his staff. When the barge was alongside the standard was struck, and to the thunder of salutes from *Duke of Marlborough*'s guns Sir Henry was piped aboard *Hellas* holding the folded standard in his arms. He advanced to where the young King stood waiting and laid it respectfully at his feet.

The Ionian Islands were now part of Greece.

Rumbold, who struck up a friendship with the young King during this voyage and the subsequent celebrations in Corfu, describes King George at this time as 'still boyish in many ways, and with a flow of animal spirits that made it sometimes difficult for his daily companions to maintain the respectful reserve and gravity due to his royal station. . . . He had a holy horror of vice, and I remember being both touched and amused one evening by his confiding in me his determination to marry as early as possible in order to be placed

---

* In actual fact the Constitution was held up for months by interminable discussions in the Chamber, to which eventually George put an end by announcing he would leave Greece if the Constitution were not voted by a certain date – a warning which had the desired effect.

at once out of reach of the many risks and temptations to which he knew he was certain to be exposed.'

Having decided to marry, King George availed himself of an invitation from the Czar to visit Russia in 1867 to seek a wife. The most suitable choice appeared to be the Grand Duchess Vera, daughter of the Grand Duke Constantine, the Czar's younger brother, but while staying with the Grand Duke at his palace in Pavlosk, George happened to look up in the hall one day and saw a young, fair-haired girl gazing down at him with great interest. It was the Grand Duke's younger daughter Olga, and it was love at first sight for both of them; they were married at the Winter Palace in St Petersburg on 27 October of that year. When they left for Greece, the newly-wedded Queen of the Hellenes took her dolls with her. She was not yet sixteen.

When King Otho arrived in Athens in 1832 it had a population of under five thousand and consisted of a few clusters of poorly-built houses scattered among the neglected ruins and tottering columns of what had once been the City of Pericles. Writing in 1844 after a visit to Greece, Thackeray described Athens as 'little better than a rickety agglomeration of larger and smaller huts', adding that he 'would rather have £200 a year in Fleet Street than be King of the Greeks'. The population of the whole of Greece numbered about 650,000 and Piraeus, today one of the great ports of the world, consisted of 'a piece of deal boarding projecting a few feet into the sea to serve as a landing stage for small boats'.

Until a palace could be built Otho took up residence in a modest one-storied house (now a tailor's warehouse in Klafthmonos Square). There was some talk of putting up a royal residence on the Acropolis itself, but the idea was mercifully scotched by the horrified veto, it is said, of Otho's classically-minded father, King Ludwig of Bavaria. A more appropriate site was finally chosen, and the vast stucco-faced edifice which now houses the Chamber of Deputies, the Prime Minister's office and several other Departments was erected and furnished for the accommodation of the Kings of Greece.

During the twelve months which intervened between King Otho's departure and King George's arrival in October 1863 there had been much rioting in Athens, and the Palace had been ransacked and looted by the mobs. When George moved in, most of the rooms were in chaos, with fittings torn out and broken furniture scattered everywhere. George had all Otho's personal belongings collected and sent to their rightful owner, and then set about putting the huge house in order – a task that took several years. While still unmarried he occupied only a small part of the Palace, many of his things remaining in their crates – a fact which enabled him on more than one occasion to bring pressure on procrastinating politicians by mentioning casually but truthfully that his bags were ready packed.

It was to this palace that the young couple came to live on returning to Athens from their honeymoon, soon settling into the routine of a happy married life. On 21 July 1868 their first child arrived – a son, the first prince of the new dynasty to be born on Greek soil. He was given the name of the last king who had reigned over the Hellenes, the warrior who had fallen on the ramparts defending Byzantium against the Infidel, the emperor who did not die but was turned into stone ready to spring to life when Constantinople was Greek once again: Constantine.

More children followed in rapid succession: George in 1869, Alexandra in 1870, Nicholas in 1872. Before she was twenty-one Queen Olga was already the mother of four. A second daughter, Marie, was born in 1876, and a third, Olga, in 1881, though she died the same year. Next came Andrew in 1882, and finally Christopher in 1888, making a gap of exactly twenty years between the first-born and the youngest.

George soon learned enough Greek to dispense with interpreters. In the first four years of his reign he travelled to every part of the country by horse-carriage, on mule-back and on foot, visiting peasants in their huts and highland chieftains in their mountain fastnesses, getting to know his people, their way of life and their problems. He had grown long flowing moustaches in the Greek fashion, and did everything he could to make himself look and behave like a Greek. He had a deep respect for the Greek Orthodox Church – to which, of course, his Russian wife already belonged – and invariably when the Bible was brought to him at the church door he would kiss it reverently and cross himself in the true Greek manner; but in the privacy of his home he practised his own religion, using the Chapel adjoining his apartments in the Palace,*

---

* During his predecessor's reign this Chapel had been used both by the Catholic King Otho and his Protestant Queen Amalia and had to be solemnly 'blessed' and 'unblessed' every Sunday when transferred from the rites of the one Church to the other.

and when he travelled he always took his Bible with him, making copious marginal notes in Danish and marking the places with strips of the red-and-white ribbon of the Order of Dannebrog.

George had no illusions concerning the true nature of the task he had undertaken: the designation 'King of the Hellenes' was not just a conventional title but a solemn pledge to bring the unredeemed Greeks into the family fold, which he took very much to heart and which he spent the rest of his life trying to fulfil.

Into the preparation and execution of this national aim George threw himself without reserve, both in the diplomatic and the military field. On the home front he decided that minimum personal entanglement in domestic politics was the best way of ensuring a healthy functioning of government, and although circumstances obliged him on occasions to take initiatives and to intervene decisively in times of crisis, non-involvement in the administration remained his basic political philosophy throughout his reign. Perhaps he was guided by the fate of his two predecessors. Capodistrias had kept everybody at a distance, governing like a Russian autocrat, and had been assassinated for his pains. Otho had gone to the other extreme, occupying himself with the most trivial minutiae of administration and trying to govern Greece on the lines of a model German principality: though conscientious and sincere, he had lost his throne. George followed neither of these courses: he placed implicit faith in his ministers, never interfering with their administrative work but always keeping himself fully informed. When State documents were brought to him for approval he would invariably sign them first and read them afterwards. It was a policy calculated to encourage native talents and was largely responsible for the emergence and gradual development of a 'political world' in a country that had only just begun an independent existence and was still in the painful process of learning to stand on its own feet.

Those early years of his reign must have been highly educational for the young King. On the eve of an election in the 1870s he was discussing the prospects with his Prime Minister Voulgaris, the old chieftain from Hydra who scorned European dress and always wore the Greek fustanella. Voulgaris was particularly anxious that his arch rival Colettis should not be elected and said so, to which the King innocently replied that if the people did not want him they would surely not vote for him. 'That is not what I mean at all,'

1 Paul's father, King Constantine the 'Soldier King', who succeeded to the
throne on the assassination of his father in 1913. Every soldier who served under
him received a copy of this signed photograph.

2 Paul's eldest brother King George II, who reigned from 1922 until Greece was declared a Republic in 1924, and was recalled to the throne by plebiscite in 1935. He died childless in 1947 and was succeeded by his brother Paul.

3 Paul's second brother Alexander, who reigned in the place of his father from 1917 to 1920, at the wheel of his favourite motor car with his Alsatian dog, Fritz. It was while trying to separate Fritz and a pet monkey that Alexander was bitten in the leg and died shortly afterwards from blood poisoning.

muttered Voulgaris, fingering the silver dirk tucked in his sash. 'We must do away with him!' Another Greek politician, Deliyannis, was indeed murdered – not for his political views but because he tried to close down the gambling houses in Athens.

George's family connexions were an immense asset to him, and every year he would go on an extended European tour visiting relatives and friends. He would spend some time at Aix-les-Bains, where everybody knew him as 'Monsieur le Roi' or just 'Monsieur Georges' and which his regular visits made fashionable in the same way that Marienbad owed its vogue to his brother-in-law the Prince of Wales. At Aix he would meet and talk with influential people from every country in Europe. In England, his favourite sister Alexandra Princess of Wales was his fervent admirer and loyal supporter in all his plans and hopes, and soon turned her husband Edward into a sympathetic ally despite the occasional remonstrances of Queen Victoria, who in 1876 invested George with the Order of the Garter on one of his family visits to the Prince and Princess of Wales. In Russia his sister Dagmar had become Czarina in 1881 when the assassination of Alexander II had placed her doting husband on the throne. The new Czar of All the Russias ('Uncle Sasha' to the family), a genial giant of a man who loved to demonstrate his colossal strength by bending massive silver trays like pieces of cardboard, was completely and happily under the domination of his wife and could be relied upon for support whenever required. There were also the annual house parties at Fredensborg, the palace in Copenhagen built in 1720 to commemorate the peace between Denmark and Sweden, where old King Christian's sons and daughters would gather from all over Europe with their wives and husbands and their children to spend Christmas with 'Apapa' and 'Amama'.

When George became King of the Hellenes the country of his adoption covered an area of some 47,000 sq. kms. and had a population of just over one million people. The Ionian Islands which he had brought with him as a gift from Britain added another 3,000 sq. kms. to the country; but millions of Greeks still remained under Ottoman rule, rendering inevitable a national policy of permanent confrontation with Turkey periodically erupting into open or clandestine war, the immediate cause of which would usually be Crete, Greece's 'Ireland in reverse'. As early as 1830

Palmerston had prophetically warned: 'I venture to predict that if Crete is not included in the Kingdom of Greece, we shall run the risk of war on account of that island before many years are past,' and events were to prove him right.

Although George's five sons all received military training, it was to Constantine, the first-born, that the eyes and hopes of the nation were turned: the deliberate choice of that name had marked out his destiny. On 27 October 1889, twenty-two years to the day after his own father's wedding, he married Queen Victoria's granddaughter Princess Sophie of Hohenzollern, daughter of the Emperor Frederick III of Germany, by whom he had six children – three sons and three daughters, just like his grandfather, King Christian IX of Denmark. The parallel could be taken further inasmuch as in both cases most of the children were to become Kings or Queens themselves. Of the six children of King Christian IX, two became Kings, two Queens and one *de jure* Queen. All three of Constantine's sons – George, Alexander and Paul – became Kings of Greece, and of his three daughters the eldest, Helen, became Queen of Roumania, and the second, Irene, Duchess of Spoleto, became for a brief moon *de jure* Queen of Croatia, though neither she nor her husband ever set foot in that country.

When her first child George was born in 1890 – again twenty-two years to the day after Constantine's own birth – Sophie decided to embrace the Greek Orthodox faith. Her brother Kaiser Wilhelm II, who had meanwhile succeeded to the German throne on the death of his father the Emperor Frederick III, was so furious that the sister of the 'Defender of Protestant Faith' should change her religion that for three years he forbade her to set foot on German soil, though his anger was probably due more to his pathological hatred of his mother, whom he suspected of supporting his sister in her decisions, than to any strong religious convictions of his own. 'My mother has no religion,' he told a bosom friend. 'Now to mortify me she encourages Sophie to change her religion – not that I care if she turned Jewess.'

In 1897, after unrest in Crete had again developed into open war with the Turks, Greece suffered a humiliating defeat. Thanks to the intervention of the Protecting Powers the consequences of this military disaster were not as harsh as they might have been for Greece, who was obliged to pay a war indemnity but had Thessaly restored to her. Another result of this settlement was that Crete was given local autonomy with Prince George, the King's second son, as High Commissioner. It had been an unequal contest: the Greek Army had very few trained officers, and at sea the Greek Navy could not exploit its superiority as the vulnerable points on the enemy coastline in Asia Minor and elsewhere were mostly inhabited by Greeks who would have been the main victims of any naval action. But the 'Thirty Days War' taught the Greeks the bitter lesson that organization and technical training were required besides courage if the unredeemed populations were to be liberated. For the next fifteen years the reorganization and building up of the Greek Army was to be the paramount concern of the King, and of the King's son and heir Constantine, who in October 1900 was appointed Inspector-General and Commander-in-Chief of the Greek Army.

⇒ 3 ⇐

In 1901 Constantine's wife Sophie lost both her grandmother Queen Victoria, who died at Osborne on 22 January, and her mother, the Empress Frederick, Queen Victoria's eldest and favourite child, who died at Friedrichshof, her home near Kronberg, on 5 August. Four months later, on 14 December, Sophie gave birth at the royal country estate at Tatoi to her fourth child, a boy, who was given the name of Paul.

Eleven years separated Paul from his eldest brother George and eight from his other brother Alexander. This gap placed him in a different age group from them, and his mother was anxious that he should mix with other boys of his own age. The royal children already had a tutor, Dr Schindler – a kindly, gentle Swiss who became so fond of his young charges that his authority over them steadily diminished until they were completely out of control. So Schindler had to go and was duly replaced by the Queen's Chaplain, Dr Hoenig, a middle-aged, dry, stern, bearded Pomeranian, a great believer in physical exercise, who had one of the rooms in the Palace converted into a gymnasium. He was also very keen on fresh air, and every morning he and his young charges would drive to Tzitzifies, a stretch of sandy beach near Piraeus, where Athenians with their children seeking refuge from the heat of the city would flock in the summer months. Bathing was strictly segregated, with a policeman in a rowing-boat patrolling the border-line separating the two sexes.

It was here that Paul first met a group of other boys who also used to go to the beach to swim and who were to become his lifelong friends.

These daily bathing-trips to Tzitzifies began as unconnected individual exercises but gradually developed into a group operation with Hoenig in firm command. Swimming instruction was on scientific lines and all the boys ended up by becoming expert swimmers. When Hoenig considered that sufficient progress had been made he would give each boy a final test: he would be put in a rowing-boat and thrown overboard fully dressed. While in the water he had to take off his clothes and lift them into the boat, garment by garment, without touching the sides, and then clamber into the boat unaided. When he could do that he was pronounced fully trained.

Hoenig was also a hiking enthusiast, and weekends were usually devoted to at least one long walk, usually in the foothills of Mt Parnes near Tatoi. As Paul's circle of friends from the Tzitzifies group gradually grew, other boys would be invited to join in these walks. Sometimes the party would split into two, with one group tracking the other through the woods. These treks were compulsory affairs at first but soon became something to look forward to and developed in Paul a love for the countryside that was to remain with him all his life.

Until the age of eleven Paul did not go to school but had private tutors to coach him on different subjects – Hoenig at first, then University professors chosen by his grandfather, King George. Very much influenced by her own upbringing and by the constant injunctions of her mother the Empress Frederick, with whom she maintained a voluminous correspondence,[1] Sophie was determined that her children should have an English education. She came up against a certain amount of opposition from her father-in-law, whose own children had all been educated in Greece and who saw no reason why it should be otherwise with his children's children, particularly those of the heir to the throne. A compromise was eventually reached: Alexander and Paul would go to a preparatory school in England, and the girls could also go to an English boarding school, but only during the summer term each year when their mother visited her relatives in England anyhow. So Helen and Irene spent seven summer terms at the Links, a boarding school for young ladies at Eastbourne, and Paul's elder brother Alexander was sent to St Christopher's Preparatory School, also at Eastbourne. Their mother would usually visit them on Sundays, travelling down from Windsor and staying the night at the Grand Hotel. Sophie's sister would occasionally come over from Frankfurt with her own children, and the two families – the two sisters had eleven children between them – would all stay together at a rented house at Seaford.

It was on one of these visits that Sophie heard of St Peter's, an offshoot of St Andrew's Preparatory School, which was then the most fashionable boys' school at Eastbourne. The popularity of St Andrew's had made a place in it much sought after, and the waiting list had grown so long that one of the assistant masters, a young man with good social connexions called Herbert de l'Isle Booth, had conceived the idea of starting a school of his own to take the overflow from St Andrew's. With another master as partner he had founded St Peter's Preparatory School for Young Gentlemen in Chesterfield Road, in the Meads district of Eastbourne.* It had a capacity of some forty boys and was already full when Sophie went to inspect it one Sunday while on a visit to her daughters at the Links nearby. She was favourably impressed, Mr de l'Isle Booth was persuaded without too much difficulty to make room for one more boy, and Paul duly arrived at St Peter's the following term.

The school building at St Peter's was a large converted private house, the boarding side being in the capable hands of the Matron, Mrs Jameson. There were four to six boys to each dormitory, Paul's neighbours being 'Rosie' (Commander Robert H. Stokes-Rees, R.N.) on one side and Tony (Group-Captain Sir Anthony Weldon, Bt) on the other. On instructions from the Headmaster, Paul was addressed as 'Pavlo' by boys and masters alike.

Paul spent the summer terms of 1911 to 1914 at St Peter's. Academically he was only an average pupil but seemed extremely proficient with his hands, and the annual exhibition of the carpentry class invariably included book-rests, foot-stools and sundry boxes of various shapes and sizes made by him. Almost every Sunday his mother would come to Eastbourne to see him and his sisters at the Links, and as often as not he would take one of his friends with him for lunch at the Grand Hotel with his family.

The outbreak of war in 1914 brought all this to an end. 'My plans are all upset by this war,' wrote the Headmaster irritably to young Weldon's mother on 20 September of that year. 'The young Prince came to me but I had to bundle him off in a hurry by special train soon after. I don't suppose I shall see him or his mother for some time to come now.'

He was quite right. Paul's school days were over.

* The school closed in 1937 and the premises were converted into a block of flats called St Peter's Court.

⇒ 4 ⇐

While Paul was broadening his education in England, events of momentous importance were taking place at home.

Since 1898 Crete had been enjoying a measure of local autonomy under a Greek High Commissioner in the person of Prince George, the King's second son, but the island still remained under Turkish suzerainty and was in a continuous state of ferment. A series of insurrections had brought to the forefront of the political scene a local politician called Eleftherios Venizelos, the son of a village schoolmaster, whose fiery patriotism, shrewd intelligence and undisguised ambition had already marked him out for bigger things. His activities had until then been confined to his native Crete but were eventually transferred to the larger scene of national politics on the mainland where the 'Military League', a group of young Army officers dissatisfied with the running of the country in general and the handling of the Cretan question in particular, had ousted the Government and seized power in May 1909. After pushing through a series of drastic reforms which included a thorough reorganization of the Armed Forces, the Military League rounded off its self-appointed task by inviting Venizelos to come over from Crete. The Military League then declared its task completed and withdrew from the scene in an act of self-immolation unique in the annals of Greek politics. By October 1910 Venizelos was Prime Minister. He dissolved Parliament and in the elections that followed was returned to power by an over-whelming majority.

Thus began an era of collaboration between King and Premier that was to double the size of Greece and bring military glory and national rehabilitation to the Greek nation.

Ever since his appointment as Commander-in-Chief, the Crown

Prince had thrown himself heart and soul into the task of re-organizing the Greek Army. A professional soldier – he had completed his military training in the Prussian Military Academy at Potsdam – utterly dedicated to the task which he regarded as a sacred mission entrusted to him by an almost mystical force of national destiny, he had set up a staff comprising the best military brains in the country.* In the first flush of reformist zeal after its seizure of power in 1909 the Military League had compelled Constantine and his brothers to resign their commissions, but on becoming Premier the astute Venizelos, who was well aware of Constantine's military abilities and was also not unmindful of the popularity and prestige he enjoyed in the Armed Forces, reinstated the Crown Prince with increased powers and responsibilities as Inspector-General of the Army. Speaking in the National Assembly on 11 June 1911 Venizelos justified the appointment in these words: 'I consider that Lt-General the Crown Prince has exceptional military abilities such as are not possessed by many senior officers. . . . I feel it my duty to inform this Assembly that as the responsible Head of Government, I regard the Crown Prince as the most suitable commander of the Armed Forces.' Working closely with the French Military Mission, Constantine devoted himself completely and exclusively to the task of Greece's military preparation, while in the political sphere Venizelos, with the King's encouragement and support, brought his considerable diplomatic skill to bear on the task of eliminating obstacles and misunder-standings between Greece and her Christian neighbours so that a united front might be achieved against the common enemy Turkey.

By the middle of 1912 military alliances had been arranged between Serbia and Bulgaria and between Bulgaria and Greece. On 1 October the state of anarchy prevailing in Macedonia provided the Balkan Allies with the justification they needed to order mobilization; the Turks immediately followed suit. On 13 October the Balkan Allies issued an ultimatum demanding radical reforms

---

* The gunnery expert on this team was Major Panayotis Danglis, an artillery officer already known to the Crown Prince from his previous service as military instructor to his younger brother, Prince Andrew. In 1893 Danglis designed a highly mobile 75mm. mountain gun that could be transported on two pack animals and could be assembled ready for action in ninety seconds flat. Known as the 'Schneider-Danglis', it was eventually manufactured for many countries by the French Schneider Company and was undoubtedly a significant contributory factor to the success of the Greek Army in the Balkan Wars.

in Macedonia, to which Turkey retorted on 17 October by declaring war on Serbia and Bulgaria; Greece declared war on Turkey the following day. In Macedonia and Thrace and the Epirus the soldiers of the Christian Allies now stood facing the armies of the Ottoman Empire. The moment for putting an end to Turkish oppression had arrived at last.

This time the Greek Army was more than ready. A few days before the commencement of hostilities the Crown Prince had assumed personal command of the Army in the field, and the moment war was declared he struck. Advancing rapidly through the mountain passes of Olympus he cut the railway between Monastir and Thessaloniki, and on 26 October* the Greek Army captured the great port, having achieved its main objective in three weeks after an unbroken series of military successes. King George entered the Macedonian capital on horseback the following day and behind him rode his son, the victorious Commander-in-Chief, the 'Son of the Eagle' as he was to be known in legend and song from now on. Through streets lined with delirious crowds they rode to the Byzantine Cathedral of St Demetrius where a solemn Te Deum was sung to the Glory of God and in celebration of the liberation of the city after four centuries of Ottoman rule.

On 3 December 1912 Turkey asked for a truce, but the conference that followed ended without result and hostilities were resumed three months later. On 21 February 1913 a Greek army, again under the personal command of the Crown Prince, captured Janina, capital of the Epirus, which had been in Turkish hands since 1430, and another dream of Hellenic irredentism was transformed into reality.

By the Treaty of London of 30 May 1913 Turkey withdrew in Europe to a line that left her not much more than Constantinople and its hinterland. But the war was not yet over. Flushed with their military successes the Bulgarians suddenly turned on their own allies and tried to wrest from them some of their spoils, but were utterly defeated at Kilkis a few days later. Roumania, until then a passive spectator, now decided to take a hand and promptly annexed the frontier province of the Dobrudja, while Turkey herself quietly reoccupied some of the territory she had earlier lost

---

* The Feast of St Demetrius, patron saint of Thessaloniki. The significance of the anniversary was not lost on the devout Greek Orthodox, who are highly sensitive to coincidences of this nature.

in Thrace, including Adrianople. The Treaty of Bucharest of 10 August 1913 awarded most of Macedonia to Greece, whose eastern frontier now reached the Aegean at the Nestos estuary. On 13 February 1914 Greek sovereignty was recognized over the Aegean Islands, which Greece had occupied anyhow during the war – with the exception of Imbros and Tenedos which command the entrance to the Straits and were allowed to remain in Turkish hands, and the Dodecanese Islands which remained under Italian occupation until their annexation by Greece in 1947.

In the space of a few glorious months the Greek frontiers reached out to include newly-liberated provinces in Macedonia and Thrace and the Epirus, the Aegean Archipelago, and far to the south to the great island of Crete. The area of the Kingdom was more than doubled. And in the eyes of every Greek two men were responsible for this miracle: Constantine, who had taken these lands at the point of the sword, and Venizelos who had consolidated these conquests at the conference table.

It was at this moment of triumphant achievement and national celebration that the Royal Family suffered a grievous blow. Since that memorable St Demetrius's Day when he had entered Thessaloniki riding his black charger, King George had taken up residence in the Macedonian capital. On 18 March 1913 he went for his usual afternoon walk accompanied by his Equerry. At a spot near the seafront where the road bends a man leaning against the wall suddenly turned as the King was passing and fired point blank at his back with a revolver. The bullet pierced the King's heart killing him instantly.[*]

King George was sixty-eight when he died and would have celebrated the golden jubilee of his reign that same year. There is evidence to suggest that he had already decided to abdicate later that year in favour of the Crown Prince.[†]

[*] The assassin turned out to be a mentally deranged alcoholic named Alexander Schinas nursing an imaginary grievance; he committed suicide while in prison awaiting trial.

[†] King George's youngest son Christopher mentions this in his book *Memoirs of H.R.H. Prince Christopher of Greece*[2] and a Danish naval friend of the King quotes him as saying to him at lunch in Thessaloniki on the very day he was assassinated: 'I am going to abdicate. It is quite time for my son to take charge. He has reached the right age and he possesses the vigour that I can no longer boast of. His popularity is now immense and he has gained for himself a position, abroad as well as at home. His time has arrived.'[3]

In the middle of a war and at the zenith of his military career Constantine unexpectedly found himself King. And the superstitious among his people were not slow to note that the legend which had kept Hellenism alive during the centuries of Turkish rule seemed about to come true: that when another Constantine sat on the throne Byzantium would rise again and Constantinople, where Constantine Paleologus had fallen defending Christendom, would once more become the Metropolis of a Hellenic Empire reborn.

At the end of his victorious campaigns Constantine sent a photograph of himself to every officer and man who had served under him. It was an informal snapshot taken by an Army photographer showing him in plain khaki uniform standing outside his field headquarters, his tunic covered with dust and his boots spattered with mud. Underneath was a handwritten dedication: 'To my gallant fellow soldiers of two glorious wars.' The signature was CONSTANTINE B (for Basileus, King, the usual adjunct to the Royal name).

The last Emperor of Byzantium was Constantine XI. Was it a calligraphic quirk, or did that B look like IB, which in Greek numerals stands for XII?

On 5 August 1913 Constantine returned to Athens from Thessaloniki, his task triumphantly completed. Under the blazing sun of a summer afternoon the battle-cruiser *Averoff*, flying the Royal Standard and escorted by the whole Greek Fleet, dropped anchor in Phaleron Bay. At the same time Queen Sophie arrived by car from Athens with her youngest son Paul, now aged twelve, sitting by her side in his sailor suit. In a few moments the King, in plain service khaki and wearing no decorations, disembarked at the pier, his two elder sons and his four brothers, all serving officers on his Staff, behind him. The Prime Minister Eleftherios Venizelos, his bright eyes beaming happily behind gold-rimmed spectacles, the blue sash of the Order of the Redeemer across the stiff white shirt of his formal dress, stepped forward. King and Premier shook hands warmly.

At the entrance to the capital, by Hadrian's Arch, a special stand had been erected for the war veterans who sat on benches and in their invalid chairs, armless, legless, sightless, cheering their commander. As the open horse-drawn landau approached, the King ordered the driver to halt. Stepping out of the carriage he walked up to the stand, stood rigidly to attention and slowly brought his hand up in salute. The men returned the salute in dead silence. A man on crutches suddenly came forward, picked up a laurel branch from the ground, hobbled unaided to where the King stood and handed it to him. Without a word the King took it, saluted once again and walked back to the carriage, the laurel held firmly in his hand.

'To my gallant fellow-soldiers of two glorious wars.' A new relationship, a special kinship, a spiritual communion almost mystical in its nature had evolved between King and soldier during those months of battle and victory. It was to dominate much of the new King's thinking and govern many of his actions in the months to come, but it was also to bring tragedy and disaster in its wake.

A few days after his return to Athens Constantine left on a European tour which included a visit to Germany to attend the German Army's summer manœuvres. On 24 August, the day before the manœuvres were due to begin, Constantine was guest of honour at a dinner at which the Kaiser proposed the health of his brother-in-law in very fulsome terms, praising Constantine's military skill but not failing to mention that he had been a pupil at the German Military Academy. He then presented the King of the Hellenes with a Field-Marshal's baton. Taken completely by surprise, and feeling very flattered by this tribute to his abilities as a professional soldier, Constantine made an impromptu speech of thanks in which he acknowledged his debt and that of many of the officers on his staff to their military training at the Kriegsakademie.

It was a speech that was to cost him dear, for it was to be cited henceforth as 'irrefutable proof' of pro-German sentiments – an allegation graphically reinforced by a photograph of him in German Field-Marshal's uniform complete with spiked helmet following the manœuvres with the Kaiser and the German High Command.* By the time Constantine returned home a month later, after taking Paul back to school at Eastbourne, the seed of suspicion had already been

---

* It is not irrelevant to recall that King George v was also a German Field-Marshal and Colonel of a Regiment of Prussian Guards. The German Emperor for his part was a Field-Marshal in the British Army, and both he and the Kronprinz held Honorary Colonelcies in various British Regiments. When it was proposed shortly after the outbreak of war in 1914 that the Kaiser and the Kronprinz should be deprived of these distinctions, King George v flatly refused to issue any public notice to that effect and eventually only agreed to their names being quietly dropped from the next issue of the British Army List.

sown, especially among the French, whose attitude from now on was to be dominated by the obsession that a Germanophil King sat on the throne of Greece.

The outbreak of the Great War in the summer of 1914 and the dilemma it created for Greece gradually produced a polarization of two diametrically opposed attitudes. There were those who believed that, after two bitter wars which had cost the country much blood and treasure, what was now required was a long period of peace for the economic and social integration of the new populations; Greece was not directly involved in the disputes between the big powers and should keep out of the war. On the other hand there were many who were firmly convinced that the task begun in 1912 had not yet been completed; unredeemed and persecuted Greek populations in the Epirus and Thrace and Asia Minor were still crying out for liberation. Only by throwing in her lot with the Entente Powers right from the beginning and sharing in the fruits of a victory regarded as inevitable, would Greece be able to safeguard her newly-won territories and achieve the ultimate dream of total national rehabilitation.

A country united as never before in its history was now tearing itself asunder over this issue, with the King resolved to keep Greece neutral and the Prime Minister Venizelos equally firm in his conviction that the future of Greece lay with the Western Allies.

This conflict of opinion came out into the open in February 1915 over the question whether Greece should join in the British attack on the Dardanelles, a venture which Venizelos wholeheartedly supported but which the Greek General Staff, and especially its brilliant Chief, Colonel John Metaxas, considered a very dubious military proposition from which Greece should steer clear. Metaxas backed his convictions by resigning as Chief of the General Staff, and the King's agreement with Metaxas's assessment of the situation left Venizelos no alternative but to resign as Premier.

The split was now irreconcilable and by September 1916 the country had become physically divided into two separate areas under rival administrations: the King's Government in Athens, still clinging to neutrality, and the 'Government of National Defence' in Thessaloniki under the Triumvirate of Venizelos, Admiral Paul Coundouriotis (the 'Nelson' of Greece) and General Panayotis Danglis (of 'Danglis Gun' fame), which only the Entente Powers recognized and which on 24 November 1916 formally declared war on the Central Powers. By this time passions had reached such heights that a 'Solemn Anathema' was pronounced against Venizelos in Athens, the public being regaled with the spectacle of the Primate of All Greece in full pontifical robes ceremonially casting a stone in the Field of Mars and pronouncing a curse upon the 'Cretan renegade' while thousands of Athenians filed past to do the same.

Meanwhile the Entente Powers, with the French always setting the pace, were increasing their pressure on Athens. Humiliating demands in blatant violation of Greece's sovereignty were followed up by arbitrary actions which, far from achieving any useful purpose, simply had the effect of alienating the sympathies of the public even more. The futility of such crude tactics and the reaction they would inevitably produce on a proud people like the Greeks were at least apparent to the King of England, who was anxiously writing to his Prime Minister, Mr Asquith, about this time expressing concern at the way things were drifting. Questioning the legality of various Allied actions in Greece, King George V wanted to know 'are we justified in interfering to this extent in the internal Government of a neutral and friendly country', and expressed astonishment at the treatment meted out by the French in Thessaloniki to regular Greek troops who, 'loyal to their King and Government, refused to join the Revolutionary [Venizelos] Movement'. In this letter, dated 4 September 1916, King George went so far as to suggest that a protest might be sent to the French Government against the French Commander's high-handed proceedings, and wound up by expressing the opinion that 'if the Allies would treat Greece kindly and not, if I may say so, in a bullying spirit, she will in all probability join them.'

In December 1916 Greece was put under blockade, and six months later on 11 June 1917 the Entente Powers, through their newly-appointed High Commissioner M. Charles Jonnart, demanded the abdication of King Constantine 'who could choose, by agreement with the Protecting Powers, a successor from among his heirs' provided it was not his eldest son George who was considered to be too closely identified with his father's policies.*

* It is interesting to compare the Allies' reactions towards Greece's neutrality in the 1914–18 War with the Allied attitude towards Turkey in similar circumstances during the 1939–45 War. Greece and King Constantine personally were reviled and denounced as Germanophil for wishing to stay out of the war; no such criticism was levelled against Turkey, whose neutrality was even praised in some quarters as beneficial to the Allied cause, though Churchill himself certainly did not share this view.

King Constantine had by now reached the limits of his powers of resistance. M. Jonnart was informed that the King had decided 'to leave the country' – the word 'abdication' was studiously avoided – and had nominated his second son, the twenty-three-year-old Prince Alexander, to take his place.

Four days later the King left Greece with his family amid scenes charged with emotion and drama; large crowds surrounded the palace and would not let him go. Appeals to disperse were ignored, and an attempt by the King to drive out of the palace was frustrated by people lying down on the road in front of the car and blocking the way. The siege continued throughout the night and into the follow-ing day; a proclamation by the King reaffirming that his decision to leave the country was irrevocable and calling on the people to accept the situation quietly and peacefully swelled the crowds even more. Meanwhile inside the palace the new King, a bewildered and pathetic young man who could not hold back his tears at the fate that lay in store for him, took the oath prescribed by the constitution in the presence of his father, the Prime Minister and the Archbishop of Athens who had been hurriedly smuggled in through a back door.

It was not until the afternoon that the King managed to leave the palace, and then only by a ruse; the royal car was ostentatiously brought round to the garden gate as if the King was about to leave from there, and while the attention of the crowd was thus diverted away from the front door the King and his family slipped out in another car. They drove to Tatoi, the royal country estate fifteen miles north of Athens, to prepare for their departure, but the public manifestations of sympathy towards the King had been a salutary warning to M. Jonnart of what he might expect if the King were to appear in public again, and at the last moment it was decided that the Royal Family should not leave from Piraeus but from Oropos, a small fishing village in the Gulf of Euboea north-east of Tatoi in the opposite direction from Athens. To make doubly sure that there would be no more demonstrations M. Jonnart also demanded that embarkation should take place as soon as the *Sphakteria* (the anti-quated royal yacht pressed into service for this occasion) arrived at Oropos at two o'clock in the morning, but the King ignored this demand and went on board at a more civilized hour. Despite the secrecy, a large crowd gathered to bid farewell, and once again there were highly emotional scenes when the Royal Family boarded the launch to be ferried out to the *Sphakteria*, many people wading out into the sea and swimming alongside the boat. At last the ship raised anchor and headed for Italy.

At the age of sixteen Paul was making his first acquaintance with exile.

From Taranto the Royal Family continued their journey by train, the King of Italy having placed his personal railway coach at their disposal, and on 19 June they arrived at Lugano, where they stayed for a week at the Palace Hotel before travelling on to St Moritz. In September the family moved to Zurich, staying at the Villa Werli, which they rented from the proprietor of the Dolder Hotel nearby, and for the next two years this was to be the pattern of their lives – the Carlton at St Moritz, the Villa Werli in Zurich – until November 1919 when the family moved to Lucerne and took up residence at the National Hotel.

Shortly after their arrival in Switzerland the Royal Family were joined by the Dowager Queen Olga, Paul's grandmother. After the outbreak of the Great War she had gone to her native Russia to establish a military hospital near her old home, and the Bolshevik Revolution had found her still there. As soon as she heard of the events in Greece she decided to go to her son but it was months before she was able, with the help of the Danish Legation, to obtain permission to leave Russia. After an adventurous journey in a train full of German prisoners of war being repatriated, she finally managed in July 1918 to join the Royal Family in Switzerland. She had lost seventeen of her Russian relatives in the Revolution, including her first cousin the Czar.

The reign of King George 1 had been a continuous process of national expansion through wars of liberation. The founder of the new Greek dynasty had known that this was how it would be when he accepted the throne, and he was determined that both he and his progeny should be intimately associated with this crusade. For this reason all his sons had been given a military education: Constantine and his brothers Nicholas, Andrew and Christopher had been trained for the Army and were all to see active service in the Balkan Wars and the Asia Minor Campaign, and King George's second son, who not only had the same Christian name as his father but also bore an uncanny physical resemblance to him, was trained in the Navy.

King Constantine, in his turn, had adopted the same policy with his three sons. George, the Crown Prince, had first studied at the Greek Military Academy – the 'School of Young Hopefuls' as it is called in Greek – and had then served for two years with the 1st Garderregiment zu Fuss, the crack German Guards founded by Frederick the Great in 1688,* and he was still in Germany when the Balkan War broke out; he immediately left for Greece to join his father's Staff. King Constantine's second son Alexander graduated from the Greek Military Academy just in time to join his father on the field too.

It had always been understood, however, that Constantine's youngest son would go into the Navy, which was just as well since from a very early age Paul was already showing a great love for the sea. His early education at a British preparatory school had been a preliminary to his entering the Royal Naval College at Dartmouth, but the outbreak of the Great War and the coolness which subsequently developed in Anglo-Greek relations as a result of Greece's neutrality and the hostile propaganda of the Allied Powers made it difficult for this plan to materialize at that particular time. King Constantine was determined nevertheless that his son should receive his training in what he had always regarded as the finest navy in the world – and the navy, moreover, in which his own father had held the rank of Honorary Admiral – and he was actually in the process of enlisting the support of King George V in this project when the events of June 1917 intervened and the whole family suddenly found themselves in exile in Switzerland.

This was the psychological moment when the German Emperor chose to indicate to his sister Queen Sophie that her son would be welcome in the German Naval Academy if he still wanted to make the sea his career. Constantine gave his consent, and not long after arriving in Switzerland Paul was on his way to Kiel.

In later years Paul was inclined to be reticent about this episode in his life, but from what little he told his family and from details obtained from other sources it is possible to piece together what happened.

After reporting at Kiel, Paul joined a special class to prepare for full entry into the Naval Academy, and in a few weeks he had made sufficient progress to be admitted as a cadet. This was the autumn of

* Frederick commanded this regiment personally throughout his life, and his injunction to all who served in it was that 'the day has twenty-four hours, and if that is not enough then you must work during the night too'.

1918, and the first rumblings of revolution were beginning to be heard in Germany. The German High Sea Fleet had been bottled up in the Baltic some months now, and prolonged inactivity coupled with the transfer of some of its best crews for service in submarines and the light flotillas had resulted in a steady deterioration of morale, especially among the units at Kiel; minor outbreaks of mutiny had already occurred in four battleships and had been sternly suppressed. The crisis came when Admiral von Scheer, who was planning a last sortie into the Channel, warned the High Sea Fleet to prepare for sea: when the order to sail came on 3 November the fleet refused to move. The mutiny soon spread to Berlin, where Soldiers' and Workers' Councils on the Soviet model were set up. Six days later the Kaiser was seeking asylum in Holland. The war was over.

The Naval Academy at Kiel was among the first institutions to be affected by the mutiny. In a loyal but hopeless attempt to help restore discipline, most of the Officer Instructors rushed to the naval base and to the ships that had mutinied, leaving the Academy to its own devices. After a day or two of confusion and hesitation the abandoned cadets decided the best thing to do was to go home, and by the end of the week they had all disappeared with the exception of two, Paul and a German boy, who were in hospital with Spanish flu and too sick to move. As soon as they could stand on their feet the two lads packed their belongings and headed for the railway station, where hundreds of other people with the same idea of getting out of Kiel were scrambling and fighting to board the train. Paul and his companion managed to get into a coach by helping each other in through the window, but Paul still felt so ill that he said goodbye to his friend and got off the train at the next station. Sick and feverish, he spent the night on the railway platform huddled on a seat in the freezing cold and woke up the following morning with a splitting headache and his nose bleeding profusely. A very fat barmaid washing beer mugs in a large tub by the platform bar saw him and beckoned him to come over. He managed to stand up and staggered across to her. She looked at him for a moment, then seized him by the scruff of the neck and forced his head into the dirty dishwater. She let him come up for breath, then pushed his head under again, repeating the process several times despite his struggles. It was drastic treatment, but it stopped the nose-bleed. The woman gave him something to eat and let him rest in the bar until the next train travelling south drew into the station. The

remainder of his journey was uneventful, and two days later Paul
was with his parents again in Switzerland.

While the Royal Family were living a life of enforced idleness in
exile, the situation in Greece was developing rapidly.

The day of King Constantine's departure from Greece his son
Alexander, now King Alexander I, had come to Tatoi to take leave
of his parents. He was closeted for nearly an hour with his father,
who explained the situation to him in detail and gave him an outline
of the problems he would be dealing with in the immediate future.
He then impressed on Alexander in no uncertain terms that the
throne he was now occupying was not properly his but rightfully
belonged to his father and, after him, to his elder brother George.
He, Alexander, was merely a *locum tenens* until such time as
normality was restored.

Alexander listened dutifully and agreed with everything his
father said. The possibility that he might one day become King had
never crossed his mind, and neither his education nor his upbringing had been calculated to prepare him for such a role. He had been
a lively but unruly boy, not particularly good at lessons and a
mediocre cadet at the Military Academy, which he had left at the
age of twenty to serve as his father's Orderly Officer at the front in
the Balkan Wars. When the war was over he was posted to an
artillery regiment where Venizelos's younger son Sophocles, destined
to become Premier himself thirty years later, was one of his fellow
officers.

Like all the members of his family – with the solitary exception of
King George I who remained faithful to the horse carriage all his
life – Alexander had a passion for motorcars verging on the pathological. The internal combustion engine fascinated him, and the
happiest hours of his life would be spent in dirty overalls in the
workshop he had rigged up at Tatoi, taking his car to pieces and
putting it together again. His appreciation of art was rudimentary –
he once frankly admitted that he had always believed Botticelli was
a kind of spaghetti – and he did not particularly care for books
either, though he could spend hours poring over a manual on the
latest 12-cylinder Packard. Country life appealed to him greatly,
and his ambition even after he became King was to retire as soon as
possible to the life of a country gentleman: he even had his eye on
the property he was going to buy, the Syngros estate on the outskirts

of Kifissia, north of Athens, with its lovely old house on the hill surrounded by many acres of woods and farmland.

A strikingly handsome man, tall and athletic with a trim military moustache and a rimless monocle invariably stuck in his right eye, Alexander cut a dashing figure in Athenian society and was constantly involved in amorous adventures entailing much climbing through windows at night and jumping over garden walls in the classic romantic manner.

This was the general pattern of Alexander's life until he met Aspasia Manos, the daughter of one of his father's equerries. It was love at first sight for both of them.

At his farewell meeting with his father at Tatoi Alexander revealed to him that he had become secretly engaged to Mlle Manos and asked his permission to marry her. Constantine was noncommittal, but insisted that in any case he should wait until the war was over. This Alexander agreed to do.

On 26 June 1917 Venizelos returned to Athens from Thessaloniki and was duly appointed Premier of a politically reunited Greece which immediately declared war on the Central Powers. Alexander, who had studiously avoided shaking hands at the swearing-in ceremony at the Palace with the man whom he considered responsible for his father's exile and with whom he hoped to have as little to do as possible, soon discovered that his constitutional duties obliged him to see a good deal of his Premier. Obsessed with the dream of expanding Greece's frontiers eastwards across the Aegean, where Greek colonists had been settled for thousands of years, Venizelos could see the golden prize of Constantinople – 'the City' as the Greeks always call it – within his grasp if Greece played her cards properly by making a major contribution towards Allied victory and thus earning for herself an advantageous bargaining position at the conference table. 'Do as I advise, leave me to do my work in my own way, help me by giving me your full support, and I promise you the City.' This was the basic theme of Venizelos's relationship with the King, and it was not very long before the impressionable young monarch found himself falling under the spell of this man as so many others had done.

At the same time Alexander lost no opportunity of reminding his parents of his desire to marry Aspasia Manos. His messages assumed a new note of urgency after an alarming experience during a visit by the Duke of Connaught, Queen Victoria's last surviving son, who arrived in Athens on 19 March 1918 to deliver into King Alexander's hands the Insignia of Knight Grand Cross of the Order of the Bath conferred on him by the King of England. After carrying out his official mission the Duke asked the King for a private audience the following day, and Alexander spent a sleepless night in anxious anticipation, provoked by what seemed to be reliable information from a friend, that the Duke was going to propose a marriage with King George v's only daughter Mary, the Princess Royal – a proposal Alexander would have found it difficult to decline without offence.* In the event, what the Duke wanted was an opportunity to make the acquaintance of Mlle Manos, about whom he had heard so much. Alexander gladly arranged an informal meeting, and was told later by the septuagenarian Duke, who had become a widower only a few months before: 'If I were a little younger I would fall for her myself.'

All this time Alexander's father was urging him to wait – 'Be patient and I will be best man at your wedding' – while his mother, who still insisted on addressing her letters to 'Prince Alexander', was completely opposed to his marrying a commoner and implored him not to irritate his father and jeopardize his health by raising the question. Venizelos also felt that the Greek people as a whole would not react favourably to the idea of one of themselves becoming Queen of the Hellenes, but when he voiced his objections Alexander retorted vehemently that he would never have expected a Greek patriot and a democrat, as Venizelos professed himself to be, to find anything wrong with the idea of the King of the Hellenes marrying a Hellene. Furthermore, he said, he was already betrothed to Aspasia Manos: was Mr Venizelos suggesting that just because Alexander was a King he was not bound by his pledged word? Venizelos managed to persuade him to leave the matter in abeyance for a while longer.

On 13 May 1919 Alexander sent a letter written in his own hand to Venizelos, who was then in Paris leading the Greek Delegation at the Peace Conference, in which after congratulating the Premier on winning recognition of Greece's claims and aspirations he announced his intention of marrying Aspasia Manos 'thus terminating an intolerable situation and putting an end to unseemly gossip reflecting on the self-respect of my royal person'. He then expressed

* Princess Mary actually married Viscount Lascelles, afterwards 6th Earl of Harewood, four years later.

the conviction that his morganatic marriage with a Greek lady would meet with approval on the part of the great majority of the Greek people, and concluded by asking the Prime Minister to give the necessary instructions for the ceremony, signing himself 'with sentiments of esteem and affection, Yours ever, Alexander'. But Venizelos was not to be persuaded. 'From this distance,' he cabled diplomatically from Paris, 'it is impossible for me to assess what the reaction of the Greek people would be in this matter, and therefore I hope Your Majesty will await my return after the signature of the Peace Treaty before taking any irrevocable decision.'

But the King was not to be put off. On 4 November 1919, with the help of his friend Christo Zalocostas (the husband of Aspasia's sister), King Alexander and Aspasia Manos were secretly married. The Palace Chaplain who was to perform the ceremony lost his nerve at the last moment and did not appear at the appointed time, and Alexander had to go and fetch him by force to Zalocostas's house in the middle of the night. The priest gabbled through the service, signed the marriage certificate and made a hasty departure. Though sworn to secrecy, he went straight to the Archbishop and told him everything. The secret was out, but it was now too late for anybody to do anything about it: Alexander and Aspasia were man and wife.

It was not until six months later that Alexander and Aspasia were able to go to Paris for their honeymoon, and then only on condition that she did not travel with him and that they did not appear together on formal occasions.

While Alexander was still in Paris his mother tried to communicate with him by telephone from Switzerland. She was finally put through to Alexander's suite at the Hotel Majestic, but the call was taken by M. Athos Romanos, the Greek Minister in Paris. Queen Sophie asked to speak to her son. Romanos waited for a moment, then told the Queen that 'His Majesty regrets he cannot come to the telephone.' Alexander was not even told about the telephone call.

While on a visit to General Milne's headquarters on the Macedonian front Alexander was given a magnificent Alsatian dog which had been found in a captured enemy trench. Nobody seemed to be able to do anything with the half-savage and unfriendly animal, but Alexander took an instant liking to it and from that day 'Fritz' became the King's inseparable companion, following him at heel wherever he went and always riding with him in his car.

On 17 September 1920 Alexander went for a walk through the woods at Tatoi, still in the dirty overalls in which he had been greasing his car. Near the gamekeeper's lodge Fritz raced on ahead and by the time Alexander reached the cottage he could hear the Alsatian barking excitedly inside and the gamekeeper's pet monkey screeching frantically at the dog. Alexander ran into the house and tried to separate the two animals, which were now snapping savagely at each other; as he pulled them apart the terrified monkey clutched at his leg and bit him repeatedly, his sharp little teeth going through the overalls and sinking deep into the flesh. The game-keeper's wife dressed the wound as best she could – bits of the trouser material had been bitten into the flesh – and a doctor was summoned from Athens later to bandage it properly. Alexander seemed more concerned about the absurdity of the situation than by the injury itself and begged the doctor not to talk about it to anyone.

But the lacerations did not seem to be healing properly; a few days later they began to fester, giving Alexander considerable pain and a high temperature. A specialist was called in, but with the condition of the leg still deteriorating there did not seem much he could do and the word 'amputation' began to be whispered, though none of the Greek doctors was prepared to take upon himself the responsibility of making such a decision. A well-known doctor was summoned from Paris; meanwhile the local doctors decided to reinvestigate the wound, lancing it open and then stitching it up again without becoming any the wiser. By 5 October even the changing of the dressings had become sheer agony, and Alexander's screams of pain could be heard by the Evzone guard outside the house. In between spells of delirium Alexander would have periods of lucidity and indulge in his favourite pastime of identifying visitors from the sound of their cars. 'That's Dr Bensis's Vauxhall . . . That must be the new equerry's little Ford.' He would even joke with the doctor dressing his leg: 'That's an awful lot of bandage you're using,' he said to him once between his groans; 'you must have shares in the company.' When the French surgeon finally arrived all he could do was confirm that pernicious septicaemia had set in and that the patient's condition was hopeless – he would not even allow the dressings to be changed any more so as to spare the dying man unnecessary suffering.

On 25 October Alexander suddenly called for his driver and asked if the brakes of the big open Packard had been repaired. 'Get the car ready,' he said, 'we're going for a spin.' His hands curled lovingly round an invisible steering-wheel, turning it this way and that as he took the car on an imaginary drive through the narrow lanes of Tatoi. Then his arms dropped back on to the bed and his eyes closed in the sleep from which there is no awakening.*

All the members of the Royal House of Greece who have departed this life lie buried on the hill at Tatoi in simple graves among the trees. King Constantine and his wife Queen Sophie, who both died abroad and were brought to Tatoi for re-burial years later, occupy more imposing tombs in a chapel built specially for this purpose by their son King George II. Alexander lies buried alongside his parents.

The inscriptions on the tombs of the Kings of Greece are brief and identical:

GEORGE I, KING OF THE HELLENES, PRINCE OF DENMARK ...
CONSTANTINE, KING OF THE HELLENES, PRINCE OF DENMARK ...
GEORGE II, KING OF THE HELLENES, PRINCE OF DENMARK ...

Only the inscription on Alexander's tomb is different. It reads:

ALEXANDER, SON OF THE KING OF THE HELLENES, PRINCE OF DENMARK. HE REIGNED IN THE PLACE OF HIS FATHER, 14 JUNE 1917 TO 25 OCTOBER 1920.

* Five months after Alexander's death his wife Aspasia gave birth to a daughter, who subsequently married King Peter of Yugoslavia.

5

Venizelos arrived in Paris in December 1918 for the Peace Conference and remained there uninterruptedly until the signature of the Treaty nearly two years later. His natural aptitude for secret negotiations soon earned him a highly influential position in the inner councils of the great Powers, with whom his views carried a weight flatteringly disproportionate to the size and status of the country he was representing. His influence was particularly strong with Mr Lloyd George, who developed a profound admiration for the Greek statesman and gave him full support in all his plans.

Venizelos's untiring efforts in Paris culminated in the Treaty of Sèvres of 10 August 1920* which recognized most of Greece's national aspirations. His work completed, he now decided the time had come to return to Athens where on 26 August he proclaimed with justifiable pride in the Greek Parliament that Greece's domains now stretched across two continents from the Adriatic to the Black Sea, with her eastern frontier poised near Constantinople. The dream of a Greater Greece had become a reality – on paper, anyhow.

With the reasonable anticipation that the Greek people on whose behalf he had laboured for nearly two years in Paris could now fairly be expected to manifest their approval of his policies, Venizelos obtained the dissolution of Parliament and proclaimed general elections for 14 November.

The death of King Alexander, which occurred a few days before the elections were due, suddenly and unexpectedly revived the dynastic problem of finding another head of state at a particularly sensitive moment in Venizelos's plans. His relations with Alexander, though difficult and strained at first, had gradually developed into a harmonious and fruitful partnership, and some similar arrangement with the King's successor was what he now ardently desired. His

---

* The Treaty of Sèvres was never ratified and consequently became inoperative.

reservations regarding King Constantine and his eldest son George still held; his sole remaining hope was now Paul, King Constantine's youngest son. Venizelos acted swiftly: Admiral Coundouriotis was immediately appointed Regent *pro tem* and on 29 October the Greek Minister in Berne, M. Kepetzis, presented himself at the Hotel National in Lucerne on instructions from his Government and asked Prince Paul to receive him on a matter of urgency. When alone with the Prince, who was then not quite nineteen, the Minister announced he had come to convey officially the sad news of the death of King Alexander and at the same time in the name of the Greek Government to invite Prince Paul, as next in line of succession in view of the exclusion of his father and elder brother, to return to Greece immediately and assume the throne. There is no record of what else the Minister may have said to Paul, but the phraseology of Paul's subsequent reply suggests that he reiterated the Government's view that King Constantine's departure from Greece was of a permanent and irrevocable nature and that he must have also indicated that the Crown Prince could perhaps be prevailed upon by Prince Paul to renounce his prior constitutional claim to the throne. Throughout the meeting the Minister insisted on addressing the young prince as 'Your Majesty'.

After hearing the Minister out Paul said that obviously he could not give an immediate reply on such an important matter but would advise him of his decision as soon as possible. He then reported the conversation faithfully to his father, who told him to put down on paper the answer he felt he ought to give: they would then discuss the matter. Paul sat down and after several attempts finally produced a draft which he took to his father. King Constantine read it very carefully and then said, with some emotion, that he did not wish to alter a single word. All he did suggest was that M. Streit, the former Foreign Minister who had followed the King into exile as his private secretary, should check the grammar and the spelling.

Paul's letter, addressed to M. Kepetzis and written in his own hand on three sheets of plain white paper, was handed to the Greek Minister next day. The text was as follows:

Lucerne, 30 October 1920

I thank you and the Greek Government for your condolences on the death of my dear brother Alexander.

In reply to your communication, please convey the following to the

Greek Government with the request that the Greek people may also be informed:

I declare that I do not share the view of the Greek Government that according to the Constitution I am called upon today to ascend the throne of Greece.

The Greek throne does not belong to me. It belongs to my august father King Constantine, whose heir according to our Constitution is my elder brother George. Furthermore, neither of them has renounced these rights, but both were obliged to leave Greece in obedience to their higher sense of patriotic duty. The irregularity of the situation created by their departure has been acknowledged by the Government both in official statements and in its communication to me through yourself.

With specific reference to the terms conveyed in this communication, the King has always maintained that his return to Greece shall be subject only to the will of the Greek people freely expressed; and the Crown Prince, who is absent at the moment,* has never made any statement on the subject, nor is it incumbent upon me to ask him to renounce his rights.

I am convinced that my views as above coincide with those of the Greek people, with whom in any case the final decision rests in the exercise of their sovereign rights, and to whose free judgement we should all submit in the interests of our beloved country.

Only by means of such a manifestation of the will of the Greek people shall it be possible to achieve fully the safeguarding of internal peace and the further strengthening of the bonds which have always bound the Greek people and the Dynasty founded by my late beloved grandfather King George, all of whose members potentially have a claim on the Greek throne.

For these reasons I should only agree to ascend the Greek throne if the Greek people decided against the return of my august father and excluded the Crown Prince from the Greek throne.

PAUL

Paul's rejection of the crown was a blow to Venizelos, who was not particularly anxious at that moment to transform the forthcoming elections into a personal contest between himself and King Constantine, though he did not fear the result. Flushed with his success at the Peace Conference, out of touch with public opinion after nearly two years' absence in Paris, misled by the adulation of Parliament – which in a gesture evocative of the age of Pericles had voted him a 'Worthy Son of Hellas' – Venizelos miscalculated the

* The Crown Prince was in Bucharest in connexion with his engagement to Princess Elisabeth, daughter of the King of Roumania.

mood of the country and failed to appreciate that after eight years of continuous mobilization the people were weary of a war which they automatically identified with the man who was now planning new military adventures in a distant land.

The outcome of the elections of 14 November 1920 was a landslide rejection of Venizelos, whose Liberal Party was annihilated. Venizelos himself suffered the crowning humiliation of being defeated in his own constituency. Shattered by the verdict of his countrymen and disgusted by what he considered their gross ingratitude, he left Greece on 17 November and went into self-imposed exile abroad.

During King Alexander's illness the Government had rejected Queen Sophie's pleas from Switzerland to be allowed to come to her son's bedside, but when his condition deteriorated they relented and gave permission for his grandmother, the Dowager Queen Olga, to come instead. Her ship was delayed by rough seas, however, and when she finally reached Tatoi Alexander was already dead. She was still in Greece at the time of the elections, and the new Government promptly entrusted the Regency to her pending a plebiscite on whether King Constantine should be invited to resume the throne.

Two days before the plebiscite the British, French and Italian Governments issued a joint declaration to the effect that if the verdict were for the return of King Constantine a new and unfavourable situation would arise in the relations between Greece and the Allies, and in such an eventuality the Powers reserved to themselves full freedom of action in dealing with the situation thus created. What this meant in effect – and the point was made abundantly clear in subsequent amplifications of the Allied statement – was that Greece could in that case expect no Allied support in her confrontation with Turkey.

If anything were calculated to affront Greek pride, it was crude political pressure of this nature: in the plebiscite of 5 December 1920 just over one million votes were cast, and all but 10,883 were in favour of King Constantine's return.*

On 19 December 1920 King Constantine made his State entry into Athens to the ringing of church bells and the welcoming cheers

* Between 1917 and 1941, King Constantine and his eldest son King George II were obliged to leave their country no less than four times: in 1917, when Constantine was ousted by the Allied Powers; in 1922, when Constantine was forced to abdicate by the Plastiras Revolution; in 1923, when George was obliged by the Plastiras Revolution to

of the whole population of the city. The battle-cruiser *Averoff* had taken the King and his family on board in Venice for the journey to Piraeus but a violent gale and snowstorm caused a change of plan and the royal party disembarked at Corinth instead and made the rest of the journey to Athens by rail. On arrival the King issued a proclamation reaffirming that his sole purpose in life was to prove himself worthy of the love of the Greek people by safeguarding their rights and interests. At the same time he announced the simultaneous engagement of his eldest son and heir George to Princess Elisabeth, daughter of the King of Roumania, and of his eldest daughter Helen to the King of Roumania's eldest son and heir Prince Carol.*

At the Spa Conference on 11 May 1920 Greece was given a mandate by the Allied Powers to occupy certain areas in Asia Minor, and Smyrna with its large indigenous Greek population had been placed under Greek administration with a Greek High Commissioner – Greek troops were already in occupation of Smyrna and its hinterland, an advance force having landed in May 1919 with the blessing of the Allies. The Treaty of Sèvres had confirmed these dispositions, but the restoration of King Constantine in defiance of the wishes of the Big Powers provided the latter with a welcome excuse to divest themselves of obligations which reappraisals of policy were rendering onerous and incapable of fulfilment. The attitude now adopted was that the Treaty of Sèvres as it stood could not be implemented, and when Greece rejected various proposed modifications in favour of Turkey the Allies promptly suspended all further financial aid to Greece.

During this time an outstanding leader, Mustapha Kemal Pasha, had emerged from the political confusion in Turkey. Setting up a Nationalist Headquarters in the heart of Anatolia and defying the

leave the country while preparations were made for the establishment of a Republic; and in 1941, when George left in order to continue the war against the Axis Powers while Greece was occupied by the enemy. In all these cases the King's departure was the result of arbitrary action, domestic or foreign, without any prior consultation of the Greek people's wishes in the matter. In contrast, on all three occasions when the King was invited to return it was in response to the desire of the people freely expressed by plebiscite: on 5 December 1920 (1,010,788 votes to 10,883); on 3 November 1935 (1,491,992 to 32,454); and on 1 September 1946 (1,166,667 to 174,411). Historical experience would seem to indicate that whenever consulted on the subject the Greeks have shown a definite predilection for the Monarchy.

* Both marriages were destined to end in divorce.

authority of the Sultan in Constantinople, Kemal now repudiated the Treaty of Sèvres and applied himself energetically to the task of building up an army to oppose the Greeks. Time was clearly not on the side of Greece and in October 1920 the order was given for the Greek Army in Smyrna to advance into the interior against Kemal's forces.

This was the situation which King Constantine inherited when he returned to Greece from exile two months later.* Greece was committed both morally and militarily in Asia Minor, and there was no going back now.

The first Greek offensive of October 1920 having petered out, a second attack was ordered in January 1921 but this also ended inconclusively. In an attempt to improve the morale of the sorely-tried troops the Government asked King Constantine to take over the supreme command himself, and on 29 May – only a few days after the Allies solemnly declared their neutrality in the Graeco-Turkish conflict – the King and his General Staff left for Smyrna after attending a Te Deum at the Cathedral in Athens to invoke the blessing of God on the Greek cause.

But Constantine in 1921 was not the 'Son of the Eagle' of the Balkan Wars; he was a sick man and during the short time he remained in Turkey he was in no fit state to take any active part in operations. Six years earlier, in April 1915, he had suffered an attack of pleurisy which had nearly proved fatal, and he had undergone a major operation involving the removal of two of his ribs – it was during this time, while his father was lying critically ill, that Paul had been closest to him, spending hours by his bedside and secretly bringing him newspapers and cigarettes which the doctors had forbidden him. Constantine had finally recovered, but the wound had never healed properly and required constant attention for the rest of his life. At the Te Deum before his departure for Smyrna the stifling heat in the crowded Cathedral had caused the dormant wound to re-open, and a dark stain had spread over the King's white tunic obliging him to sit down in order to hide his condition from the congregation. It was in this state that he made the journey by

---

* General Sir Henry Wilson, Chief of the British Imperial General Staff, recounted that at a meeting with Venizelos he 'told him straight that he had ruined his country and himself by going to Smyrna'. Winston Churchill, though no less critical, spreads the blame a little more evenly: 'I cannot understand to this day how the eminent statesmen in Paris – Wilson, Clemenceau, Lloyd George and Venizelos – could have been betrayed into so rash and fatal a step.'[4]

sea to Smyrna, and the arduous living conditions at the front soon proved too much for his weakened constitution. Less than four months after his arrival in Smyrna he collapsed and on 29 September 1921 was obliged to return to Athens.

On 20 October 1920 Greece's ally France signed an agreement with the Turks under which, in return for certain considerations of a commercial nature, Kemal was to receive ample supplies of arms and military equipment.* Britain, to whom Greece now turned for help, strongly urged that the Greek Army should hold on to its positions pending a conference with her French Allies. The outcome of this conference, which did not take place until the following March, was the offer of an armistice in return for various concessions on the part of Greece including the abandonment of any claim on Smyrna and the partitioning of Eastern Thrace between Greece and Turkey. Greece accepted these terms but the Turks refused any armistice unless Asia Minor were evacuated by all foreign troops within four months – a condition which both Greece and the Allies found unacceptable.

The stalemate continued until July 1922 when two Greek divisions were suddenly withdrawn from Smyrna and landed at Rodosto on the Sea of Marmora with the intention of seizing Constantinople and thus strengthening Greece's bargaining position in future negotiations. This project had to be abandoned, however, when the Allies firmly warned Greece that they would resist by force of arms if necessary any attempt to take Constantinople.

In January 1915 Colonel John Metaxas, then Acting Chief of Staff, had prepared a memorandum evaluating the case for and against Greek expansion in Asia Minor, in which he had said *inter alia* that the annexation of any territory in Anatolia would inevitably entail long and arduous operations into the interior in extremely unfavourable conditions:

The invading army would find itself obliged to pursue the Turks into the heart of a country inhabited by a hostile population and bristling with physical obstacles. . . . Even if successful in the initial stages of the campaign, the Greek Army would gradually see its strength dwindle owing to the necessity of guarding its flanks and its lines of communications . . . Sooner or later a point would be reached where

---

* 'A few weeks later the Greek army upon the Anatolian plateau were being shelled by the guns of Creusot and bombed by aeroplanes provided to Kemal from French sources.'[5]

equilibrium would be established between the opposing forces. From that moment onwards the Greek Army would be forced to act on the defensive, the initiative passing to the enemy. The Turks, fighting on interior lines in their own country, would be able to bide their time so as to attack the Greek Army when it was deployed over a vast front, finally dealing it a crushing blow.

In the event, Metaxas's assessment proved uncannily accurate and the summer of 1922 found the situation developing exactly as he had foreseen. Kemal decided to make his stand in defence of Ankara on a strong position north of the Sakkaria. With the Greek Army's communications and lines of supply stretched tenuously across nearly four hundred miles of desolate country, and with his own forces mustered on ground of his own choosing and equipped with all the arms they needed, Kemal launched his offensive along the whole front on 25 August 1922. The Greeks managed to absorb the first shock of the assault but before long their lines broke under successive waves of Turkish infantry who hurled themselves against their positions. Unable to contain the Turkish attack the Greek troops began to withdraw, in good order at first but later in confusion degenerating into panic as they retreated westward to Smyrna, where thousands of Greek refugees fleeing before the advancing Turks were already converging, blocking the roads and swelling the population of the city.

The Turkish Army entered Smyrna on 9 September 1922. For the next five days Kemal's soldiery were turned loose on the city, slaughtering every Greek man, woman and child they could find and then setting fire to the Greek quarter and burning it to the ground. The Archbishop of Smyrna was brought before the Turkish Commandant who hurled him bodily from a balcony to be literally torn to pieces by the Turkish mob below. In the harbour there were indescribable scenes of horror as people tried to get away in anything that would float, and thousands drowned as they plunged into the sea to escape the pursuing Turks or as overloaded boats capsized a few yards from the quayside.*

In the consuming flames and the seething waters of the ancient Aeolian city, three thousand years of Hellenic civilization perished for ever.

---

* The exact number of Greeks who lost their lives in Smyrna during these five days has never been ascertained, but the figure of 300,000 men, women and children is generally accepted as accurate.

4 Paul the schoolboy arriving in England to continue his studies at St Peter's Preparatory School, Eastbourne, in the summer of 1913. Left to right: Paul, his sisters Helen and Irene, his brother George (*behind*), his father King Constantine and his brother Alexander. All four men in the photograph became kings.

5 Paul (*left*) on a climbing expedition with a friend in 1936.

6 The Royal Palace, Athens.

⇒ 6 ⇐

On his return to Greece with his father in December 1920 Paul had
set about picking up the threads of his life and resuming his interrupted studies. His abortive initiation into cadet life in Germany
had not altered his determination to follow a naval career, nor
diminished his eagerness to continue his training as soon as possible,
and within a few days of his arrival in Athens he enrolled at the
Greek Naval Academy. A special rank of Dokimos Simaioforos,
half-way between cadet and midshipman, had been created to
accommodate students whose training had been interrupted for
political or other reasons and who could not be expected to start
from the bottom again, and Paul was placed in this class. King
Constantine himself brought him to the Academy the first day and
in the full hearing of staff and cadets the King impressed on everybody that his son was just another cadet and was to be treated as
such. The King then shook Paul's hand and left; for the next two
years the huge barracks on the Castella overlooking Piraeus harbour
was to be Paul's home.

Cadets at the Naval Academy slept in big communal dormitories,
but the senior cadet each year traditionally had a room to himself
and the only concession made in Paul's case was that he shared this
room with the senior cadet instead of using a dormitory. He was
addressed as 'Ypsilotate', Your Royal Highness, and in the polite
form of the plural, but this in no way inhibited his instructors from
reprimanding him in class when necessary in the usual naval
manner ('Your Royal Highness, you are a clot').

Paul would arrive at the Academy punctually at 7.45 on Monday
morning and stay there until midday on Saturday when he would be
picked up and driven to Tatoi for the weekend with his family.
From Monday to Saturday he would lead the life of an ordinary
cadet – lectures, naval drill, P.T., technical training – and in July

and August there was the annual spell of duty on board ship with all the scrubbing of decks, polishing of brasses and stoking of boilers that went with it. This was the first instance in its history that the Greek Naval Academy had a Royal Prince among its cadets, and inevitably there was an initial period of embarrassment while both sides adjusted themselves to the situation, but it was not very long before Paul could relax and feel completely at home. This was the first time in his life that he was living for long periods away from home and outside the environment of the Court, and the fact that he could be accepted and liked for his own self, instead of just being respected because of his rank, was a revelation that was to stand him in good stead in his dealings with people later on in his life when the responsibilities of kingship devolved on him.

Smoking was strictly prohibited inside the Academy, but the cadets often felt the urge to indulge in this forbidden pleasure and it seemed only logical that Paul – who had not yet begun smoking, though he was to become a chain smoker before long – should be asked to stand guard and give warning if an officer should be approaching. On several occasions when there was active opposition to some irksome regulation Paul took his place among the cadets as a matter of course, and duly suffered the same punishments.

But it was on the sea that he found himself completely in his element right from the start. He was a born sailor and could handle a boat with that instinctive sense of wind and current that no amount of coaching can impart if it is not inborn.

In 1922, having completed his shore training, Paul was posted to the cruiser *Elli* with the rank of sub-lieutenant. The Commanding Officer of the ship was Captain Joannides,* a personal friend of King Constantine, who repeated to him the instructions he had given to the Naval Academy as to how Paul should be treated. Captain Joannides, known in the Greek Navy as 'Kapetan Fysaroufas' (Captain Puff-and-Blow), needed no such injunction: Greece was at war with Turkey, and in any case war-time discipline was always maintained on his ship.

Paul did not see much action on the *Elli*: the Turkish fleet seldom ventured out to sea, and on the occasions when the *Elli* was under fire it was from enemy shore batteries when she ventured too close to land. In the evacuation of Smyrna she covered the embarkation of

---

* Vice-Admiral Pericles Joannides who married Princess Marie, Paul's aunt, on 16 December 1922. He died on 7 February 1965.

Greek troops with protective fire from her guns before finally withdrawing to Greek waters in Samos.

On 8 September 1922, the day before the Turks entered Smyrna, the Government in Athens resigned after ordering general de-mobilization. A few days later a revolution broke out among dis-contented officers on the islands of Chios and Mytilene, where remnants of the Greek Army had taken refuge after the evacuation of Asia Minor. The revolution was led by Colonels Stylianos Gonatas and Nicholas Plastiras who issued a proclamation – copies of which were dropped from an aeroplane over Athens – demanding the abdication of King Constantine, the dissolution of Parliament and the appointment of a new emergency government.

Broken in health and spirit, Constantine consulted his old friend and comrade-in-arms of the Balkan Wars Colonel John Metaxas, who advised him to accede to the demands of the revolution.* Three days later, from the same fishing village at Oropos where five years before he had begun his first exile, King Constantine sailed away once again, his eldest son having been sworn in as King George II.

This time Constantine did not return. A few weeks later, on 11 January 1923, he died from haemorrhage of the brain in a hotel room in Palermo, a small leather pouch containing Greek earth clutched tightly in his hand.

As soon as the news of King Constantine's death reached Athens Metaxas, now generally accepted as leader of the Royalist faction, wrote to General Gonatas, the Premier, demanding that the body of the King should be brought to Greece and given a State funeral. Venizelos, whom the Government thought wise to consult in the matter by telegram, replied advising that permission should be given provided the body was brought ashore at Oropos and taken direct to Tatoi for private interment. This proposal was put to King George who rejected it out of hand: if his father could not be buried in Greece with the full honours due to a King, then he was not going to be buried in Greece at all – not for the time being, anyway. Paul went to Italy to make alternative arrangements.

* In his monumental diary published posthumously in four bulky volumes – *Metaxas: To Prosopiko Tou Imerologio* (*Metaxas: His Personal Diary*)[6] – there are the following entries for 14 September 1922: 'Summoned urgently to Palace in evening. Advised King abdicate immediately to avert worse evils for the Monarchy. King decides abdicate and asks me to draft letter of abdication and proclamation. Then Constantine says goodbye to me. I am moved to tears.'

Constantine's body was taken first to Naples, where the funeral service was held in the presence of as many members of the family as could be mustered, and then to Florence, where it was placed in the crypt of the Russian Orthodox Church.*

One of the first acts of the Revolutionary Government after it was installed in Athens was to arraign before a military tribunal a number of individuals whom it regarded as personally responsible for the Asia Minor disaster, namely the former Premier, four Cabinet Ministers and the Commander-in-Chief of the Greek Army in Anatolia. After a trial lasting fourteen days they were all sentenced to death on 28 November 1922 and summarily shot.† A wave of revulsion swept through Europe against this senseless act of reprisal, and Britain severed diplomatic relations with Greece. Prince Andrew of Greece – younger brother of King Constantine and father of Prince Philip Duke of Edinburgh – who had been in command of an Army Corps in Asia Minor with the rank of lieutenant-general, was also arrested and would probably have shared the fate of the others had it not been for the timely intervention of his first cousin the King of England, who secured his release and had him evacuated from Greece with his whole family on board H.M.S. *Calypso*.‡

Before putting Gounaris and his colleagues on trial the Revolutionary Council had taken the precaution of divesting the new Sovereign of his constitutional prerogative of mercy, so that when the verdict came out he was powerless even to commute the death sentences. Overwhelmed by frustration at his helplessness King George decided to follow his father's example and abdicate but Metaxas, whose loyalty to the monarchy could not be disputed, once

---

* When King George II returned to Greece after the restoration of the monarchy in 1935 he brought back for burial the remains of his father, his mother and his grandmother, who had all died in exile. They were given the State funeral which they had been denied at the time of their death, with all the solemn ritual of the Greek Orthodox Church, and were finally laid to rest at Tatoi. By one of those ironies of fate with which Greek history seems to abound, Venizelos was also brought to Greece the same year. He too had died in exile; he too had breathed his last in a hotel room in a foreign land. He was taken by sea from Brindisi direct to Canea and buried privately in his native Crete.

† These men have passed into Greek history as 'The Six'. They were D. Gounaris, P. Protopapadakis, N. Stratos, G. Baltazzi, N. Theotoky and General G. Hadjianestis. Gounaris was ill throughout the trial and had to be strapped to a chair to face the firing squad.

‡ This mission was expertly carried out by Captain Gerald Talbot, R.N., to whom King George V showed his personal appreciation by appointing him a K.C.V.O.

again intervened and advised the King not to abandon the country to the chaos that would assuredly follow if he were to remove himself from the scene at that moment. George was persuaded to stay, a lonely and isolated figure, seeing nobody and seldom venturing outside the Palace.

The elevation of his childless elder brother to the throne had placed Paul next in line of succession and he was now accorded the official designation of Diadochos (literally Heir to the Throne or Crown Prince) that was to be his for the next twenty-five years. At this time he was serving in the Navy as a lieutenant.*

On 22 October 1923, a few weeks before elections were due, a military counter-revolution broke out under the leadership of three senior Army officers – Major-General G.Leonardopoulos, Major-General P.Gargalides and Colonel G.Ziras – but was quickly suppressed by the Athens Government. Metaxas had been told the details of this project in advance and had been so appalled by its amateur planning that he had tried to dissuade its organizers from going through with it, but without success. He finally decided to throw in his lot with them anyhow, and after the collapse of the coup managed to escape to Italy on board a Norwegian ship which luckily happened to be sailing that day from Patras.

Convinced that the King was also implicated in the coup – Metaxas's links with the Palace were no secret – the extremist republican elements in the Revolutionary Council led by Major-General Theodore Pangalos and Captain Alexander Hadjikyriakos, who between them controlled the Army and the Navy, now began to bring pressure on the Government to depose the King on the grounds that he no longer enjoyed the confidence of the Armed Forces. This demand was put in even more drastic form – that the monarchy should be abolished and a republic be installed in its place – immediately after the elections of 16 December 1923, and Gonatas duly wrote to the King saying that as the newly-elected National Assembly was about to examine the question of the regime,

---

* Students of Greek events of this period may be perplexed by certain discrepancies in the matter of dates due to the fact that until 1923 Greece still used the Old Style calendar, which is thirteen days behind. On 1 March 1923 Greece adopted the Gregorian or New Style Calendar like the rest of the world – as the newspaper *Kathimerini* put it in an editorial, 'the Greek nation which went to bed last night fondly believing that it was Wednesday, the 15th day of February 1923, will be surprised to learn that today is indeed Thursday, the day after Wednesday, but the first day of March 1923.'

it was considered desirable that during this time 'Your Majesty should be graciously pleased to absent yourself abroad on leave.'

On 19 December 1923 King George left Greece with the Queen, ostensibly on a visit to his wife's parents in Roumania.* With them went his brother, Crown Prince Paul. They were seen off by the Prime Minister and Madame Gonatas, who wept profusely as she presented the Queen with a large bouquet of flowers.

The new National Assembly, which now included most of the leading members of the Revolutionary Council, met on 2 January 1924 and immediately invited the self-exiled Venizelos to come back to Greece and assume the premiership. Bowing to the general wish Venizelos returned from Paris and formed a Government with the declared intention of holding a plebiscite in two months' time to decide whether Greece should be a monarchy or a republic, and then holding fresh elections under the regime finally chosen. But this procedure was too legalistic for the more impatient elements in the new Chamber, and the acrimonious debates so exasperated Venizelos that on 4 February, after some particularly heated exchanges, he stormed out of the Chamber and resigned in disgust. A month later he quit Greece for the second time and went to live in France, where until he returned to Greece in 1928 he was to devote his energies to producing a scholarly rendering into modern Greek of Thucydides' *History of the Peloponnesian War*.[7]

On 25 March 1924, the National Assembly passed a resolution – proposed by the new Government under the republican Alexander Papanastasiou – abolishing the monarchy, declaring Greece a republic and depriving all members of the reigning dynasty of their Greek nationality and their rights to the Greek throne. In addition, the resolution provided for the compulsory expropriation of property belonging to members of the deposed dynasty, and also stipulated that property which had come into the possession of the Royal Family in the form of gifts from the State, local municipalities, etc. should revert automatically to the previous owners without compensation. This qualification led to the belief that compensation would be paid at least for private property belonging to the Crown, but in the event all property, irrespective of how it was acquired,

---

* On 14 February 1921 George had married Princess Elisabeth, daughter of King Ferdinand of Roumania, in Bucharest, and arrived in Athens a fortnight later just in time to attend the wedding of his eldest sister Helen to his wife's elder brother Carol, Crown Prince and subsequently King of Roumania. King George's marriage with Elisabeth was childless.

was confiscated without compensation. This included Tatoi, the royal estate on the slopes of Mount Parnes purchased piecemeal from the Scarlatos-Soutsos and the Syngros families by King George I from 1872 onwards out of his private funds. In his will King George I had stipulated that Tatoi should always belong to the reigning King.*

* The estate consists of some nine thousand acres of pine forest, but large areas of woodland were destroyed in the big fire on 30 June 1916 – which also destroyed the original house and nearly cost King Constantine his life – and by clandestine tree-felling during the occupation of 1941–4, when most of Athens obtained its winter fuel by poaching timber from the abandoned estate. Tatoi was restored to King George II by Act of Parliament on 22 January 1936 after the re-establishment of the monarchy. It now includes a dairy farm, a market garden and a winery.

⇒ 7 ⇐

The abolition of the monarchy in 1924 and the establishment of a republican regime meant the dispersal of the Greek Royal Family, all of whose members were expelled from Greece. Having been deprived of their Greek nationality they were left without passports but this difficulty was circumvented with the help of their kinsman the King of Denmark, who invoked the ingenious but impeccable argument that as all members of the Greek Royal Family were also Princes of Denmark they were fully entitled to Danish passports.

Paul's brother King George was in Bucharest with his Roumanian wife when he received the news of his dethronement. They were staying as guests of his father-in-law King Ferdinand at the Villa Cotroceni, the royal residence in the Roumanian capital, but after a while they moved to a rented house on the Calea Vitoriei. The marriage was not a success and was already beginning to show signs of strain. The couple now steadily grew further apart and George's journeys abroad – to Florence to visit his mother, to Spain, but mostly to England – became more frequent and his absences from Bucharest longer. In 1932 he left Elisabeth for good and moved to London, accompanied only by his friend and equerry of many years, Major Dimitri Levidis, and his faithful manservant 'Mitso' Panteleos. He lost all contact with his wife after that, and when Elisabeth divorced him on 6 July 1935 the first he knew of it was when he read the news in a London newspaper.

Paul's grandmother, the Dowager Queen Olga, was staying in London with her youngest son Prince Christopher, who had recently married a young American widow, Mrs Anastasia Stewart Leeds. Prince Christopher's wife died suddenly on 29 August 1923, and the Dowager Queen then stayed for a while with her daughter Princess Marie, also living in London in a rented house overlooking

Regent's Park. The prematurely widowed Prince Christopher decided to make a permanent home for his mother in Rome where the climate would suit her better, and Queen Olga joined him there after he bought a house which he named Villa Anastasia in memory of his wife. His mother's health was failing, however, and on 18 June 1926 she died in Rome at the age of seventy-five, her body being taken in due course to join that of her son Constantine in the crypt of the Russian Orthodox Church in Florence.

After his mother's death Prince Christopher stayed on in Rome. On 11 February 1929 he married again, his second wife being Princess Françoise, daughter of the Duc de Guise, the Pretender to the throne of France. The youngest and most sophisticated of King George I's eight children, Christopher led a colourful and cosmopolitan life that included the offer in 1912 of the throne of Portugal, which he declined for the very good reason that the deposed King Manoel was a friend of his and because 'nothing under the sun would induce me to accept a kingdom; a crown is too heavy a thing to put on lightly; it has to be worn by those born to that destiny, but that any man should willingly take on the responsibility in these troubled times, not being constrained by duty to do so, passes my comprehension.' Not long afterwards he was offered the throne of Lithuania, which he also declined with the excuse that 'my head is too bald to prevent the crown from slipping off'.

Christopher died in Rome on 21 January 1940.

Three of Paul's uncles made Paris their home in exile. Prince George – 'Uncle Jakob' of the flowing moustaches and a quarter-deck vocabulary in four languages – who had married in 1907 the Princess Marie Bonaparte, great-granddaughter of Napoleon's brother Lucien, already had a second home in Paris, where he now established himself with his family.

To Paris also came Paul's uncle Nicholas with his wife the Grand Duchess Helen, daughter of the Grand Duke Vladimir of Russia and their three daughters Olga, Elizabeth and Marina, all of whom married in exile: Olga to Prince Paul of Yugoslavia, Elizabeth to Count Toerring-Jettenbach and Marina to the Duke of Kent. While in Athens the family had occupied a magnificent palazzo in the centre of the city, a wedding gift from the Czar,* but in Paris

* It is now the Italian Embassy.

their reduced circumstances made it necessary for Prince Nicholas to find some means of supplementing his small income, which he did by giving lessons in painting and selling his own work, which he truthfully but misleadingly signed 'Nicolas le Prince'.

The third uncle, Andrew – whose links with England through his marriage with Princess Alice, daughter of the Marquess of Milford Haven, were destined to be cemented even more closely many years later through the marriage of his son Philip with Queen Elizabeth II – had already left Greece with his family in December 1922 after being arrested by the Revolutionary Government in the aftermath of the Asia Minor disaster. After visiting their relatives in England Andrew and his family settled in a small house at St Cloud on the outskirts of Paris.

Paul himself had gone to Bucharest with his brother King George in December 1923 and was staying with his sister Helen, the wife of Crown Prince Carol of Roumania, when the republic was proclaimed in Greece. The opulence of the Roumanian Court and the sophisticated superficiality of Roumanian society life were not particularly to his taste, however, and after a while he left Bucharest and went to stay with his mother, who after King Constantine's death in Palermo had made her home in Florence with her two younger daughters, Irene and Katherine.

Although Paul was always on the move during the next few years, in between his travels he would always return to the Villa Bobolina on the via Bolognese. It was in Florence that his love of music received its first deep awakening, and he began to take lessons from Signor Volterra, a former concert pianist of some repute. Even in the family atmosphere and the beautiful surroundings of Florence, however, Paul found the prolonged inactivity intolerable and he was soon on his travels again, this time to England.

In London Paul immediately began looking up old school friends like 'Rosie' Stokes-Rees and the Weldon brothers and various other people he had met in Athens. One of these was Henry Drummond Wolff who had been to Greece in 1922 in connexion with an order for aircraft for the Greek Air Force. To him Paul now unburdened himself, asking if he could help him find a job, preferably something to do with cars or aircraft. Drummond Wolff had family connexions with the giant Armstrong-Siddeley combine, his sister being Lord Armstrong's wife, and after talking the matter over with the Chairman, Sir John Siddeley, he was able to tell Paul that if he was not above working as a factory hand, a job could be found for him in the company's plant in Coventry. Paul immediately accepted on condition that his identity should not be disclosed; he would prefer to be known as plain Mr Paul Beck.

He had driven to England from Florence in his most prized possession, a Lancia Lambda, but as the ownership of such a car by a factory worker was bound to arouse suspicion he sold it and bought a humbler vehicle, a second-hand Morris Cowley. He had been told that most of the people who worked at Coventry lived in Leamington Spa near by, so he drove there in the Morris and set about finding somewhere to live. After looking around he found just what he was looking for – a room in a house in Clarendon Square, practically next door to a garage where he could keep his car.

For the next ten months Paul settled into a routine consisting of driving to Coventry from Leamington every morning, putting in a full day's work at the factory, and driving back to Leamington in the evening. His pay was £3·50 a week, the standard rate for an apprentice. To begin with he was assigned to the Instructor and Chief Pilot of Armstrong-Whitworth's, Alan Campbell-Orde, to familiarize himself with aircraft and aero-engine construction. Campbell-Orde and the other two test pilots with whom Paul worked saw a good deal of each other after working hours, and as they all lived at Leamington they would often go to Paul's room and sit talking till the early hours of the morning. Campbell-Orde and his two colleagues soon discovered the identity of their apprentice, but this did not affect the easy relationship that had already developed between them. Occasionally Paul would drive to London for the weekend to see visiting relatives – his brother King George, his mother Queen Sophie, his Aunt Marie – but he would always return to Leamington in time to be at the factory first thing on Monday morning.

After three months on airfield work under Campbell-Orde he put in another three months on factory organization and administration and ended up with a spell in the engine assembly shop. Throughout this time he was also perfecting his knowledge of motor cars, tinkering about with his own Morris in the garage in Clarendon Square or helping Mr Hodgkins and his two sons whenever a particularly interesting repair job came in. It was not until many years later that the Hodgkins family discovered the identity of the tall young man from the house next door who would spend hours in their garage giving them a helping hand.

After about a year at Coventry Paul gave up the job at the factory and returned to London, where he took a small flat near Victoria. He sought relaxation for a while by plunging into the social round, and for the next few months the tall good-looking prince with the booming laugh and the rimless monocle stuck firmly in one eye was to be seen at all the fashionable parties in London and at country weekends – with the Tredegars in Wales, shooting stag with Lord Massereene and Ferrard in the Isle of Mull, sailing at Cowes. He was a member of the Royal Air Force Club in Piccadilly and when in London he would drop in practically every day for a meal or a drink. He was also an honorary member – the only one – of the Artists' Rifles Association Club in Craven Street, off the Strand, and made many friends among its officers, especially Lt-Col. F. Alan Parker, who as a young subaltern at the time, shared a flat with a brother officer in Regent's Park Terrace, not far from where Paul's Aunt Marie was living. Paul was a frequent visitor at the flat, where he would spend hours at the piano – something he lacked in his own flat – and Parker gave him a key so he could go there and play whenever he felt like it.

Paul's zest for life and his passionate interest in everything that was going on around him was the first thing that struck those who met him. One day at a dinner party he found himself sitting next to Dr Webb-Peploe, a house surgeon at St Thomas's Hospital. Paul was fascinated by the doctor's description of the activities in a big London hospital; could he visit St Thomas's one day? Webb-Peploe was actually going on to the hospital after dinner that very night and offered to take Paul with him. They boarded a bus to Westminster and Paul was taken on a conducted tour of the whole hospital, finishing up at an emergency operation in the theatre which Paul watched with fascinated interest. Dawn was breaking by the time he arrived home.

Despite the pleasant distractions which London society life had to offer, this was the worst period of Paul's exile. A gregarious person by nature, he now found himself leading a very lonely existence and before long the inevitable happened: he developed an emotional attachment for a young Englishwoman who returned his affection. Essentially a family man, Paul now began seriously to think in terms of marriage but before he could make any final decision his mother arrived unexpectedly in London – she had heard rumours and had come to find out for herself. Paul explained the situation and was distressed to find Queen Sophie firmly opposed to any idea of marriage. The Queen had very strict ideas about the conventions in such matters and felt that one morganatic marriage in the family was enough. Furthermore, a marriage in the circumstances would be widely interpreted as a tacit acceptance of the unlikelihood of the restoration of the monarchy in the foreseeable future and would consequently be a blow to the hopes and aspirations of the supporters of the monarchy and more particularly her elder son King George. Paul was now greatly concerned about his mother's health and was anxious to do nothing that might hurt her. He agreed to postpone any marriage plans for the time being, and under the pressure of all these inhibiting influences the affair petered out after a few weeks.

At a dinner party at the Ambassadors Club in London in the spring of 1930 Paul happened to run into Captain Frederick Wessel, whom he knew slightly. Wessel was Danish by birth but had been to school in England, and when the First World War broke out he took out British nationality – it cost him exactly twenty-five pence – and joined the Royal Fusiliers, later transferring to the Royal Flying Corps. After the war he stayed on in England doing various jobs in the City and later, after his father died leaving him a considerable amount of money, doing nothing in particular and leading a life of leisure in London society. In the course of conversation with Paul at the party Wessel mentioned that he was going on a cruise to the Greek islands in his motor yacht later in the summer. Immediately Paul was seized with nostalgia: he had not set foot in Greece for seven years, and memories of his naval cadet days and of his home at Tatoi came flooding back. He took Wessel to one side and asked him point blank: could he come with him on the cruise? Wessel was taken completely by surprise but the suggestion appealed to his sense of adventure; at the same time he had no particular desire to end up in a Greek jail for bringing a prohibited person into the country, so he asked for time to think it over. Next day he told Paul he would be happy to take him along under certain conditions: first, Paul would have to conceal his identity; second, he should abstain from any political activity while in Greece; and third, he would have to pull his weight on board the yacht. Paul immediately accepted, and a rendezvous was arranged on the French Riviera where the *Frefrada* was being fitted out for the cruise.

On the appointed day Paul presented himself at Villefranche. He had grown a beard, the monocle was gone, and he was now the proud possessor of a brand new Danish passport. 'I am your cousin Peter Wessel,' he announced to the astonished and delighted Freddy Wessel, 'and you have hired me as a deck-hand for this cruise.'

On 10 July 1930 the *Frefrada* left Villefranche at 10.30 a.m. on the first leg of the voyage. On board were Freddy Wessel and his English wife Frances, Paul, the other deck-hand Bill Hedgley with his brother-in-law Watson who was in charge of the galley, and Teddy, a wire-haired terrier who was always doing little tricks, like standing on his head. Everybody on board knew who 'Peter Wessel' was but they had been sworn to secrecy and all addressed him as Peter.

The *Frefrada* was a 64-ft twin-engined motor yacht of 44 tons, built at Cowes the year before. She had two 70-h.p. Parsons engines and carried fuel for a thousand miles at eight knots, though she could work up to eleven knots if pressed. The name *Frefrada* was an amalgam of the names of Frederick Wessel, his wife Frances and his son David.*

Ten hours after leaving Villefranche *Frefrada* arrived at Calvi in Corsica, where the travellers spent four days due to rough weather. On 15 July they started off but a strong head wind and heavy seas forced them back to Calvi. Next day they tried again and this time they managed to make Ajaccio, where they refuelled and set off again, reaching Bonifacio the following morning. They did not like Bonifacio: 'It is dirty to the ninth degree and flies are to be encountered in plagues,' wrote Hedgley in the record he kept of the cruise. From Bonifacio they headed for Naples via the Ponza Islands, off which they were surprised to see a pair of huge turtles surfacing alongside. They put in at Porto Nuovo di Santa Lucia, where visits were exchanged with people Wessel knew from the

* Not long afterwards the Wessels divorced and the name of the yacht was changed to *Dania*.

Naples Yacht Club. That evening there was a dinner party on board
to which several local dignitaries were invited. Fortunately none of
them knew Paul, who was particularly anxious that his identity
should not be revealed at this stage as the Greek authorities might
be warned of his impending arrival.

From Naples *Frefrada* went on to Capri where again several
visitors came on board, including an old army friend of Wessel's,
Ivone Kirkpatrick,* but nobody suspected that the tall bearded
sailor was not what he was introduced as, the owner's cousin. On
30 July they arrived at Messina, but a German ship unloading to
windward sent clouds of coal dust over them so they decided to sail
across the straits to a cleaner anchorage at Reggio on the other side
of the channel. While in Messina Hedgley recorded disapprovingly
that the local agent 'wore loud squeaking yellow boots which he failed
to wipe when coming aboard'.

On 2 August *Frefrada* arrived at Corfu and anchored close to the
old Venetian fort, opposite the fosse separating the citadel from the
main town. This was their first call on Greek territory, and as Paul
knew many people on the island he had to be particularly careful
not to betray his identity; but the disguise of the beard proved very
effective, and although the party went ashore several times Paul was
not recognized. They visited the Palace in the centre of the town
built in the 1820s during the British administration of the Ionian
Islands as the Chancery of the Order of St Michael and St George,
which was founded in Corfu, and had a look at the royal villa of Mon
Repos. They also went on picnics and excursions in the interior of
the island, being very careful to give a wide berth to the Ropa area
where the Theotoky family, many of whose members had close links
with the Crown and were well known to Paul, had their country
estate. Despite Wessel's injunctions not to talk politics, discussions
on the political situation were inevitable at meetings with Greeks,
but from Paul's happy expression when he came back to the yacht
from these excursions it was obvious that what he was hearing was
most welcome – which was scarcely surprising, since Corfu has
always been staunchly monarchist in sentiment.

After spending three days in Corfu the voyagers were under way
again down the west coast of Greece, into the Gulf of Patras and on
to the Corinth Canal, through which they passed on the afternoon

* Later Sir Ivone Kirkpatrick, Permanent Under-Secretary of State at the Foreign
Office.

of 7 August without incident until they came out the other end, when the water circulation in the port engine suddenly stopped and they had to continue on one engine to Phaleron Bay, where they finally anchored for the night. It was not a happy choice. 'The wind off shore at night brings an awful stench,'* wrote the fastidious Hedgley in his diary, 'and if the wind is in the bay during the day it soon pushes up a sea which makes it rather uncomfortable.'

While waiting at Phaleron for a new pump from England the Wessels and their guest made frequent sight-seeing trips to Athens. They went up to the Acropolis, they visited the museums, they took walks in the streets of the city including a stroll past the Palace in Herod Atticus Street which the President of the Republic was now using for his official entertaining, though he did not actually live there.

Then one day Paul said he would like to see Tatoi once more. They hired a car – Tatoi is fifteen miles from Athens – and when they arrived at the main gate they asked the driver to wait while they went in. The woods surrounding Tatoi Palace were open to the public so there was nothing unusual in two men and one woman in yachting clothes, obviously foreign tourists, wandering about in the grounds. There did not seem to be a guard near the house, so Paul went to the side door and rang the bell. After a while the door was opened by an elderly caretaker who asked the callers what they wanted. He looked at them inquiringly, then he saw Paul and his eyes opened wide: he recognized him immediately, despite the beard. Paul explained the situation after pledging him to secrecy, and the old man gladly asked them in and showed them round the house, including Paul's own room. Everything was in dust sheets as Tatoi was **very** rarely used by the President.

On the drive back to Athens the taxi-driver seemed to develop a sudden interest in his passengers, and turning to Wessel who was sitting in front he asked him who the people at the back were. Wessel said they were his wife and his cousin, but the driver still seemed curious: 'He looks very much like the Diadochos,' he said, pointing at the passenger in the rear. At this point Paul joined in the conversation. 'What is the Diadochos?' he asked. The driver explained that the Diadochos was the Crown Prince, the King's

---

* This is scarcely surprising since the main sewer from Athens debouches into Phaleron Bay, polluting its waters and making its lovely sandy beach unsuitable for bathing to this day.

brother Paul. Wessel thought this was very funny and laughed; so did his wife and Paul at the back. The driver joined in and said no more.

That evening they went to dinner at the Grande Bretagne Hotel in Athens. While having drinks at the bar Wessel was hailed by another old friend, Oliver Harvey,* who had been a contemporary of his at Malvern and was now First Secretary at the British Legation in Athens. He was invited to join the party at dinner; half-way through the meal Wessel confided to Harvey that the man on his left was not his cousin Peter Wessel but the Diadochos. Harvey carried on as if he had not heard but over coffee he leaned across to Wessel and said to him quietly: 'Freddy, get the hell out of here, somebody is bound to recognize him, and there is nothing we could do if you got into that kind of trouble.' As soon as they returned to the yacht later that night they weighed anchor and headed for Vouliagmeni further along the coast on one engine.

In those days Vouliagmeni was just an anchorage with no houses at all. 'There are no means of buying provisions, these have to be procured from Athens,' notes Hedgley in the diary, adding prophetically: 'It looks as if it will be a popular resort in the future.' There the party spent a lazy but pleasant ten days, sailing the dinghy, swimming, fishing, going for walks ashore and sunbathing – Paul had a habit of rubbing himself with lemon juice, which he claimed to be the most effective protection against sunburn.

Throughout the voyage Paul had been doing his watch regularly just like the others – four hours on, eight hours off, day and night – and had insisted on doing his full share of the work, which included engine-maintenance, deck-scrubbing, underwater hull-scraping, shopping expeditions ashore and any odd job that needed doing. The atmosphere on board was a little strained at times as the Wessels' marriage was showing signs of breaking up and a yacht at sea is no place for two people to be cooped up together when they get on each other's nerves. Paul took it all in his stride, however, and tried not to be affected by the situation.

On 19 August *Frefrada* moved on round Cape Sounion and then north to Chalkis, where the island of Euboea is joined to the mainland by a swinging bridge. Here they found a message that the new pump had arrived from England and Wessel immediately

* Later Lord Harvey of Tasburgh, G.C.M.G., G.C.V.O., C.B.

went by train to Piraeus to fetch it. With both engines now working perfectly *Frefrada* continued her cruise, calling at Skiathos and Skyros on 25 August and at Kymi, on the east coast of Euboea, the following day. Their next stop was Andros, where a sudden squall hit them carrying away the awning, bending several stanchions and ripping the canvas. Provisions were running low, too – melons, bread and five eggs was all Paul could find at Andros – so they put in at Syra to repair the damage and take in supplies. 'We were pleased to think we had at last reached a place where provisions were plentiful and good,' wrote Hedgley. 'Syra seemed to breathe an air of friendliness . . . A stroll on shore upheld our first impressions . . . Tout le monde can be seen in the cool of the evening, parading up and down or sipping their aperitifs at the café tables,' adding somewhat ambiguously that 'some of the ladies' toilets were extremely smart'.

From Syra they moved on to the volcanic island of Santorin where according to Hedgley 'the grandeur of the scene is almost beyond description', and on 29 August *Frefrada* arrived at Suda Bay in Crete for a stay of ten days. A squadron of the Greek Navy was anchored in the bay, and as the trim little motor yacht passed by she gravely dipped her British ensign in formal salute. Next day a pinnace from the Greek flagship came over to *Frefrada* to pay a courtesy call in accordance with international maritime etiquette. Looking through the binoculars Paul suddenly recognized the officer on board the pinnace, so he discreetly kept out of sight in the forecastle while Wessel entertained the Greek party in the saloon. Fortunately the Greek squadron sailed away the following morning and the risk of similar embarrassments was thus removed, but on 4 September a British squadron sailed into the bay led by the battle-cruiser *Ramillies*, with which *Frefrada* again exchanged the usual courtesies. 'Would you like to come aboard for a hot bath?' was the next signal from *Ramillies* – an invitation which was gladly accepted. On the ship they were received by the officer of the watch, to whom Wessel presented his cousin Peter Wessel. They were then invited to the Captain's cabin for a drink, and to Captain Fairbairn also Paul was introduced as Peter Wessel, but under the mellowing influence of the Captain's liquor the Master of the *Frefrada* gradually forgot his inhibitions and revealed Peter Wessel's true identity to Captain Fairbairn as they were leaving, apologizing for deceiving him in the first place. Immediately after the visitors had returned to their own ship, the Captain's barge was seen putting out from H.M.S. *Ramillies*, heading majestically towards *Frefrada*. When the barge was close enough Captain Fairbairn could be seen standing in the cockpit, in full summer uniform with three other officers similarly attired, and it was clear that the call was being returned in official style. Hedgley happened to have a bosun's whistle, and as Captain Fairbairn transferred from the barge to *Frefrada* he was piped aboard in the regulation manner. Conversation was somewhat formal at first, but supplies of liquor on board *Frefrada* were plentiful and before long everybody relaxed and the official visit soon developed into an uproarious party in true naval tradition.

Next day *Frefrada* weighed anchor and headed out to sea, passing H.M.S. *Ramillies* to port. The battleship was flying a signal which read: 'Goodbye. Fine weather go with you. Pleasant voyage.'

The rest of the cruise was uneventful. After calling at Navarino and Argostoli for supplies *Frefrada* set out on 12 September on the longest leg of the whole cruise, from Argostoli to Malta, a matter of 330 miles which they managed to do non-stop in just under thirty-six hours. On arrival at Malta they were not allowed to moor to the quayside until they had obtained pratique, and as the doctor could not be found they had to wait until the following day – 'this seemed a queer procedure in a British port,' comments Hedgley indignantly. All formalities finally completed, the voyagers spent the next eight days in Valetta where as Hedgley records 'Captain Wessel, his wife and guest were entertained lavishly by both Services at Government House and on board ships that were still in port.' This hospitality was returned on 20 September with a big party on board *Frefrada*, which sailed out the following evening on the final stage of her cruise. Palermo, the next stop, was quite a come-down after Malta for Hedgley. 'What a filthy harbour!' he writes in the diary. 'Coal dust and oil mixed with several kinds of offal covered the surface of the water, and the stench from the fishing fleet lying near was well-nigh unbearable.'

Palermo was the end of the journey for Paul, who had arranged to visit his mother after the cruise. He said goodbye to his friends on the *Frefrada* and left by train for Florence.

Paul was in London again the following year when a message arrived from his sister Irene that their mother was ill. There was an underlying note of anxiety in his sister's letter and Paul decided to leave immediately for Florence, travelling by car and driving hard all the way without stopping for the night. On arrival he realized that his mother's illness was even more serious than he had feared: cancer had been diagnosed and the doctor in Florence strongly advised that Queen Sophie should be taken to Germany for special treatment. Next day they left for Friedrichshoff, the old home of Queen Sophie's mother, and Paul went on to Frankfurt to make arrangements for the patient to enter Professor von Norden's clinic. At the same time Paul sent a telegram to his brother George and his sister Helen advising them to come to Frankfurt as soon as possible. Paul met them at the railway station in Frankfurt and told them that an operation had been performed the previous day: it had revealed general cancer at a very advanced stage* and their mother had only a few days to live. He took Helen's hand gently in his and said to her: 'You will have to be mother to us all now.'

On 13 January 1932 Queen Sophie died, all her children by her bedside during her last moments. For a few days her body lay in state in the great hall of Friedrichshoff, where her own mother had lain some thirty years before. Then Paul took her to the Orthodox Church in Florence and placed her in the crypt alongside his father Constantine and his grandmother Olga to await re-burial on Greek soil.

On several occasions when Helen was staying with her mother in Florence, Queen Sophie had taken her to Fiesole in the hills overlooking the city and had shown her a villa there, set in the woods of San Domenico. 'If we had to stay here permanently, that is where I should like to live,' she had said. Helen made inquiries about the estate and discovered that the lovely fifteenth-century villa had originally belonged to the Frescobaldi family, whose name it bore, but had changed hands several times since then and was now owned by an American named Wilkins, who was prepared to sell the property. There were nearly twenty acres of grounds with three small cottages.

When Helen went to Frankfurt in 1931 she told her mother that she had decided to buy the house she liked so much at San Domenico so they could all go and live there. The news cheered the ailing

---

* Both Queen Sophie's parents, the Emperor Frederick III and his wife Victoria, daughter of Queen Victoria, died of cancer.

Queen, who actually showed signs of improvement for a while; but the inevitable relapse came shortly afterwards, and after her mother's death Helen wanted nothing more to do with the house. Her exclusion from Roumania had now become definite, however, and after a while she decided that the time had come, if only for reasons of economy, to give up the rented house in Florence and make a permanent home for her sisters and her brother. She had some money – in her absence Carol had sold some property she owned in Roumania but refused to give her the proceeds unless she went to live abroad – and Mr Wilkins was still prepared to sell. So the villa on the hillside at Fiesole was bought and Helen with her brother Paul and their sisters Irene and Katherine moved into the house, which they renamed Villa Sparta. This was now to be the family home.

After protracted negotiations between Helen and Carol over their son's custody a compromise had been reached by which the boy would live in Roumania with his father but would visit Helen abroad every six months, and it was to the Villa Sparta that Michael would come twice a year to stay with his mother.

For Paul also the Villa at San Domenico came to be a place he could at last regard as home – perhaps the proximity of his parents patiently waiting in the city below to be taken to their final resting place at Tatoi gave him a feeling that some of his roots were here with him, that he was no longer an exile in a foreign land.

⇒ 8 ⇐

The Greek Republic lasted eleven years, almost exactly the same length of time as Britain's unique experiment in republican government under Oliver Cromwell. During that period from 1924 to 1935, there were twenty-three changes of government, one dictatorship, and thirteen coups varying in degree from simple pronunciamentos by ambitious generals to active civil war with rival armies and fleets ranged against each other.

In June 1925 General Theodore Pangalos overthrew the Government and assumed dictatorial powers, in the exercise of which over the next few months he involved Greece in a war with Bulgaria – from which the country was extricated through the intervention of the League of Nations and the payment of an indemnity to Bulgaria – and also sought to safeguard the nation's morals by decreeing that women's skirts should not be higher than fourteen inches from the ground – an edict for the enforcement of which every Greek policeman was equipped with a tape measure. Pangalos was overthrown by another General, George Kondylis, with the assistance of the Athens garrison. New elections produced a coalition government which remained in office until the spring of 1928 when Venizelos decided he could no longer resist the lure of Greek politics. On 3 July 1928 the Cretan statesman – who had during his absence abroad married a very rich member of the Anglo-Greek community in England, Elena Schilizzi* – became Premier once again and remained in office for four years. General elections on 25 September 1932 produced a stalemate, and another election on 5 March 1933 gave the Populists and other monarchist parties a clear majority displacing Venizelos's tenth, and last,

---

* She was his second wife. He was first married in 1890 to a Cretan girl, Maria Catelouzou, who died four years later while giving birth to their second son, Sophocles.

Government. As soon as the results became known General Plastiras staged another coup and tried to seize power, but lacking popular support he was obliged to abandon the attempt and flee abroad.

The new Government under the Populist leader Panaghis Tsaldaris managed to survive for two years against a background of growing political strife which was now crystallizing into the simple issue: monarchy or republic. Venizelos, who had survived another attempt on his life, withdrew in high dudgeon to his native Crete in protest against the dilatoriness of the authorities in bringing his assailants to justice. He was still there when another military insurrection broke out on 1 March 1935, ostensibly to curb the growing tide in favour of the restoration of the monarchy. The mutineers received short shrift in Athens, but the flagship *Averoff* and some other units of the Greek Navy joined the insurrection and sailed to Crete where Venizelos, perhaps out of a distorted sense of loyalty, placed himself at the head of the rebels. The only support forthcoming from the mainland was in Macedonia where several garrisons mutinied, but the prompt arrival of the Minister of War, General Kondylis, soon put an end to that. Venizelos fled to the Dodecanese, adding to the humiliation of defeat the ignominy of surrendering the flagship of the Greek Navy to the Italians.* From Rhodes Venizelos went to Naples and then to Paris, where he died in exile a year later.

Kondylis had now emerged as the 'strong man' of Greece, and shortly after the suppression of the revolution he became Deputy Premier. The republicans abstained from the elections of 9 June 1935, so the Chamber was now overwhelmingly monarchist in sentiment. The new Government had already pledged itself to hold a plebiscite on the regime, but Kondylis was becoming impatient. A typical example of the Greek soldier-politician of the 1920s George Kondylis, traditionally a staunch republican, had by 1935 become the leading figure of the monarchist camp. Explaining his conversion from militant republicanism to constitutional monarchy in a speech in Parliament on 5 July 1935 he said:

Everybody knows that I was one of the warmest supporters of the republic and was among those who fought for its establishment. But after

---

* To his wife who fled the country with him on the *Averoff* Venizelos said philosophically but without false modesty: 'Big men make big mistakes.'

eleven years' experience of a republican regime, I now see that instead of internal peace it has brought us civil war, the undermining of respect for the State, spiritual anarchy. So what would you have me advise the Greek people? I shall ignore the abuse of those whose vested interests are involved and I shall say to the Greek people that the only thing to do is to bring back the well-tried system of constitutional monarchy.

Kondylis's blunt and uncomplicated approach undoubtedly represented the sentiments of the majority of the Greek people at this time; on 10 October 1935 he ousted the Prime Minister and assumed the premiership himself. The National Assembly thereupon passed a resolution in favour of the restoration of the monarchy and Kondylis was promptly nominated Regent *ad interim*.

For the last three years King George had made London his home, having broken completely with his wife Elisabeth in Bucharest. He now occupied a small two-room suite in a modest hotel in Mayfair, scrupulously abstaining from any involvement in politics. To emissaries from Greece who came to his little sitting-room in Brown's Hotel he made it quite clear that only if the Greek people manifested their desire for the restoration of the monarchy by plebiscite would he return home. He was not prepared to go back at the behest of any single political party but as King of all the Hellenes, and this was the reply he also gave to the Greek Minister in London when the latter formally called to announce to him the resolution passed by the National Assembly restoring the monarchy: he would only go back if invited to do so by the people.

The plebiscite was held on 3 November 1935: the voting was 1,491,992 for the monarchy and 32,454 for the republic. The result was immediately communicated to King George in London. Meanwhile Brown's Hotel had hoisted the Greek Royal Standard over its porch and the Court Circular, reporting a luncheon at Buckingham Palace at which King George was present, no longer referred to him as King George of Greece but as the King of the Hellenes.

On 14 November King George and his brother Paul left for Greece, the Prince of Wales and other members of the British Royal Family coming to Victoria Station to see them off. In Paris the following day King George and Paul were received with full honours and were entertained at an official banquet by the President of the Republic. Their next stop was Florence, where King George and Paul were joined by their sisters and other relatives at a memorial service for their parents in the Russian Orthodox Church. They spent the night at Villa Sparta and then continued their journey to Rome, where the King of Italy invested both with the Order of the Annunziata. At Brindisi they embarked on the Greek cruiser *Elli*, and on 25 November they were back home in Greece after twelve years' exile.

Waiting to greet the King and Paul when they disembarked at Phaleron was Kondylis, who had automatically ceased to be Regent the moment the King had set foot on Greek soil but still remained Prime Minister. He handed the royal proclamation he had prepared to the King, who read it slowly and deliberately line by line with everybody watching and then told Kondylis to make certain changes in the text – and the following day all the newspapers carried a photograph showing the King holding the text in his hand and clearly giving instructions to an abashed and uncomfortable Kondylis who was listening dutifully to what his Sovereign was telling him. As King George went to enter the open car for the drive to Athens Kondylis made to get in also but the King indicated that only Paul was to ride with him and motioned to Kondylis to follow in another car. King George was making it abundantly and publicly clear from the very start, even over trivial matters, that he was not returning to Greece as the puppet of General Kondylis.

Next day the Prime Minister formally submitted his resignation to the King, who requested him to continue in office for the time being, invested him with the Grand Cross of the Order of George I – Greece's second highest honour – and instructed him to prepare for signature a Royal Decree granting a general amnesty. Kondylis demurred and recommended that the political and military leaders of the revolt of March 1935, especially Venizelos and Plastiras who were living in exile in France, should be excluded from the amnesty, but the King was adamant that the amnesty should be unconditional – 'I consign the past to oblivion' he had said in his proclamation – whereupon Kondylis again submitted his resignation, which this time was accepted. The King then asked Dr Constantine Demerdzis, a Professor of Civil Law at Athens

University, to form an interim 'service' government whose first act after being sworn in was to promulgate the amnesty. The effect was immediate: within the hour the leader of the Liberal Party, Mr Themistocles Sophoulis, who had up to that moment studiously avoided any contact with the King, called at the Palace to sign the book and was duly summoned to audience with the King whom he solemnly assured that his party – which had played a leading role in the dethronement both of King George and of his father Constantine – was now, like the King, ready to forget the past and cooperate for the restoration of unity among the Greek people. The Crown and the republicans were at last reconciled.

The new atmosphere created by the amnesty and the re-appraisal of attitudes encouraged by it convinced the King that a fresh mandate from the people was desirable: Parliament was dissolved and general elections held on 26 January 1936. The result was a stalemate, with the 'Venizelist' parties winning 142 seats and their combined opponents mustering 143. Holding the balance in between were 15 Communists.

The new Parliament was formally opened on 2 March 1936 by the King, who appealed to its members to hearken to the people's demand for a strong administration. But irreconcilable attitudes and the almost identical numerical strength of the two opposing parliamentary groupings made the formation of a government an impossible task. Before long both sides were beginning to make overtures to the Communists for their crucial votes and persistent rumours were now circulating that the Liberals had actually reached a working agreement with the extreme left. This was enough to provoke an immediate reaction from the military: at a secret meeting of the Commanders of the Armed Forces and the Security Services, the Minister of War, General Alexander Papagos, was authorized to report to the King that the Armed Forces would in no circumstances tolerate a government that rested on the Communist votes. The King listened without comment to what Papagos had to say and when he had finished requested his resignation. He then sent for Metaxas and asked him to take on the task of restoring discipline in the Army.

Metaxas agreed on condition that he should be sworn in there and then as Minister of War and that his appointment should not be made public for a few hours. A priest was hastily summoned from a nearby church to administer the oath and was not allowed to leave in case he should talk. Metaxas, who was an old hand at this game, waited at the Palace till three o'clock before walking the few yards up the road to the Ministry of War; as he had anticipated, everybody was out at lunch and the place was deserted. He showed his Warrant of Appointment to the Duty Officer and promptly installed himself in the Minister's office, summoning the commanders of the Athens garrison to report to him at once; he also telephoned the Corps Commanders throughout the country. From each and every one he obtained a pledge of loyalty; one or two doubtful commanders he immediately replaced with men he could trust. By five o'clock he was firmly in the saddle and in complete control of the situation.

Though not a popular figure personally, Metaxas enjoyed immense prestige even among his opponents for his undoubted military abilities and his loyalty to the Throne. His forays into politics had not been particularly successful but his judgement in military matters was faultless as events had invariably proved both on the occasions when his advice had been taken and, even more convincingly, when it had been ignored. His devotion to the monarchist cause had sent him and his family to exile more than once in his lifetime, but he had always returned more firmly convinced of the righteousness of his beliefs. Never the leader of a big party – in the elections of 26 January 1936 he held only 7 seats in an Assembly of 300 – he was nevertheless regarded as someone to reckon with, and there was general relief that he should now be entrusted with the difficult task of putting a firm rein on the military. He was the right man in the right place at the right time, and even Venizelos heartily applauded the appointment. 'I cannot tell you how happy I am that the King has entrusted the Ministry of War to Metaxas,' he wrote to his friend Loukas Kanakaris-Rouphos on 9 March 1936 in a letter that was to become famous as setting the seal on the final reconciliation between Venizelos and the Crown. 'By this action the King has safeguarded his prestige, which is so indispensable to the reestablishment of the spiritual unity of the Greek people and the definite return of the country to a normal political life . . . From the bottom of my heart I cry: Long Live the King.'

The Liberals being the largest single party in the new Chamber, the King now called on Sophoulis to form a government, but after a few days the Liberal leader abandoned the attempt and recommended another government under Demerdzis. The new Cabinet was duly sworn in on 14 March: Metaxas was now not only Minister of War and Air but also Deputy Prime Minister.

Four days later Venizelos died in exile in Paris. The Government wished to give him a State funeral but the more fanatical anti-Venizelist elements threatened disturbances if the funeral were held in the capital. Despite Metaxas's assurances that he was quite capable of maintaining order the Prime Minister and the Liberal leaders were finally persuaded that the body should be taken direct to Crete.

On 27 March 1936 the Greek destroyer *Hydra* arrived at Canea with the mortal remains of the Cretan statesman, and huge crowds gathered at the funeral, at which the King was represented by the Crown Prince, this being Paul's first official duty after his return to Greece. Drawn by Cretan warriors in national dress, the gun carriage bearing the body of modern Greece's greatest son was hauled to Akrotiri, where nearly forty years earlier he had led his first revolution, and there was laid to rest.

On 13 April 1936 the Prime Minister Constantine Demerdzis was found dead in his bed: he had collapsed during the night from heart failure.* The King immediately appointed Metaxas, the Deputy Premier, as Prime Minister in his place.

At the age of sixty-five Metaxas had finally realized the ful-filment of his ambition, but the climax of his career was still to come.

On 22 April Parliament reassembled, with Metaxas now occupying the Premier's seat. In the course of the debate it came to light that the leader of the Liberal Party, Sophoulis, had reached an agree-ment with the leader of the Communist Deputies, Sklavainas, by which the Communists undertook to support a Liberal administra-tion in return for various benefits which such a Liberal government undertook to grant to them. Quite unabashed by these disclosures the Liberals in their turn revealed that parallel, though un-successful, negotiations had been going on at the same time

---

* Death took a heavy toll of Greek politicians that year. Kondylis died of a stroke on 31 January; Venizelos on 18 March; Demerdzis on 13 April; Panaghis Tsaldaris, leader of the Populist Party, on 16 May; Alexander Zaimis, twice President of the Republic and ten times Premier of Greece, on 15 September; and Alexander Papanastassiou, the republican leader, on 17 November. Admiral Paul Coundouriotis had already died on 22 August 1935.

between the right-wing Populist Party and the Communists.* In the midst of these accusations and counter-charges Metaxas demanded and obtained the confidence of Parliament by a comfortable margin of 241 votes to 16. Parliament then prorogued itself for five months after considerately providing Metaxas with the authorization to govern during this period by decree subject to a small parliamentary committee which reflected the numerical strength of the various parties in the Chamber. If this arrangement was intended to break the political deadlock it certainly did not succeed in its objective, since party strife was simply transferred from the floor of the Chamber to the narrower confines of the committee. True, with Parliament in recess the Communists were deprived of their bargaining position but this did not prevent them from diverting their activities to stirring up labour unrest and fomenting disorders in various parts of the country. In May a tobacco workers' strike assumed such violent proportions in Thessaloniki that the police were obliged to intervene, using firearms and inflicting casualties – twelve dead and nearly three hundred wounded. A Government proposal to institute compulsory arbitration in labour disputes provoked more opposition and the Communists now openly declared that the workers were ready to fight in the streets to impose their demands. To lend greater force to the threat a general strike was proclaimed for 5 August.

But Metaxas had had enough. On 4 August 1936 he summoned his ministers to a Cabinet meeting at eight o'clock in the evening and informed them that he was going to seek the King's consent to the immediate suspension of certain articles of the Constitution and the dissolution of Parliament without provision for new elections. These were the unmistakable hallmarks of dictatorship. Three of the ministers would have none of it and resigned on the spot, but with his customary thoroughness Metaxas had posted guards outside with orders not to let anyone leave the building

---

* In all fairness it should be said that pacts of this nature are not uncommon in Greece, where frequent changes in the electoral law make it tactically expedient at times for parties at opposite ends of the political spectrum to collaborate at the polls. In the elections of 19 February 1956 for example, when the electoral system favoured large groupings at the expense of individual parties, a common front was formed comprising seven parties ranging from the right-wing Populists to the extreme left-wing Union of the Democratic Left. Having served its purpose this unholy alliance predictably broke up into its various component parts immediately after the elections.

without his permission. At 10 o'clock Metaxas went to the Palace and returned shortly afterwards with the King's signature on the two decrees. He then ordered the arrest of several political leaders and issued a proclamation announcing that martial law was now in force throughout the country and that any opposition to the Government would be crushed at once.

The Metaxas dictatorship, which came to be known simply as 'the Fourth of August', had begun.

It has been a matter of controversy whether the Fourth of August was sprung on King George at the last moment or whether the King was already aware of Metaxas's intentions and had in fact signified his approval in advance. Those who subscribe to the latter view cite as evidence a cryptic entry in Metaxas's Diary under the date 27 February 1936: 'Evening with B.* Long discussion. Hesitant. But he is coming round to my solution.' There is also an entry on 3 March which reads: 'Let this cup pass from my lips. But Thy will be done', heavily underlined. Taken in the context of other entries in the Diary during this period the 'solution' probably refers to a non-party service government under Metaxas himself, which was one of the alternatives under consideration at the time of the parliamentary deadlock following the elections of 26 January 1936. Unfortunately no further clarification is forthcoming from Metaxas himself as there is a gap in the Diary from 7 March 1936 to 9 November 1937. Bitterly disillusioned by what he regarded as the utter selfishness of the politicians and their seeming inability to put aside their petty interests and personal ambitions, King George decided to put the seal of his approval to the Metaxas dictatorship having convinced himself that there was no other way of maintaining peace and order in the country. In a Europe seething with unrest – the Spanish Civil War had already broken out, Hitler had just reoccupied the Rhineland, Italy was celebrating her conquest of Ethiopia and consolidating her position in Albania – the King had come to the conclusion that democracy, especially as practised in Greece, was a luxury the country could not afford at that moment. It was a decision reached reluctantly and in sorrow: his long stay in England had instilled in him a genuine admiration of the British system of government, and his actions

* B = Basileus = King.

during the period between his restoration and the Fourth of August demonstrated even to the most sceptical that if democratic institutions could not be made to function in Greece it was certainly through no lack of encouragement or effort on his part.

It was in keeping with King George's character that having consented to the dictatorship he should now give Metaxas his complete trust and full support. He was under no illusions as to the consequences of his decision, and was well aware that it automatically brought him into conflict with most of the political elements of the country, who would henceforth identify him with the new regime and all the odious aspects of authoritarian rule.

In his private life also the King had been no less unfortunate. His hopeless marriage with Elisabeth of Roumania had disintegrated some years previously as a result of total incompatibility of temperament and the absence of any mutual interests that could have kept them together. During the latter part of his exile he had developed a strong attachment towards an English woman J— whom he had met while on a visit to India as the guest of the Viceroy, Lord Willingdon. King George's sentiments were reciprocated by this extremely attractive and highly intelligent lady, but though the relationship helped to fill the emotional vacuum in his life and was to endure until his death, the need to keep it secret imposed an additional strain.

King George's strict sense of duty now compelled him to devote his energies exclusively to the role which had devolved on him through the inexorable process of inheritance and which he obediently accepted as a sacred trust from which there was no deviation or escape. Never demonstrative in his feelings, he now maintained an even more austere aloofness towards everyone with whom his status brought him into contact, withdrawing increasingly into himself in self-imposed isolation. 'Poor Georgie,' his mother had said when he was still a boy, 'his little heart is all locked up inside.' He could not unlock it now – not even to his own brother.

⇉ 9 ⇇

Since his return to Greece* Paul had been staying with the King at the Palace in Herod Atticus Street, but though living under the same roof as his brother he was finding it increasingly difficult to establish any close relationship with him. During the years of exile the two brothers had been forced by circumstances to lead completely separate lives and had never been together in the same place for any length of time though their paths had constantly crossed. Paul had hoped that the situation in which they now found themselves and the fact that his brother, like himself, was unmarried would perhaps bring them closer together, but as the months went by without any sign or gesture from the King he gradually resigned himself to being excluded from any serious participation in affairs of State and began to turn his attention to other activities where he felt he was not intruding into his brother's sphere of interests.

Paul had already rejoined the Navy with the rank of lieutenant-commander and was attached to the Chief of Staff on special duties involving frequent spells at sea, but his functions and duties as heir to the throne precluded his being put on full-time service.

The Fourth of August had not had any immediate repercussions on him – he had not been consulted in the matter, nor was he personally involved in its establishment.† This, however, did not

* Exhausted after the long ceremonies of welcome on their arrival in Athens, the King and his brother discovered at the last moment that nobody had thought of preparing the bedrooms in the semi-derelict Palace. When they were ready to retire for the night there was nowhere for them to sleep, and they had to wait while a couple of beds were hastily made with linen borrowed from a hotel.

† 'It would be a mistake to imagine that the Metaxas regime aroused anything like the fierce hostility throughout the country that Greek politicians would have you think. . . . There is no doubt that when Metaxas became Prime Minister Greece badly needed a strong administration. . . . It is easy for anybody who has been intimately associated with Greek politics to understand why King George, who returned to Greece with a desire to reign as a constitutional monarch, was led to accept Metaxas.'[8]

prevent him from reacting with repugnance towards certain manifestations of the dictatorship which impinged on him personally.

From a very early age Paul had taken a keen interest in recreation and the activities and problems of young people generally. Himself a great lover of sport and open-air life, he had joined the Boy Scouts when still a boy and had taken such an active part in Scouting that on coming of age he had been made Chief Scout of Greece. The Royal Family's exile after the establishment of the Republic had meant a halt to his activities in that sphere, but while in England he had availed himself of the opportunities available there to familiarize himself very thoroughly with the organizational and training aspects of Scouting so that when he returned to Greece in 1935 he felt well equipped to interest himself in the resuscitation of the Greek Scout Movement of which he was still nominally Chief.

It was then that he found himself in conflict with the dictatorship. Metaxas's military training had instilled in him a disciplinarian approach to life which found its ideal expression in the Fourth of August, drawing its inspiration from the Sparta of Leonidas rather than the Athens of Pericles. Parallel to this aspect of his character there was an almost maudlin sentimentality in his attitude towards family, children and education, and the channel through which he was able to give full rein to this side of his nature was the National Youth Organization (E.O.N.), his most cherished brain-child, on the creation of which he lavished his personal attention from the moment he came into power. Less than a month after the establishment of the dictatorship Metaxas instructed the Minister of Education to draft the necessary legislation. For this purpose the Minister sought inspiration and guidance by studying details of other youth movements abroad, and as at that time the only countries which had concerned themselves with the organization of youth at government level as envisaged by Metaxas were Germany and Italy, the E.O.N. when it finally began to take shape inevitably bore many of the hallmarks of the Hitler Youth and the Fascist Ballila.

The clash between Metaxas and the Crown Prince was not long in coming. Paul was becoming increasingly aware of pressures being brought to bear on Scouts to quit their own movement and join E.O.N. instead, and in his dealings with the authorities in his capacity as Chief Scout he could not fail to notice that he was now meeting with deliberate lack of cooperation and undisguised obstruction. Paul was highly resentful of these irritating encroachments in a sphere which he regarded as his special province and for which he considered he held personal responsibility. He made no secret of his feelings and Metaxas, who maintained an excellent network of information, was not kept in ignorance of Paul's attitude, which he had reason to believe was shared by his brother.

'They say E.O.N. displeases the King. I don't believe it, but we shall see,' writes Metaxas in his Diary on New Year's Day in 1938, and a few weeks later he records his satisfaction in an entry on 25 March in which he refers to the annual Independence Day celebrations: 'Yesterday went to the Field of Mars for the E.O.N. rally. It is my creation, something I achieved in spite of great opposition! Nearly 18,000 children from Athens and Piraeus, the suburbs and the provinces. Spoke a few words to them . . . Army parade today excellent. In the afternoon, march past of school-children, Boy Scouts and E.O.N. All in uniform, about 12,000 to 14,000 of them. Terrific impression on everybody.' But whatever the crowds may have thought, Paul was still unconverted. 'More intrigues against E.O.N., or rather against me,' writes Metaxas in his Diary on 9 April 1938, 'but they don't dare come out in the open.' A week later there is another entry: 'Troubles with E.O.N. Crown Prince running it down . . .' And there is another resentful and rather self-pitying entry on 9 June 1938: 'Athletes' parade. What real use is my work to anybody? Everything is superficial. Crown Prince insulting about E.O.N. Much personal opposition.'

It was at this stage that a solution to the problem was found through the intervention of Lord Lloyd, the recently appointed Chairman of the British Council.* At the request of the Prime Minister, Mr Neville Chamberlain, and the Foreign Secretary, Lord Halifax, Lloyd had visited Greece and had met Metaxas, who had complained to him about the hostile attitude of the British press towards the Fourth of August. Lloyd promised to use his good offices with various newspapers with which he had connexions, and also managed to persuade Metaxas to sign a

* Lord Lloyd of Dolobran, G.C.S.I., G.C.I.E., D.S.O., British High Commissioner in Egypt 1925–9, Secretary of State for the Colonies 1940–41.

cultural treaty which gave Britain a bridgehead, albeit only a cultural one, in a part of the world which Hitler was assiduously cultivating and to which Britain had not been giving much attention.

Lloyd had already met Paul during the latter's visit to England for the coronation of King George VI and had discussed with him the problem of E.O.N. Knowing Paul's views on the subject, Lloyd raised the question with Metaxas and proposed that as one of the practical applications of the Anglo-Greek Cultural Treaty, the physical training of E.O.N. should be entrusted to Britain. Metaxas, who was no fool and who clearly must have known that the matter had already been discussed between Lloyd and Paul, agreed on condition that the Scouts should amalgamate with E.O.N. and that the Crown Prince should accept the leadership of the enlarged E.O.N. – a compromise which Lloyd strongly supported and to which Paul finally consented.

The successful outcome of these negotiations was recorded by Metaxas in his Diary in an entry covering the period 21 October to 11 December 1938: 'Scouts and Guides approached us in last few days seeking a compromise with E.O.N. and we told them plainly to merge with us. Finally the Crown Prince asked for me and we discussed the matter for two hours. He is ready to come back to E.O.N. And I shall bring him back in triumph as its beloved Chief ... Today, 11 December, this miracle was achieved. A magnificent rally in the Field of Mars. New colours presented by the Crown Prince. Terrific enthusiasm. My children, my dear little boys and girls of E.O.N. I have led them to victory.'

Paul's work in the aircraft factory in England had awakened in him a keen interest in flying, and soon after his return to Greece he began to take flying lessons. His instructor was Wing-Commander Charalambos Potamianos, a regular officer in the Royal Hellenic Air Force, to whom Paul took an instant liking and whom he appointed his equerry.* Potamianos took Paul through the standard training syllabus using an Avro Tutor and a 626, and made such a

* When he succeeded to the throne in 1947, Paul appointed Potamianos his Private Secretary. Now holding the rank of Air Vice-Marshal, he became Chief of Air Staff in 1948 and served as Minister of National Defence in the 'caretaker' government of 1961. In 1964 he resigned all his official appointments and founded the 'New Democratic Movement'.

good job of coaching him that Paul, who had a remarkable aptitude for mechanical things anyway, was able to pass all the routine tests without difficulty and receive his wings in record time. Metaxas had given instructions personally to Potamianos that on no account was the Crown Prince ever to fly alone, not even for the final test. These instructions were known to the Officers' Panel who examined Paul for his qualifying tests and who assumed that Potamianos was in the aircraft with Paul as it performed the prescribed take-off and forced landing practice, followed by an unscheduled display of aerobatics and inverted flying. It was only when the plane taxied to a stop that it was realized that Paul had been flying solo. Metaxas, who did not like having his orders disobeyed, had Potamianos confined to barracks for a week and then promoted him half a stripe for his excellent work in coaching the Crown Prince.

Parallel to his interest in flying Paul now began to devote a good deal of his recreation to a sport for which he had always cherished a special love but which circumstances and lack of financial means had hitherto prevented him from indulging: sailing. He joined the recently formed Royal Hellenic Yacht Club, sailing a 'Star' class yacht – a type only adopted by the Club in 1935 – and by 1938 he was able to carry off three firsts in the international regatta at Phaleron Bay. As a result of his performance he was elected Honorary President of the Club and took a very active part in its contests to the end of his life.

In November 1936 Paul went to Florence to arrange for the mortal remains of his parents and his grandmother to be brought to Greece. The three coffins which had lain for years in the crypt of the Orthodox Church in Florence were placed on a special train which the King of Italy made available and taken to Brindisi where they were transferred on board the Greek battle-cruiser *Averoff*. King Constantine's personal standard, which had been draped over his coffin in the crypt in Florence, was hoisted on *Averoff* and on 17 November the coffins were disembarked at Piraeus and brought to Athens. Drawn by sailors and escorted by kilted Evzones of the Royal Guard with arms reversed, the three catafalques passed through silent crowds to the Cathedral, eighty white-bearded Metropolitans of the Church of Greece in their magnificent vestments and their jewelled crowns walking majestically behind, their serpent-topped golden croziers swinging rhythmically in step as they intoned the prayers for the dead. For six days the coffins lay in state in the Cathedral while the people filed past to pay homage. On the seventh day they were taken to Tatoi and laid to rest among the other members of their family.

Part Two

1936-1941

The origins of the House of Guelph stretch far back into European history, but the earliest member of the family of whom there is actual documentary reference is the Bavarian Count Welf I, a contemporary of Charlemagne. Through marriage with the heiress of Magnus, the last Billung Duke of Saxony, the Guelphs brought the Saxon lands into the family and the son of this union, Henry the Proud, added to them the entire fortune of the Emperor Lothair by marrying his only daughter Gertrude. Their son Henry the Lion, Duke of Saxony, fell foul of the Emperor and suffered the dismemberment of his Duchy so that only the Saxon hereditary possessions remained for his descendants. In 1235 the Emperor Frederick II, wishing to end the feud with the Guelphs, recognized these lands as a separate Duchy and since that time every member of the House, male or female, bears the title of Duke or Duchess of Brunswick-Luneberg. With the passage of time the lands were subdivided time and time again to endow new branches of the family, one of them being the Dukes of Luneberg-Celle from whom were descended the Electors of Hanover.

When Queen Elizabeth I of England died in 1603 she was succeeded by King James of Scotland, who united the two kingdoms under the House of Stuart. In 1613 his daughter Elizabeth married Frederick V, Elector Palatine of the Rhine and King of Bohemia, by whom she had eleven children. The youngest of these was Sophia who in 1659 married Ernst August, Duke of Brunswick-Luneberg and Elector of Hanover; and it was their eldest son George who eventually succeeded both his father as Elector of Hanover and the childless Queen Anne as King of Great Britain by right of inheritance through his mother the Electress Sophia, who had predeceased Anne by one year. The Stuarts were thus displaced as the reigning House by the Guelphs in the person of King George I, who brought the Electorate of Hanover and the Kingdom of Great Britain under the same crown.

During the Napoleonic Wars Hanover was annexed to the Kingdom of Westphalia, but the Congress of Vienna restored its independence in 1814 and elevated the Elector to the dignity of King.

The Kings of Great Britain continued to be also Kings of Hanover until 1837 when Victoria succeeded her uncle William IV as Queen of Great Britain. Since the order of succession in Hanover was through the male line only, Victoria did not automatically also succeed to the throne of Hanover as her predecessors had done though she was born, and throughout her life remained, a Duchess of Brunswick-Luneberg and a Princess of Hanover; the Crown of Hanover passed to her eldest surviving uncle, Ernest Augustus, 1st Duke of Cumberland – the eighth of King George III's fifteen children – the two kingdoms thus becoming separated after a union of 122 years, with King Ernest founding a new line in Hanover. His blind son George who succeeded him as King of Hanover and 2nd Duke of Cumberland in 1851 opposed Bismarck's policy of a federal German Empire and sided with Austria instead, as a result of which Prussia invaded Hanover and annexed it in 1866. King George spent the remainder of his life in exile and died in 1878, being buried in St George's Chapel, Windsor. He was succeeded by his only son Ernst August, 3rd Duke of Cumberland, who lived on a property he had bought at Gmunden in Upper Austria and who maintained after his father's death the claim of his House to the throne of Hanover. In 1878 he married Princess Thyra, sister of King George I of the Hellenes.

When William, hereditary Duke of Brunswick, died without issue in 1884 this Ernst August – who as a Guelph bore the dignity of Duke of Brunswick-Luneberg as well as his own title of 3rd Duke of Cumberland – claimed the Duchy of Brunswick as next of kin, but the German Federal Diet disallowed the claim because he would not relinquish his concurrent claim to Hanover, which was now part of Prussia. In 1906 the Duke of Cumberland renounced his claim to Brunswick in favour of his youngest son, also called Ernst August, while maintaining for himself the claim to Hanover. This Duke had three sons: George, Christian and Ernst August. Of these, Christian died of appendicitis in 1901 in his sixteenth year. The eldest, George, was killed in a motor accident in Germany in 1912 while on his way to Copenhagen for the funeral of King Frederick VIII of Denmark. Although the Hohenzollerns and the Guelphs had not been on speaking terms for nearly fifty years the Kaiser went out of his way to observe all the courtesies on this occasion, sending one of his sons with a detachment of the Imperial Bodyguard to render honours. In response to this gesture the Duke of Cumberland sent his sole surviving son Ernst August to convey his appreciation to the Kaiser in person in Berlin. There the dashing young prince, who was reputed to be the handsomest man in Europe, met and fell in love with the Kaiser's only daughter, the Princess Victoria Louisa. They were married on 24 May 1913, thus healing the feud between the two families. A few months later the bridegroom pressed his claim to Brunswick. This time it was recognized, and on 3 November 1913 Ernst August made his State entry into Brunswick as its reigning Duke.

On the defeat of Germany in the First World War Ernst August abdicated in common with all the other reigning princes of the German Empire who gave up their thrones at the same time as the Kaiser. Since then the family carry the titles of Prince of Hanover and Duke of Brunswick by courtesy only as part of their name.

Ernst August and Victoria Louisa had four sons and a daughter, Frederica Louisa, who was born on 8 April 1917. At the age of twenty she became the wife of Paul, Crown Prince of Greece.

On one of his periodical visits to relatives in 1927 during the exile years Paul went with his mother and sisters to stay for a few days with the Duke of Brunswick at his home, Schloss Hubertihaus in Austria. It was on this trip that Paul first met Frederica, who was then ten years old.

Their next meeting was five years later. Frederica was now a grow-ing girl, rather wild – the only girl in a family of four boys – and with a fondness for practical jokes. She took an instant liking to the enormous man with the friendly smile and booming laugh, and whenever he went into the bathroom she would put her gramo-phone outside the door and play jazz records, which she knew he disliked.

He talked to her of his life in England and of his experiences in the Armstrong-Whitworth aircraft factory at Coventry, where he had worked as a mechanic, using the name Beck.

'I might open a garage of my own if I could find a partner to put up the money,' he mused half-seriously.

'His name would have to be Mr Call,' she said, keeping a straight face.

During this period she was going to boarding school in England at North Foreland Lodge near Broadstairs, where with her inborn intelligence and her bounding energy she had inevitably become Head Girl, though her rebelliousness against some of the school regulations had occasionally caused trouble. Life at home in the Hartz Mountains had toughened her physically but she could still not see why the dormitory windows at school had to be left wide open at night in midwinter for the snow to come in, just because the regulations so decreed. Despite these occasional clashes with authority, or perhaps because of them, she was extremely popular both with the teaching staff and with her fellow pupils, and when financial difficulties and the stringent currency regulations in Germany made it impossible for her family to keep her on at the school, the Headmistress insisted that Frederica should stay another year free of charge to complete her studies.

On a visit to his sisters at the Villa Sparta in Florence Paul again met Frederica, now no longer the skittish tomboy he remembered but a mature young woman studying history and the arts at the American College. They went for long walks and car drives in his little Morris, and as the days went by they gradually realized that they were becoming emotionally involved with each other. He was quite certain in his own mind, but she was not quite so sure. Her intellectual development was at a stage where she firmly believed that mutual attraction, even love, was not a sufficient basis for marriage; there had to be something more. So when he said goodbye the situation between them remained unclear.

They met again in Berlin when Paul went there for the Olympic Games in 1936. This time he actually proposed to her but she was still not sure, and as she felt she had to be absolutely certain before taking such an important step in her life she was obliged to refuse him.

A whole year passed before they met again, when he was on another visit to her parents at Hubertihaus. On one of their walks in the woods she suddenly asked him:

'Do you believe in miracles? Because I don't.'

He did not answer for a while, then he said to her gently:

'Look around you: look at the trees, look at the flowers, look at yourself. Can you honestly say you don't believe in miracles?'

They talked in that vein for a long time and she discovered they had a lot more in common than she had realized: very early in life he had become interested in religion in the widest sense of the word and he now found himself effortlessly at home with the idea of God. His feelings towards God were veneration, not fear; he talked of God freely and without embarrassment as of a wise and kind friend. The idea of God was deeply rooted inside him, induced by solitude during much of his life and the need for solace from the misfortunes he and his family had suffered. He was a devout Christian and a practising member of the Greek Orthodox Church, but his religion was completely devoid of sectarian bigotry, and he was always ready to join a discussion on the subject – he was thoroughly familiar with the Bible and had also read many books on other faiths.

He had to go back to Greece for the annual naval manœuvres so again there was nothing definite between them, though this time they agreed to consider themselves unofficially engaged.

Flying had become a new passion with him by now and while his ship was at Thessaloniki he spent much of the time taking brother officers up in his plane, which he had conveniently arranged to have transferred from Athens to the air base at Sedes near by. Some of the younger officers who had never flown before found this new experience intoxicating, especially the aerobatics with which Paul was only too happy to oblige – he had got over the initial feeling of fear he used to have in the past whenever he flew as a passenger, and now greatly enjoyed trick flying. The week before his arrival at Thessaloniki he had taken part in an air display with his squadron at Janina, and one of the planes had crashed in flames, killing the pilot – a detail Paul was careful not to mention in his letters to Frederica. But flying had not diminished his love for the sea and he was overjoyed to be with the fleet once more, though this meant long spells of duty with very little sleep in between.

The naval manœuvres concluded, Paul returned to Athens and told his brother that he was going to propose to the Duke of Brunswick's daughter. The King was very pleased with the news. He did not know Frederica personally as the last time he had seen her she had been a small child, but he did know the Duke and the Duchess, who were both related to him and Paul: their own grandfather, King George I, and the Duke's mother, Princess Thyra, had been brother and sister, while the Duchess's father, Kaiser Wilhelm II, and Paul's mother, Queen Sophie, were also brother and sister. Dynastic reasons made it highly desirable that the heir to the Greek throne should marry soon since King George's own marriage to Elisabeth of Roumania had been childless, and the prospect of a young and highly suitable wife for his only brother, now approaching his forties, was most welcome.

On 26 September the Greek press reported briefly that the Crown Prince had left for Vienna on a private visit. But Schloss Hubertihaus and not Vienna was his ultimate destination. On 27 September he formally proposed to Frederica, and that same afternoon the King in Athens summoned the Prime Minister to inform him of the engagement. The official announcement made headline news in the newspapers the following day.

Paul left Hubertihaus not long afterwards as large-scale army manoeuvres were being held in northern Greece and all members of the Royal Family who held commissions in the Armed Forces were obliged to attend. Living conditions during the five-day exercise were rough: accommodation for Paul and the King consisted of a railway coach drawn up at a siding near Serres, and to these cramped quarters the brothers would return at the end of the day, hot and sweaty and exhausted. Washing facilities on the train were primitive, so in the evening before dinner they would drive into town for a bath at the local hotel.

On 13 October Paul was back in Athens, where the first difficulties concerning the wedding arrangements were beginning to manifest themselves. To begin with, the date of the wedding had not yet been finally decided: 7 January had been suggested, but nine was Paul's lucky number and, furthermore, 9 January was a Sunday, a more suitable day of the week than Friday.

No sooner had the matter of the date been settled than another little problem came up: the State landau had last been used on the occasion of the wedding of Paul's mother in 1889, since when it had been lying derelict in the Palace stables. The harness and the springs had gone to pieces and could not be made good in time, so another conveyance would have to be found.

Most important of all, there was the problem of where they were going to live. The Government had proposed a house in Athens but when Paul inspected it he found it was quite unsuitable.

Then there was the matter of the bride's name. Name-days are more important in Greece than birthdays, and as there is no Saint Frederica in the Greek Orthodox Calendar it had been suggested that the Crown Prince's future wife should adopt an official name which could be celebrated annually on the appropriate Saint's Day according to Greek custom. Olga and Sophia, the names of Paul's grandmother and mother, had been proposed by the Archbishop: in point of fact the ten names with which Frederica had been christened* already included both of these, but she herself felt it would be presumptuous to adopt either of them and promised to find a more appropriate one. In the end the whole idea was tacitly dropped and Frederica retained her own name.

Where should they go for their honeymoon? His boyhood friend Johnny Serpieri had offered them 'Tour la Reine', his country estate near Athens, for the first few days after the wedding, but nothing had yet been decided about afterwards.

Meanwhile the guest-list was getting longer and longer, and all sorts of problems were cropping up. It was not so much a question of accommodation, since many of the guests were going to stay at hotels or were being put up in private houses, but of seating them in the Cathedral and at table for meals. The huge edifice in Constitution Square built in King Otho's time had not been used as a royal residence since King George I had died in 1913, and now there would not be enough servants to cope with the influx of foreign guests. Paul suggested that some soldiers from the Guard should be trained in various domestic tasks: they were not very adept at first and Paul began to be haunted by visions of soup being spilt over crowned heads, but everybody was counting on the uncanny way Greeks have of coping somehow in the end.

There was also the problem of the old Kaiser, who from his hermit's retreat at Doorn in Holland had suddenly begun to take an interest in his granddaughter's marriage. He could not come to the wedding himself, of course, but whom would he be sending to represent him as Head of the House of Hohenzollern? Frederica had reassuring news on this point: Prince August Wilhelm, the Kaiser's fourth son, was coming, and they both knew 'Auwi' and liked him very much.

At the end of October King George left on his annual trip abroad,

---

* Frederica Louisa Thyra Victoria Margaret Sophia Olga Cecilia Isabella Christa.

from which he did not return until the week before Christmas. Meanwhile another petty annoyance had come to vex Paul, who was acting as Regent in his brother's absence: he had asked Frederica to send him a Hanoverian flag so that it could be copied for the street decorations, but she had replied that only the flag of the German Reich was allowed to be flown abroad, and as her father was already in disfavour with Hitler great care had to be taken not to create more problems for the Duke in Berlin.

In the middle of these preparations a family tragedy occurred. On 16 November an aeroplane taking Prince George, hereditary Grand Duke of Hesse and the Rhine, to England for the wedding of his brother Prince Ludwig to Lord Geddes's daughter Margaret crashed near Ostend killing all its occupants. The wedding had been originally fixed for 26 October but had had to be postponed because of the sudden death of the old Grand Duke. Besides the new Grand Duke himself, the victims of the crash included his wife, Princess Cecilie of Greece,* his six-year-old son and heir, his other son aged four, and the Grand Duke's mother, herself widowed only a month earlier.† To add a macabre note to the horror of the tragedy, evidence was discovered among the wreckage that the Grand Duchess had been in an advanced state of pregnancy. The Greek Court went into mourning for eight days but Paul, who had always believed that it was unseemly to parade one's private feelings of sorrow on the death of a relative, refused to use black-bordered writing paper in his letters to Frederica.

All this time official duties were keeping Paul very busy. Metaxas, whose military intuition had convinced him as far back as 1936 that war in Europe was inevitable in the not too distant future,‡ was feverishly engaged in patching up Greece's deficiencies in military

* Paul's first cousin and a sister of the Duke of Edinburgh.

† The sole remaining member of the Grand Duke's own family, his one-year-old daughter Princess Johanna who was not on board the aeroplane, died two years later from natural causes. The Grand Duke's brother Prince Ludwig who now inherited the title died childless in 1968, when the Great House of Hesse and the Rhine ceased to exist.

‡ In his book, *The Naval War of 1940*, Vice-Admiral E. Cawadias, Commander-in-Chief of the Royal Hellenic Navy during the last war, recalls a meeting of the Supreme Naval Council in the autumn of 1936 under the chairmanship of Metaxas in his capacity as Minister of National Defence, in the course of which Metaxas was asked point blank if war was envisaged, and if so against whom. After long hesitation, Metaxas replied as follows: 'What I am going to tell you is not to be repeated outside this room. I foresee war between the British and the German blocs, and this war will be much worse than the last one. I shall do all I can to keep Greece out of it, but this will not be possible.

equipment and was giving urgent attention to the country's air force, which was virtually non-existent in the matter of modern aircraft. This was a problem very close to Paul's heart and one to which in his capacity of Regent he could now give his personal attention.

'Last night,' Metaxas was cabling the King in London in code on 20 November 1937,

Supreme Council of National Defence met to choose type of bomber. Crown Prince presided at his own request.... After exhaustive and completely objective discussion lasting seven hours Council decided order 24 French Potez bombers of latest type.... There remains question of ordering another 12 bombers which we shall negotiate with Blenheim representative due here 23 October. Would relieve our finances of great burden if Blenheim agreed payment by instalments, and hope Your Majesty may find it possible to recommend to the British to be more accommodating in the matter of payment...

And I say again that what I tell you now must not be repeated outside these four walls: our place in this war will be by the side of Britain.' Shortly before this King Edward VIII visited Greece during his Mediterranean cruise with his future wife Mrs Simpson on the yacht *Nahlin*. While in Athens on 27 August 1936 he saw Metaxas, whose report on this meeting to King George in Corfu included the following: 'King of England tonight received me in audience lasting one and a half hours.... We spoke of traditional Anglo-Greek friendship, which I assured His Majesty will endure for ever.'

⇒ 11 ⇐

It had been arranged that Paul would go to Blankenburg as early as possible in December and also visit various relatives of his future wife, including her grandfather the Kaiser at Doorn, before spending Christmas with Frederica and her family, but King George's prolonged absence made a change of plans necessary. The King had stopped in Rome and Paris for talks with the Italian and French leaders and had only arrived in London on 7 November. After staying the customary three days at Buckingham Palace he had moved to his beloved Brown's Hotel from where he would sally forth daily to visit friends and browse among the antique shops. In between, in his usual discreet manner, he was seeing the British Prime Minister and Service Chiefs concerning supplies of arms and equipment for Greece's armed forces, which was the main purpose of his journey abroad.

On 18 December the King returned at last to Athens. The very next day Paul, accompanied by his equerry 'Babbi' Potamianos, left by train for Blankenburg.

Meanwhile, someone had remembered that Princess Frederica was thirty-fourth in line of succession to the throne of England and thus came within the provisions of the British Royal Marriages Act of 1722, according to which the prior consent of the King of England is required for the marriage of all descendants of King George II of England and Hanover. So the Privy Council held a hurried meeting at Buckingham Palace on 26 December 1937 and gave formal assent to the marriage.

Exactly two weeks after leaving for Blankenburg Paul was back in Athens, and two days later he was off again to the Graeco-Yugoslav frontier to meet and escort his fiancée and her family, who were coming by train from Austria, on the last stage of their journey to Athens. Heavy snow had been falling for some days in Central

Europe and the train was late. At Idomeni, the railway station just inside the Greek frontier, Paul sat in the station-master's office until three o'clock in the morning, when the train drew into the station. Before the train had stopped he was racing down the platform to the royal coach and leaping up the steps to greet his bride. An hour later the coach, coupled to the royal train on which Paul had travelled up from Athens, was heading south to the Greek capital, where it arrived at five o'clock in the afternoon.

The day before the wedding Paul and Frederica went to see the villa at Psychiko that had finally been chosen as their home. Paul's sister Irene had been getting the house ready: various repairs and alterations had had to be made, fittings were being installed, furniture was arriving, curtains were being put up. The place was in chaos, but at least Frederica could have an idea what her future home was going to be like. Many of the wedding presents were going to be very useful – the Mayor of Athens had given a silver dinner service, a textile firm had made a gift of household linen, and a well-known Athenian store had undertaken to embroider everything with the royal couple's ciphers.

Sunday, 9 January, dawned under heavy skies. At 7.30 the battery on Mt Lycabettus in the heart of Athens fired a signal for the various contingents of troops to start moving towards their allotted positions along the route: by nine o'clock the guests themselves had begun to arrive at the Cathedral. At 10.30 the guns on Lycabettus fired a twenty-one-gun salute, the signal for the procession of the royal guests to start from the Palace. Car after car entered the Palace forecourt through the entrance gate on the right and drove up the crescent-shaped drive to pick up its passengers in their proper order at the front door under the portico, coming out through the other gate and turning into Herod Atticus Street, which was lined along its whole length with Evzones of the King's Bodyguard in their white pleated kilts, gold-embroidered jackets and long-tasselled scarlet caps. With a clatter of hooves came a squadron of Horse Guards with the King's Standard, followed by the last car carrying King George and the bride's mother, the Duchess of Brunswick.

The State landau, hastily repaired and refurbished after all, now trundled laboriously through the narrow gates and with much groaning of springs and creaking of leather turned up the street, drawn by six white horses and carrying the bride with her father, the Duke of Brunswick, a trim handsome figure in military uniform.

The light drizzle that had been falling since daybreak had by now become a steady downpour.

Just about the time that the royal procession was starting off from the Palace another procession had debouched from a side street into the Cathedral square: fifty Metropolitans of the Greek Orthodox Church in their full episcopal regalia and with their glittering domed crowns on their heads walked slowly the short distance to the steps and into the Cathedral, taking their places on each side of the altar.

A few moments later the State landau drew up in front of the Cathedral, and while the postillions steadied the horses the Duke stepped down and helped his daughter to alight. The bridesmaids who had been waiting on the steps of the Cathedral picked up the bridal train, and to the strains of Byzantine chanting coming through the open doors the bride entered the Cathedral on her father's arm.

An hour later a 101-gun salute from Lycabettus and the peals of the bells of every church in Athens announced to the people that Princess Frederica was now the wife of the Diadoch.

At the Palace, where the State landau arrived after taking the newly-married couple through the streets of the capital to acknowledge the cheers of the crowds, there was another marriage service in the private chapel according to the rites of the Protestant Church to which the bride still belonged.* The couple then proceeded to the 'Old Palace' in Constitution Square and there, in the Trophy Room on the *piano nobile*, received the congratulations of the Government, the Diplomatic Corps and hundreds of other officials who filed past.

The size of the crowds which turned out in the streets despite the weather, and the manifestations of affection and joy along the whole procession route left no doubt as to the popularity of the marriage, and provided a very welcome surprise for the King, who issued a proclamation to the Greek people to express his appreciation:

> Your warm participation in the joy of my Royal House and of the Ducal House of Brunswick-Luneberg on the happy occasion of the marriage of my dear brother Paul and the Princess Frederica of Hanover is a token of the happiness which I pray Divine Providence may have in store for them. Deeply moved, I address to you from the bottom of my heart my warm thanks for the sentiments of love and devotion you have

* Frederica was received into the Greek Orthodox Church as a full communicant on 20 October 1946.

always manifested towards my House, which now includes a new and dear member, the spouse of the Heir to the throne.

There was no secret about where the newly-weds were going for their honeymoon: at 4.30 in the afternoon they drove in an open car to 'Tour la Reine'. On 21 January they left by ship for Brindisi, en route for Switzerland. After that they stayed a week with Paul's sisters at the Villa Sparta in Florence, then visited Frederica's grandfather the Kaiser at Doorn, and went on to England for a few days. On Sunday, 6 March, they returned to Athens and took up residence at Psychiko.

The house was still nowhere near ready. A fortnight later Paul's old schoolmate at St Peter's, Tony Weldon – now Sir Anthony Weldon, Bart. – happened to be passing through on his way home from a trip in the Middle East. He sent a message to Paul to say he was in Athens, and was immediately invited for a drink. 'The rooms are not even properly furnished yet,' wrote Weldon in his diary, 'and H.R.H. apologized profusely for not asking me to stay to dinner but they are, as yet, not installed in the house.'

On a more practical note, he records that his wedding present to Paul, an 'aquaflorium' he had obtained from America, had been smashed in transit – 'this means another present!'

On 25 March Paul and Frederica made their first official public appearance together at the Independence Day celebrations, driving in an open car with the King to the Cathedral for the Te Deum. On the same day it was announced that the Crown Prince had been promoted to Lieutenant-Colonel in the Infantry, full Commander in the Navy and Wing-Commander in the Air Force.

At the end of October 1938 King George left for his annual visit to England, and for two months Paul was again Regent during his brother's absence.

It was during this period that a crisis broke out in the Church. On 22 October Archbishop Chrysostomos of Athens, Primate of All Greece, died at a very advanced age, and the Synod met to elect his successor. There were two candidates: the saintly Chrysanthos, Metropolitan of Trebizond, whom Metaxas respected and liked and who also enjoyed the support of Nicoloudis, the powerful Minister of Information; and the ambitious and politically-minded Damaskenos, Metropolitan of Corinth, who was backed by the Minister of Education, Georgacopoulos. In the election of 5 November Damaskenos had emerged as the victor by one solitary vote, but it then transpired that a certain bishop who had been deposed from his See by the Ecclesiastical Court some months earlier, and was therefore ineligible to vote, had in fact taken part at the election and had cast his vote in favour of Damaskenos. Metaxas, who was furious at the intrigues of his Minister of Education, had the whole matter referred to the Council of State, the Supreme Court of Arbitration in Greece, which promptly nullified Damaskenos's election and found in favour of Chrysanthos. In the middle of all this Metaxas, who was ill in bed, had to go to Turkey for the funeral of Kemal Ataturk, who had died on 10 November from cirrhosis of the liver brought on by chronic alcoholism. As soon as he returned to Athens Metaxas used the 'Archbishop crisis' as a pretext to dismiss Georgacopoulos and three other ministers on whose loyalty he could no longer depend. On 17 December Paul, as Regent, received in the Throne Room at the Palace the affirmation of Archbishop Chrysanthos as Primate, and the following day

Chrysanthos was enthroned in the Cathedral with all the splendid ceremonial of the Greek Orthodox Church.*

Metaxas's relations with the Palace were passing through a delicate phase about this time. Though sufficiently sure of his grip on the country by now not to feel unduly worried as to the security of his own position, Metaxas always remained highly susceptible to any indications of royal disfavour. On the whole the King appeared to let Metaxas have his way in all matters concerning domestic policy, but the Dictator was always highly suspicious of the attitude of certain Court officials, especially the King's Private Secretary, Dr Th. Angelopoulos, who according to Secret Service reports reaching Metaxas seemed to be lending too willing an ear to the complaints of sundry politicians against the regime. The yardstick by which Metaxas usually measured his status with the Palace was the annual 'Fourth of August' celebration which had been declared a national holiday for compulsory observance throughout the country. On the first anniversary in 1937 King George, who was vacationing at the time in Corfu, had sent Metaxas a telegram in which he recalled the conditions of crisis which had 'necessitated the taking of emergency, and I trust temporary, measures' and concluded by expressing the wish that it would soon be possible 'for all to cooperate in concord for the common good'. The implications of this message were too obvious at a time when Metaxas was sending politicians to exile in remote islands, and the censorship had therefore forbidden publication of the King's message. On the second anniversary in 1938 Metaxas anxiously waited for a royal message that did not come. 'Until late this evening no telegram received like last year,' he records sadly in his Diary on 3 August, and the entry for the next day reads: 'Ceremony at Stadium. Visited various centres, everywhere received with enthusiasm. But still nothing from Corfu . . .'

It was while still under the influence of this atmosphere of uncertainty that Metaxas received a copy of the programme issued by the Court for the official welcome of King George on his return from abroad on Christmas Day. Metaxas read it with rising anger: there

---

* This affair was to have its sequel immediately after the occupation of Greece when the Germans deposed Chrysanthos for refusing to administer the oath of office to the collaborationist Premier Tsolakoglou and appointed Damaskenos as Primate in his place. Although Damaskenos's behaviour during the Occupation was in other respects impeccable, his acceptance of the primacy in these highly dubious circumstances was something he was never able to live down.

are reasons to believe he thought that Paul, who was then Regent and with whom Metaxas's relations still remained frigid over the Youth Movement business, despite the recent formal reconciliation of the two men had had a hand in drafting it. Metaxas could scarcely complain to Paul personally on a question of protocol, so he sat down and wrote the following letter to Mercati:

Athens, 24 December 1938

The Premier and Minister of Foreign Affairs
to
The Grand Marshal of the Court

On the occasion of the circulation by the Royal Household of the programme for the reception of H.M. the King on his return from abroad, I have the honour to request that whenever instructions are received from H.M. the King relating to the civil, military or ecclesiastical authorities which come under my jurisdiction, you should convey these instructions to me as the sole competent person to communicate them to the authorities under me and ensure their proper execution, thus avoiding unnecessary irregularities.

With specific reference to the above programme, I have the honour to draw your attention to the fact that according to our institutions the Government takes precedence over all civil, military or ecclesiastical authorities in the country, and consequently over the Archbishop of Athens also. It is therefore the desire of the Government that programmes which do not observe this order of precedence should not be issued. In any case, the Government does not wish matters of protocol affecting itself or its members to be regulated without its knowledge or consent.

I have the honour also to draw your attention, not only in my capacity of Prime Minister but also as Minister of Foreign Affairs, to the fact that the Heads of Diplomatic Missions are not accredited to the Court but to H.M. the King and the Greek Government.

The King arrived the following day. 'By way of greeting,' writes Metaxas ruefully in his Diary, 'he informed me that somebody had told him I had fainted at Kemal's funeral. I assured him that I was in excellent health.' On 26 December there is a more cheerful entry: 'This afternoon with the King. My suspicions completely unfounded. He received me warmly and gave me a nice Christmas present.'

But Metaxas's anxieties regarding the King's attitude were never completely dissipated and remained a constantly recurring theme in his Diary; as for his relations with Paul, they seldom progressed beyond the stage of formal correctness, relapsing occasionally into unconcealed antagonism. Although the Crown Prince was now nominally Chief of the Youth Movement, his heart was not in the venture and the sole reason he persevered with this equivocal position was his wish to avoid an open rift with Metaxas, which would have been an embarrassment to his brother the King at this critical time.

The year 1939 was a period of acute tension for Greece and for Europe. Emboldened by the policy of appeasement adopted by Britain under Neville Chamberlain and by France under Daladier, Hitler tore up the agreement he had signed at Munich six months earlier and on 15 March 1939 occupied Czechoslovakia, not even bothering to tell his Axis partner until the day of the actual occupation.

To the Italians these bloodless victories of their German allies were particularly galling. 'It is useless to deny that all this worries and humiliates the Italian people,' writes Count Ciano, the Italian Foreign Minister, in his Diary that same day, adding ominously: 'It is necessary to give them satisfaction and compensation: Albania.'⁹ On 7 April 1939 – Good Friday – Italian forces landed in Albania and occupied the mountainous little kingdom on Greece's north-west frontier, thus establishing a bridgehead on the Balkan peninsula.

The following day a message arrived in Athens from the Greek Military Attaché in Rome to the effect that the Italians were planning to occupy Corfu in two days' time. The message reached Metaxas as he was leaving his office to go to the midnight Resurrection Service, and he put it in his pocket. Outside the Cathedral Metaxas saw Sir Sydney Waterlow, the British Ambassador to Athens, who had come with his First Secretary, Mr Henry Hopkinson (later Lord Colyton), to see the Service. Metaxas drew them aside and showed them the telegram. 'I told them that I have made the decision to resist to the end even if the war should spread to the whole of Greece, and that I would prefer the total destruction of my country to dishonour,' writes Metaxas in his Diary. Waterlow and Hopkinson hastened to their Embassy to cable the Foreign Office. Next day they visited Metaxas and told him that Mussolini had given assurances about Greece to the British Government, who had advised the Italian Government to repeat these assurances to Athens. Sure enough, an hour later the Italian Chargé d'Affaires, Signor Fornari, asked to see Metaxas and conveyed a personal message from Mussolini to the effect that 'Fascist Italy reaffirmed her intention to respect absolutely the integrity of both the Greek mainland and islands.'

For Britain and France also the occupation of Albania had been the last straw. On 12 April 1939 – Metaxas's sixty-eighth birthday – Waterlow called on the Greek Premier and gave him the text of the announcement which Mr Neville Chamberlain was to make in the House of Commons the following day:

In the event of any action being taken which clearly threatened the independence of Greece and which the Greek Government considered it vital to resist with their national forces, His Majesty's Government would feel themselves bound at once to lend the Greek Government all the support in their power.

In the midst of this tension the engagement was announced of Paul's sister Irene, who was still living at Villa Sparta near Florence, to the Duke of Spoleto, cousin of the King of Italy. The marriage took place in the Cathedral in Florence on 1 July 1939, but the felicity of the occasion did not inhibit the Italian authorities from demonstrating their growing hostility towards Greece by forbidding the flying of any Greek flags. King George, who only heard about this after his arrival in Florence, was so affronted by the discourtesy that he would have returned to Athens immediately without waiting for the wedding, but was finally persuaded to stay in order not to precipitate a crisis with Italy which Metaxas was particularly anxious to avoid at this stage.

For the same reasons Metaxas was also greatly concerned that Greece's relations with Germany should not be exacerbated, and while King George was in England at the end of 1938* a message was received from Metaxas proposing that on his way home the King should visit Hitler. King George was entirely opposed to this suggestion, which he considered most inopportune at a time when Greece was trying to obtain military aid from her Western Allies; at the same time he did not wish to offend Metaxas by reacting with a flat refusal. So he sent for the Press Attaché to the Greek Embassy

* It was during this visit that King George was appointed a Knight of the Garter on 7 November 1938.

in Paris, Spyro Cosmetatos, whom he had known for many years and who was related to Metaxas, and asked him to convey the following message to the Premier personally:

I prefer not to reply to the Prime Minister through the official channels in order to avoid possible indiscretions. I have no desire to visit Hitler at Berchtesgaden, and I have no intention of making a pilgrimage such as certain other Heads of State have been doing. However, if it is indeed considered necessary for me to see Hitler, which I would find most distasteful, I would agree to go to Frankfurt to visit my aunt who lives there. If Hitler should choose to be in Frankfurt at the same time I could then call on him, as would be right and proper according to international courtesies when two Heads of State happen to be in the same place.

Metaxas did not pursue the matter further, and nothing more was heard of the proposal.

Paul was now also becoming increasingly involved in Service matters and was assisting the King by following at close hand the Government's efforts to make up the deficiencies in the Navy and to meet the more immediate requirements of the Air Force. Two new Hunt class destroyers had been ordered in Britain and in February 1939 Paul paid a flying visit to inspect progress at the shipyard and also to expedite deliveries of some aircraft which had also been ordered in Britain.

Satisfied and content that he was at last doing something useful and interesting, Paul was also completely happy in his private life. The house at Psychiko where Paul and Frederica had set up home had been re-decorated and furnished to their requirements and on 2 October 1938 their first child, a girl, had been born, and had been christened Sophie at the Cathedral on 9 January 1939, their first wedding anniversary.

But there were more difficulties between E.O.N. and the Scouts. Metaxas decided that the time had come for this problem to be dealt with once and for all, and on 16 May he summoned the Governing Council of the Scouts – Paul, who was still Chief Scout, ostentatiously did not attend – and told them bluntly that they were going to be absorbed by E.O.N. without further delay; and on 27 May 1939 a laconic communiqué announced that the merger had taken place. Paul had kept completely aloof from these developments, but the sad fate of Greek Scouting was not calculated to improve his relations with Metaxas, which were now reduced to a state of icy formality – recording in his Diary that he attended a reception given by the Crown Prince on 21 June 1939, Metaxas significantly makes no further comment except that the weather was very hot that day.

➳ 13 ⬄

On 23 August 1939 a shocked and bewildered world heard the news
that Nazi Germany and the Soviet Union had signed a non-
aggression pact. Nine days later Germany invaded Poland. On the
same day Britain and France issued an ultimatum calling on Germany to withdraw her troops. Hitler did not deign to reply, and at 11.0
a.m. on Sunday, 3 September 1939, the Second World War began.

In Greece, at the other end of Europe, developments in the
West were being followed with growing concern as regards the
attitude of Italy, with whom Greece now had a common frontier in
Albania. In his usual manner Hitler had waited until the last moment
before advising his Axis partner of his plans, and Mussolini had
made it clear in his reply that in the event of war Germany could
count on Italy's 'non-belligerency' and no more – the excuse the
Duce had given to Hitler for not coming in at once was that 'in our
previous meetings war was envisaged after 1942, and on this date I
should have been ready on land, by sea and in the air according to
our agreed plans'. This did not necessarily mean that Mussolini
might not attempt a local diversion in the Balkans, especially as the
attitude of the Italian Government and the State-controlled press
towards Greece was becoming increasingly hostile. Metaxas was
not the type of man to take chances where military matters were
concerned, and already on 24 August he had ordered partial
mobilization, alerted the fleet and placed all anti-aircraft defences on
a war footing. On 29 August he was able to note in his Diary with
evident satisfaction: 'Mobilization carried out in perfect order,' adding grimly, 'the machine works without a hitch.' On 1 September,
the day of the German invasion of Poland, there is a laconic entry:
'War! Italy neutral!' On 4 September, after Britain and France
had declared war on Germany, there is an identical entry: 'War!
Italy neutral!'

Despite this natural anxiety as to what the future might hold in store, there was no lack of confidence as regards Greece's ability to cope effectively with any attack from across the Albanian frontier. In an assessment prepared on 2 September 1939 General Alexander Papagos, Chief of the General Staff, dealt with various eventualities and said – prophetically as events in 1940/41 were to prove – that in the event of any serious Italian thrust from Albania 'we might be able to undertake offensive action intended to throw the Italians out of Albania' and went on to elaborate that 'the first phase of such offensive operations on our part would aim at the capture of Southern Albania' adding that Greek troops in the Epirus had accordingly been reinforced.[10]

This self-assurance did not prevent Metaxas from seeking some sort of *modus vivendi* with the Italians, who seemed equally anxious to avoid an open rift at this stage; he was adamant, however, that no improvement in Graeco-Italian relations was possible while Italian troops were massed on the Albanian frontier. After lengthy negotiations agreement was reached on this vital point and the following communiqué was issued simultaneously in Athens and Rome on 20 September 1939:

The Royal Government of Greece and the Royal Government of Italy have thought it expedient, in the present state of European affairs, to make a thorough examination of the mutual relations between the two countries. They are glad to be able to testify that these relations continue to be sincerely friendly and are inspired by a spirit of complete and mutual confidence.

Practical proof of these feelings has been given in the decision of the Italian Government to withdraw their military forces from the Graeco-Albanian frontier and in the similar steps being taken by the Hellenic Government.

In implementation of this agreement Italian troops in Albania were withdrawn to a depth of twenty kilometres from the Greek frontier; for his part, Metaxas reduced Greek forces proportionately in the Epirus, Western Macedonia and Corfu.

For the moment at least the atmosphere of crisis seemed to be subsiding. On the last day of 1939 Metaxas wrote:

Another year gone by – a momentous year for me, for Greece, for the world. . . . My conscience is clear. I have done my duty . . .

During the course of the year that followed, the fortunes of the

Western Allies suffered a series of setbacks. The 'phoney war' that had lulled Europe into a sense of false security for months suddenly erupted into violent and devastating warfare. On 8 April 1940 Norway and Denmark were invaded and occupied by Germany; on 10 May Belgium and the Low Countries were attacked;* on 14 May Rotterdam was blitzed by the Luftwaffe; on 18 May the Germans entered Brussels, and ten days later the Belgian Army surrendered. Sweeping everything before them the Germans reached the Channel ports, and the British just managed to evacuate the remnants of their expeditionary force from the beaches at Dunkirk. On 4 June 1940 Churchill made his famous speech of defiance:

Even though large tracts of Europe and many old and famous States have fallen or may fall into the grip of the Gestapo and all the odious apparatus of Nazi rule, we shall not flag or fail. We shall go on to the end. . . . We shall fight on the beaches, we shall fight on the landing grounds, we shall fight in the fields and in the streets, we shall fight in the hills; we shall never surrender.

This was the moment chosen by Mussolini to abandon at last the role of passive spectator. On 10 June 1940 Italy entered the war, attacking a France already prostrate.

'I solemnly declare,' announced the Duce in a public speech that same afternoon, 'that Italy has no intention of dragging into the conflict other nations who are her neighbours by land or sea. Switzerland, Yugoslavia, Greece, Turkey and Egypt should take note of these words.' Almost immediately after these words were spoken Italy launched a propaganda campaign against Greece coupled with a policy of intimidation based on accusations that Greece was tolerating and conniving at violations of her neutrality by allowing British warships to use Greek waters in their operations against the Italian Navy. Italian protests and official *démarches* followed each other with increasing frequency and mounting intensity; Greece's explanations and assurances were brusquely rejected or brushed aside.

In the midst of these anxieties another happy event took place at the little villa at Psychiko: on Sunday, 2 June 1940, a second child, a boy, was born to Frederica. A salute of 101 guns from Mt

---

* On the same day Winston Churchill became Prime Minister and formed the coalition that was to govern Britain for the next five years.

Lycabettus just before six o'clock in the evening gave the Athenians the news that a son had been born to the Crown Prince. King George, who was at Psychiko with the other members of the family when the child was born, appeared to be much moved by the event and in a rare display of emotion warmly embraced his brother. On 20 July the baby prince was baptized at the Cathedral and given the name Constantine.

About this time the Germans made an attempt to intervene in Graeco-Italian affairs. Already, during his meeting with Ciano in Milan on 6 May 1939 shortly after Italy's occupation of Albania, von Ribbentrop had hinted that Italian pressure on Greece would be facilitated if King George, who was known to cherish no particular love for the Axis, could be ousted from the Greek throne. Italy's entry into the war in the summer of 1940 and the steady deterioration of Graeco-Italian relations as a result of the Italians' anti-Greek propaganda made it palpably clear that an Italian incursion into the Balkans was now a matter of time. With their attention focused on their plans for the invasion of Britain, the Germans were very anxious to avoid the distraction of a second front at the other end of Europe at this particular moment: a compromise between Italy and Greece that would avert such an extension of the war was therefore highly desirable. With this end in view a senior Nazi Party official approached the Counsellor of the Greek Legation in Berlin, M. Tziracopoulos, and asked him to convey to the King and to Metaxas in person that Germany was prepared to use her good offices to dissuade Italy from attacking Greece, and might even be expected at the end of the war to give support in respect of certain Greek aspirations – clearly a reference to Greece's claim on Northern Epirus in the southern part of Italian-occupied Albania – if Greece were to discard British influence and observe a benevolent neutrality towards the Axis for the remainder of the war. As British influence was exercised through King George – so continued the German argument – he should abdicate in favour of Crown Prince Paul, whose abstention from any political activity made him an unknown quantity so far as his sentiments were concerned and whom the Germans assumed to be less biased towards them because of his marriage to a German princess.

Tziracopoulos immediately proceeded to Athens and sought an audience with the King to whom he conveyed the German proposal.

7 Paul as a Commander in the Royal Hellenic Navy at the time of his marriage in 1938.

8 Home again after the war. King George driving into Athens with Paul and Frederica, September 1946.

9 Paul and Frederica on a visit to the front during the guerilla war. To the left: Field-Marshal Papagos (holding stick) and General van Fleet (with binoculars).

10 Paul at the wheel of his M G sports car with his young son Constantine.

King George heard Tziracopoulos out in silence, then said to him in a voice of suppressed fury: 'Go back and tell them that so far as the throne is concerned I don't give a damn, but they had better not stick their noses into this country's business if they know what's good for them.' It is recorded that this is the sole occasion on which King George lost his self-control to the extent of banging the desk with his fist.

During the three months that followed, events built up inexorably to a climax. The Fourth of August anniversary came and went without incident except that Metaxas again had occasion to complain, in the privacy of his Diary, about the attitude of the Palace: 'Feel very strongly about King, Crown Prince, Royal Household staying away from anniversary celebrations,' he wrote on 6 August. A few days later he had more important things to worry about.

The Feast of the Assumption of the Virgin on 15 August is observed in Greece as a public holiday, with a traditional pilgrimage to the island of Tinos, where an ikon of the Virgin credited with miraculous powers of healing is taken in procession through the streets of the town. On this day in 1940, early in the morning, an unknown submarine fired three torpedoes at the Greek cruiser *Elli*, lying at anchor half a mile outside the mole of Tinos harbour. Two of the torpedoes missed the ship and exploded against the mole, causing some damage but no casualties; the other struck the *Elli* amidships setting her on fire and killing one member of the crew and injuring twenty-nine others. The explosion holed the ship, which sank in a few minutes.

There could be no illusions as to the identity of the submarine responsible for this outrage against a neutral country; if any doubts existed they were quickly dispelled by a naval committee of inquiry which established six days later that fragments of the two torpedoes which had exploded against the mole had markings on them revealing their Italian origin. The act was deliberate and clearly aimed at provoking Greece into war with Italy. Metaxas, who had no intention of falling into the trap, suppressed the committee's report – it was only released to the press, together with photographs of the Italian markings on the torpedo fragments, the day after Greece entered the war – and re-affirmed Greece's neutrality.

Meanwhile Italian forces were taking the offensive in Africa. At the beginning of August British Somaliland was occupied, and on 13 September an Italian army in North Africa invaded Egypt and advanced across the frontier to Sidi Barrani.

On 28 October – a day of happy omen for Mussolini, whose march on Rome took place on that date, but also the anniversary of Italy's humiliating defeat in the First World War at Caporetto – at three o'clock in the morning Metaxas was awakened at his modest villa in Kifissia near Athens: the Italian Minister Signor Grazzi was at the door asking to see the Prime Minister urgently. Metaxas put on his dressing-gown and went into the sitting-room where Grazzi handed him a note: it was an ultimatum from the Italian Government demanding the right to occupy various unspecified strategic points in Greece for the duration of the war against Britain, and announcing that Italian forces would begin their advance into Greek territory in three hours' time. Metaxas looked up from the note he was reading, and Grazzi recalled later that there were tears in the eyes of the short, plump little man who faced him.

'The answer is NO,' said Metaxas simply. 'This is war.'

He courteously escorted his visitor to the door, then telephoned the King and told him what had happened. At five o'clock in the morning he was presiding at an emergency meeting of the Cabinet. Later that day the Greek General Staff issued its first War Communiqué:

Since 5.30 this morning Italian military forces have been attacking our advanced units on the Graeco-Albanian frontier. Our forces are defending the national soil.

In the first phase of the Graeco-Italian war the strategic aim of the Greek Army was to absorb the first shock of the Italian attack by falling back to carefully-selected defensive positions in the mountain passes according to a pre-arranged plan; this delayed the Italian advance and gained precious time for full mobilization and deployment of the troops to the front.

On 14 November the Greek Army was able to launch a general offensive. The dramatic developments of the next few days are best summarized by Churchill himself:

In the northern [Macedonian] sector the Greeks advanced into Albania, capturing Koritza on 22 November. In the central sector of northern Pindus an Italian Alpini division was annihilated. In the coastal zone, where the Italians had at first succeeded in making deep penetrations, they hastily retreated from the Kalamas river. The Greek Army, under General Papagos, showed superior skill in mountain warfare, outmanœuvring and outflanking their enemy. By the end of the year their prowess had forced the Italians thirty miles behind the Albanian frontier along the whole front. For several months twenty-seven Italian divisions were pinned in Albania by sixteen Greek divisions. The remarkable Greek resistance did much to hearten the other Balkan countries and Mussolini's prestige sank low.[11]

In North Africa the British also now took the initiative: in a series of wide outflanking sweeps their troops struck deep into Libya. On 9 December Sidi Barrani was recaptured, on 3 January 1941 Bardia fell, on 22 January Tobruk was taken. In six weeks the British Desert Army advanced two hundred miles across waterless desert capturing 133,000 prisoners and over seven hundred guns.

⇉ 14 ⇇

The day Greece entered the war King George assumed Supreme Command of all the Armed Forces. For him this was no mere constitutional formality: he brought to this role all the unswerving strength of purpose of which his character was capable and all the physical energy he could muster, presiding at day-to-day meetings of the War Council, conferring constantly with Metaxas and the Services chiefs, pressing Greece's war requirements on the Allies and providing the spiritual and moral leadership which an embattled nation requires in moments of crisis.

Paul and Frederica also had an important part to play. The King's all-absorbing preoccupation with the prosecution of the war at the military and diplomatic level demanded his continuous presence in Athens and prevented him from visiting the front. This duty devolved on Paul, whose mission it became to inspect the advanced positions in the various sectors and to keep the King informed on the situation generally. His inspections of the naval base and various operational units of the fleet naturally held special interest for him – he was officially serving as a Captain in the Navy at the time. While in Athens he regularly attended with his brother the meetings of the War Council in the Grande Bretagne Hotel in Constitution Square where it had established its headquarters and where both he and the King had rooms when late sessions prevented them from returning to Tatoi, where all the family were now living.

Frederica, who had already begun to take an interest in hospital and welfare work as a matter of course in the tradition of the ladies of the royal family, now found that these activities had assumed a new urgency. Hearing from Paul after one of his visits to the front of the privations of the soldiers in the frozen mountain fastnesses of the Pindus, Frederica launched an organization for collecting and distributing warm clothing and other comforts for the troops, recruiting for this purpose only women volunteers, mostly members of Athenian society who welcomed the opportunity of demonstrating that they too could do useful work in assisting the war effort.

Throughout this period Germany had maintained an attitude of aloof non-interference in the Graeco-Italian conflict: diplomatic relations between Germany and Greece continued as normal, with the Greek Minister still in charge of the Legation in Berlin and with the German Minister, Prince Erbach, carrying on with his duties in Athens and trying to avoid any contact with the British and other Allied envoys in the Greek capital.

There are conflicting views as to whether Hitler had any fore-knowledge of the Italian attack on Greece; he was certainly given no notice of the actual date, which Mussolini saw fit not to communicate to his Axis partner in advance, perhaps in apprehension that Hitler might try to stop him. But the prolongation of the Albanian war was proving highly inconvenient to Hitler, who had his own plans for Eastern Europe and who was now obliged to look on helplessly while the weeks and months went by with no sign of progress in Albania and with the prospect of Italy's expulsion from the Balkan peninsula altogether becoming a distinct possibility. Some means other than military force had to be found to wind up Italy's Albanian adventure.

On 2 January 1941 a certain Dr von Angerer, a personal friend of Field-Marshal Goering, arrived in Athens from Berlin bringing the German Legation's diplomatic bag. Dr von Angerer had visited Greece before and had met the Crown Prince and Frederica socially. He now sent a message to Frederica saying he had brought her a letter from her father and would like to hand it to her personally. Frederica received him the same day: he gave her the letter and said he also had various personal messages which he would like to give to her and Paul together after they had both had time to study the contents of her father's letter. Frederica said she would consult her husband and contact him again later.

In the letter the Duke of Brunswick paid tribute to the Greek Army's achievements in Albania but at the same time stressed the futility of further resistance, which would only oblige Germany to intervene in support of her Italian ally. If on the other hand a face-saving formula could be found to bring the Graeco-Italian conflict to an honourable conclusion, Greece could withdraw from the war with her honour unsullied and could look forward to the sympathetic understanding of a magnanimous Fuehrer when the day of reckoning came at the end of the war.

Frederica read the letter in shocked surprise. She knew what her father's sentiments were towards the Nazi regime, and the tone of the letter was the precise opposite to what she would have expected. She examined the letter carefully to see if perhaps it was a forgery, but there was no mistaking her father's handwriting nor the writing paper with the family crest at the top. Then she noticed that the letter began 'My dear daughter' and was signed 'Your affectionate father'. At once she became suspicious: her parents invariably addressed her as 'Frederike Baby' in their letters and always signed themselves with the diminutives 'Papi' and 'Mami'. She told Paul of her suspicions, and he advised her to clarify the point by speaking to her father in Germany.

It was several hours before the telephone call was put through but eventually she heard her father's voice at the other end. They spoke about family matters, then Frederica suddenly said:

'I have received your letter.'

It was quite certain that the call was being intercepted, but she had to know.

'Which one?' he asked.

'The one where you give me a lot of advice,' she said.

'Oh, that one,' laughed her father. 'Well, Frederike Baby, I had to tell you what I think, but then you never listen to your Papi, do you?'

For a while she said nothing, overwhelmed by relief that the letter clearly did not represent her father's real views and had obviously been written under pressure.

'Can you hear me?' asked her father anxiously.

'Yes, I hear you,' she said.

'And do you understand?' he insisted.

'Yes, I understand perfectly,' she said.

When von Angerer came again he was received by Paul and Frederica together, as he had asked. He told them that he knew what was in the letter and had been instructed to amplify its contents verbally and in the strictest confidence as follows: the German Government appreciated that such a radical change of policy as was proposed could only be carried out by a new leadership, as King George's Anglophil sentiments were too ingrained to allow a change of loyalties at this stage and Metaxas himself was too deeply committed with the Allies to change course in mid-stream; it was therefore suggested that a suitably-engineered 'palace revolution' should force King George to abdicate. Paul would automatically succeed to the throne, and in accordance with constitutional practice the Prime Minister would automatically submit his resignation to the new King. The new King, however, would not ask Metaxas to carry on but would accept his resignation and entrust the mandate to form a new Government to someone else who would be willing, with Paul's blessing, to put into effect the new 'peace with Italy' policy.

'What makes you think we would be prepared to play such a role?' demanded Paul indignantly.

Von Angerer began to say something about it being well known that Paul did not get on with Metaxas and about Frederica being German, but she cut him short.

'I am Greek,' she said furiously. 'Will you understand that? The day I married my husband I became Greek, and I am more proud of it now than ever before. Go back and tell them that.'

As soon as von Angerer had gone Paul saw the King and told him everything; the Prime Minister was also informed at once. Writing in his Diary on 4 January 1941 Metaxas refers to reports of concentrations of German divisions in the Balkans and continues: 'Now I understand significance of latest German approaches to Crown Prince and threats through her father to Frederica that we should submit to Hitler! We would sooner die.'

Metaxas did not live to see his words come true; on 29 January 1941 a shocked world heard that he had died that afternoon. Greece and the whole free world mourned the elderly little dictator who had upheld the honour of Greece in the manner of his ancestors and who had given the sorely-pressed Allies their first victories of the war; and in England flags flew at half mast over public buildings – a rare instance of such a tribute being paid to a foreign statesman who was not a Head of State.*

All indications now were that a German attack on Greece was in preparation. About a month before his death Metaxas had seen the German Minister in Athens, Prince Erbach, who in the course of conversation had asked him if Greece's alliance with Britain was

---

* The only other instance I am aware of is that of Foch, who was a Field-Marshal in the British Army as well as being a Marshal of France.

directed against Germany also, to which Metaxas had replied: 'If you touch us in the Balkans, it certainly is.' Two days after von Angerer's approach to the Crown Prince, Metaxas was instructing the Greek Minister in London to stress to the Foreign Secretary, Mr Anthony Eden, the grave threat that was building up in the Balkans as a result of the concentration of German forces in that area, and to state that 'in the event of an attack, even if she remain alone, Greece will certainly resist to the end'.

On 22 February 1941 Anthony Eden arrived in Athens for talks with the Greek leaders.

I dined with the King in a small party, including his brother and sister-in-law Prince and Princess Paul of Greece. The presentations were somewhat mumbled by the King, English fashion, and I was pre-occupied by the discussions of this extraordinary day. After dinner there was some talk about German behaviour in the war and I made comments which, though no doubt critical, did not seem unduly so to me in the atmosphere of that time. As we left for the final meeting of the conference, the King said somewhat quizzically to me: 'Rather severe on my sister-in-law, weren't you?' I had to confess that, though struck by her beauty, I had not known who she was, which was not a good mark for my diplomacy.[12]

On 8 March 1941 Mr George Vlachos, editor of the Athens newspaper *Kathimerini*, published an 'Open Letter to Hitler' in which the sentiments of the Greek people were eloquently interpreted:

It appears that the Germans want to invade Greece. We ask you why. Would not all the world say that 45,000,000, after attacking our 8,000,000 were now begging for the help of another 85,000,000 to save them? Perhaps you will say to us, 'What about the British?' Do you wish us to tell them to go? But tell whom? The living? For we can hardly dispatch the dead, those who came here and fell here and found tombs here. Your Excellency, there are some infamies that are not done in Greece. We can send away neither the dead nor the living. Instead we will stand beside them till some ray of light shines again and the storm finally passes . . .

Small or great, the free army of the Greeks will stand in Thrace as it stood in Epirus. It will fight. It will die there too. In Thrace it will await the return of that runner from Berlin who came five years ago and received the light of Olympia, and has changed it into a bonfire to bring death and destruction to a country small in size but now made great, and which after teaching the world how to live must now teach the world how to die.

On 6 April 1941 the German Army struck from across the Bulgarian frontier. The Greek forts facing Bulgaria held out till the end, but German forces advancing rapidly through Yugoslavia in the west outflanked the Greek line of fortifications and reached Thessaloniki on 9 April. The Greek forces withdrew to a defensive position further south on the Aliakmon River where they were joined by British and Commonwealth troops which had meanwhile landed in Greece.

On the day of the invasion German bombers also raided Piraeus, and that night the whole of Athens was shaken by a terrific explosion in the port. Paul, sleeping at Tatoi nearly twenty miles away, was almost thrown out of his bed and immediately guessed that this was not a bomb but something much bigger. He was right. The British cargo ship, *Clan Fraser*, lying alongside the quay at Piraeus with 200 tons of T.N.T. on board caught fire during the raid and blew up, sinking another eleven ships in the vicinity and putting the whole port out of action.

Under heavy pressure from the advancing enemy the Greek and Allied forces fell back from the Aliakmon line and took up defensive positions further south at Thermopylae on 17 April. The situation was clearly hopeless, and next day the Prime Minister, Koryzis, saw King George and advised capitulation. The King had issued an Order of the Day only three days earlier ruling out any such eventuality: 'The honour and best interests of Greece and the fate of the Greek nation preclude any thought of capitulation, the moral calamity of which would be incomparably greater than any other disaster,' he had said. 'It must not be forgotten also that the British forces continue to fight in defence of the Greek soil.' To be told now by his own Prime Minister that Greece should surrender was too much for the King, who rounded furiously on Koryzis and told him that this was not the advice he expected from any Greek, least of all from the Prime Minister. Koryzis accepted the King's admonishment in silence and took his leave after emotionally kissing the King's hand. After he had gone King George began to feel worried about the Premier's unusual behaviour and asked Paul to go after him. He was not at his office, so Paul went on to his home, but he was too late. As soon as he had reached his house Alexander Koryzis had gone to his study and shot himself.

Finding a successor proved no easy task; nobody was particularly anxious to form a government with the enemy at the gate. For three days King George was his own Prime Minister until on 21 April Emmanuel Tsouderos, a Cretan banker, accepted the King's mandate.

On the same day the decision was taken for the King and the Royal Family to move to Crete, where the seat of Government was to be established and to which a large proportion of the Allied forces from the mainland were also being evacuated.

In the private chapel in the Palace where the King usually worshipped all the members of the Royal Family gathered for a last service together, those who were leaving and those who were staying behind. They all took Holy Communion, King George grim-faced and dry-eyed, the others in tears.

On 22 April 1941 Frederica was evacuated by flying boat to Crete with her two children, Sophie aged two and a half years and the ten-months'-old Constantine. Paul's sister Katherine and King Alexander's widow Aspasia with her daughter Alexandra were also in the plane but Paul himself remained behind with the King.

The flight itself was uneventful, but as the passengers were being ferried to the shore by launch after arriving in Suda Bay about two hours later German planes suddenly appeared and divebombed the anchorage and the town itself. Frederica and her children just managed to scramble ashore and dash to a slit-trench; the others stayed in the flying-boat tossing about until the raid was over. Nobody was hurt and after refuelling the Sunderland took off again for Athens to evacuate the King, the Crown Prince and the Prime Minister, who all arrived at Suda Bay next day.

The stay in Crete was brief as on 20 May the German airborne attack began and it soon became evident that the island could not be held. The Sunderland was soon taking off again from Suda Bay, this time heading for Alexandria and with a much bigger load which included, besides the Crown Prince and his family, the Commander-in-Chief of the British forces, General Sir Henry Maitland Wilson, and several of his senior officers and staff.

As dawn was breaking Paul and Frederica looked back at the fast-disappearing mountains of Crete. It was to be their last glimpse of Greece for five years.

King George's escape from Crete was more perilous. When the attack began and selective air-bombing showed that his whereabouts had become known to the enemy, the King left Canea where he had set up his headquarters and moved on to another house, but German air-bombing continued and he was obliged to move again. General Freyburg, the Allied Commander in Crete, now insisted that the King should be evacuated to a safer place – 'If the King is killed it can't be helped; what we have to avoid at all costs is his being taken prisoner,' was the blunt way he put it. Evacuation could only be effected by sea from the south coast, so King George and his party, which included his cousin Prince Peter, the Prime Minister and several others escorted by a platoon of New Zealanders, made their way southwards over the hump of the White Mountains. Some of the time the King rode on a mule but most of the laborious journey was on foot. Finally, after three days and nights of constant climbing and several narrow escapes from German parachutists, the party reached the coast at Sphakia where they were picked up by the British destroyer *Decoy* and taken to Alexandria on 1 June.

For his courage under enemy fire during this operation King George was awarded the British D.S.O., the only reigning sovereign ever to receive this decoration. Being the King and constitutionally 'the fountain of all honour' he could scarcely confer a Greek award on himself but on 26 June 1941, soon after his arrival in Egypt and while technically on Greek territory in the Greek Legation in Cairo, he signed a warrant conferring the Greek Military Cross on his brother Paul.

Part Three

1941-1946

⇒ 15 ⇐

After a brief stay in Alexandria the King, the Crown Prince and his family and the Greek Government left for Cairo where King George set up his headquarters at the Greek Legation, the Crown Prince and his family took up residence at the Mena House Hotel and the others were accommodated by various Greek families in their private houses.

A few days later Paul and Frederica were invited to supper at the house of a former Egyptian Premier. During dinner a message was passed to Frederica that King Farouk's beautiful young wife Farida was upstairs and would be delighted to see her – as a Moslem she was not allowed to participate in such functions. She was in a small boudoir on the first floor, and the two young women sat at the window chatting and smoking and watching the people in the garden below. After a while one of Farida's ladies came in hurriedly and said the King was coming up the stairs. 'He doesn't like me smoking, what shall I do?' whispered Farida frantically. Frederica promptly tipped the ashtray out of the window; meanwhile Farida sprayed scent on her fingers and in her mouth. The door opened and Farouk walked in. He presented himself to Frederica – they had not yet met officially – and then looked pointedly at Farida, who immediately said goodnight and withdrew, closing the door after her and leaving the two alone. Farouk walked deliberately from lamp to lamp switching off the lights, then draped himself over the arm of the chair where Frederica was still sitting.

'I like pretty women,' he said to her.

'That's nice,' she said.

He pointed out of the window at the people in the garden below.

'Do you see those girls down there?' he said. 'Well, I know most of them.' The way he said 'know' left no doubt as to what he meant.

She said nothing.

He put his arm round the back of her chair and over her shoulders. She thought very rapidly: what would happen if she smacked his face? Visions of diplomatic incidents and international complications rose before her. Then she had an idea.

'Do you know my husband?' she asked him.

'No, I haven't met him yet.'

She leaned out of the window. 'Do you see that man over there in naval uniform – the big tall one with the broad shoulders? That's him, and I am very much in love with him.'

'You are?'

'Yes, I am, and he is with me.'

He got up from the armchair. 'I'm very much in love with my own wife, too,' he said. 'Goodnight.' And went out.*

The question of finding an alternative seat for the Greek Government in the event of enemy occupation had already been broached before the evacuation of Greece by Churchill, who on 13 April 1941 sent a message on the subject to General Maitland Wilson in Athens:

I am also glad to hear that the King is not leaving Greece at present. He has a great opportunity of leaving a name in history. If, however, he or any part of the Greek Army is forced to leave Greece every facility will be afforded them in Cyprus, and we will do our best to carry them there.

A few weeks later the question was raised again, this time in Crete by the new Greek Premier, Mr Tsouderos, who told the British Minister that should they be obliged to evacuate Greek territory altogether the Greek King and Government would prefer to seek refuge in Cyprus. Mr Tsouderos elaborated on the suggestion by proposing that Britain should cede Cyprus forthwith to Greece in the person of the King of the Hellenes, as had been

* This story leaked out some years later in an American magazine. Farouk was still king, and a demand for an official denial was lodged by the Egyptian Ambassador in Athens. Sophocles Venizelos, who was Prime Minister of Greece at the time, thought the whole thing a huge joke but after consultation with Paul it was decided that the Greek Government should issue a formal denial. This did not seem to satisfy Farouk, who now demanded that the denial should come personally from Frederica. This was too much. A message was conveyed to Farouk that if he insisted on a personal statement from Frederica she would be obliged to confirm the story, not deny it, since it was true. Nothing more was heard from Cairo and the matter was tacitly dropped. When President Nasser paid a State visit to Greece after Farouk's dethronement some years later he told Frederica that he knew all about the incident except that he had always understood that she had actually slapped Farouk's face.

done with the Ionian Islands which had been similarly ceded by Britain to the King's grandfather King George I in 1863. The existing British administration of the island would be retained for the duration of the war, but the King and his Government would be establishing themselves in Cyprus as Greeks among Greeks and not as refugees in a foreign country.

The reply was not long in coming. Faced with the stark reality of Greek hopes and expectations affecting a British colony, the British Government had second thoughts about the proposal – which it had itself put forward in the first place – and the British Minister duly informed the Greek Premier that his Government could not discuss the Cyprus question at the moment and did not wish the Greek Government to seek refuge in Cyprus, since its establishment there would provide the Germans with justification for attacking the island – an eventuality which Britain wished to avoid as Cyprus was unfortified and defenceless. Why the Germans should require an excuse to attack British territory at a time when they were already at war with Britain was a detail on which the British Minister volunteered no explanation.

With the arrival of King George and the Greek Government in Cairo from Alexandria the problem of finding a more congenial refuge became more pressing. This was a time when the Government of King Farouk was beginning to be difficult with the Allies. Various facilities could scarcely be refused to Britain, whose troops were virtually in occupation of Egypt, but with the exiled Governments of small countries in Nazi-occupied Europe things were different. It had been hoped that Greece might prove an exception: after all, the Greek community was the biggest foreign colony in Egypt and had long enjoyed a privileged status. The cotton industry had been created out of nothing and developed into Egypt's main source of wealth by a handful of Greeks whose descendants were still the leading figures in the business life of the country and whose munificent gifts and lavish endowments had transformed the city founded on the delta by Alexander the Great into a cosmopolitan metropolis with imposing buildings and magnificent churches and up-to-date hospitals and schools. For psychological reasons besides solid practical considerations, both the British and the Greek Governments regarded it as highly desirable that King George and his Government should be established as near as possible to occupied Greece, so as to constitute both a focus for military activity in the Eastern Mediterranean basin and an inducement to leading personalities in the motherland to escape across the archipelago and offer their services to the Allied cause.

These hopes were soon dashed by the attitude of King Farouk and his Government headed by the Italophil Sirry Pasha, who both made it abundantly clear that the continued presence of the Greek King and Government on Egyptian territory was not welcome. King George's personal letter of thanks to the King of Egypt for his hospitality remained unanswered by Farouk, who simply left a visiting card on King George a week later, while at government level the Egyptian Premier confined himself to a frigid call on the Greek Premier at the Greek Legation. In the circumstances an invitation from the British Government to move to London, where most of the other Allied Governments-in-exile were already established, was gratefully accepted by the Greek Government, and on 27 June 1941 King George and the other members of the Royal Family, together with the Greek Government and senior officials, sailed from Port Said on the liner *Nieuw Amsterdam* for England via the Cape.

An offer of hospitality to the Greek Royal Family had also been received from the South African Government, and after long discussion it had finally been decided that only the King and the Crown Prince should go to England and that the other members of the Royal Family, including Frederica and the children, should remain in South Africa.

On 7 July the *Nieuw Amsterdam* arrived at Durban, where the whole of the Greek party disembarked – some to stay on in South Africa, the others, including the King and the Crown Prince, to await another ship that would take them to England. During this short period in between ships Paul and Frederica looked for a house where she could stay with the children but nothing suitable could be found, and it was to the temporary hospitality of the Governor-General's home at Westbrooke, near Cape Town, that Frederica returned after seeing Paul off on the *Durban Castle* on 25 August.

On 21 September 1941 the *Durban Castle* arrived at Liverpool, where the Greek royal party were welcomed by the Duke of Gloucester on behalf of the King of England. When the train bringing King George, the Crown Prince and the Prime Minister of Greece drew into Euston Station that afternoon, King George VI and Queen Elizabeth together with Mr Winston Churchill and the British Cabinet were waiting at the platform to greet them.

The King took up residence at Claridge's Hotel, moving into the corner suite on the first floor that was to be his home off and on for the next five years. The Crown Prince occupied two rooms next to the King, and six flats in Aldford House, a modern block in Park Lane overlooking Hyde Park, were rented to accommodate the Greek Government-in-exile.

The organizational and coordinating activities into which Paul immediately threw himself left little time for letter-writing, and for the next few weeks communication between the fretting husband in England and the isolated wife with her children in South Africa was confined to laconic cables. One of these cables from Frederica broke the news to Paul that he was going to become a father again, and he was delighted. He was now just forty and feeling extremely young and healthy – on board ship on the long journey from Cape Town he had done a lot of physical exercise and soon after his arrival in England he had taken up squash, which he played regularly to keep fit. He had also looked up some of his old chums from his Eastbourne school days, especially 'Rosie' Stokes-Rees, now a Commander in the Royal Navy, who was able to arrange tours for him to various establishments and munitions factories. Another place he visited was an operational bomber squadron, where he spent the whole night in the operations room until the planes came back from a raid early next morning.

Paul had been hoping to join his family for Christmas but on 11 December he cabled that the journey would have to be postponed for the moment, 'don't know for how long'. On 24 December he sent another cable with Christmas wishes and the somewhat forlorn prayer 'Hope we will be back home this time next year.' He also mentioned in this cable that he was doing a broadcast on Christmas Day at 7.15 in the evening.

In this radio message Paul addressed himself to the seamen of Greece:

Let none of us forget, neither those who are in Greece nor those who are with the Free Greek Forces, that we all belong to the Greek Navy and are part of its honourable and glorious history.

Let us not underestimate ourselves. The whole world – yes, even our enemies – admires Greece today. There is a proverb that says: He who loses his money has lost little; he who loses his honour has lost much; but he who loses his courage has lost everything. We never had any money to lose, and we have always held our honour high; but who is there besides ourselves who is fighting with thirty-five-year-old cruisers and thirty-two-year-old destroyers and seventeen-year-old submarines that still return to their base covered with glory?

⇒ 16 ⇐

The few weeks immediately following Paul's departure for England were not uneventful for Frederica. Until she could find a house she had been offered the hospitality of Westbrooke, the official residence of the Governor-General, but her stay was cut short by a big fire which gutted the part of the house where she and her children were living.

On hearing of the fire General Smuts, the Prime Minister, offered Frederica the hospitality of his own house, Groote Schuur – Cecil Rhodes's old home at Rondebusch near Cape Town – and here she stayed for three months while looking for somewhere else to live. Cape Town was flooded with refugees at this time and the housing shortage was very acute, but Frederica finally managed to find a hotel in Somerset West, a residential area some forty miles out of Cape Town, which had suitable accommodation consisting of a barn that had been converted into a self-contained apartment annexed to the hotel.

It was here that Frederica and her family spent their first Christmas in South Africa, and a very unhappy and uncomfortable Christmas it was: rats scurrying about the house kept them awake at night, it was nothing unusual for a mouse to run out from under the sofa, and cockroaches infested the bathroom and lavatory. The food provided by the hotel was also unsuitable for the children.

All this time the house-hunting had continued, and at last a small house, 'Kenwick', had been found at Claremont, a suburb of Cape Town. It was going for £100 a month, fully furnished, but this was more than Frederica could afford. After a certain amount of bargaining the owner agreed to let her have it for £65 which was still more than she had been prepared to pay, but cheaper than staying at the hotel. She took it.

In London Paul was going about his duties, seeing old friends whenever he could get away. One of these occasions was the christening of the son of his old school-mate Stokes-Rees, who had asked him to be godfather. At the christening party, which was a rollicking affair in true naval tradition, everybody had to do a turn. Paul sat stiffly in a chair, draped a white handkerchief over his head, put a teapot lid on top of that, folded his arms over his lap, blew his cheeks out, and there was his great-grandmother, Queen Victoria.

On 10 April the Belgian Embassy in Cape Town forwarded to Frederica a telegram from Paul sent via the Governor-General of the Belgian Congo a week before, advising her he was stranded in Leopoldville: he was travelling to Cairo from London when one of the engines of his aircraft had stopped. The plane carried on for over two hours on three engines and had finally made a safe landing at Leopoldville where they had to wait a week until another aircraft could fly out a repair crew. Eventually he reached Cairo and on 17 April Nicoloudis, the Greek Ambassador to South Africa, telephoned Frederica to tell her that Paul would be joining her soon.

Next day was Frederica's twenty-fifth birthday. Early in the morning a telegram arrived from Paul bearing the magic date-mark: CAIRO. He sent her his love and best wishes for her birthday and told her he would be arriving in a week.

The same day a letter arrived from England from Queen Mary, posted from the Duke of Beaufort's country home, Badminton in Gloucestershire, where she had been evacuated. The Dowager Queen had heard that Frederica was expecting another baby, and as it was impossible to send baby clothes she had instructed a bank in Cape Town to hand Frederica £100 and hoped 'this little help would be acceptable.' What a dreadful war this was, said Queen Mary, adding sadly: 'I feel so sorry for you with your heart divided and with your great anxiety about so many dear ones' – an echo of what her own feelings must have been when she found herself in a similar situation during the First World War.

⇢ 17 ⇠

On 11 May 1942, a few days after Paul rejoined his wife at Cape Town, their third child – a girl – was born, and they decided to ask the South African Premier, General Smuts, to be godfather, which is the greatest compliment a Greek can pay to a friend.* The new baby's christening – General Smuts chose his favourite name of Irene (Peace), which was also the name of his beloved farm near Pretoria – provided an opportunity for the two families to get to know each other on a more personal basis, and proved to be the foundation of a friendship that was to have a profound influence on the life of Frederica.

Three weeks after the birth of his daughter Paul received orders to return to Cairo immediately. He left promising Frederica he would send for her very soon, but on 24 July he wrote explaining that King George had instructed all officers not to bring their female relatives to Cairo – the British had evacuated all officers' wives and the King felt he should follow their example. King George's youngest sister Katherine, who was in South Africa with Frederica, had written to her brother saying she wanted to go to Cairo and work there, but the King had instructed her too not to do so. Paul was furious, but eventually he calmed down and assured Frederica he would manage to get her to Egypt somehow or other very soon.†

The uncertainty of his position and the vagueness of his status in the Armed Forces also irked Paul considerably. He had applied for some sort of post – anything, he did not mind what it was – but the answer had been equivocal and evasive: such a posting would

* In the Greek Orthodox Church godparenthood actually establishes a family relationship: a man and a woman who have the same godparent but are in no way related by blood cannot marry each other without special dispensation from the Church.

† He was over-optimistic – it was not until 1944 that Frederica and her children were able to join him in Egypt.

restrict his general activities, and the King would want to discuss the matter with him anyway before any decision could be made. Paul took that to mean that he was going to be summoned to London to see his brother, but the days went by and nothing happened. What he dreaded was some desk job in London that would take him away from the Greek Armed Forces in the Middle East. This he was determined to avoid at all costs.

On 12 August Frederica received a telegram from Paul:

JUST RETURNED FROM TOUR ALL OUR UNITS STOP
HAVE RECEIVED PERMISSION TO STAY

He had won his battle.

Following the christening of her daughter, Frederica saw more and more of Smuts and very rapidly a close spiritual relationship developed between the impressionable young woman and the old Boer soldier-statesman whose later years were becoming increasingly preoccupied with philosophical and metaphysical matters. When shortly afterwards Frederica was obliged to quit 'Kenwick' at Claremont because the owner needed it for himself, Smuts immediately invited her to move with her family to his official residence in Pretoria, which he seldom used as he preferred to stay at his farm, 'Irene', outside the town. He would come up regularly to attend Parliament and deal with official business, and gradually it became almost a routine that whenever he was in town he would lunch with Frederica and go for long walks with her; they also wrote to each other regularly, at least once a week. Despite the great difference in age – Frederica was twenty-five at this time and Smuts in his seventies – they seemed completely attuned to each other spiritually and mentally. Their approach to various questions and their reactions to events and situations were invariably the same. He would seek her out at receptions or dinners and insist on sitting next to her, making no secret of the fact that he considered her the most interesting person there. Beginning from this period a state of perfect friendship, of ideal spiritual love, developed between them and continued until his death.

Until the middle of March 1943 both King George and his Government were based in London, but most of the Greek Armed

Forces were stationed in the Middle East. These consisted of all the units of the Greek Navy still afloat and such remnants of the Greek Army and Air Force as had managed to be evacuated from Greece, their numbers being steadily augmented by the conscription of Greeks living abroad and by a steady stream of refugees who managed to escape from occupied Greece and make their way in small boats across the Aegean to the Asia Minor coast from where they were assisted to Allied Headquarters in Egypt.

This was the manner in which Panayotis Kanellopoulos arrived in Egypt in April 1942. The nephew of Gounaris (the Greek Premier executed by the Revolutionary Committee in 1922), he had abandoned his academic career as Professor of Sociology and founded the National Unionist Party soon after the restoration of the monarchy in Greece in 1935. He had been arrested in February 1937 for his opposition to the Metaxas dictatorship and had been exiled to various islands until Greece's entry into the war on 28 October 1940, when he cabled Metaxas demanding his release so that he might serve his country. He was freed four days later and immediately joined the Army, refusing a commission and serving in the ranks on the Albanian front.

The most distinguished of the politicians who had so far escaped from occupied Greece, Kanellopoulos was immediately offered the vice-premiership with jurisdiction over all three Service ministries. He did not join the rest of the Greek Government in London but remained in Cairo so as to be near the Greek forces.

Meanwhile, in occupied Greece itself the various guerrilla organizations were rapidly assuming a violently political character, with the Communist 'National Liberation Front' (E.A.M) dominating the scene, its guerrilla army (E.L.A.S.) having forcibly absorbed or brutally liquidated most of the other guerrilla bands with the notable exception of E.D.E.S. under its colourful black-bearded leader, General Napoleon Zervas, who managed to preserve his independence in the mountain fastnesses of the Epirus.

In accordance with Allied policy of aiding all underground organizations operating against the Axis occupation forces, G.H.Q. Middle East was providing substantial assistance in arms and money to all and sundry guerrilla bands in occupied Greece irrespective of political complexion, and British military missions were attached to both E.L.A.S. and E.D.E.S.

The dangers of this indiscriminate support had been repeatedly

brought to the attention of the British authorities by the Greek
Government, especially as events were clearly demonstrating that
the Greek Communists who controlled E.L.A.S. were far more
interested in preparing the ground to take over the country after
the liberation than in engaging in effective military operations
against the Axis forces. But an ambivalent situation had gradually
developed in the British attitude towards the legitimate King of
Greece and his Government. 'His Britannic Majesty's Government,'
writes Sir Reginald Leeper, British Ambassador accredited at the
time to the King of the Hellenes in exile, 'in their Greek policy
were speaking with two voices. The political voice, i.e. the Foreign
Office, was giving full support to King George and his Government;
the military voice, i.e. G.H.Q. Middle East, was giving support
with arms and gold sovereigns to the King's worst enemies in
the Greek mountains . . . Many of the people who advised the
British military authorities on Greek affairs were republican in
sympathy.'[13]

The British Intelligence services which were responsible for
assisting escapees from occupied Greece and whose help was
indispensable to reach G.H.Q. Middle East were by this time
showing a marked predilection for persons with republican
sympathies, especially officers who had been cashiered for taking
part in the abortive Plastiras revolution in 1935. Having himself
forgiven and forgotten the political past when he offered his
services to Metaxas in 1940 at a time of national crisis, Kanellopoulos
was prepared to attribute the same patriotic motives to all who
behaved in similar fashion and to accept the offer of their services
without question.*

The infusion of these republican elements into the Greek
Brigades – where because of their previous rank and past experience
they were usually appointed to positions of authority – coupled
with intensive E.A.M. propaganda among the troops, soon brought
the inevitable result: on 26 February 1943 the two Greek Brigades

---

* In his Memoirs, *Ta Chronia Tou Megalou Polemou 1939–44*, published in Athens
in 1964, Kanellopoulos recalls that Tsouderos – himself an old republican but a man of
longer political experience – warned him against his 'excessive confidence' towards
officers dismissed from the Army in 1935, and admits his mistake in not listening to this
advice. 'But I was young,' he confesses, 'I had no experience of administrative authority
and I had just arrived from occupied Greece. I believed that all sincerely shared the
tribulations of the Greek people. I could not bear the idea of making distinctions
between Greeks.'

mutinied. Kanellopoulos immediately sped to the Lebanon where the First Greek Brigade was on a mountain warfare course, but the situation was too far advanced and he returned to Cairo, cabling his resignation en route.* The mutiny was suppressed by units of the British Ninth Army without loss of life but with considerable diminution of Greek prestige.

It was to this state of affairs that King George and his Cabinet returned from London in March, having decided it was time for the Government to transfer its seat to Cairo in order to be able to deal at close quarters with the political repercussions and military implications of the mutiny.

Soon after its arrival in Cairo the Greek Government was reshuffled; only then was it realized how high had been the price of appeasement. 'Those who had inspired the mutiny had really won,' writes Leeper,[14] 'because Tsouderos had found himself forced to accept sweeping changes in his Government which made it strongly republican in character. Two new Ministers, Roussos and Karapanayotis, made no secret of their strong republican views and yet they occupied the two important posts of Vice-President of the Council and Minister of War respectively ... The King found himself in the anomalous and embarrassing situation of having to swear in a Government of which nearly every member was an avowed republican.'

Paul was now installed in the room he had occupied before in the Greek Legation in Cairo, sharing the same quarters as his brother the King who had also taken up residence in the Legation. Because of the continuing ambiguity of his position – he still held no official appointment except his status as Crown Prince – he was not completely 'in the know' about what was going on and could only formulate hazy ideas and conclusions about the situation. He sent regular reports to Frederica, not so much to keep her informed as to enable her to pass everything on to General Smuts, who was keeping a watchful and anxious eye on developments in the Middle East.

Paul had no doubts as to the causes of the mutiny. Most of the Greek officers brought out from occupied Greece were men who

---

* On the journey back Kanellopoulos was ambushed by mutineers of the Second Greek Brigade near Tel Aviv. He and his escort of two officers managed to break free and made a dash for their jeep, only to find the driver had been knifed. One of the officers seized the steering wheel and drove the jeep full speed through the mutineers to safety.

had taken part in the 1935 revolution: if any others also managed to escape – usually with much greater difficulty and at their own expense – they would be kept back in Turkey for weeks and when they finally reached Cairo they would be pushed into the background – for which Paul blamed 'the Levantines' widely employed by the British authorities at the time.* These elements had worked steadily among the troops, undermining their morale and making them discontented; Communist agitators had also infiltrated the units. Mutiny was the inevitable culmination of this calculated process.

A British brigadier was put in command of each of the two Greek Brigades, and on 21 March King George left on a tour of inspection of the re-formed units. The King had been in two minds about spending Greek Independence Day (25 March) with troops that had just been brought back to discipline, since his presence among them might be interpreted as condonation of their insurrection, but he had finally been persuaded that his visit would have a good effect. To emphasize the support of the British Government Mr Richard Casey, the British Minister of State in the Middle East, accompanied the King on this tour.

While these disturbing developments were taking place Paul found himself at odds with his cousin Prince Peter, only son of Prince George of Greece. In 1939 the Prince had married Mme Irene Ortchinnikov, a Russian lady who had already been married and divorced twice. The marriage was not officially recognized: members of the Greek Royal Family must obtain the consent of the Head of the House, i.e. the reigning King, before they can marry, and in the case of Prince Peter such consent had not been sought from King George nor had it been forthcoming after the event.† Some minor misunderstandings had already arisen between Paul and Prince Peter's wife, who had launched an appeal of her own in Cairo: this had led to a certain amount of confusion between this

* 'Levantine' is an expression used disparagingly by Greeks to denote persons of obscure near-eastern or Armenian origin with no particular loyalties and with exceptional linguistic, commercial and conspiratorial abilities.

† Both Paul and his son Constantine in their turn adopted the same attitude in this matter when they succeeded to the throne, and this difference resulted in the estrangement of Prince Peter from the Royal Family. The dispute came out in the open in September 1964 when Prince Peter called a press conference in Athens and revealed his conflict with the Royal Family over the status of his wife.

appeal and the Crown Princess's Fund, and Paul had some reason
to believe that nothing was being done to dispel this confusion, with
the result that donations intended for the Crown Princess's Fund
were going to the other appeal. Prince Peter's wife hotly denied these
allegations and invited Paul to dinner to discuss the matter. The
King happened to be alone that evening and to keep him company
Paul declined the invitation, explaining the reason, but apparently
his refusal had given great offence. Some weeks later the King,
Paul and Peter were all invited to see the film *Desert Victory*. The
party, which included Prince Mohammed Ali, was for men only,
but much to the King's embarrassment Prince Peter brought his
wife with him. She avoided Paul most of the evening, but finally
he took her aside and had it out with her. The essence of her
complaint was that members of the Court were speaking against
her – especially Levidis, the Master of the Household, and Paul's
equerry 'Babbi' Potamianos. Paul pointed out he could scarcely be
held responsible for other people's actions, though he felt sure her
complaints were without foundation, and the discussion ended
inconclusively on that note.

Paul mentioned the matter to Levidis, who explained that on two
occasions he had been asked to say what the status of Prince Peter's
wife was. He had replied that she was not a Princess of Greece and
therefore not entitled to a curtsy – as it was his duty to say, that
being the lady's position. Potamianos also denied he had ever
spoken disparagingly about her to anybody. At Paul's request they
both telephoned Prince Peter's wife but she was not to be mollified,
and the conversation between her and Levidis, who could be very
acid on occasions, ended up with him saying that if she would ask
him to tea one day he would give her some good advice about
correct behaviour – a remark not calculated to improve the
situation.

On another occasion, driving home with the King and Paul from
a charity performance, Prince Peter turned suddenly to King
George and said that these occasions did not amuse him and if he
could not bring his wife along he would rather stay at home. The
King replied quietly that this was a men's party and anyway there
was a war on and this sort of thing was not intended for amusement.
Paul was furious – he himself would never have dreamt of speaking
like that to his brother and he was amazed that the King should
have allowed his cousin to address him in that manner without

blowing him up. 'Some situations are not settled just by blowing up,' answered the King wearily, changing the subject.

In between these distractions Paul spent Easter in Jerusalem as guest of the Greek Orthodox Patriarch. He attended church throughout Holy Week and the combined effects of the anti-typhoid injection he had received just before leaving Alexandria and the long services several times a day almost prostrated him. As soon as he returned to Alexandria it was time for the second injection, the after-effects of which were even more devastating.

In the Navy, with which his links always remained very intimate, curious and disturbing things were happening. The Captain of the *Coundouriotis*, a fine officer and an old friend of Paul's from his Naval Academy days, was suddenly removed from his command and replaced by one of the newcomers from Greece, a man notorious for his involvement in every revolution in Greece in recent years. Quite apart from the political implications, Paul knew that the British, under whose over-all command the Greek Navy had been placed immediately after the evacuation of Greece, were very unhappy about postings of this nature: warships were now a mass of complicated machinery and sophisticated instruments, and to put men with no recent training or experience in command of such vessels was courting trouble. At the same time competent and well-trained officers who happened to be loyalist were being transferred to relatively unimportant posts as far away from the fleet as possible. One such case was that of Paul's former Naval A.D.C., Captain John Vlahopoulos, who had suddenly been packed off to London as Naval Attaché.*

The same insidious tactics were being adopted in the Army. Under the excuse of training, loyalist officers were being sent off to Palestine and Lebanon and their places with the fighting units taken over by others. Such treatment was creating much resentment among these officers, among whom the feeling was steadily growing that they had been abandoned by their natural leaders. The King for his part did not consider it incumbent upon him to intervene, even if he could: any such initiative, he felt, would be misconstrued as a step towards the creation of a 'King's Party' and the last thing he wanted to do was to foster any such illusions.

* Captain Vlahopoulos, a fine swimmer, was drowned in the sinking of the passenger-ship *Cheimarra* on 19 January 1947 while trying to help his wife who could not swim. Nearly four hundred lives were lost in this disaster.

Paul took a different view. The Greek Government was not responsible to Parliament – there was no parliament to be responsible to – nor had it been elected by the people: it owed its legal existence to the King, who alone was now responsible to the Greek people. If things went wrong it would be the King who would be blamed, not the Government: it was therefore the duty of the King to take such action as he considered necessary in these abnormal circumstances, since the responsibility for the consequences would be his anyway.

On 6 May Paul met for the first time another recent arrival in Cairo: Sophocles Venizelos, younger son of the liberal statesman, whom the outbreak of war had found in the United States looking after his business interests. A soldier by profession, he had left the Army before the war after attaining the rank of colonel, and had gone into shipping, showing little or no interest in politics. He now appeared in Cairo and offered his services. Anyone bearing the magic name of Venizelos was an invaluable asset to any Greek Government, and he was immediately offered a post in the Cabinet. A short, trim, handsome man in his late forties, he spoke English and French perfectly and had the distinction of being a bridge player of international repute. Paul took an immediate liking to him and the two soon became friends: in later years after Paul had succeeded to the throne Venizelos found himself in political conflict with Paul on more than one occasion but his behaviour towards the King was always impeccable.

At the other end of the African continent Frederica had been obliged to move house again and was now more or less comfortably installed in 'Blencathra', at St James. She had been taking driving lessons and at last felt sufficiently confident to take the driving test. There was no difficulty with the actual driving part of the examination but the oral test was something of a fiasco. She was asked how far away from the kerb a car should be parked: she said thirty feet. Did she not mean thirty inches? said the examiner helpfully. She pondered the matter and agreed that she did mean inches. The next question was, how far from a bus stop could a car be parked? Thirty inches, she replied immediately. Did she not mean feet? said the patient examiner. Yes, she meant feet, of course. Much to her surprise she passed the test and was now the proud possessor of a driving licence.

She was seeing General Smuts frequently, going on long walks and holding lengthy discussions with him on Holism,* but she was more determined than ever that the family should be reunited again, and ways and means of achieving this aim were a constantly recurring theme in the correspondence between husband and wife. Paul raised the matter once more with the King, coupling his request with an offer to take a reduction in his civil list if he did not have to maintain two homes.† He also availed himself of the opportunity to raise the whole question of Frederica's potentialities, which he felt were not being utilized to full advantage: she had put her heart and soul into everything that had to do with the country and the Royal Family, and she could be of immense help in all sorts of ways if the King would only use her more. In this respect her presence in Cairo would be an invaluable asset as there were many aspects of relief and social welfare work that could best be handled by a woman. The King was adamant, however, that until the situation improved officers' wives were not to join their husbands in Egypt, but he raised no objection to Frederica coming to Egypt on a visit.

In June 1943 Frederica arrived in Cairo, and immediately threw herself into the task of organizing her fund, setting up committees, launching appeals, visiting Greek communities in Egypt and generally working up interest in the plight of the Greek people and the need to have a relief organization ready to move into Greece immediately after liberation. In November she returned to South Africa. Paul again remained in Cairo, but this time it was agreed that Frederica and the children should join him in Egypt for good the following February.

---

* Holism is the theory which makes the existence of 'wholes' a fundamental feature of the world and regards natural objects, both animate and inanimate, as wholes and not merely as assemblages of elements or parts. General Smuts became increasingly absorbed in this theory and in 1926 published a philosophical treatise on the subject entitled *Holism and Evolution*, in which he develops the theory that matter, life and mind do not consist of fixed and unalterable elements and that there is another factor, the whole, which science does not recognize at all and which has an influence and an effect all its own.

† The King and the Diadoch are the only members of the Greek Royal Family who receive a civil list from the State, fixed by Parliament.

11 The only reigning Orthodox Monarch visits the Supreme Head of the Greek Orthodox Church. King Paul and Queen Frederica with the Oecumenical Patriarch in Constantinople during the State visit to Turkey in 1952.

12 Dancing at the Yacht Club. Paul is wearing the informal evening dress – black trousers and cummerbund, white open shirt and no jacket – which he introduced for greater comfort during the hot summer months.

13 In the grounds at Tatoi.

⇒ 18 ⇐

Though quickly suppressed, the mutiny of March 1943 had produced a chain reaction of political developments resulting in various changes in the Greek Government, which now included several elements sympathetically disposed towards E.A.M. Pressure on the King for gestures of appeasement was steadily mounting.*

In order to counter leftist propaganda in occupied Greece and abroad to the effect that the Allies were going to 'impose' a government after the liberation, King George made a broadcast to the Greek people on 4 July 1943 in which he promised that general elections would be held as soon as security had been restored, that the Greek Government in Cairo would resign when it arrived in Athens, and that meanwhile the 1911 Constitution would be in force, this last assurance being tantamount to a repudiation of the Metaxas regime.

But the Left now had the bit between its teeth. On 13 August a guerrilla delegation arrived in Cairo from occupied Greece – a secret airstrip had been cleared at Neraida in Thessaly, and this was the first time it was being used – and demanded that the King should issue a proclamation announcing that he would not return to Greece unless specifically invited by plebiscite.† King George referred this new development to Churchill and President Roosevelt and asked for their advice. 'My present personal inclination,' he cabled on 19 August, 'is to continue the policy

---

* 'In Cairo the King had a government which was mainly republican, but the republican ministers who had taken the oath to the King were all the more anxious to show that they had not lost their republican faith by pushing the King as far as they possibly could to make statements which he did not wish to make for fear they might damage his cause and discourage his supporters in Greece.'[15]

† The King did not wish to receive the E.A.M. delegates officially, but a private meeting was arranged by Leeper in his flat where he entertained them to lunch and where the King arrived just as coffee was being served.

F

agreed between us before I left England. I feel very strongly that I should return to Greece with my troops.' Churchill's reaction to this message was passed on to Eden, the Foreign Secretary, the same day: 'If substantial British forces take part in the liberation of Greece, the King should go back with the Anglo-Greek Army . . . In any case, he would make a great mistake to agree in any way to remain outside Greece while the fighting for the liberation is going on and while conditions preclude the holding of a peaceful plebiscite.'

General Smuts, who was being constantly briefed on the situation by Paul and King George, was even more categorical. In a message to Churchill dated 20 August 1943 he said:

King George has always been strongly pro-Ally and sacrificed much for the Allied cause and we have every reason to stand by him in this crisis. It seems to me sound policy that you should once more make it quite clear to the Greek Government that the U.K. Government stands by the King at least until such time as the Greek people, under proper conditions of public tranquillity, are able to decide on their future regime. A plebiscite or general election on the regime immediately on the Allied occupation of Greece should be ruled out as likely to lead to civil strife, if not to civil war, in the existing bitterness of feeling. I very much fear that, in the inflamed conditions of public feeling, not only in Greece but in other Balkan countries, chaos may ensue after the Allied occupation unless a strong hand is kept on the local situation.

Thus fortified, Churchill cabled direct to King George on 26 August saying that the King's statement of 4 July was adequate and advising against any further statements. The message ended with the assurance that whatever the King's decision in this matter, he could count on the support of the British Government. On 7 September Roosevelt cabled on similar lines.

The Italian collapse a few days later greatly strengthened the military position of E.A.M., most of the arms and equipment of the surrendering Italian units in Greece falling into the hands of the Communist guerrilla forces. This made them less dependent on Allied aid and correspondingly less amenable to Allied persuasion. Pressure continued on King George to reconsider his attitude, and on 8 November 1943 he was induced to write a letter to his Prime Minister Tsouderos, in which he stated *inter alia* that 'when the cherished hour strikes I shall examine anew the question of the date of my return to Greece in agreement with the Government'.

The text was released for publication, but in the process of translation from the Greek original the three significant words 'the date of' were omitted, so that in the translated version which appeared in the press the King seemed to be saying that he was ready to reconsider not simply the date of his return but the whole question of whether he should go back or not. A correction was issued, but the initial impression inevitably remained.

The position of the British Government was clarified on 9 November by Churchill, who in the course of a statement in the House of Commons declared:

> In accordance with the principles of the Atlantic Charter, it will be for the Greek people to decide on the future government of their country. . . . Until the Greek people can express their will in conditions of freedom and tranquillity, it is the settled policy of H.M.Government to support the King of the Hellenes, who is at once our loyal ally and the constitutional Head of the Greek State.

The Italian surrender also changed the whole strategic situation in south-east Europe; the certainty of a German withdrawal from the Balkans now rendered a major Allied operation in that theatre superfluous. This meant that such armed forces as were already on the spot, i.e. the Communist guerrillas, would have a much bigger say in developments than would otherwise have been the case, and the British accordingly shelved the idea that King George should return to Greece with the liberating forces. At the same time it was strongly felt that there had to be a Head of State, an ultimate source of legitimacy, from which the administrative machinery of State could draw its authority in the period immediately following liberation.

While in Cairo for an Allied conference in December 1943 Mr Eden proposed to King George that Archbishop Damaskenos of Athens should be appointed Regent. Although the circumstances surrounding his appointment as Primate were highly dubious,* Archbishop Damaskenos was at this time the only person of any recognized stature in occupied Greece, and his high ecclesiastical office, if nothing else, made him acceptable to most of the political

---

* When the Axis Powers occupied Greece, Archbishop Chrysanthos was Primate. His courageous defiance of the Axis authorities and his refusal to administer the oath of office to the 'quisling' government resulted in his dismissal, Damaskenos being appointed Archbishop of Athens and Primate of All Greece in his place.

leaders. Nevertheless, King George rejected the proposal: he had led the nation against the enemy when Greece was invaded, and he felt it was his right and his duty to return to his country with his Government and his troops when the day of liberation came. To accept the idea of the appointment of a Regent for an unspecified period immediately following the liberation was to accept his own exclusion from participation in the liberation, and that he was not prepared to do. In this attitude he was supported by President Roosevelt, so the Regency proposal was dropped for the time being – only to be raised again by the British in the form of an ultimatum a year later.

Various things were occupying Paul's interest. One was a proposal sponsored by General Stanotas, a retired cavalry officer, to organize sabotage in occupied Greece on military lines. The General's idea was to build up a network of officers throughout Greece as local operational centres for various activities: meanwhile, a joint Anglo-Greek Staff would have to be set up ready to move into the country when the moment came. Another aim of this organization besides sabotage would be to muster as many men as possible under military discipline so that a reliable force capable of preserving law and order might be at hand in the chaotic conditions that would assuredly follow the withdrawal of the occupation forces. Paul thought the scheme a very sensible one and put General Stanotas in touch with the appropriate British services, but in the end nothing came of it – mysterious forces were at work in Cairo, and any plan calculated to reinforce the existing order had a habit of being pigeonholed and forgotten.

Another scheme in which Paul became involved was the preparation of relief for Greece by an organization set up under General Hughes. The basic principle was not so much to cope with immediate needs but to help the Greeks help themselves on a more long-term basis. Cattle would be supplied for breeding purposes, artificial insemination methods would be introduced to expedite re-stocking of farm animals, seed would be distributed for planting, caiques were being equipped as floating ambulances for inter-island use. This was something in which Frederica's Fund could help, and a considerable sum was immediately donated to equip one of these mobile sea-borne hospitals in readiness for the happy day of liberation which both Paul and Frederica firmly believed the coming year would bring: nine was their lucky number, and 1944 added up to twice nine.*

The year closed with an incident that brought pride and joy to all Greek hearts. The *Adrias*, a Hunt-class destroyer of the Royal Hellenic Navy, struck a mine near the island of Leros and had her bows completely blown off. Her commanding officer, Commander John Toumbas, was on the bridge at the time and was thrown up in the air by the blast: this probably saved his life as the explosion also blew the gun turret clean off the foredeck smashing it against the bridge where Toumbas had just been standing. He came down on top of the mass of twisted metal, injuring his chest and legs but still conscious. He managed to beach the damaged vessel so that the gaping hole where the bows had been could be patched up and then sailed the crippled ship five hundred miles to Alexandria, fighting off air attacks on the way – a remarkable achievement for which he was awarded the Greek equivalent of the V.C. as well as the British D.S.O. Paul went to Alexandria to greet the gallant ship, which limped into port to the sound of the sirens of every ship in the harbour paying tribute to a splendid feat of seamanship.

The *Adrias* incident awakened Paul's nostalgia for the sea and he obtained the King's permission to go on board a destroyer on its next mission. He was so thrilled by the prospect of going to sea again that he cabled Frederica, who was expected in Cairo about that time, to postpone her departure for a fortnight so that he could be there to welcome her when she came.

At the beginning of March 1944 Frederica arrived in Egypt from South Africa with her children, and the family was at last reunited after nearly three years of separation. They took up residence in a rented house in the Smouha district in Alexandria which was to be their home until their final return to Greece in September 1946.

Just about the time of Frederica's move to Egypt, on 6 March, Prime Minister Tsouderos cabled King George, who was on a visit to London, that a secret emissary from occupied Greece had brought with him messages to the effect that the various political leaders in Greece were demanding the immediate appointment of Archbishop

---

* This number was associated with many significant events in Paul's and Frederica's lives. They were engaged on the 27th and married on the 9th. Paul's aircraft during his Air Force days carried the number 9, and the street-number of the house where they went to live after they were married was 9. Frederica herself was born on the 18th, and the Royal Family finally returned to Greece in 1946 on the 27th day of the 9th month.

Damaskenos as Regent. Tsouderos urged the King to accept but this the King was not prepared to do. 'The proposed immediate appointment of Archbishop Damaskenos as Regent is unacceptable,' cabled King George to Tsouderos on 10 March. 'I consider myself mandated by the Greek people to continue the struggle against the enemy and to safeguard the rights of the nation while it is under foreign occupation and unable to express its free will. I do not desire, nor have I the right, to surrender this mandate and to negotiate with anyone before the Greek people can freely and without pressure express its sovereign will.'

But the political situation was moving to a crisis from a different direction. On 26 March 1944 the formation was announced of a 'Political Committee of National Liberation' in occupied Greece – clearly the first step towards the setting up of a rival authority to the Tsouderos Government in Cairo. As Tsouderos seemed disposed to enter into negotiations with this Committee, and in fact sent a conciliatory reply to the message announcing its formation, King George cabled him from London on 18 March not to assume any obligations committing him in any way until he had had time for further consideration.

Meanwhile the intensive Communist propaganda among the Greek Forces in Egypt was beginning to bear fruit and the first ominous rumblings were making themselves heard. On 8 March Brigadier Beaumont-Nesbitt, Chief Liaison Officer with the Allied Armies, wrote to the Greek Minister of War expressing anxiety at reports of subversive political activity in the Greek Army by officers involved in the mutiny of March 1943, and asking what steps were being taken to deal with these activities. To this letter Mr Karapanayotis, whose appointment as Minister of War had been one of the aftermaths of the mutiny of March 1943, replied reassuringly that discipline in the Greek Army was secure, that all fears were unfounded and that the situation was completely under control.

Just two weeks later the storm broke. On 31 March a group of officers demanded to see Tsouderos and handed him a memorandum signed by several Army and Air Force officers pledging support to the Communist-controlled 'Political Committee of National Liberation' in occupied Greece. This was the signal for open mutiny in several units of the 1st Greek Brigade, which was encamped at Bourk-el-Arem near Alexandria, fully equipped and ready for embarkation to the Allied front in Italy. Five ships of the Greek Navy joined the mutiny and demanded the resignation of the Government. In Cairo itself the guard at the Provost-Marshal's Headquarters seized control and freed the mutineers who had been arrested and were being held there.

Under pressure from his colleagues Tsouderos cabled his resignation to the King in London and recommended Sophocles Venizelos, the Minister of Marine, as his successor; but the King replied that the restoration of law and order was what mattered most at the moment and Tsouderos should carry on for the time being. In this view he was supported by Churchill, who was even more blunt: 'I was much shocked to hear of your resignation, which seems to leave Greece forlorn at a moment of peril for her national life,' he cabled Tsouderos. 'The King, whom I have just seen, tells me he has not accepted your resignation. He is coming out to Alexandria next week. Surely you can await his arrival.' Tsouderos agreed, and at the same time urged the need for the King's immediate return to Cairo.

This was not the view of the British Ambassador, Leeper, who on 7 April cabled the Foreign Office in London that 'the King of Greece's return here at present would certainly provoke fresh trouble. Tsouderos and all his colleagues are strongly of this opinion.* He would find himself isolated and unable to do anything and would be a grave embarrassment to us. In the circumstances in which we are living here at the moment the advice of people on the spot should, I submit, be accepted. My views are shared by everybody here.'

Churchill promptly invited King George to lunch and showed him Leeper's telegram. He then sent the following message to Leeper:

I have discussed the situation with the King. He is resolved to return to Cairo, leaving by air Sunday evening, and notwithstanding your telegram I consider he is right to do so. If, as you say, what is happening in Cairo is a Greek revolution, I cannot advise him to stay away and allow the issue to be decided in his absence. All local Greek politicians and agitators should at the same time be warned that we shall not hesitate to take adequate measures of security to prevent agitation and demonstrations which might threaten law and order in Egypt and the position and authority of the King and the Greek Government.

* This was quite untrue. Tsouderos had just cabled King George: 'Cabinet begs Your Majesty to expedite your return to Cairo to deal with crisis.'

The next day Churchill sent another cable to Leeper:

Weather permitting the King will leave Sunday night. Meanwhile it is Mr Tsouderos's duty to stand to his post. Of course if he can get M. Sophocles Venizelos to stay with him all the better. When the King arrives the British Security Service must ensure his personal safety. He may require a few days to make up his mind and must on no account be hustled. . . . You should stick to the line I have marked out and not be worried about the consequences. You speak of living on the lid of a volcano. Wherever else do you expect to live in times like these? Please however be careful to follow very exactly the instructions you are receiving from me, namely, first in priority: order and discipline to be maintained in the armed forces; secondly, the safety of the King's person to be ensured; thirdly, every effort to be made to induce Tsouderos to hold office till the King returns and has had time to look around; fourthly, try to get Venizelos to remain with Tsouderos; fifthly, celebrate Easter Sunday in a manner pious and becoming.

And the day after that, 9 April, Churchill sent Leeper a more detailed statement of policy for use in his discussions with the Greeks:

Our relations are definitely established with the lawfully constituted Greek Government headed by the King, who is the ally of Britain and cannot be discarded to suit a momentary surge of appetite among ambitious émigré nonentities. Neither can Greece find constitutional expression in particular sets of guerrillas, in many cases indistinguishable from banditti, who are masquerading as the saviours of their country while living on the local villages. . . . Our only desire and interest is to see Greece a glorious, free nation in the Eastern Mediterranean, the honoured friend and ally of the victorious Powers.

The King is the servant of his people. He makes no claim to rule them. He submits himself freely to the judgment of the people as soon as normal conditions are restored. He places himself and his Royal House entirely at the disposition of the Greek nation. Once the German invader has been driven out Greece can be a republic or a monarchy, entirely as the people wish.

Early in the morning of 10 April King George arrived in Cairo by air from London. Paul met him at the airport and briefed him on the latest developments.

The King received Tsouderos later that day, and over the next forty-eight hours saw all the members of the Government and also all the Greek politicians in Cairo at the time. On 13 April the King appointed Sophocles Venizelos Prime Minister.

The mutiny in the Greek Brigade had by now reached its climax. On 7 April the British Commander-in-Chief Middle East, General Sir Bernard Paget, had assumed personal command of the Brigade, and had forbidden the Greek Minister of War, Karapanayotis, any contact with the Greek Army before arresting and deporting him to the Sudan. British troops surrounded the mutinous Greek Brigade, which still refused to be disarmed. Churchill's instructions to Paget were firm and clear: 'You will have achieved success if you bring the Brigade under control without bloodshed. But brought under control it must be. Count on my support.' His instructions to Leeper were equally categorical: 'There can be no question of making terms with mutineers about political matters,' he cabled on 12 April. 'They must return to their duty unconditionally. They must submit to be disarmed unconditionally. It would be a great pity to give any assurances about the non-punishment of ringleaders. The question of clemency would rest with the King.'

In characteristic fashion, Churchill in London was not only sending instructions on how to cope with the situation but was actually directing the military operations against the mutineers. On 22 April he cabled Paget:

If you find it necessary to fire on the mutineers' camp, you should consider whether you might not start with a few ranging shots directed on their batteries which are aiming at you. If they make no reply, after an appropriate interval let them have a stiffer dose, and at the same time tell them the weight of fire which you are ready to direct on them if they persist. We are prepared to use the utmost force but let us avoid slaughter if possible.

Paget found it expedient to enter into the spirit of the thing and kept Churchill fully informed of even the smallest details. In a cable the next day he explained:

In order to get close observation of their camp, we must first capture two Greek posts on high ground. This will be done by infantry only just before dawn. When it is light we will lay a smoke-screen over their camp for ten minutes. Then there will be a pause for the smoke-screen to clear away, after which leaflets will be dropped. They will state that there will be a further smoke-screen for half an hour, under cover of which all who wish should leave camp and come over to our lines. If mutineers are still holding out after this a few shells will be fired at one of their batteries, followed by a further pause to allow for surrender. We shall continue this process until all their guns are knocked out. If the mutineers still will not surrender it will be necessary to make an infantry assault on the camp under covering fire from artillery and tanks.

These tactics proved completely successful. There was not much stomach for a fight on the part of the Greek rebels, who had been completely misled by Communist propaganda and never imagined that it would ever come to facing British troops over their gunsights. On 23 April the Greek Brigade surrendered and was evacuated to a prisoner-of-war cage after the ringleaders had been arrested. The only casualty was one British officer killed.

In the Navy things were a little more difficult. The destroyer *Ierax* and two corvettes were refusing to obey orders and were being covered by the guns of shore batteries and British ships in Alexandria harbour. Churchill had cabled the British Naval Commander-in-Chief that he should leave the mutineers in no doubt that force would be used if necessary, and on 16 April Admiral Sir John Cunningham advised the new Premier Venizelos that he would not hesitate to sink the mutinous Greek ships if he were left with no other alternative. Venizelos called a conference of all the Greek politicians to tell them of the Admiral's decision, and persuaded them all to sign a protocol authorizing him to try and seize the rebel ships by force, but using only loyal Greek units for that purpose. Venizelos then appointed Vice-Admiral Peter Voulgaris Commander-in-Chief of the Greek Navy and gave him a free hand. Voulgaris immediately organized a boarding party consisting almost exclusively of naval officers, and personally led a raid in Alexandria harbour during the night of 22/3 April, taking the rebel ships by storm. Some of the mutineers offered resistance and there were some casualties – eleven dead and thirty wounded. By morning the mutiny was over. It had lasted just three weeks.

⇒ 19 ⇐

During Frederica's stay in Egypt in the summer of 1943, a scheme which had been germinating in Paul's mind for some time began finally to take shape. Already several months earlier he had conceived the idea of going to occupied Greece to join the resistance movement but the split in the guerrilla forces and the emergence of the Communist-controlled E.L.A.S. as the dominant element had frustrated that plan in its genesis. Later on, he had revived the idea in a different form: he would go to Greece and join Zervas, whose E.D.E.S. group was strongly established in the Epirus and whose attitude towards G.H.Q. Cairo had been impeccable. Zervas had been discreetly sounded on this project, and though a republican by conviction he had not only readily agreed but had even offered to place his forces under the command of the Crown Prince as the King's representative.

The next step was to find out the reactions of the Allied C.-in-C., so Paul saw General Maitland Wilson and put the idea to him. Wilson commended the Crown Prince's patriotic sentiments but said the risks were too great. 'Look,' protested Paul, 'if I get killed there will be a couple of lines in *The Times* obituary column and by next day everybody will have forgotten all about it.' But it was the possibility of Paul's capture, not his death, that was worrying Wilson. He promised to think about it, but as the days went by without further news Paul decided to invoke the help of his friend General Smuts, and on 9 September 1943 he asked Major-General Frank Theron, South African Minister to the Greek Government, to send a message to the General – Theron had his own channels of communication and used a code of which only Smuts and his closest associates, including Churchill, had the key.

In this message Paul put forward the argument that the collapse of Italy provided an opportune moment for a bold and imaginative

155

stroke in Greece. He had accordingly urged General Wilson to allow him to go to Greece at once to rally the country in the name of the King. Wilson was sympathetic but thought the time was premature; for his part Paul believed that now was the right moment, and he felt certain of success. He had not yet discussed this plan with the King as he did not wish to tell anybody until the logistics of the operation had been worked out in greater detail and until he could also say to his brother that he had Smuts's support, for which he now appealed to the General. He also asked if he might take Theron with him on this mission – the South African soldier-diplomat was very *persona grata* with the British and would be most useful as a contact with them, especially as he would be acting with General Smuts's full authority.

To this message Theron added the following personal comment: 'I think I can help the Crown Prince if you will agree to his request. The gallantry of Greece stirs me intensely and the adventure appeals to my Theronides blood from ancient Greece.'*

The reply came quickly: Smuts instructed Theron to give full support and provide all facilities that might be required. He also promised to take up the matter with Churchill at their next meeting.

At this stage the logistics of the operation began to assume rather larger proportions than Paul had originally anticipated and he now decided to bring into the scheme his equerry, Wing-Commander 'Babbi' Potamianos, and his orderly officer, Captain 'Johnny' Serpieri, both of them close and trusted friends who had followed him to exile. With their help and with the close cooperation of Theron three alternative plans were prepared.

The first entailed the use of a Greek destroyer; with his many friends in the Navy Paul had no difficulty in selecting a captain whom he could fully trust. It was the same with the second plan, which involved the use of a submarine. Both officers pledged their support and promised to be ready to put the plan into effect at short notice. However, as the Greek Navy was at sea most of the time and the two ships could not be guaranteed to be in port when required, an alternative means of transport, an aircraft, had to be arranged. Here things were more difficult as the Greek Air Force at this time consisted mostly of training squadrons which were not based in Egypt at all.

* This was a private joke – Theron had become so devoted to the Greek cause from the very start that Paul had once remarked that he must have Greek blood in him.

This was where Theron came in. There was a South African squadron of Dakotas based at Cairo West military airfield, and as a full Ambassador and a Major-General to boot Theron could pull rank when required. The plan was that, with the airfield Commander's connivance – and a confidential order from Smuts himself instructed the Commander to cooperate fully with Theron – a Dakota piloted by Potamianos would be 'hi-jacked' from the South African base at Cairo West and drop Paul and his companions by parachute at Zervas's secret headquarters in North-West Greece. This was where the first real difficulty arose: though an excellent pilot with a fine war record, Potamianos had never flown a Dakota before. Theron promptly arranged for the omission to be rectified: for the next two weeks Potamianos reported regularly every day at Cairo West for flying instruction on Dakotas from one of the South African pilots. Another problem was that the Crown Prince had had no parachute experience and could not take a crash course now as that would arouse suspicion and might give away the whole plan; but Paul was prepared to take the risk of a parachute drop without previous training. The only other member of the party without parachute experience was Serpieri, and Theron arranged for him to go to Italy to do his regulation three drops. In a week he was back in Cairo, a bright new parachutist flash on his shoulder.

Having completed his plans, Paul decided to tell his brother about the scheme and asked for permission to put it into operation. The King did not oppose the idea, but the political situation was now so delicate and involved that he was anxious to avoid further complications and Paul's scheme was bound to cause controversy. Finally he gave his consent subject to approval by Allied G.H.Q.

At the last moment, Allied consent was not forthcoming: the Crown Prince was told that the risk of capture was too great. To make certain he did not defy the veto, specific prohibitive instructions were issued to all concerned.

Frustrated and impotent, Paul was once again obliged to revert to the role of passive spectator as events moved inexorably to the tragic climax of the insurrection of April 1944.

⇒ 20 ⇐

The day after the suppression of the mutiny Sophocles Venizelos submitted his resignation, having held the premiership for just eleven days. Only a week earlier on 15 April 1944 the politicians in Cairo had been joined by George Papandreou, leader of the Democratic Socialist Party, who had been brought out of Greece by the British 'escape' organization. He appeared on the scene at the right psychological moment.* He was the most recent arrival and brought with him the views of other politicians still in occupied Greece; he had a long political record, having been one of the collaborators of the great Eleftherios Venizelos; most important of all, he was fresh blood, untainted by the plots and intrigues of the Cairo scene. The King immediately appointed him Prime Minister.

Meanwhile more politicians and representatives of the guerrilla organizations were being brought out of Greece for a round table conference, without much hindrance from the Germans, who either did not bother to interfere or were by this time incapable of patrolling every little cove and island in Attica and the Archipelago. By the middle of May all the delegates had gathered in the Lebanon where they were now joined by Papandreou and the other politicians from Cairo.

The actual conference began on 17 May; there was no time limit for each speaker and for three days each and every one of the twenty-five delegates had his say. There was a good deal of plain speaking – when General Stephen Sarafis, a former regular Army officer who had gone over to the Communists, made some remark about being 'the elected leader of E.L.A.S.', George Kartalis, representing a guerrilla organization which had been wiped out and whose leader

---

* 'He could not have chosen his moment to enter on the stage better had he been a famous actor, and there are few actors who in the Greek language can command the eloquence and vocal persuasiveness that Papandreou can command.'[16]

had been brutally murdered by E.L.A.S., leaned across the conference table and said to Sarafis contemptuously: 'You were never elected leader of E.L.A.S., you were spat into the leadership' – but after long and heated discussions an agreement named 'the Lebanon Charter' was finally signed laying the foundations for a Government of National Unity. Papandreou formally submitted his resignation to King George, who entrusted him with the mandate to form another government embodying the principles of the Lebanon Charter.

Article 5 of the Charter dealt with the question of the regime by stipulating that once the country had been liberated and order had been restored, the Greek people would decide both on the constitution and on the government of their choice. In order to satisfy the republican elements in his Cabinet, Papandreou issued a statement on 12 June 1944 to the effect that it was the view of the Government that the King should await a popular vote before returning to Greece, especially as he had already agreed to this in his letter of 8 November 1943 to Tsouderos – the letter in which the significant words 'the date of my return' had mysteriously disappeared in translation – and by his acceptance of the Lebanon Charter, in which this policy was implicit. This statement committed the King much further than he had been prepared to go, but in the circumstances he had no choice but to accept.

As soon as its delegates returned to Greece, E.A.M. began to make fresh demands, which were finally narrowed down to the insistence that Papandreou should be replaced as Premier by some other person. Papandreou himself was prepared to stand down, but the British would not have it. 'Surely we should tell M. Papandreou he should continue as Prime Minister and defy them all,' Churchill cabled to Eden furiously on 6 August. 'The behaviour of E.A.M. is absolutely intolerable . . . We cannot take a man up as we have done Papandreou and let him be thrown to the wolves at the first snarlings of the miserable Greek Communist banditti.' But it was not until 3 September that E.A.M. finally took up the six portfolios allotted to them in the new Government on the basis of the Lebanon Charter.

In August 1944 Papandreou was summoned to Rome to see Churchill, who was in Italy at the time. Churchill had been receiving anxious messages from Smuts concerning future developments in Europe generally and the Balkans in particular, and as the day of the liberation of Greece was clearly imminent he wanted to have a talk with Papandreou, whom he had never met.

While still in Naples, and five days before seeing Papandreou, Churchill had sent a message on 16 August to Eden outlining the attitude he intended to adopt:

I am not aware of, and certainly never consciously agreed to, any British Cabinet decision that the King of Greece should be advised not to return to Greece until after the plebiscite has taken place, but to come to London. It would be much better to see how events develop, particularly as it may not be possible for a plebiscite to be held under orderly conditions for many months.

He also found it prudent to send a similar message to President Roosevelt the following day:

The War Cabinet and Foreign Secretary are much concerned about what will happen in Athens, and indeed in Greece, when the Germans crack or when their divisions try to evacuate the country. If there is a long hiatus after German authorities have gone from the city before organized government can be set up, it seems very likely that E.A.M. and Communist extremists will attempt to seize the city and crush all other forms of Greek expression but their own. You and I have always agreed that the destinies of Greece are in the hands of the Greek people, and that they will have the fullest opportunity of deciding between monarchy or republic as soon as tranquillity has been restored, but I do not expect you will relish more than I do the prospect either of chaos and street-fighting or of a tyrannical Communist government being set up. . . . I therefore think that we should make preparations through the Allied Staff in the Mediterranean to have in readiness a British force, not exceeding 10,000 men, which could be sent by the most expeditious means into the capital when the time is ripe.

Roosevelt readily agreed, and even offered American transport aircraft for the operation.

The meeting between Churchill and Papandreou took place in Rome on 21 August, and one of the matters discussed was the position of the King. Churchill told Papandreou that there was no need for any new declaration by the King since he had already said that he would consult his Government before going back to his country; but 'the British nation felt friendly and chivalrous towards him for his conduct at a difficult moment in both our histories'. Britain had no intention of interfering with the solemn right of the

Greek people to choose what regime they liked, 'but it must be for the Greek people as a whole, and not a handful of doctrinaires, to decide so grave an issue'. Churchill also suggested that the Greek Government should transfer its seat as soon as possible from Cairo to somewhere near the Headquarters of the Supreme Allied Commander, which was now established near Naples.

Suitable accommodation was promptly found at Cava dei Tirreni, a summer resort five miles out of Salerno and about fifty miles from Caserta, and Papandreou returned to Cairo, only to find a new crisis on his hands: four of his ministers, including Venizelos, resigned because they had not been consulted about the meeting with Churchill. Meanwhile, King George had left for London after appointing Paul as his Regent and official representative in the Middle East.

Paul's first official act in this capacity was to swear in the six E.A.M. ministers who had finally agreed to join the Government. Three days later Papandreou and his colleagues left Cairo and established the seat of the Greek Government at Cava.

Later that month the two principal guerrilla commanders, General Stephen Sarafis of E.L.A.S. and General Napoleon Zervas of E.D.E.S., were brought from Greece to Italy for consultations concerning the command and disposition of the Greek forces. On 26 September 1944 the 'Caserta Agreement' was signed – by Papandreou and the two guerrilla leaders for Greece, and by General Wilson and Mr Harold Macmillan, who had just been appointed British Minister Resident in the Mediterranean, for Britain. The essence of this agreement was that all guerrilla forces in Greece placed themselves at the disposal of the Greek Government which, in its turn, placed them under the orders of Lt-General Sir Ronald Scobie, nominated by the Allied Command as G.O.C. Forces in Greece.

By early October reports began to come in that the German withdrawal from Greece had begun; any moment now the order would be given setting in motion the process of liberation of the country. An atmosphere of eager expectation, a sense of personal participation, began to infuse everyone involved in Greek affairs now that the journey home was clearly in sight.

To Paul in Cairo it seemed grossly unjust and totally wrong that the one person who had remained steadfast to the Allied cause from the very beginning, the King, should be excluded from his rightful place at the head of the liberating forces. He asked his brother in London for permission to make one last attempt: if the Allies were adamant about letting King George go, then he wanted to ask to go himself. The King agreed, and authorized him to go and see the Supreme Allied Commander in Italy.

But getting from Cairo to Caserta was another matter. Paul first approached Leeper and asked him to arrange transport, but after a week had passed without anything being done – Leeper had meanwhile transferred to Cava dei Tirreni with the Greek Government – he went to the British Air Commander in Egypt, Air Chief Marshal Sir Keith Park, and asked for transport to Italy. Park told him he could have a plane, but clearance had to be obtained first from the Foreign Office. Paul knew what that meant, so he went to General Paget and explained to him in confidence the purpose of his journey. The Commander-in-Chief promised him a plane for the following day, but later the same evening Paul received a message from Paget saying the arrangements had been cancelled by order of the Foreign Office. 'Suggest you send a stinker to General Wilson,' Paget added helpfully and privately, and Paul followed his advice. Three days later he was on his way to Italy.

The plane was early and there was no one to meet him when he landed, but a young officer with a car who happened to be there drove him to General Wilson's villa at Pasilipo. It was raining heavily.

Paul's meeting with the Allied C.-in-C., at which Macmillan and Leeper were also present, was not a success. Paul asked Wilson to explain the military situation with regard to Greece, and then gave his own views concerning the matter he had really come to discuss. He was firmly convinced, he said, that the presence of the King on Greek soil at this juncture was indispensable, and as the King was prevented from going for reasons known to them all it was his intention to demand from the Greek Prime Minister that he himself, as Diadoch and the King's nearest relative, should go in the King's place. Leeper intervened at this point to say that if Paul made such a demand in his capacity of Regent – which he still was in the King's absence in London – the Prime Minister would very probably resign and E.A.M. would go off on their own and cause endless trouble. Macmillan agreed with Leeper but put it more brutally: if Paul had been a Communist agent, he said, he could not have presented a better case for total disruption. Paul bit his tongue but said nothing, though later at lunch he complained bitterly to Leeper about Macmillan's offensive remark. After further lengthy discussion it was agreed that the matter depended on what the King and Churchill, who were due to meet in London, finally decided between them.*

In London, where he arrived the following day, Paul made no further progress. The King had accepted the British Government's firm advice that he should wait until the situation had clarified before even considering going to Greece, and this also applied to his brother. Without wasting any more time, Paul returned to Egypt.

It was actually as he sat brooding in the plane on the flight back that Paul had the idea of making one final effort, and as soon as he landed in Cairo he drove straight home to Alexandria and told Frederica of his new plan.

As from midnight on 13 September, all forces that were going to be used for the landing in Greece – operation 'Manna' – had been placed on a forty-eight-hours' alert. Paul's plan was that, just before the fleet sailed for Greece, he would go on board the Greek flagship and demand to be taken along. If the Commander-in-Chief was agreeable, well and good; if not, then Paul and his companions – Potamianos, Serpieri, 'Bouly' Metaxas (Paul's Orderly Officer) and the Equerry – would overpower the Admiral and lock him up in his cabin until the fleet was well on its way. The Captain of the flagship

---

* Leeper describes this incident as follows: 'While the Greek Government was still at Cava the Crown Prince came over from Egypt at the King's request. The King had not yet abandoned his wish to go into Athens with his Government but if that were not possible he would have liked the Crown Prince to take his place. Both brothers felt very keenly their exclusion from the triumphal return to Athens. It was therefore not very agreeable for us to have to oppose their wishes. The all-party Government would have dissolved on this issue. At the last moment there would have been no Greek Government, and E.A.M. would certainly have seized power in Athens. The Crown Prince only stayed a day or two in Italy and then joined the King in London.'[17]

Macmillan also recounts this incident, though less charitably than Leeper: 'The Crown Prince, or Diadoch, called to see General Wilson on the morning of 30 September. Leeper and I were also present. I felt sorry for the Prince. He was obviously sincere and anxious to do his best for his brother and the dynasty. But I fear he suffers under the usual illusions of royalty. He believes that he has only to show himself in Greece for a "landslide" to take place. We tried to explain to him that if he were to go now to Greece, the carefully constructed Government of Papandreou would fall to pieces. The only beneficiaries would be E.A.M./E.L.A.S. who would take over the country. A long and rather painful discussion followed. . . . In spite of his disappointment at our attitude, the Crown Prince behaved with exquisite courtesy, and the luncheon that followed went off well.'[18]

had to be let into the plot, but as he happened to be an old friend of Paul's there was no obstacle from that direction. Once on Greek soil Paul was confident he would have no difficulty in remaining there, as he was still invested with the powers of Regent and could therefore legitimately refuse to take orders from anyone except the King.

Having made all the arrangements, Paul decided to tell his brother what he intended to do. The King, who had given an undertaking to Churchill and whose own loyalty was now involved, ordered Paul to abandon his plan and expressly forbade him from any similar projects in the future. Paul abided by the King's decision and never raised the subject again.

What Paul did not know, and indeed was not told until much later, was that in her determination not to be left behind Frederica had also made plans to go to Greece. She had already taken a crash commando course in Cairo with Paul – 'just to keep you company while you are doing it,' she had told her husband – and could also handle firearms, having practised in South Africa with a pistol Smuts had given her for her personal protection. She now persuaded the commander of another destroyer to take her secretly on board when the fleet sailed so that she should arrive in Greece at the same time as her husband. At the last moment she decided to confide in a close friend, who strongly advised her against the project for a number of reasons, one of them being the risk that Paul might not be able to get to Greece after all, in which event she would arrive on her own. Reluctantly, she abandoned the idea.

On the morning of 4 October British forces occupied Patras, the main port in south-western Greece, and on 14 October they entered Athens, hot on the heels of the retreating Germans. On 18 October the Greek Government arrived and established itself once again on Greek soil. By 11 November the last of the German forces had left the country, and Greece was again free after three and a half years of enemy occupation.

It was not long, however, before those who had fondly believed that the policy of appeasement would assuage the Communists suddenly began to realize that their hopes were not going to be fulfilled. What the Communists were seeking was complete power, which they could only hope to achieve through force; as they were now virtually the only element in the country equipped with arms, the moment for action had clearly arrived.* Under various pretexts E.L.A.S. refused to disarm as agreed and began instead to converge on Athens, the only area in Greece that was not already under their control. On 1 December the six E.A.M. ministers resigned from Papandreou's coalition government, and the break was complete. Two days later the first clash occurred in Athens. General Scobie immediately ordered E.L.A.S. to evacuate Athens. E.L.A.S. replied by launching an all-out attack on the capital, concentrating first on police and gendarmerie stations, most of which were quickly overwhelmed and their defenders butchered.

On personal instructions from Churchill, British troops were ordered to intervene. 'Do not hesitate to act as if you were in a conquered city where a local rebellion is in progress,' was Churchill's succinct order to General Scobie on 5 December. 'We have to hold and dominate Athens. It would be a good thing for you to succeed in this without bloodshed if possible, but also with bloodshed if necessary.'

Bloodshed *was* necessary. Through sheer weight of numbers and the advantage which a guerrilla force inevitably enjoys over regular troops, especially in street fighting, E.L.A.S. was able to seize most of Athens until only a small enclave in the centre of the city remained under the control of the British troops supporting the Greek Government. At the same time E.L.A.S. bands in the Epirus launched an all-out attack on Zervas's forces, which had to be evacuated by sea to the island of Corfu to prevent their complete annihilation.

But Churchill was determined to see the business through, despite the bitter criticisms to which his action was being subjected by an ill-informed press and a vociferous left-wing group in Parliament. Field-Marshal Alexander, who had just been appointed Supreme Allied Commander, Mediterranean, arrived in Athens with Eden to examine the situation on the spot. 'The British forces are in fact beleaguered in the heart of the city,' bluntly cabled the Field-Marshal, who proposed that Piraeus and the road to Athens should be secured, reinforcements be brought from Italy, supply dumps be built up, and then Athens and Piraeus be methodically cleared. He

---

* 'In Greece, as elsewhere, the resistance movements had been presented by our propaganda as bodies of romantic idealists fighting with Byronic devotion for the freedom of their country. In fact, with all their genuine patriotism, they had become the instrument of Communist ambitions.'[19]

was given a free hand, and the 4th British Brigade was diverted to Greece. The tide soon began to turn.

On 14 December Churchill received a message from Smuts, who throughout this period was receiving day-to-day reports of the developments in Greece from Paul in Cairo:

We may, I fear, find, if private partisan armies and underground movements are kept alive, the peace degenerating in civil convulsions and anarchy not only in Greece but elsewhere also in Europe. At this stage firmness is in any case essential, and weakness in dealing with the partisans may end in real civil war at a later, more inconvenient, stage. . . . My own view, for what it is worth, is that after the suppression of the E.A.M. revolt the Greek King should return to discharge his proper constitutional functions, and the onus of practically running Greece should no longer be borne by His Majesty's Government.

Smuts's message, or at least that part of it concerning the King's return, was no doubt induced by the resuscitation by Leeper of the proposal that the Archbishop of Athens should be appointed Regent. This had been rejected both by King George in London and by Papandreou and his Ministers in Athens,* but on 15 December Field-Marshal Alexander had also urged that the best chance of getting a settlement quickly was through the Archbishop. To this Churchill had replied on 17 December:

The King of Greece has refused categorically in a long and powerfully reasoned letter to appoint a Regent, and especially to appoint the Archbishop, of whom he has personal distrust. I have heard mixed accounts of the Archbishop, who is said to be very much in touch with E.A.M. and to have keen personal ambitions.† We have not yet decided whether or in what way to overcome the King's resistance. If this cannot be overcome there will be no constitutional foundation other than an act of violence to which we must become parties. The matter would be rendered more complicated if, as it may prove and as the King asserts, he is advised not to appoint a Regency by his Prime Minister and Government. In this case we should be punishing the King for obeying his constitutional oath and be ourselves setting up a dictator. The

* Eden disputes this, and even casts aspersions on King George's veracity in the matter: 'More evidence in morning that King of Greece is not telling us the truth about evidence he is getting from Greece on Regency. Aghnides (Greek Ambassador in London), whom I trust, gives a different version to that of the King.'[20] On the other hand Macmillan, who was on the spot in Athens, fully supports the King's version: 'Later in the evening I went to see Papandreou. He said that *all* the leaders of the parties were against a Regency.'[21]

† The former of these charges may not have been true, but the latter certainly was.

Cabinet have therefore decided to await further developments of the military situation before taking final and fateful decisions.

Two days later, on 19 December, Churchill cabled Alexander again:

The Cabinet feel it better to let the military operations to clear Athens and Attica run for a while rather than embark all our fortunes on the character of the Archbishop. Have you looked up his full record? It is a hard thing to ask me to throw over a constitutional King acting on the true advice of his Ministers, apart from British pressure, in order to instal a dictator who may very likely become the champion of the extreme left.

Alexander's reply was grim: it was certainly possible for the Athens-Piraeus area to be cleared and held, but E.L.A.S. would still have the run of the Greek mainland. The Germans had been unable to keep their communications open during the occupation with seven divisions on the mainland and four in the islands, and the British could not spare anything like that number now. The answer therefore had to be found in the political, not the military, field.

To Smuts, Churchill replied on 22 December that the return of King George to Greece would provide no basis for a British policy. 'I have serious doubts about the Regency,' he continued, 'which may well assume the form of a dictatorship . . . All Leftist forces and our people on the spot have certainly given their support to it.'

Torn between his own sentiments and the advice he was receiving from Greece, and in view of the conflicting information about the Archbishop, Churchill decided to go to Athens and see for himself. He arrived with Eden at noon on Christmas Day, and after a conference with Alexander, Macmillan and Leeper he went on board the *Ajax* where they were joined by the Archbishop.* The result of the *Ajax* discussions was that a meeting was summoned next day of all the political leaders and E.L.A.S. representatives under the

---

* 'All preparations had been made by the ship's company for a jolly evening. The sailors had a plan for a dozen of them to be dressed up in every kind of costume and disguise as Chinese, Negroes, Red Indians, Cockneys, clowns. . . . The Archbishop and his attendants arrived – an enormous tall figure in the robes and high hat of a dignitary of the Greek Church. The two parties met. The sailors thought he was part of their show of which they had not been told, and danced around him enthusiastically. The Archbishop thought this motley gang was a premeditated insult and might well have departed to the shore but for the timely arrival of the Captain who, after some embarrassment, explained matters satisfactorily.'[22]

chairmanship of the Archbishop, who had already made a very favourable impression on Churchill.

The decisions of the conference were summarized in a cable sent by Churchill to Roosevelt on 28 December:

The Greek conference was unanimous in recommending a Regency. ... I am therefore returning with Anthony [Eden] to England to press upon the King of Greece to appoint the Archbishop Regent. ... I should greatly hope that you would feel yourself able to send a personal telegram to the King of Greece during the next few days supporting the representation we shall make to him, of which we shall keep you informed. My idea is that the Regency should be only for one year, or till a plebiscite can be held under conditions of what is called normal tranquillity. ... In the meanwhile we have no choice but to recommend creation of a new and more competent executive Government under the Regency of the Archbishop, and to press on with our heavy and unsought task of clearing Athens from very dangerous, powerful, well-organized and well-directed elements which are now pressing into the area.

On 29 December Churchill was back in London, and next day sent another cable to Roosevelt after seeing King George:

Anthony and I sat up with the King of Greece till 4.30 this morning, at the end of which time His Majesty agreed to the following announcement. ... This has been a very painful task to me. I had to tell the King that if he did not agree the matter would be settled without him and that we should recognize the new Government instead of him.

The proclamation to which King George was finally induced to put his signature was as follows:

We, George II, King of the Hellenes, having deeply considered the terrible situation into which our well-loved people have fallen through circumstances alike unprecedented and uncontrollable, and being ourselves resolved not to return to Greece unless summoned by a free and fair expression of the national will, and having full confidence in your loyalty and devotion, do now by this declaration appoint you, Archbishop Damaskenos, to be our Regent during this period of emergency; and we accordingly authorize and require you to take all steps necessary to restore order and tranquillity throughout our kingdom. We further declare our desire that there should be ascertained, by processes of democratic government, the freely expressed wishes of the Greek people as soon as these storms have passed, and thus abridge the miseries of our beloved country, by which our heart is rent.

To Roosevelt went another message from Churchill the following day, the last day of 1944: 'The Greek King behaved like a gentleman and with the utmost dignity.'*

On 3 January 1945 the Archbishop, now invested with the powers of Regent, accepted the resignation of the Papandreou Government and appointed General Nicholas Plastiras Premier. A vehement republican, Plastiras had led the revolution which deposed King Constantine in 1922, and had led unsuccessful revolutions in 1933 and 1935, since when he had been living in exile in France. He was brought back to Greece by the British in December 1944 at the height of the fighting in Athens. His Government, which was sworn in by the Archbishop in his capacity as Regent, consisted almost exclusively of republicans.

Meanwhile E.L.A.S. were fighting a losing battle against the British forces, and were beginning to withdraw from Athens, taking hostages with them. Many of these hostages perished during the forced march in bitter weather, and those who could not keep up were shot out of hand by their captors.†

On 11 January 1945 E.L.A.S. emissaries asked for a truce, which came into effect four days later. The 'Second Round' was over. On 12 February, after three weeks of negotiations, an agreement was signed at Varkiza which provided for an amnesty, the demobilization of E.L.A.S., the release of hostages, a purge of collaborators, and the holding of a plebiscite and elections under Allied supervision.

* The same could scarcely be said of Churchill and Eden. On the night of this dramatic meeting I was summoned by telephone to take certain documents to the King at 10 Downing Street (I was serving as his Secretary at the time). After delivering the documents I was instructed to wait in an adjoining room where, although my hearing is defective, I could hear through the door the voices of Churchill and Eden, particularly the latter, raised in anger at the King. In the middle of this heated argument the door was flung open and the King stormed out, his face white and taut. He had been told bluntly that he had until 2 a.m. to appoint the Archbishop as Regent; if he refused, the British Government would recognize the Archbishop as Head of State anyhow, would accredit their Ambassador to him, and would withdraw recognition from King George, who would be allowed to remain in England only as a private individual. In the car as we drove back to the hotel the King would not trust himself to speak; after recovering his composure he went back to Downing Street and informed Churchill and Eden that he had no choice but to acquiesce to their demands. He did extract from them a definite promise, however, that the insurrection would be suppressed at all costs and that the helpless mass of the Greek people would not be abandoned to the mercies of an armed Communist minority.

† In a debate in the House of Commons on 19 October 1945 the Minister of State, Mr Hector McNeill, stated that the bodies of 8,752 hostages taken by E.L.A.S. had been found in Attica and the Peloponnese alone, and that the total of those who died was certainly much higher.

The remarkably lenient terms of the Varkiza Pact allowed the Greek Communist Party (K.K.E.) to continue its subversive activities with the full protection of the law. The leader of K.K.E., Nikos Zachariades – who had spent the war years in an internment camp in Germany – was actually brought to Greece on 30 May 1945 in a British aircraft. The Communist newspaper resumed publication, and Communist infiltration into the trade unions was intensified. Although E.L.A.S. forces were ostensibly demobilized, large numbers made their way into friendly Communist countries across the northern frontiers, and large quantities of arms were carefully cached in readiness for the 'Third Round' that was to come.*

The Plastiras Government lasted just three months and was succeeded by a 'service' government under Vice-Admiral Peter Voulgaris, the man who had suppressed the naval mutiny in Alexandria in April 1944. In July 1945 elections in England brought the Labour Party into power after a landslide victory at the polls, and the Regent was invited to London for discussions with the new Government. One of the decisions reached at these talks was that elections should precede the plebiscite on the regime: the question of the date, however, was not decided. The British Government wanted them as soon as possible; so did King George, who in a statement from London on 27 October 1945 said:

I ask for no more than that the will of the people should be ascertained as quickly as possible, and that subsequently a Government should be formed representative of the popular will. As one who led his country to victory in the war I surely had the right to return to my country immediately after its liberation, just as did other Heads of

---

* 'On thinking over events in Greece,' writes Harold Macmillan in his autobiography, *The Blast of War*, 'I feel that the King of the Hellenes is the real villain of the piece. Had he written a clear letter (and not an equivocal one) saying that he would not return until called upon by a vote of the people, this powerful weapon of anti-monarchical propaganda would not have been available to the extremists.' In the light of subsequent events and taking into consideration the fact that Mr Macmillan occupied a high and responsible position from which he could reasonably be expected to have some awareness of the realities of the Greek situation as well as accurate information on Communist long-term plans and strategy, such an assessment of the Greek problem can only be described, at best, as naïve and disingenuous. It is perhaps what one would expect from someone who refers to the thousands of hostages taken by the Communists in the following calculating terms: 'E.L.A.S. have retained the Greek hostages. I am sorry for the people but it will prove a useful weapon for us. It damages E.L.A.S. politically at home; and it should enable us to persuade the Greek Government of the necessity for a general amnesty.'

State. But I agreed to submit myself in advance to my people's verdict so that the tendentious impression spread abroad that a large section of my people is against me should be ended once and for all.

The Archbishop, however, was not so keen – it was no secret that he much enjoyed the role of Regent and was not particularly anxious to relinquish it. On 9 October the Voulgaris Government resigned over this issue, and the Regent had such difficulty in finding a successor that he was obliged to take over the premiership himself for a while. A stop-gap administration formed under Mr Kanellopoulos lasted only nineteen days, but eventually the eighty-five-year-old Liberal leader, Themistocles Sophoulis, agreed to form a government which immediately proclaimed an amnesty for all political and criminal offences, except murder, committed between April 1941 and the Varkiza Agreement of 12 February 1945.

At the same time the Regent announced that the plebiscite on the return of the King would not be held until 1948. This brought an angry protest from King George, on 21 November 1945:

> The postponement of the plebiscite for three years creates a completely new situation. When Greece was liberated I agreed, at the suggestion of my Government and on the advice of the British Government, to return to my country only after the freely expressed consent of the Greek people. For this reason I entrusted to the Archbishop-Regent the exercise of my royal duties for the time of emergency resulting from the civil war. The Varkiza Agreement specifically laid down that the plebiscite would be held before the end of 1945 and that it would precede the elections. In September, however, it was decided that elections should precede the plebiscite, which was to be held at a future unspecified date. Now it is unilaterally decided that the plebiscite should once again be postponed for three years, and in the meantime a Government has been formed made up exclusively of republicans. . . . The repudiation of every decision that has so far been taken compels me to regulate my future attitude without any reservation other than the interests of my people and the respect of its sovereign will.

The publication of this statement provoked the resignation of the Regent, but it did not require much pressure from the British and American Ambassadors in Athens to persuade him to withdraw it.

It also provoked a retort from Mr Bevin in the House of Commons two days later: 'It has been suggested,' he said, 'that in supporting a proposal to postpone the plebiscite we have broken pledges given to the King of Greece by the Prime Ministers and

Foreign Secretaries of former Governments. I cannot agree that H.M. Government have ever been committed to any particular date for the plebiscite, or any particular order in which the election and plebiscite should be held.' At this point Mr Churchill – now leader of the Opposition – was compelled to intervene. 'I feel it absolutely necessary to place on record my own personal view,' he declared, 'namely, that a delay of two or three years in the holding of a plebiscite on the question of monarchy or republic in Greece would not be a *bona-fide* interpretation of the pledges and understandings we have given, not only to the King but to the Greek people.'

The elections were held on 31 March 1946 on the proportional representation system and under the supervision of an Allied Mission consisting of British, American and French observers. The result was a clear victory for the Populist (royalist) party and its allies who won 231 out of the 354 seats in Parliament. The Communists abstained, but the report issued by the Allied Mission calculated this abstention at less than fifteen per cent.

On 17 April 1946 the first Greek Government to be freely elected by the Greek people for ten years took office under Constantine Tsaldaris, the Populist leader, and at the opening session of the new Parliament on 13 May the Regent, in his Speech from the Throne outlining the Government's policy, announced that the plebiscite would take place later that year.

The referendum was held on 1 September 1946. In an exceptionally high poll – 90 per cent of the registered electors – the voting was 69 per cent in favour of the return of King George, 20 per cent against the King's return (but not against the monarchy as such), and 11 per cent in favour of a republic.

On 5 September the Prime Minister arrived in London and formally announced the result of the plebiscite to King George, who issued a proclamation to the Greek people:

By your vote of 1 September, you have confirmed the ancient ties between Crown and people. At the same time, your verdict should be interpreted as a solemn injunction to put a final end to a long-standing division which has weakened our nation and presented us abroad in a false light. We cannot, however, hope to carry out the nation's mandate except by faithful adherence to democratic principles and by the normal employment of all the national forces. . . . International complications have drawn Greece into the vortex of great conflicts which today make this task of national unity not simply a question of mere economic and political well-being, but of self-preservation itself. . . . I do not count on miracles, but I do believe in the strength of your patriotism and in the willingness of the nation to follow those who, in all conscience, demand of it the sacrifice of personal ambitions and private interests.

After five years in exile, the King and the Royal Family were now free to go home.

Part Four

%

1946-1950

⇉ 21 ⇇

On Thursday, 26 September 1946, the Greek destroyer *Themistocles* sailed from Alexandria with Paul and Frederica on board. Before their departure they had attended a solemn Te Deum at the Cathedral of St Sava where the Patriarch of Alexandria and the Greek community had wished them God-speed. After inspecting a guard of honour of Egyptian troops at the quayside and taking leave of Greek and Egyptian officials, Paul and Frederica boarded a launch which took them out to the destroyer anchored in the middle of the harbour. At eleven o'clock precisely *Themistocles* weighed anchor for Greece.

It had been agreed that the two brothers – Paul travelling from Alexandria by sea and King George flying direct from London – should rendezvous in Eleusis Bay on 27 September in the evening and enter Athens together the following morning. Exactly twenty-four hours after *Themistocles* left Alexandria, King George drove out to Heathrow Airport and after saying goodbye to Greek Embassy officials and members of the Greek community boarded the four-engined Lancastrian that was to take him back to Greece.*

After a non-stop flight the plane touched down at Eleusis at five

---

* It is one of those inexplicable quirks of British behaviour that no member of the British Royal Family – with the exception of Princess Marina Duchess of Kent, who was a close relative – nor any Cabinet Minister was at the airport to bid farewell to the King, in stark contrast to his arrival in England five years earlier almost to the day when he had been met at Liverpool by the Duke of Gloucester and at Euston Station in London by the King and Queen and the other members of the Royal Family as well as Churchill and most of the Cabinet. The most charitable explanation would be that the Greek King had probably expressed his customary desire for 'no fuss', but it seems hardly credible that such a wish could have been taken so literally that the most elementary courtesies should have been totally dispensed with. The British authorities did not even provide transport for the King: the aircraft he used had to be paid for by King George out of his own pocket – the charter fee and other expenses were actually defrayed at the time by the Greek Embassy in London, but the amount involved was subsequently deducted from the King's Civil List.

o'clock in the afternoon. It taxied up to the apron, and as soon as the engines were silent the door opened for the King to disembark. Nobody had foreseen that the hatch of the Lancastrian would be a good fifteen feet off the ground, and Eleusis was a military airfield with no passenger gangway. For several minutes the King stood at the open hatch looking down at the officials below, who stared back in embarrassed silence until someone appeared with a step-ladder. This was just long enough to reach the hatch-way and the King slowly clambered down with as much dignity as he could muster in the circumstances. Unloading the baggage was an even more complicated operation, as the luggage compartment was located in the nose of the aircraft which was even higher up in the air. A table was placed on the ground in front of the plane, a smaller table was put on top of it, and a chair was balanced on top of that. Then an aircraftman climbed on to the chair and standing on tiptoe just managed to lift himself into the nose of the plane from where he lowered the luggage, piece by piece, to another aircraftman standing on the chair.

While all this was going on the King boarded the destroyer *Miaoulis* lying at anchor in Eleusis Bay. The *Themistocles* had already arrived from Alexandria, and the Crown Prince joined his brother on the *Miaoulis* to discuss the final arrangements before returning to his own ship for the night. Shortly afterwards another launch drew alongside the King's ship, a tall black-robed figure standing erect in the cockpit: it was the Archbishop coming formally to surrender his powers as Regent, which had automatically lapsed the moment King George set foot on Greek soil.

Early next morning Paul and Frederica joined the King on board *Miaoulis* which then weighed anchor and steamed through the Straits of Salamis and round the promontory of the Castella into Phaleron Bay, escorted by *Themistocles*, *Kanaris* and *Adrias*. At ten o'clock the royal party disembarked to a salute of 101 guns – King George in Service khaki, Paul in Admiral's summer uniform and Frederica in a white dress and blue feathered hat. After the Prime Minister had presented his Cabinet King George, Paul and Frederica boarded an open and rather decrepit vehicle – the only open car that could be found at short notice with a rear seat wide enough to accommodate three people. With Frederica squeezed tight between her husband and her brother-in-law, the car started off along the dead-straight Syngros Avenue towards Athens, a cavalcade of cars with the King's suite, the Government and other notabilities following behind. The royal party drove straight to the Cathedral for the Thanksgiving Service conducted by Archbishop Damaskenos who had by now reverted exclusively to his ecclesiastical duties, and then proceeded to Constitution Square where the King laid a wreath at the tomb of the Unknown Warrior before climbing up the steps to the Parliament building above to receive in the Trophy Room the congratulations of the civic and military authorities and the Diplomatic Corps. In the vast square below a large crowd cheered and called for the King to come out on the balcony.

It was nearly two o'clock before Paul and Frederica could get away to Psychiko, to the home they had not seen for five years.

Two weeks later Frederica left again for Alexandria in the destroyer *Kanaris* to bring back her children. On 18 October the whole family was reunited at last and took up residence again at Psychiko.

A few days before leaving for Greece, King George had a lengthy meeting in London with the Foreign Secretary, Ernest Bevin, with whom he discussed his plans and hopes for the future.

His main aims were twofold: first, to safeguard the independence of Greece from the Communist threat which, though temporarily checked by the British military intervention in December 1944, was beginning to manifest itself again in the form of marauding bands raiding the more remote areas of the country from across the northern frontiers; and second, to restore and consolidate parliamentary government and political normality, which Greece had now lacked for ten years. Meanwhile the country, exhausted by war and revolution, desperately needed foreign aid. Measures of appeasement were necessary, and it was the King's intention to begin by commuting all outstanding death sentences. If that had the desired effect, he would proceed further to a reduction of prison sentences and then to a general amnesty. As regards the purely political aspect, it was his intention to encourage the formation of a coalition government and to prepare for fresh elections in a reasonable time.

Bevin listened sympathetically to the King's plans and promised full support.

Immediately after his arrival in Athens King George received the

Prime Minister, Constantine Tsaldaris, and entrusted him with another mandate to form a coalition government. This was easier said than done, however, and when the new Government was sworn in before the King four days later it was again a one-party administration, Tsaldaris having been unsuccessful in his efforts to broaden it. King George continued pressing for a more widely-based administration, being supported in these efforts by the U.S. Government, which was now beginning to interest itself more intimately and openly in Greek affairs.

Although the political leaders were unanimous on the desirability of a national government, however, they could not come to any agreement on the allocation of portfolios and particularly on who should hold the premiership, to which Themistocles Sophoulis, the octogenarian Liberal leader of the opposition, laid vigorous claim.

The King's choice finally rested on Demetrius Maximos, a retired banker and former Foreign Minister, who had been out of active politics long enough to make him acceptable to most of the others, and on 27 January 1947 a national coalition government was sworn in comprising all the parties represented in Parliament with the exception of the Liberals, whose leader Sophoulis still refused to participate.

Meanwhile, the situation in northern Greece was steadily deteriorating. Only a few days before the King's return to Greece a band of irregulars two thousand strong had attacked a mountain village in Thessaly, forcing the Government forces to withdraw and wait for reinforcements before the village could be recaptured; elsewhere in the north, guerrilla bands, armed and supplied from across the frontiers by the Communist regimes of Yugoslavia, Bulgaria and Albania, were terrorizing and plundering the countryside. Operating under the crippling disadvantages of regular troops fighting guerrillas who are uninhibited by established rules of warfare, the Government forces were unable to assert their presence in the affected areas, with the result that civilian morale was sinking very low. A tour by the King to boost morale was highly desirable, but the King could not absent himself from Athens, where political and administrative problems required his continuous presence. King George asked his brother to go instead.

Paul had already visited Patras on 30 November for the annual celebration of the patron saint of the city, St Andrew, and had been pleasantly surprised by the genuinely warm welcome he had received. Frederica had gone with him and from now on she was to be constantly at his side whatever he did and wherever he went. She accompanied him also on this northern tour, which began on 8 January and lasted twelve days.

They set out from Thessaloniki, to which they travelled by destroyer as the road from Athens was still in a very poor state and it was quicker and safer to go by sea.* While Paul inspected Army units and frontier posts in Macedonia, Frederica visited hospitals, welfare centres, women's and children's homes and similar organizations, listening to their needs, offering suggestions and making arrangements for assistance and future cooperation. It was her first personal experience of the stark conditions then prevailing in the countryside, her first contact at close quarters with the total disruption and chaos brought by years of enemy occupation and civil war. And in her mind the skeleton of a plan began to germinate for a nationwide organization with the necessary authority and resources to meet this great challenge.

On returning to Athens Paul, who had been promoted Lieutenant-General by Royal Decree on 14 January while still on tour, gave a detailed report on the situation to the King and also told him of Frederica's ideas for a big relief organization, which they had discussed in some detail on the journey back from Thessaloniki. King George agreed with the basic plan, and not long afterwards Frederica launched her 'Northern Provinces Welfare Fund', the forerunner of the vast Royal Welfare Fund (Vasiliki Pronoia) which was to become the main preoccupation of her life in later years.

Shortly afterwards Paul was again called upon to deputize for the King, this time at Janina for the annual celebration of the liberation of the Epirote capital on 21 February. The pattern of the northern tour was repeated, with Paul inspecting frontier garrisons on the Albanian border and Frederica visiting the villages and hamlets in the area.

The winter of 1946/7 saw a further intensification of guerrilla activity: large-scale military operations against Communist bands were now becoming necessary in Macedonia and Thessaly in the

* 'The main railway line from Athens to Thessaloniki is out of action, tunnels and bridges have been blown up. . . . Of the 10,000 kilometres of Class A highways, only 5 per cent are in good condition, 35 per cent are usable but the remaining 60 per cent are almost impassable. . . . It takes twenty-two hours to travel by jeep from Athens to Thessaloniki, a distance of 220 miles.'[23]

north and the Peloponnese in the south. In Athens the war-time nationalist guerrilla leader General Napoleon Zervas – now Minister of Public Order in the coalition government – was taking drastic measures to curb Communist subversive activities, left-wing sympathizers being arrested in large numbers and deported to the islands.

On 21 February 1947 – the day on which Paul and Frederica were attending the Liberation Commemoration Service in the Cathedral at Janina – the British Embassy in Washington informed the U.S. State Department that the British Government found itself no longer able to carry the burden of economic and military aid to Greece, and that British troops would be withdrawn as soon as convenient. This decision set in motion a sequence of events which culminated in the United States taking over from Britain the role which the latter had played in Greece for over a century, and found its formal expression in a message to Congress by President Truman on 12 March 1947. 'I believe that it must be the policy of the United States to support free peoples who are resisting attempted subjugation by armed minorities or by outside pressures,' declared President Truman, who asked Congress to approve aid for this purpose amounting to $400 million over the next twelve months, of which $300 million was to go to Greece, half of it for economic and the other half for military purposes; military equipment should be urgently transferred to the sorely-pressed Greek Armed Forces; and U.S. military missions should also operate in Greece in an advisory capacity.

Congress duly approved these proposals, which subsequently came to be known as the 'Truman Doctrine'.

Although King George had fought tenaciously for his constitutional right to return to Greece at the end of the war, his efforts had been a compulsion of duty rather than a labour of love. The thought of being plunged once again into the soul-destroying arena of political strife that he could still remember from before the war, added to the strains and bitter disappointment of the recent years, was a prospect too painful for him to contemplate. Already during the months in London before the plebiscite he had been seriously considering abdication – not as an immediate step, which his rigid dedication to duty would not allow him to take while the status of the Crown still remained in abeyance, but as a future course of action to be put into effect when the monarchy had re-established itself sufficiently firmly in Greece that a dramatic act such as he was contemplating could do no injury to the throne of which he regarded himself as no more than the transient incumbent.

There was another consideration: his emotional attachment to J—, the Englishwoman who had been sharing his life for some years now, had become an increasingly important factor in his calculations, and he was no longer prepared passively to contemplate a future in which this relationship could only continue furtively and inter-mittently as in the past. What he now yearned for was to be able to abandon the turmoil and the responsibilities of high office and be free to lead the quiet and dignified life of an English gentleman to which his character and temperament made him ideally suited.

His plans even reached a practical stage: early in 1946 he bought the lease of a house in Chester Square, in the fashionable Belgravia district of London, and for the next few months devoted much of his time to furnishing and decorating it, lovingly selecting the furniture and carpets and materials with the help of J— and frequenting public auctions where he could pick up old silver and pictures for his house.

He even laid down a modest wine cellar, and when at last he returned to Greece later that year the car he had bought during his stay in London was left behind for future use.

For family reasons J— had been unable to join King George in Athens immediately. She was also suffering from persistent bouts of migraine – the first manifestations of the dread Parkinson's Disease of which she was soon to become a tragic and helpless victim. The King had taken up residence in the Athens Palace, where he lived completely alone at first until he was joined by his youngest sister Katherine, who was still unmarried; Tatoi, where he would have preferred to live, was uninhabitable.

Life for the King during these first few months in Athens was very lonely indeed, and his health was also beginning to show the strain under which he was living. On 11 March 1947 he wrote to J—:

I'm afraid I had a mild sort of breakdown, which I tried my best to keep to myself. Those beastly old nerves were trying to get the upper hand, with those stupid pains in my chest, headaches, giddiness etc. In exasperation I called in old Anastasopoulo [the Royal physician] who only repeated what all the doctors in London had told me before. Nothing organic is wrong, only a question of nerves brought on by over-work. Of course my existence is not one to improve all this. I hardly get out at all, irregular meals and maddening worries.

During the next few days the chest pains of which he had been complaining became more frequent, making him feel very tired and depressed. On Sunday, 30 March, he was expected for dinner as usual at the Crown Prince's house at Psychiko, but at the last moment he telephoned to excuse himself saying he did not feel very well. Next day he felt no better, but he went to a charity performance of the film *Henry V* in the evening, having promised some weeks previously that he would attend; during the performance he complained to Frederica, who was sitting next to him, that he felt a strong pain in his side, but he insisted on staying until the end of the film.

The following day – Tuesday, 1 April 1947 – the King went through his normal routine in the morning and then prepared for lunch. Half-way up the wide staircase he seemed to be out of breath and sat down on the steps for a while before continuing to the dining-room on the first floor. He said he was not hungry and asked for some soup and nothing else, but before it had arrived he got up and went to the drawing-room next door, asking for a glass of water. When the footman arrived with the water he found the King lying unconscious, his head resting on a handkerchief which he had carefully spread over the arm of the sofa.

Paul and Frederica were immediately summoned but by the time they reached the Palace the King was already dead. He had died at 1.55 p.m. from heart failure brought on by coronary thrombosis. He was fifty-six.

Six hours later,* in the Throne Room at the Palace, Paul took the prescribed oath before the Archbishop of Athens, the Prime Minister and other officers of State, swearing

. . . in the name of the Holy, Consubstantial and Indivisible Trinity to protect the established religion of the Hellenes, to guard the Constitution and the Laws of the Greek Nation, and to preserve and defend the national independence and territorial integrity of the Greek State.

At the age of forty-five, Paul was King.

The death of King George was so sudden and unexpected that the news was received with incredulity at first – some people thought it was a sick April Fool's Day joke, others who heard the church bells tolling in the afternoon thought they were for the Oecumenical Patriarch, who had been lying gravely ill in an Athens clinic for some days.

The official announcement of the King's death was broadcast by Paul himself over the radio that evening:

It is with a heavy heart that I announce to you the untimely death of my beloved brother, our King, George II. He leaves this world with a clear conscience that there was no sacrifice he did not make in the service of his country.

Called upon today to continue his work, I declare myself ready to devote all the strength of my soul for the good of the nation.

After lying in state in the Cathedral for three days King George's body was taken to Tatoi for burial. It is a tradition initiated by King George I when he bought the estate that all members of the

---

* Greece is not the only country where such indecent haste is observed in the transfer of constitutional power: President Kennedy's widow was still wearing the blood-stained dress in which she had comforted her assassinated husband when Vice-President Johnson was sworn in as the new President at Houston on 22 November 1963.

Royal Family should choose for themselves the precise spot in the grounds where they wish to be laid to rest. It is also a tradition that the reigning monarch shall place a stone each year on the spot he has chosen for himself. King George had followed this custom, selecting a quiet shaded place under the trees not far from the tiny chapel on the hill-top and it was to this spot that his body was brought on 6 April. Only the members of the family were present for the simple burial service, but when the moment came to lower the coffin into the ground Frederica looked round, searching for someone. She went over to where J—, who had been brought from London for the funeral by Princess Marina, was standing discreetly in the background; putting her arm round her, Frederica helped the weeping woman to the graveside among the members of the family.

⇒ 23 ⇐

On 7 April 1947 Pipinelis, who had been asked by Paul to stay on as Political Adviser, submitted a thirteen-page memorandum in which he set out the political and other problems confronting the new King.

First and foremost was the Communist insurrection – 'the bandit war' – on the successful outcome of which depended the very existence of the State and the Monarchy. Greece was fighting this war with inadequate means and with lukewarm allies, and the basic policy was the restoration of law and order coupled with measures of appeasement and clemency for the benefit of those who genuinely desired to return to the national fold. Respect for the law and the dignity of the State had to be restored at all costs, however, and on this point Pipinelis quoted Bolingbroke's advice to the Patriot King: 'He must pursue in arms those who presume to take up arms against him, but he will pursue them like rebellious children. He will beat down the violence of this flame by his valour, and extinguish even the embers of it by his lenity.' Within its constitutional framework, the Crown had a decisive role to play in keeping the nation united and firm against the internal and external foe.

The King's second task was to ensure stability of government by bringing into the administration all the main political forces of the country. The coalition government of Mr Maximos largely fulfilled this aim, and any efforts to widen its basis further by the additional inclusion of the Liberals under Mr Sophoulis would have to be pursued with skill and tact so as not to jeopardize such collaboration as had already been achieved.

On 24 August 1947 the Maximos coalition disintegrated following the resignation of several of its members over the re-organization of the Cabinet. This was Paul's first experience as King of a government crisis, and he handled it with scrupulous regard for

187

constitutional procedure. First he summoned Tsaldaris, leader of the majority party (the Populists), and asked him to form a broadly-based coalition government. To facilitate Tsaldaris's task he then summoned the other political leaders and told them that if Tsaldaris failed he would then be obliged to entrust the mandate to Sophoulis, Leader of the Opposition (the Liberals); meanwhile, if the other political leaders could agree on such a coalition under some other Premier, the King was willing to dispense with the constitutional formula of entrusting the mandate to one leader after another and give it instead to the particular person they had agreed upon; with the proviso that such a government would have to enjoy the confidence of Parliament. In conclusion he asked to be informed by that same evening if such a solution was agreed upon.

But such a solution was not forthcoming, nor was Tsaldaris any more successful in his own efforts, and on 29 August an exclusively Populist Government was sworn in with Tsaldaris as Premier. Inter-party negotiations continued behind the scenes, however, suitably encouraged by the American Embassy in Athens, which made no secret of the strong desire of the U.S. Government that a broadly-based government should be formed as soon as possible to administer the massive aid under the Truman Doctrine. On 5 September agreement was finally reached between the two main parties, and two days later a Liberal-Populist coalition government was sworn in with Sophoulis as Premier and Tsaldaris as Vice-Premier and Foreign Minister.

Within a fortnight the new Government had reached agreement with the American Aid Mission for increasing the strength of the Greek land forces to 200,000, of whom 150,000 were to be regular army and 50,000 a National Guard specially trained and equipped to protect the countryside from rebel bands. All the necessary material would be supplied by the U.S.A.

In November 1947 Princess Elizabeth of England married Prince Philip, only son of Prince Andrew of Greece. Paul had been greatly looking forward to attending his first cousin's wedding not only because of the happy occasion of a union between the two royal houses – though Prince Philip was obliged to renounce his nationality, his religion and even his status as a Prince of Greece before he could become the consort of the heir to the British throne – but also because the gathering in London of many world leaders would provide an invaluable opportunity to put Greece's case to her powerful and influential friends. Shortly before the wedding, however, Paul was taken ill with typhoid fever and Frederica had to go to London alone. But the potentialities of the occasion were too valuable to let pass, and before Frederica left Athens she was thoroughly briefed by the King so that when suitable opportunities occurred she should be able to utilize them to the full. She showed herself a very adept pupil, with a quick grasp of essentials and a remarkably retentive memory, and in the event this exercise proved to be a highly successful operation which laid the pattern for a system of collaboration between husband and wife that was to be put into use repeatedly in the future with remarkably fruitful results.

On 21 November – the day after the royal wedding in London – the Greek Ambassador gave a dinner for Queen Frederica at Claridge's to which several of the people who had played a prominent role in Greek affairs, including Churchill, Smuts, Eden, General Scobie and others, were invited. After dinner Frederica took Churchill by the arm and led him to a sofa at the end of the room where they could talk privately.

Churchill began by mentioning some photographs he had seen in the newspapers of Greek guerrilla bandits being executed; public opinion did not react favourably to such scenes, he said, shaking his head gravely as he puffed at his cigar. Frederica agreed, but pointed out that these were men who had been found guilty of the most abominable crimes after proper trial. That is as it may be, said Churchill, but it was still very bad propaganda. 'Well, Britain and Greece have never been any good at propaganda for themselves, have they?' she said.

How was American aid coming along? asked Churchill. Well, said Frederica choosing her words carefully, it was sufficient as regards maintenance supplies, but very little actual combat material was coming through. 'You should tell General Marshall about that,' he suggested. 'He is here in London.' Frederica said she would not know how to talk to an American Secretary of State; anyway he would be too busy to see her. 'Don't worry, I'll arrange a meeting for you,' offered Churchill.

The following day Frederica flew to Germany to visit her parents, whom she had not seen for eight years. On her return to London she found a message from Churchill's secretary to the effect that General

Marshall was only free for a few minutes that same day at 6.45 p.m. if Frederica could see him then. Frederica replied she would be glad to see him, and punctually at 6.45 p.m. the Secretary of State of the United States was shown into her sitting-room at Claridge's.

It was the first time the two had met, and after she had been talking with him only a few minutes she felt – as she had felt in somewhat similar circumstances when she first met Smuts – that here was a man whom one could instinctively trust without reservations, a man of firm determination coupled with gentleness and compassion; above all, a man of vision and imagination. For his part, General Marshall was rather taken aback on being confronted by a smiling and very attractive young woman who appeared to be in her teens.

'I know you have only fifteen minutes, so I will come straight to the point,' she said quickly, trying to hide her acute embarrassment by plunging into her subject without any preliminaries. 'We need heavy artillery and mountain guns. We cannot fight the Communist bands with only forty-seven heavy field guns and fourteen mountain guns.' Marshall expressed surprise: surely military equipment was arriving in Greece from the United States. 'No,' said Frederica, 'you are sending us food and maintenance supplies but no heavy material.' Marshall was still doubtful, but Frederica, who had done her homework very thoroughly, insisted that if he made inquiries he would find that she was right. Why did the Greek Government want *mountain* guns, Marshall was curious to know. Because the Greek Army was used to them and fought better with this type of artillery, she said; most of the operations were taking place in mountainous country, and mountain artillery would give the Greek Army a big advantage over the bandits. Marshall, who was evidently conversant with this problem, still did not appear to be convinced. There were two schools of thought on this point, he said: one supported the arguments the Queen had been expounding, the other believed that guerrilla fighting was usually waged at close quarters with light portable weapons. No, replied Frederica, on whom Paul had impressed the importance of this particular point; that might be correct in theory but it was not so in the case of Greece, where the terrain played a vital role in view of the fact that the bands were operating, and were being supplied, from across the northern and western frontiers, which were completely mountainous.

Evidently impressed by the logic of the Queen's argument

Marshall now began to ask technical questions concerning the Greek Army command, but Frederica replied evasively that these were matters on which she was not competent to speak; the fact that she was discussing military matters at all was simply due to her husband's inability to do so himself because of his illness. This did not seem to deter Marshall from continuing the discussion. Things were going to get much worse, he confided to her; the Russians were conducting a total war of nerves in Europe, and the prospects were that guerrilla activity in Greece would be intensified in the near future. U.S. Army officers were being attached to the Greek Forces in an advisory capacity, and perhaps their presence would provide psychological encouragement for the Greek troops. The Greeks were in no need of psychological encouragement, she retorted spiritedly; what they wanted was arms, and the American officers would at least be able to ascertain the requirements on the spot.

Feeling that perhaps she was being a little ungrateful, she turned to more general matters and said that Europe could look to the future with greater optimism now that America was manifesting in a practical manner her readiness to play a leading role in the world. Yes, but did Europe have the necessary spiritual reserves to derive benefit from American aid and leadership? Marshall wondered. Certainly, was her immediate and earnest reply. So far as her own country was concerned, Greece was now the last frontier between the Eastern bloc and the Western world, and the Greeks would defend that position in any circumstances. 'And if war should come again,' she said passionately, 'this time my husband and I will stay behind with our people.'

Marshall seemed greatly cheered by this conversation. He had frankly despaired of the Greek political leadership, he confessed to her, but now he felt more hopeful and confident for the future. America was determined to defend the line Italy–Greece–Turkey–Persia at all costs and the mistakes of the Hitler era were not going to be repeated.

The Secretary of State then felt in duty bound to speak a little of the American political scene, 'but by this time I was so tired I could not make head or tail of what he was saying,' Frederica frankly admitted in the long and detailed report she sent to Paul that same evening via the Greek Embassy code.

Before Marshall took his leave, he promised Frederica to look into the matters they had discussed and write to her. Despite the original stipulation that he could only spare fifteen minutes, he had stayed for one hour and a quarter.

Later that evening Frederica had a telephone call from Smuts, who recounted to her an incident that had occurred at the Claridge's dinner. He had been sitting alone with Churchill, who had been partaking liberally of champagne throughout the meal and who suddenly leaned over to Smuts and said to him in a stage whisper as he nodded towards Frederica: 'Now, there's a Fascist woman!' Smuts had been surprised and shocked by this remark and had launched into an indignant defence of Frederica, expressing amazement that Churchill should have believed the scurrilous allegations against her in the Communist press. Churchill had seemed a little puzzled by Smuts's reaction, but after a while the explanation dawned on him: 'I said faschinating, not faschist,' he said sibilantly, guffawing at Smuts's embarrassment.

The closing days of 1947 saw the operations of the Communist bands building up to a high pitch. On Christmas Eve the rebel leader 'General' Markos Vafiades, a Greek refugee tobacco-worker from Asia Minor, announced the setting up of a 'Provisional Democratic Government of Greece', the announcement coinciding with the launching of an all-out assault on Konitsa, a mountain town strategically situated near the Albanian frontier, clearly with the intention of making it the capital of the newly-formed rebel administration.

Konitsa had already been the object of repeated rebel attacks for some time and its garrison of about nine hundred men was virtually in a state of siege. Helped by heavy rain which impeded the movements of Army reinforcements from the south, the guerrilla forces – three thousand strong, using artillery and mortars – succeeded in capturing the heights around Konitsa, and for a whole week, from Christmas Day to the last day of the year, the rebels pounded the beleaguered town. On 31 December units of the 8th Mountain Division made contact with the defenders after storming the rebel-held heights surrounding Konitsa one by one in actions reminiscent of the Graeco-Italian war, suffering many losses but also inflicting heavy casualties on the Communists who were eventually obliged to withdraw across the frontier and seek refuge in Albanian territory.

The relief of Konitsa, the first major defeat inflicted on the Communists, found the King still confined to his bed with typhoid fever – it was not until 30 January 1948 that he was well enough to appear in public. His disappointment at being prevented from going to Konitsa to congratulate the troops and boost the morale of the harassed population was so poignant and frustrating that Frederica volunteered to go in his place.

The visit was kept absolutely secret, and when the Queen arrived by destroyer at Preveza the next day she was ostensibly on one of her normal welfare visits to the provinces.

As soon as she was alone with the Corps Commander, Frederica told him the real purpose of her journey. The General demurred that Konitsa was still very much a theatre of military operations, and he could not assume the responsibility of taking her there. 'Very well, let us go to Janina then,' said the Queen. In the staff car driving to Janina Frederica kept asking questions about roads and distances, and after scribbling in her notebook she tore out the page and handed it to the General without a word. On it she had written:

SCHEDULE

02.00   Departure from Janina by car.
06.00   Arrival at Voidomati Bridge. Transfer to mule.
10.00   Arrival at Konitsa on mule-back. Inspection of Konitsa.
14.00   Departure from Konitsa by mule.
18.00   Arrival at Voidomati Bridge. Transfer to car.
18.02   Departure for Janina.

and underneath she had put her signature: FREDERICA R.

The General smiled indulgently and explained that such a journey was out of the question as the road was still heavily mined and under constant fire from Communist batteries: the garrison Commander himself, Brigadier Dovas, had just been blown up by a land-mine on this very same road, two other officers in his jeep being killed instantly and he himself suffering multiple injuries. But Frederica was not to be deflected from her purpose, and in the end the Corps Commander was forced to agree.

After the visit to Konitsa, on the proposal and at the insistence of the Army Command, King Paul conferred on Frederica the Greek Military Cross, which is awarded only for bravery under fire. For their part, the inhabitants of Konitsa erected a life-size statue of Frederica, in the centre of the town.

⇒ 24 ⇐

After the inevitable initial difficulties, the Liberal-Populist coalition of September 1947 had gradually developed into a working partnership, with the American Embassy intervening discreetly – and sometimes not so discreetly – as and when necessary to eliminate misunderstandings so that the war against the Communist guerrillas could be pursued without domestic distractions.

With their traditional republican background the Liberals had been cautiously suspicious during the early stages of their collaboration with the royalist Populists, but the frequent working sessions between the King and the elderly Liberal Premier as well as other members of his party in ministerial positions soon brought about a fundamental reappraisal of the role which the Crown was being called upon to play in the particularly difficult circumstances then prevailing; more specifically, a new evaluation of the personality and character of King Paul as an individual was gradually taking shape.

It was about this time that a British writer,* gathering material for a book on Greece, was asked by King Paul what people he had already seen. On being told their names the King pointed out that they were all avowed monarchists; surely some prominent opponents of the institution should also be interviewed so that a more balanced picture might be obtained. The writer followed the King's advice, and one of the people he saw was Sophoulis, a dedicated and life-long republican. The Premier did not speak a word of English, and the person who had actually proposed Sophoulis as a leading spokesman for the anti-monarchist point of view acted as interpreter at the interview. Much to the British author's surprise, Sophoulis launched into a well-reasoned and convincing argument in favour of the monarchy, until the embarrassed interpreter was obliged to

* Air Vice-Marshal Arthur S. Gould Lee.

194

interrupt and explain to Sophoulis that what his interviewer was expecting from him was the case *against* the monarchy.

Note what I say carefully [replied Sophoulis, who subsequently insisted on checking and initialling the transcript of his remarks]. I became a republican in my youth in reaction to the extreme monarchism of my professor in a German university, and I have fought against the monarchy ever since. At every plebiscite I have declared for a republic. At the 1946 referendum I proclaimed my opposition to the return of King George, but when the results showed that the people wanted the King I accepted their decision and declared that the question of the regime was settled. . . . Now I acknowledge that the new King and Queen have only one desire, which is to serve Greece. I have talked often with them both and watched them in their activities, and I give them my full support, for although I remain a republican by conviction I can still approve of a constitutional monarchy. . . . In order to obtain the adherence of all his subjects the King must be the first democrat among them, and that is what King Paul has shown himself to be. As for the Queen, every day she is showing her desire to help Greece, just as she did when she was Crown Princess.

Although the Army was invariably successful whenever it managed to come to grips with the Communists, the hit-and-run tactics of the guerrillas were having a demoralizing effect on the exposed populations in the frontier regions, where the Communists enjoyed the additional advantage of being able to seek refuge across the border inside Yugoslavia, Albania and Bulgaria, immune from further harassment by the Greek Army which could not follow them into foreign territory without international complications.

The sense of frustrated impotence induced by this state of affairs was beginning to have its repercussions inside the Government: the differences of opinion as to the ways and means of coping with the situation were giving rise to great stresses within the coalition, while in Parliament itself violent scenes, leading to blows on the floor of the Chamber, were becoming a common occurrence. On 5 May the Premier Sophoulis and the Vice-Premier Tsaldaris together saw the King and recommended the adjournment of Parliament for a further period of one month beyond the normal Easter recess. The two leaders were quite frank about their dilemma: if they were to appear before Parliament themselves and ask for such an adjournment, they were almost certain not to get it; therefore the King should use his constitutional prerogative and adjourn

Parliament on his own authority. The King replied that since Sophoulis and Tsaldaris jointly represented the parliamentary majority through their parties, he would accede to their recommendation. He asked them, however, to formulate their request in writing, which they did within the hour. At the same time there was a reshuffle of the Government, some of the less successful ministers being replaced by more energetic colleagues. One of these was the Populist Deputy for Serres, a forty-year-old Macedonian called Constantine Karamanlis, who was transferred from the Ministry of Labour – which he had held since November 1946 – to the highly important Ministry of Transport.

A Government crisis was averted – but not for long.

To their raiding and sabotage activities the guerrillas were now adding a new dimension of warfare: 'Paidomazoma', the abduction of young children between the ages of two and fourteen, forcibly taken from their homes and removed as hostages across the border to various 'Iron Curtain' countries where they would be given a Communist upbringing away from their parents. In its Report of 21 May 1948 the U.N. Special Committee on the Balkans emphasized that these abductions were no isolated incident but part of a concerted design

a) to terrorize the Greek families into giving their support to the Communists;
b) to imbue the children with the Communist ideology; and
c) to destroy the Greek race, to dislocate agricultural production by forcing families to abandon their fields and seek safety for their children in the towns.

With its highly-stretched lines of communication the Army was in no position to provide continuous protection against this danger to the village populations along the country's six hundred miles of frontier in the north; the only effective measure was to evacuate the children to the safety of the interior, away from the guerrillas' reach, as quickly as possible.

With three young children of her own, Frederica could understand all too readily the anguish of parents living under the shadow of this inhuman threat. It was a challenge which she grasped with a passionate determination and vigour that only a personal identification with a cause can provide. The full resources of her Northern

Provinces Welfare Fund were immediately brought into operation.
Women volunteers were sent out to the exposed areas to bring the
children away, with their parents if they insisted on coming too,
alone if their parents felt they could not completely abandon their
homes. Using Army trucks and hired vehicles, the volunteers
collected the children from the villages and brought them to safe
towns in the interior.

When Frederica launched her Northern Provinces Welfare Fund
on 5 July 1947 she broadcast an appeal to the nation – her first
direct communication with the Greek people as Queen. After
describing the pitiful condition of the destitute populations of the
frontier provinces she had recently witnessed with her own eyes,
she called on the more fortunate ones to give generously. 'I do not
ask for what you can spare,' she said. 'I am asking you to deprive
yourselves. Any sacrifice you make will be small compared to the
sacrifices suffered by the people of the northern provinces.' The
response had been overwhelming: in a country still in the throes of
ruinous devaluation and the crushing after-effects of war and
occupation, nearly £500,000 had come in within a few days.

One of the uses to which Frederica had put these funds was the
establishment of 'Paidoupolis', Children's Communities where
boys and girls orphaned or left destitute by the guerrilla war could
be given a home. The statutes of the Paidoupolis defined their
purpose as being 'to provide a temporary shelter and welfare for
orphans and children abandoned, destitute or needing immediate
help and originating from the countryside and the regions considered unsafe owing to present tragic circumstances', and went on
to elaborate that the term 'welfare' covered food, clothing, medical
attention, education and entertainment.

Within a month of Frederica's original appeal the first
Paidoupolis, providing accommodation for 640 evacuated children,
was inaugurated in Thessaloniki; three weeks later six more
communities were functioning at Ianina, Larissa, Volos, Lamia,
Cavalla and Stylis, accommodating another 2,860 children.

But the new call on the resources of the Fund arising from the
urgent need to evacuate children threatened with abduction was on
a much bigger scale than its financial means were designed to meet;
Frederica decided to make another nation-wide appeal for this
specific purpose. With its inevitable emotional overtones, such an
appeal could not fail to evoke universal response. In addition to

individual donations from the public, including one day's pay from all workers and employees, the Government also contributed with a five per cent surcharge on cinema and theatre tickets, restaurant bills and luxury articles. In a remarkably short time there were fifty-two Paidoupolis operating in requisitioned buildings or in tent encampments set up for this purpose throughout the country.

Frederica's personal role in initiating and operating this scheme was duly recognized by the grateful women of Greece, who saw nothing incongruous in conferring on a thirty-year-old woman the affectionate title of 'Mother of Greece'.

Meanwhile King Paul was having his own problems with the Government, both on the political and the military plane.

On 9 July 1948 the Prime Minister, Sophoulis, asked for an urgent audience with the King at which he proposed that General Papagos should be appointed Supreme Commander of the Armed Forces. The idea had already been mooted some weeks earlier, but the Government had subsequently formed the opinion that a change in the whole command structure which such an appointment would entail was inadvisable in the middle of the campaign. The King had shared these reservations, and the matter had not been pursued any further. The stalemate in the military operations, however, had induced second thoughts on the part of the Premier, who had now been converted to the view that any side-effects of such an appointment would be more than compensated by the advantages of having a man of the prestige and acknowledged military ability of Papagos in overall charge of the country's war effort.

On 13 July Sophoulis again saw the King and reported that he had raised the question of Papagos's appointment in the Supreme Council of National Defence, where he had encountered unexpected opposition from the Ministers of the Army and of the Navy. Sophoulis wanted to press on with the matter nevertheless, but the King advised him to put the proposal in abeyance.

A few days later there was another emergency: Sophoulis telephoned the King's secretary on 25 July and said he had to see the King urgently. The secretary explained that the King was out of town and would be back in Athens in two days' time, but the Premier insisted that the King should be requested to return immediately as a crisis had arisen. At 9.30 p.m. the King received Sophoulis, who said that certain members of his own party were

no longer supporting him and that General van Fleet* was demanding the replacement of certain army commanders, to which the
Government was opposed while military operations were in
progress. In the circumstances, Sophoulis wanted to submit his
resignation. The King was determined to preserve the coalition
which had been achieved with such great difficulty, and told
Sophoulis that a political crisis at a time when the Army was
fighting a bitter war was totally inadmissible; nor was the withdrawal of the support of nine deputies sufficient cause for the
Government's resignation. Sophoulis was not convinced. The King
then put it to him that his resignation would serve no practical
purpose. In such a situation the King was constitutionally required
to ask his Prime Minister for advice as to what the next step should
be, and this the King was now doing: what did Mr Sophoulis
advise? Sophoulis said that the King should consult Mr Tsaldaris,
leader of the largest party, and then himself as leader of the
opposition (as he would be after he had resigned), and then
successively the leaders of the other parties in Parliament. This, he
admitted on being pressed by the King, would merely prolong the
crisis and could finally lead to no other result than the formation of
a similar government to the present one. Then why go through all
this rigmarole for nothing, demanded the King, laughing.
Sophoulis laughed too and agreed to withdraw his resignation, but
for reasons of political expediency he insisted that a statement
should be issued to the effect that he had submitted his resignation,
which the King had refused to accept.

Two days later another crisis arose, for which this time the
responsibility lay with the King himself.

On 12 May 1948 the British Government announced proposals
for constitutional reform in Cyprus, which had had no constitution
since 1931 when disturbances in favour of union with Greece
('Enosis') had led to the abolition of the Legislative Assembly and
the substitution of government by Orders in Council. The new
proposals provided for an elected legislature which, however, was
specifically forbidden to discuss the status of Cyprus within the
British Commonwealth. This was the moment chosen by Lord
Winster, the Governor of Cyprus, to make an announcement that
the question of 'Enosis' was definitely and irrevocably closed.

'I repeat that no change in the sovereignty of the island is

* Chief of the U.S. Military Mission to Greece.

intended,' he said. 'Anything to the contrary which you may hear, either here or elsewhere, designed to make you believe that the question is still open, or that negotiations are contemplated, is untrue.'

This statement had given rise to anti-British demonstrations in Cyprus, and Archbishop Makarios, Head of the Church and the elected 'Ethnarch' or National Leader of Cyprus, had called upon the Greek Cypriots (who comprise nearly eighty per cent of the population of the island) to reject the British proposals and had appealed to Britain to permit the union of Cyprus with Greece 'as an act of justice and in fulfilment of the national demand'.

With public feeling now running high in Greece on this issue, King Paul felt constrained to make reference to it in an interview with Mr Cyrus L. Sulzberger of the *New York Times* on 28 July in the following words:

Greece certainly desires and will continue to desire the union of Cyprus with the rest of Greece. It is difficult to understand why this has not yet been effected. The argument that this might interfere with British security is not valid. Were Cyprus to be given to Greece, as the vast majority of its population desires, this would in no way interfere with any military or other bases Britain has established there. Furthermore, if it could be arranged under the United Nations, Greece would be prepared to offer further base facilities to Britain or the U.S.A. in Crete or elsewhere. . . . Such bases could only benefit Greece and the world, and at the same time the establishment of Greek sovereignty over Cyprus would be in accord with the desires not only of the Greek population of that island but of Greeks all over the world.*

No sooner had the King's remarks appeared in the press than Tsaldaris, who was Minister of Foreign Affairs as well as Deputy Premier, sent a message to the Palace that he was going to resign because he had not been consulted in advance concerning the King's remarks. He was, in truth, in a rather awkward situation, having received from the British Foreign Secretary, Mr Ernest Bevin, only a few days earlier an appeal that the Greek Government should not raise the Cyprus question. But the King was firm: it was high time somebody voiced the feelings of the Greek people on this national issue, and if the Government was not going to do it he would do it

* These were, in fact, precisely the security arrangements finally agreed when Cyprus became an independent State in 1960.

himself. And if Mr Tsaldaris still wanted to submit his resignation, the King would accept it without argument.

That was the end of the matter so far as the Greek side was concerned, but on 31 July the British Chargé d'Affaires in Athens delivered to the Prime Minister an *aide-mémoire* in which the British Government protested against the King's remarks:

That His Majesty King Paul or his Government should make public statements of this kind can, in the view of His Britannic Majesty's Government, only cause embarrassment and misunderstanding and encourage both Greeks and Cypriots to indulge in a type of agitation which in present circumstances can only be described as a dangerous luxury.

The *aide-mémoire* went on to stress that such agitation would not move the British Government from its declared policy on Cyprus, and expressed the view that King Paul had 'done a disservice to the cause of Anglo-Greek cooperation in this untimely reiteration of Greek claims'. In conclusion, the British Government asked that the Prime Minister should

... find an early opportunity to make it clear by a public statement that the Royal Hellenic Government not only do not envisage pressing Greek claims to the union of Cyprus to Greece, but that they consider agitation to that end is against the interests of Greece and can only redound to the profit of Greece's enemies.

Mr Sophoulis was not prepared to go quite as far as that, but on 3 August he did issue a statement to the effect that the King had merely repeated the national feelings already expressed in the Greek Parliament, but in view of the present delicate situation and in view of Greece's desire to maintain sincere collaboration with her great Allies, the Greek Government was of the opinion that further discussion on the question of Cyprus would be liable to prejudice Greece's international relations.

On 26 October the King went to Thessaloniki for the annual celebration of the liberation of the Macedonian capital. On his return to Athens next day he received the Prime Minister, who reported that he had again raised the question of the appointment of General Papagos as Commander-in-Chief. The King agreed with the proposal, but suggested that before the matter was finally put to the Supreme Council of National Defence, General Papagos himself should be asked whether he would be prepared to accept the appointment, and if so on what terms. It would also be necessary to ascertain the views of the British and the Americans, especially the latter, who were entitled to be consulted in such matters by virtue of the American aid agreement between the two countries.

Sophoulis immediately wrote to Papagos, who after considering the matter very carefully replied to Sophoulis on 11 November setting out his conditions, which in brief were as follows:

1. The powers of the C.-in-C. should be the same as those he had held during the 1940–41 war in the matter of planning and directing military operations, the composition of military units, appointment and transfer of officers, and the recall of officers from the reserve.

2. The Allied Military Missions should confine their activities to training and supply, and should not intervene in administration, organization or operations.

3. Martial law should be maintained throughout the country, with the imposition of strict censorship to safeguard military information.

4. The gendarmerie should be placed under the orders of the C.-in-C.

5. Naval and Air Force cooperation in military operations should also be under the C.-in-C.

The above considerations were for immediate application. As regards long-range objectives, Papagos emphasized in his letter that if the Greek question was not going to be solved by international agreement through the United Nations, then the burden of suppressing the Communist rebellion would naturally fall exclusively on the Greek Armed Forces:

For a rapid termination of the struggle [he continued] I do not consider that the forces we actually dispose of are sufficient. Bearing in mind that the solution of the problem with regard to the forces required does not only depend on the numbers of the rebels but also on the area and the nature of the terrain over which the rebels operate, on the objective of the operations – which should be their encirclement and annihilation or capture – and finally on the requirements of the State to protect certain inhabited regions, communications, public installations etc., I consider it necessary to have an Army of at least 250,000 men, with corresponding equipment of all types, and if possible with an increased percentage of front-line troops.

All this time an atmosphere of crisis was building up in Parliament, where dissatisfaction over the Government's apparent inability to bring the guerrilla war to a successful conclusion was steadily growing. To the ranks of opposition politicians voicing these criticisms was now added Mr Sophocles Venizelos, Deputy Leader of the Liberal Party, who had always maintained an independent line and had consistently declined office in the Liberal-Populist coalition.

On 11 November Venizelos and a group of dissident Populists, together with the Democratic Socialist Party under George Papandreou, announced they were withdrawing their support from the Government. This was the signal for Sophoulis to resign.

On 15 November Venizelos wrote a personal letter to the King explaining and justifying his attitude. The collapse of the Coalition Government, he said, was the inevitable consequence of its own failure. Its total inability to provide the necessary leadership after fourteen months in office was having a paralysing effect on the national effort at a time when the full mobilization of the nation's energies and resources was imperative. The only way to achieve this was the formation of a non-party government consisting not of politicians but of experts.

On 12 November Sophoulis formally submitted his resignation to the King, and advised him to call on Tsaldaris, as leader of the largest party, to form a government. On 13 November the King received Tsaldaris and entrusted the mandate to him. After five days of intensive negotiations, however, Tsaldaris admitted failure in his efforts, and on 18 November a new government consisting of Liberals and Populists as before under Sophoulis, with Tsaldaris as Deputy Premier, was sworn in. Three days later the new Government obtained a vote of confidence in parliament by a majority of two, with the Venizelist Liberals voting against it.

In this crisis a decisive role was played by Spyros Markezinis, who had broken away a year earlier from the Populist Party with some twenty Deputies to form the 'New Party', and who now threw his support decisively behind the new Government. Markezinis was an ardent admirer of Papagos, and his action in enabling the coalition to secure a further lease of life, albeit with an infinitesimal majority, was not unconnected with the conviction that the appointment of Papagos as Supreme Commander was most likely to be achieved under such a Government.

The temporary nature of the compromise which had enabled the Liberal-Populist coalition to continue in office was rapidly becoming evident, and Papagos now informed the King that he was not prepared to accept appointment under an administration that inspired no confidence in him or in anyone else for that matter. On 22 December 1948 Venizelos asked to see the King, to whom he repeated the view that the Government as then constituted could not remain in power much longer. The King advised him to discuss with Sophoulis and Tsaldaris the possibilities of broadening or reconstituting the Government before taking any drastic action.

It was against this background of incipient crisis that the new year dawned, and during the first few days of 1949 discussions took place with a view to broadening the complexion of the Government by the inclusion of other parties. These negotiations came to nothing, and on 15 January Sophoulis submitted his resignation, advising the Sovereign to summon all the political leaders together and call on them to provide a parliamentary solution to the problem. The King accepted this advice, and once again the appropriate constitutional procedure was set into motion.

First of all, and in order to forestall any argument as to who did or did not qualify for the title of political leader, the King's Private Secretary, 'Bouly' Metaxas, called on the Speaker in order to ascertain the current party strengths in the Chamber of Deputies. The Speaker knew the figures by heart, but Metaxas insisted on a written list with the Speaker's signature on it. The position was as follows:

Populist Party (Tsaldaris)	131
Venizelist Liberals (Venizelos)	54
Democratic Socialist Party (Papandreou)	30
Liberal Party (Sophoulis)	29
National Liberal Party (Gonatas)	24
National Party (Zervas)	21
New Party (Markezinis)	19
Nationalist Party (Turcovasilis)	10
National Unionist Party (Kenellopoulos)	8
Independents	28
	354

Metaxas then notified the party leaders in the list one after the other that the King would receive them the following day at 12 noon.

Later that same evening the Populist leader Tsaldaris telephoned Metaxas that he and three other party leaders – Venizelos, Papandreou and Kanellopoulos – had agreed on a basis of cooperation among themselves, and asked for an urgent audience of the King. Metaxas told Tsaldaris that the King had already left for Tatoi, but a few minutes later Tsaldaris again telephoned to tell Metaxas that to save time he and the other three leaders were proceeding to Tatoi anyhow in the hope that the King would receive them there.

The King, who was duly informed of these developments by Metaxas over the telephone as soon as he arrived at Tatoi, decided not to deviate from his original plan, since all the other party leaders had already been summoned for the following day and it would be discourteous as well as politically inadvisable to cancel the audience in the circumstances. When the four politicians arrived at Tatoi, therefore, they were informed by the equerry on duty that the King was resting and could not receive them at such short notice.

Punctually at 12 noon on 16 January the political leaders were shown into the King's presence in the Palace at Athens. King Paul received them standing, and without any preliminaries proceeded to read to them an exhortation to the drafting of which he had devoted considerable effort.

They were the elected leaders of the Greek people, he said, and it was their duty to find a solution to the political crisis. There was no time to waste in futile discussions; a strong national government was needed to rally the nation behind the army and to convince friend and foe alike that party politics had been put aside for the duration of the war. Petty interests which divided the political parties were nothing before the national interest; the war had to be won at all costs. He was confident they would show themselves worthy of the trust of the Greek people, but if no national government were forthcoming within twenty-four hours then he would be obliged to look elsewhere for some other solution. 'Once again I appeal to your patriotism,' he concluded. 'Hearken to the voice of the nation as expressed through me. You are the leaders. Show yourselves worthy of leadership.'

When he had finished, the King indicated that there should be no further discussion in his presence but that the political leaders should confer among themselves and give him their answer as soon as possible. He was actually leaving the room when Kanellopoulos asked whether the King insisted on the participation of *all* the parties, but the King was not to be drawn. 'I have said all I am going to say to you,' he said firmly as he opened the door. 'And may the Almighty give you guidance,' he added as an afterthought in the traditional Greek manner before closing the door firmly behind him.

The King's ominous reference to 'some other solution' was not lost on the politicians: if Parliament could not provide a government, the King was now ready to look elsewhere. Nor would he have very far to look: across the road from the Palace was the office of his Great Chamberlain, General Papagos.

A general discussion followed the King's exit from the audience chamber, but it was soon apparent that no immediate consensus of opinion could be reached, and the party leaders dispersed.

The King had requested that the final decision of the politicians should be conveyed to him by one of their number, but agreement proved impossible even on who this spokesman should be, and in the end they each submitted their views to the King individually in writing. The replies revealed that opinion had crystallized into two groupings: one consisting of Tsaldaris, Venizelos, Papandreou and Kanellopoulos, who said they would agree to serve in a government headed by Mr Alexander Diomedes – a former Governor of the

Bank of Greece and a leading economic expert – and the other consisting of most of the other parties, who proposed Sophoulis as premier.

Since Papandreou was opposed to the appointment of Papagos as C.-in-C., whereas everybody else considered it eminently desirable and Sophoulis himself was actually making it a condition, some means had to be found of reconciling Sophoulis and the 'Four'. For this purpose Metaxas called on Sophoulis to sound him as to whether he would be prepared to form a broadly-based government of national unity. Sophoulis, whose political acumen had not been impaired either by his advancing years or by his recent grave illness and who kept his ear close to the ground, replied that he was ready to accept the mandate provided Diomedes was included in the government as Vice-Premier and provided Papagos was appointed Commander-in-Chief immediately. Metaxas proposed that Diomedes's reaction should be ascertained forthwith. Sophoulis promptly telephoned Diomedes to come to his house at once, and after a few minutes' private conversation between the two men Metaxas was called in and told that Diomedes had agreed to serve. An hour later Sophoulis was received by the King who formally entrusted him with the mandate, and immediately afterwards the Royal Secretariat issued this statement:

Following the resignation of the Government under Mr Sophoulis, the appeal by the King to the parliamentary party leaders and the views expressed by the party leaders, the King has entrusted to Mr Sophoulis the mandate of forming a broadly-based coalition government in the spirit of his appeal. Mr Sophoulis accepted the mandate, and at the same time expressed the desire that Mr A. Diomedes should be appointed Vice-Premier with overall supervision of economic matters, and that General Papagos should be appointed Commander-in-Chief. The King was graciously pleased to accept the above wishes of Mr Sophoulis. Mr Diomedes has agreed to participate in the Government on the above basis.

On 19 January 1949 the King signed a Decree appointing General Alexander Papagos Commander-in-Chief of the Armed Forces and promoting him to Field-Marshal, a rank never previously held in Greece except nominally by the Sovereign. The following day the new Government was sworn in. It consisted of 11 Tsaldaris Populists, 8 Sophoulis Liberals, 4 Venizelos Liberals, 3 Markezinis New Party and 2 Kanellopoulos National Unionists, with Sophoulis as Premier and Diomedes as Vice-Premier and with the five party leaders forming a policy-making Inner Cabinet. The new Government duly appeared before Parliament and on 4 February received a vote of confidence by 245 to 50, with 58 Deputies absent; after which Parliament went into recess until 1 June.

⇒ 26 ⇐

The military operations against the guerrillas were greatly intensified under the vigorous leadership of Papagos, and a series of action in various parts of the country had resulted in heavy casualties being inflicted on the Communist forces, both in killed and wounded and in men captured.

In the north, a guerrilla force two thousand strong managed to seize the industrial town of Naousa and held it for forty-eight hours before being driven out by the Army on 16 January. During their brief occupation of the town the Communists had sacked it, looting the shops and burning down all Government buildings and several factories. The Mayor and a number of leading citizens had been executed – eighty-seven bodies were subsequently found in the rubble – and about four hundred people, half of them women and young girls, had been carried off as hostages.

On 21 January another strong guerrilla force captured the mountain town of Karpenisi, in the Agrafa mountains 125 miles north-west of Athens, and held it until driven out on 7 February by Government forces which had been unable to reach the area earlier owing to the worst snowstorm for many years.

Paul and Frederica immediately decided to go to these two towns, and spent several days in that area. The visit was a psychological landmark in Frederica's emotional development. The cumulative effect of the impact on her of the misery and the ravages of the guerrilla war had been building up inside her over the months, and the stark horror of what she had seen with her own eyes at Naousa and Karpenisi proved to be the breaking point. The haunting memory of the weeping women clinging to her and pleading for their abducted children to be given back to them, the black-clad widows standing outside their burned-out homes silently beating their breasts, the sight of strong men broken by grief for their slaughtered sons – all this suddenly became too much for her. Being with other people became unbearable and she would burst into uncontrollable tears at the slightest provocation.

Paul was not blind to these signs. The Duke of Brunswick was in Switzerland at this time for medical treatment, and Paul insisted that Frederica should go to her ailing father for a while. She did not have the willpower to resist, but the experiment was not particularly successful: instead of the carefree, well-ordered and comfortable life in Switzerland proving a healing distraction, the contrast of her new surroundings to the conditions she had left behind had the opposite effect and drove her into a mood of black depression. She returned to Athens as soon as she could, but the familiar loved surroundings of her home and her family did not make her feel any better. She now yearned for a solitude she could not easily have, avoiding official functions whenever she could – driving with Paul one day she stopped the car and ran back home. For the next few days the King kept her as busy as he could, sending her to visit three islands on one day where part of the journey was on mule-back and where she had to mix with the people at very close quarters. It made her feel better, but she still needed something to occupy her mind.

It was then that she began to develop an interest in nuclear physics. She read as much as she could on the subject and gradually began to find that the scientific approach provided a spiritual outlet which was the best means of restoring her peace of mind. It was an interest that was to have an increasingly important influence on her life and prove a boon in times of distress and spiritual confusion.

On 16 March 1949 the General Staff issued a communiqué announcing that the entire Peloponnese had now been cleared of Communist guerrillas, and on 27 March the King and Queen left Athens again on a seven-day tour of the Morea.

The King had scarcely returned to Athens before another political crisis broke out. The forceful personality of Markezinis was proving a little too much for his fellow ministers in the Cabinet – especially for Tsaldaris, from whose party Markezinis had seceded with his splinter group – several of whom were threatening to dissolve the coalition unless Markezinis left the Government, which the latter was refusing to do. These dissident elements now asked the Vice-Premier Diomedes to convey the situation to the Palace with the plea that since the coalition was very much the personal creation of the King, he should now indicate to Markezinis to withdraw in the general interest. This the King was not prepared to do, and in the end a compromise procedure was adopted: on 12 April Sophoulis sent Paul a letter saying that the unity of the Government could no longer be maintained, and it had become necessary to re-examine the structure of the coalition; for this purpose, and in order to have greater freedom of action, he was submitting his resignation. The King replied, accepting Sophoulis's resignation and entrusting him again with the mandate to form another government; and the new Government which Sophoulis promptly formed proved to be identical with the previous one, except that it no longer included Mr Markezinis.

But fate now intervened. On 24 June 1949 Sophoulis collapsed and died of heart failure. He was buried with full national honours, his funeral being attended by the King and Queen.

The demise of the Premier automatically entails the resignation of the Government, and again the constitutional procedure was put into action. The largest parliamentary group was still the Populist Party, so the King summoned Tsaldaris and asked him to form a new Government. Tsaldaris, whose 131 supporters did not give him an overall majority in a Chamber of 354 deputies, approached Venizelos and Papandreou with a view to forming a coalition, but negotiations broke down over the premiership, which Tsaldaris claimed for himself as leader of the largest party; an offer to Venizelos, who had succeeded Sophoulis as leader of the Liberal Party, that the premiership should alternate between himself and Tsaldaris at three-monthly intervals proved insufficient to tempt the new Liberal leader. In the end Alexander Diomedes, Vice-Premier in the outgoing administration, succeeded in forming a coalition Government of which the complexion was almost identical with that of the last Sophoulis Government.

Shortly afterwards an event of profound significance for Greece took place in Yugoslavia. Marshal Tito's independent policy had already brought about Yugoslavia's expulsion from the Cominform a year earlier, and relations with the Soviet Union and the satellites of the Eastern bloc had progressively deteriorated almost to breaking point. In a speech at Pula on 10 July 1949, Marshal Tito now announced that Yugoslavia was closing her frontier with Greece. This meant that the Greek Communist guerrillas were being deprived of their main channel of arms and supplies and were being denied access to their principal training centres, while at the same time Greek Government forces hitherto deployed along the 150-mile border with Yugoslavia could now be released for operations elsewhere.

The effects of these developments were not long in making themselves felt. After a week's hard fighting Greek Government forces dislodged the guerrillas from all their strongholds in the Kaimaktchalan range on the Yugoslav frontier, inflicting heavy casualties and forcing the remainder to flee into Yugoslavia – whence, under Tito's new ruling, they could no longer re-enter Greece. On 6 August Government troops launched a major offensive in the Grammos range on the Albanian frontier, and on 10 August another further north against the main rebel strongholds in the Mt Vitsi and Lake Prespa area, where nearly eight thousand guerrillas held fortified positions; by 16 August all organized resistance in this last area had ceased. On 23 August Mt Beles, the main rebel stronghold on the Bulgarian frontier, was occupied after a four-day battle. The Grammos offensive was renewed on 25 August, extensive use being made of recently-delivered American 'Helldiver' aircraft, and by 30 August complete Government control had been established over the whole area.

On 2 September the Greek General Staff announced that not more than five thousand guerrillas remained on Greek soil: the guerrilla war was over. On the same day King Paul sent the following personal letter to Field-Marshal Papagos:

> On the occasion of the great victory of the Armed Forces, I wish to extend to you my warmest congratulations.
>
> The confidence placed in you by myself and by the Greek people has once again been fully justified.
>
> Under much more unfavourable conditions, you have carried on the work and the traditions of my father.
>
> The nation rightly expresses its gratitude to you and to the men who fought under your inspired leadership.

It is the custom in Greece for the King to issue a proclamation to the people on New Year's Day. The text is usually prepared in collaboration between the Prime Minister and the King's Private Secretary, on general lines indicated by the King, but in 1950 Paul decided to draft the message himself. It ran as follows:

Hellenes,

I send you all my warmest good wishes for the New Year.

My life and my thoughts are dedicated to my people, and I feel the joys and the sorrows and the hopes of you all as if they were my own.

May God forgive me when I say that I am a happy King, because my happiness springs from the hearts of my people.

On Greek Independence Day nearly two years ago I declared our country to be in peril.

A year ago I asked the nation to declare 1949 the Year of Victory.

Today I am proud and grateful to my people that they have once again performed a miracle and made 1949 indeed the Year of Victory.

The guerrilla war lasted a little over three years and cost the country many lives and much destruction. In the armed forces, 1,032 officers and 11,745 other ranks were killed, in addition to 4,527 officers and men missing; the wounded numbered 2,313 officers and 35,419 other ranks. Civilian casualties were also heavy: 4,289 (including 165 priests) were executed by the Communists, and 931 were killed by land mines. Material losses included large numbers of livestock and the destruction of 915 road and railway bridges, the burning of 80 railway stations, and the complete destruction of 24,626 dwellings, 15,139 farm buildings, 50 churches and 139 schools, as well as the partial destruction of another 22,000 houses.

⇒ 27 ⇐

During the guerrilla war various experiments had been initiated by Paul and Frederica for the re-education of individuals who had been forcibly recruited into the ranks of the guerrillas against their will or who had been lured into the Communist camp by propaganda or by sheer force of circumstances. Many of these 'reluctant warriors' had seized the first opportunity to surrender during the fighting, others were among prisoners taken by the Army; some of them turned out to be youths in their teens who could scarcely be dealt with on the same basis as hardened adults. The psychological and physical plight of these young people had immediately struck a responsive chord in Paul, whose long connexion with Scouting had rendered him particularly sensitive to problems of this nature.

Not long after his accession to the throne in 1947 Paul had launched a project that was to play an increasingly important role in his life: the National Foundation, of which the basic aim as defined in its Charter was 'to raise the moral, social, educational and living standards of the Greek people'. The work of the foundation was to be primarily educational but in the widest sense of the word. One of its main aims was to make Greeks, from village level upwards, more conscious of the fact that they played an integral part in the life of the nation, and to bring home even to the most humble that they, no less than the more eminent members of the community, contributed to the general well-being of the country. It based its activities on the principle of helping people to help themselves, with the ultimate goal of assisting the population as a whole towards becoming more active and self-helping. In these aims the foundation avoided competing with private enterprise and at the same time sought full and harmonious cooperation with the authorities when necessary, from municipal to ministerial level. Bearing in mind that over half the population of the country looked to agriculture for its livelihood, the foundation directed its energies mainly to the rural element, which was not only the largest but also the most needy.

Within this general context the foundation developed over the years a dynamic activity in various directions – education, agricultural assistance, community development, tourism, etc. – and fulfilled its purpose beyond the most sanguine expectations; but its first big test came during the guerrilla war when Paul entrusted to it the task of 'bringing back into the national family', as he put it, the young men who had for one reason or another found themselves fighting against their own country. These boys were sought out in prisons and internment camps all over the country and brought to the island of Leros, where accommodation was available in the empty barracks and hangars left behind by the Italians who had used Leros as a naval base during their thirty years' occupation of the Dodecanese. Here some twenty technical schools were soon functioning. The boys were organized in troops on Boy Scout lines, and most of the people running the scheme were personally known to Paul and selected by him for this work. At first the boys lived in tents put up by the Army, but as they acquired the skills they had chosen for themselves the derelict buildings were gradually made habitable and occupied by the bricklayers, the carpenters, the house-painters and the electricians putting into practical use the trades they were learning. By the time each group left the island at the end of their vocational training they had found their self-respect once again and were ready to lead useful lives among their fellow citizens.

Just about the time that the Leros experiment was being initiated, Paul also asked the National Foundation to help in a matter very near to his heart: the education of his son and heir, the Crown Prince Constantine.

On succeeding to the throne in 1947 Paul had moved with his family to the Palace in Athens and to Tatoi, which was gradually being repaired and brought back into use. The villa in Psychiko which the family had occupied while Paul was Crown Prince had been turned into a private school for the royal children: it had three classes, one for boys and two for girls, and each of the classes had one of the royal children as a pupil, the others being local boys and girls from all walks of life. The school was staffed by regular teachers under the direction of the Crown Prince's English tutor, Mr Jocelyn Winthrop Young.

This arrangement continued until 1948 when at King Paul's instigation the National Foundation was instrumental in founding 'Anavryta', a secondary school for boys run on English public-school lines. The King took an intimate personal interest in the creation of Anavryta right from the start, the first meeting of the Board of Governors being held in his study at the Palace under his chairmanship. He had taken a decisive attitude in the matter of the basic principles that were to be the guidelines of the new school, using as his model the school founded at Salem by the distinguished German educationalist Dr Kurt Hahn, of which Frederica's brother, Prince George of Hanover, was now headmaster. Paul began the proceedings at this first meeting of the governors with the remark: 'It's about time Plato came back to his own country', and this set the tone that was to dominate all subsequent meetings, at which Paul invariably presided.

Anavryta was established in the Syngros estate, a property of 250 acres situated at Kifissia, ten miles from Athens, which the Greek philanthropist Andrew Syngros had bequeathed to the State in 1899. At first the original Syngros mansion was sufficient for the school's needs, but as the intake of boys increased more classes were established and by 1954, when the first graduates left the school, Anavryta had nine classes with 150 pupils, of whom over a quarter had been granted scholarships by the National Foundation. Meanwhile, new buildings had been erected in the wooded grounds – dormitories, a library, a gymnasium, laboratories, a lecture hall, and finally an open-air theatre on the classical model, built by the boys themselves.

The curriculum at Anavryta was broadly the same as that of other Greek schools of the same level, particular emphasis being laid on the development of a sense of responsibility and self-reliance. Crown Prince Constantine was among the initial group of twenty-nine boys, and his tutor Winthrop Young, who had been a pupil at Gordonstoun – the school in Scotland also founded by Dr Hahn – was the first headmaster of the school. Throughout his nine years at Anavryta, Constantine received exactly the same treatment as the other boys, boarding in during the week and spending the weekends at home.

With the guerrilla war definitely ended – on 15 October 1949 the Communist 'Provisional Government of Free Greece' publicly admitted defeat with a face-saving announcement that the guerrilla forces had 'ceased operations in order to avoid the complete annihilation of Greece' – and with the influence of a common cause in a national crisis now removed as a cohesive factor, the pressures that had made possible a certain amount of collaboration between the parties began to disappear. The cessation of hostilities also meant that there was no longer any physical obstacle to the holding of elections, especially as the normal four-year term of the existing Parliament was drawing to a close anyhow in a short while.

Nobody could seriously dispute that the Chamber elected on 31 March 1946 had been a disappointment. No single party had emerged with a clear majority, and such inter-party alliances and combinations as had been arranged before the elections had quickly disintegrated into their original separate entities, proliferating a few additional parties in the process. Nor had the quality of the human element been particularly high, which perhaps was not very surprising in view of the fact that the plebiscite was still to come when the elections were held in March 1946 and many of the candidates had been nominated not so much on the strength of their parliamentary abilities as for their attitude towards the highly emotional issue of the regime. Given the mixed nature of the Chamber, only a combination of two or more parties had ever been able to secure a working majority, and in the four years of its existence the Parliament of March 1946 had thrown up ten such coalition Governments, all of which had been hamstrung from the start by conflicting party interests and by the petty personal ambitions of its constituent members, whose main inducement to collaborate with their political rivals was the desire to share in the spoils of office. Clearly this Parliament had ceased to have any useful purpose; only a new Chamber could provide a strong leadership based on healthy parliamentary support which the country so badly needed.

The signs were clear for anyone to see, and Paul began to prepare for the situation that would arise when the time came for the government to go.

His immediate concern was to ensure an impartial administration during the intervening period between the dissolution of parliament and the new elections, and for this he felt that what was required was a 'service' government consisting of experts with no party political connexions. With this in mind he sounded John Theotokis, a member of the original triumvirate that had guided the Populist Party before the 1946 elections, an elder statesman whose long tenure of office as Speaker of the Chamber of Deputies had by the very nature of things inured him from the wear and tear of party politics. Theotokis came from a patrician Corfiote family which had been at the forefront of Greek national life for many generations: he responded immediately to the King's approach, and even indicated which persons he intended to include in his 'caretaker' government – all of them individuals with high technical qualifications and no political affiliation. To make his own status clear, he also tabled a formal declaration in the Chamber to the effect that he was no longer a member of the Populist Party but an Independent, at the same time assuring the King that when the moment came he would announce that neither he nor any members of his Government would stand for Parliament at the elections. He then retired to his estate in his native Corfu, there to await the royal summons.

The break-up of the coalition actually came on 5 January 1950, when the Liberal leader, Sophocles Venizelos, wrote to the Prime Minister, Diomedes, that his party was no longer willing to continue its collaboration with the Populists, whose leader Constantine Tsaldaris he accused of making political speeches in violation of the agreement between the parties that there should be no electioneering while the coalition remained in office. Papagos also became incensed at a reported remark by Tsaldaris to the effect that the Field-Marshal had accepted the Supreme Command only after he, Tsaldaris, had ensured that the necessary arms and supplies would be forthcoming from the Americans; and although the Populist leader denied having made any such allegation, the Field-Marshal considered himself affronted and submitted his resignation as Commander-in-Chief.

The moment had come: Diomedes had no alternative but to resign. On 6 January the King summoned Theotokis to the Palace and asked him to form a 'caretaker' government. At the same time the King personally requested Papagos to withdraw his resignation, which the Field-Marshal agreed to do. And on 7 January King Paul signed a decree dissolving Parliament and proclaiming general elections.

In conformity with the wishes of the major parties, the elections
were held on 5 March 1950 on the proportional representation
system, and nearly 3,000 candidates representing 26 parties contested the 250 seats of the new Chamber (reduced from 354 in the
previous one). To the existing major political parties was now
added a newcomer, the National Progressive Union of the Centre
(EPEK), a left-of-centre group jointly led by two former premiers
staging a political comeback: General Nicholas Plastiras and
Mr Emmanuel Tsouderos.

Hopes that the elections would produce a self-sufficient government with a clear overall majority were dashed with the
announcement of the results:

Populist Party (Tsaldaris)	62
Liberal Party (Venizelos)	56
EPEK (Plastiras-Tsouderos)	45
Democratic Socialist Party (George Papandreou)	35
Others	52

The big question mark in the new situation as it was now
crystallizing was Plastiras, about whose intentions there were
widely conflicting reports and conjectures. The General's past, and
more especially the role he had played after the débâcle of the Greek
Armies in the Asia Minor campaign of 1922, had given him a big
following among the Greek refugee elements from Anatolia, whose
political orientation was largely left-wing and from among whose
ranks most of the Communist leaders had sprung. Not un-
naturally, Plastiras was regarded by more conservative opinion as
being sympathetically inclined towards these elements; this
automatically rendered him suspect to the majority of the population which, after fighting the Communists for many years, was in
no mood to see them back in the political arena now that they had
finally been defeated. In addition, some of Plastiras's election
speeches, with their broad hints of amnesty and changes in the
military command, had confirmed these suspicions.

Already, during the period preceding the elections Plastiras, who
had played a leading role in the establishment of the republic in
1923 but now claimed to be fully reconciled with the monarchy,
had shown some reservations towards the Crown. On 21 February
1950 he had written a curt letter to the 'caretaker' Premier
protesting that the King's visit to Epirus at the time had a political

character in view of the impending elections and asking that, since the Government constitutionally bears the responsibility for all the King's actions, it should take appropriate steps in the matter. Theotokis had replied courteously but firmly rejecting the interpretation which Plastiras sought to place on the King's visit to Janina, which was an annual event in celebration of the liberation of the Epirote capital from the Turks in the Balkan Wars; 'and you, as an old soldier,' added Theotokis, 'cannot but appreciate the national significance of the commemoration of such an anniversary, which in the annals of our country may be compared with Marathon.'

In the proportional representation system of voting the results cannot be definitely assessed until all the votes have been counted. This meant that the final figures for the elections would be delayed for several days until the returns from the more remote rural areas could all be collected and counted. Even the preliminary figures, however, clearly showed that Plastiras was strategically placed to play a decisive role in any attempt to form a government, and this advantage he was not slow to utilize. On 12 March a letter addressed to the King personally and signed by Plastiras, Tsouderos, Venizelos and Papandreou was handed in at the Palace. It ran as follows:

We have the honour to inform Your Majesty that we, the undersigned party leaders constituting a majority in Parliament, have agreed to form a Government whose policy will be as defined in the attached Note.

To the letter was annexed a memorandum laying down certain general principles to which nobody could take exception, namely: recognition and support of the regime as a constitutional monarchy; coordination of Greek foreign policy with that of the Western democracies; full support of the United Nations; effective use of American aid for national reconstruction; the balancing of the budget; wider measures of social security; and the development of friendly relations with Greece's northern neighbours.

The King was not to be stampeded by manœuvres of this kind, however. On his instructions 'Bouly' Metaxas sent an identical letter of reply to each of the four politicians saying:

The King notes with pleasure that you and the other signatories have reached agreement on forming a government.

The King will bear this in mind while the final election results are being assessed, during which intervening period His Majesty will, in accordance with usage, consult all the party leaders with a view to the formation of a new government.

On 15 March the King began his consultations. Meanwhile, the honeymoon of the four political leaders was turning slightly sour over the question of the premiership: the Liberal Party – the largest of the three groups, with 56 seats – was naturally sponsoring its own leader Venizelos, while EPEK and the Democratic Socialists with 80 seats between them supported Plastiras.

On 22 March the King asked Tsaldaris, as leader of the largest party, to form a government. Tsaldaris sounded Venizelos whether he was prepared to collaborate in a two-party coalition, but the Liberal leader declined on the grounds that he still felt himself bound by the agreement he had made with Plastiras and Papandreou; whereupon Tsaldaris saw the King again later the same day and relinquished the mandate.

The King then summoned Venizelos as leader of the next biggest party: to everyone's surprise Venizelos agreed to form a government, and the new Cabinet was sworn in the following day. It was recruited exclusively from the Liberal Party with the addition of Panayotis Kanellopoulos, leader of the 'National Regeneration Front' with seven seats in Parliament, who was appointed Vice-Premier and Minister of National Defence.

At this stage the Americans entered the scene. During the preliminary negotiations the State Department and the U.S. Embassy in Athens had manifested their anxiety at the prospect of a minority government that would be at the mercy of a snap vote in the Chamber at any moment; they would have preferred a centre coalition with an assured parliamentary majority, and blamed Venizelos for frustrating such a solution through his opposition to Plastiras as Premier. In their irritation at the way the situation was developing the Americans had even turned on the King, and in a stormy interview with the King's Private Secretary, 'Bouly' Metaxas, the American Chargé d'Affaires in Athens, Mr Henry Minor, warned that the Plastiras solution had been widely expected in America and had received much publicity; if Plastiras were now left out it would create disillusion and resentment, and would also provoke criticism of the Crown. Metaxas replied vigorously that the King's course of action in such matters was prescribed by constitutional procedure: the Sovereign was obliged to entrust the mandate to the leader of the largest party in Parliament and then, if he was unsuccessful in his efforts, to the leader of the next biggest party until a government could be formed. That was precisely the procedure the King had followed, and now there was nothing more to be done but wait until the new Parliament assembled to see if Mr Venizelos would obtain a vote of confidence.

The situation, however, was suddenly changed by a dramatic development. On 31 March the U.S. Ambassador, Mr Henry Grady, addressed a letter to the new Premier, Sophocles Venizelos, the text of which he took the unusual step of simultaneously releasing to the press.* In this letter the Ambassador began by saying he felt obliged to bring to the attention of the Prime Minister, the new Parliament and the Greek people the fact that a critical period had been reached in the recovery of Greece. American aid was designed not only to help establish peace, but also to meet the basic needs of the Greek people and to create new productive enterprises so that Greece might become independent of foreign aid in the future. Military security and relief of distress had been attained, but the effort to make Greece self-sustaining and to establish new industries had hardly begun, and 'it should be frankly recognized that an important reason for the delay has been a less than satisfactory performance by the Greek Government in its conduct of economic affairs'.

The American people, continued the Ambassador, were entitled to expect that any Greek government which hoped to continue to receive American aid should utilize this assistance to the fullest degree; only a stable and efficient government supported by the people and by Parliament would be able to act with the courage and firmness of long-term policy which were essential to the wise use of the aid offered.

The Ambassador then proceeded to enumerate in some detail the things which should be done in the economic, military, administrative and industrial fields, and called for decisions to enforce an adequate financial plan and to achieve an improvement in government efficiency:

The foregoing measures, which we regard as essential to the successful fulfilment of a major capital investment programme, should it seems to

* Venizelos read it in the press handout issued by the American Embassy five hours before he received the actual letter.

me be proposed by the Greek Government to parliament at the earliest possible date. Parliament of course may modify, enact or reject all measures proposed to it, in accordance with what the deputies believe to be the will of the people. But we in the American Missions regard parliamentary approval of major recovery measures to be essential, not only as a validation of the democratic process of government but as an assurance that the hard tasks of reconstruction have the willing support of the sovereign Greek people.

It is in the hands of the Greek Government and the Greek Parliament to decide whether or not they wish to continue to receive American aid and hence to accept the responsibilities that will attain its purpose. It is the obligation and intention of the American Government with regard to all Marshall Aid countries to decide whether or not the performance of the recipient governments, whether Greek or any other, justifies a continuance of the aid on the scale heretofore contemplated.

The tenor of the letter and the manner of its delivery allowed no doubts as to the U.S. Government's sentiments towards the government of Mr Venizelos, who could scarcely ignore such a manifestation of hostility from Greece's main ally and benefactor: he promptly resigned.

The King called on Plastiras, as leader of the next biggest party, to form a government. The Liberals and the Democratic Socialists now agreed to participate, and on 15 April a new administration was sworn in, comprising 6 EPEK, 5 Liberals and 5 Democratic Socialists. Still smarting under the American snub, Venizelos himself did not participate but left on a trip abroad – a stratagem he found highly convenient on more than one occasion when he wanted to avoid an unpalatable decision.

On 17 April the King opened Parliament, and in his speech from the throne declared that the new Government would cooperate fully with the American Mission and carry out a programme of large-scale economies, improved administration and fiscal reforms. On 28 April Plastiras received his vote of confidence.

All this time the tragic fate of the abducted Greek children, the 'Paidomazoma', had been occupying Frederica. The United Nations Balkans Committee had made strenuous efforts in the matter but had been completely unsuccessful in securing the repatriation of even a single one of these 28,000 unfortunate children scattered beyond the Iron Curtain – 12,000 in Yugoslavia, 4,000 in

Roumania, 3,000 each in Hungary, Bulgaria and Albania, 2,000 in Czechoslovakia and 1,000 in Poland. All the endeavours also of the International Red Cross to bring these children back to their homes had come up against a blank wall; only by mobilizing world opinion could some pressure perhaps be brought to bear on the guilty nations.

29 December 1949 was declared a national day of mourning for the abducted children: special services were held in churches throughout the country, the newspapers appeared with black mourning borders, all amusement centres remained closed for twenty-four hours.

On the day before, Frederica spoke about the 'Paidomazoma' over the radio. She had insisted on drafting the broadcast herself, and after much effort she had produced a text which was a mixture of English and Greek; only then did she ask for assistance in putting the speech into good Greek, and even then she insisted on using some of her own original Greek words:

Like most of you who have a happy family life, I celebrated Christmas with my children. Their happy laughter still rings in my ears. It should have warmed my heart and made me feel contented. But I keep thinking of those other Greek mothers whose children have been abducted by the Communist bands and forcefully taken into the countries that lie beyond the Iron Curtain.

In the name of the whole Greek nation, especially in the name of the stricken families, I ask the civilized world today: 'Pray with me for the fate of these 28,000 abducted children.' Their mothers have come to me and asked for help. I have seen into their desperate eyes and listened to their heartbroken sobs. It is with their tortured souls and their empty arms that I turn today to all of you and beg you for God's sake and your children's sake: 'Help me rouse the conscience of the world, add your voice to ours to bring back our children to their mothers' arms.' Too long has the civilized world remained silent. Silence in the face of such an outrage can only add to the crime itself and turn us all into culprits.

Have you forgotten that some years ago the fate of one little boy called Lindbergh shocked humanity as a whole? In Greece we mourn the fate of 28,000 little Lindberghs. Their fate is no less tragic. They have not only been physically torn from their families and beloved surroundings, but their innocent little souls are being systematically poisoned against their parents, their country and our God.

This Christmas no loving mother has told them the story of the smiling Jesus Child. No message of love can come to them in the concentration camps behind the Iron Curtain. But they are waiting to be saved by all of us who still believe and have faith in the Christ Jesus when He said:

'Suffer the little children to come unto me, and forbid them not. For of such is the Kingdom of God.'

She made no attempt to hide her emotion, and the people listening could hear her sobs as she struggled to speak the words through her tears.

If the Americans thought that by ousting Venizelos and supporting Plastiras they were ensuring the establishment of a stable and cooperative government, they were soon disabused in their expectations. On 17 July 1950 Dimitri Levidis, who had succeeded Papagos as Great Chamberlain at the Palace, went to Athens airport to bid goodbye to General James van Fleet, who was leaving Greece on relinquishing his post as Chief of the American Military Mission. Before boarding his plane van Fleet took Levidis to one side and confided to him – with the request that he should convey the information to the King personally and to nobody else – that in his final report to the U.S. Secretary of the Army he had given it as his opinion that:

1. With the Plastiras Government in office, Greece was running grave security risks.

2. In the event of international complications, the present Greek Government would constitute virtually a fifth column.

3. According to his own observations, the Armed Forces and the Security Services were rapidly disintegrating under the present Government.

4. Again according to his own observations, the Communists were being allowed to infiltrate into the public services.

At diplomatic level also the Americans were beginning to have second thoughts. After the stormy meeting between the King's Secretary, 'Bouly' Metaxas, and the American Chargé d'Affaires, Mr Henry Minor, at the time of the crisis over the appointment of the Venizelos Government, relations between the Palace and the Embassy had been virtually suspended, and it was not until 11 May that the two resumed their severed contact. The Americans were not happy about the Plastiras Government, Mr Minor confessed; it lacked drive and stability, mainly as a result of Venizelos's continuing abstention and also due to personal squabbles within the Government. He was being pressed by the State Department to persuade Venizelos to join the Government – the Deputy Premiership and the Ministry of Foreign Affairs were still being kept open for him – but it appeared that Venizelos was still nursing a grievance over the 'Grady letter' and had studiously avoided any contact with the Embassy since that memorable 31 March.

At a subsequent meeting between Metaxas and Henry Minor on 17 July, the American Chargé d'Affaires was at pains to point out that the recent dramatic developments in the international situation – hostilities had broken out in Korea on 26 June – had created a state of affairs where the slightest incident could start off another war. In such conditions Greece was particularly vulnerable and would surely find it necessary to take effective precautionary measures which a government such as that now in power, with its basic instability and the ambivalent attitude of its leader towards the extreme left, would find it difficult to undertake. The interests of Greece and the Western cause as a whole, he said bluntly, would be better served if the Plastiras Government were to make way for a more dependable administration, and in the prevailing circumstances the obvious head of such an alternative government would be Papagos.

Though the King shared the reservations of the Americans concerning the Plastiras Government and would naturally have preferred a stronger administration, he was not particularly anxious to have Papagos relinquish the Supreme Command, where it would be more difficult to replace him than it would be to find another Premier to replace Plastiras. He therefore inclined to the view that developments should be allowed to take their natural course, unless the international situation should take a dramatic turn for the worse, in which case it was his intention anyhow to dissolve Parliament and appoint a government of national emergency under Papagos; meanwhile Papagos should be sounded as to what his attitude would be in the various eventualities that might arise. The Field-Marshal had demurred at first saying that he had no particular desire to enter politics, but had finally indicated that if all efforts failed to form a viable government under one of the political leaders, he would be ready to answer the King's call.

All this time the atmosphere within the Cabinet itself was becoming increasingly difficult, with Plastiras straining at the leash to widen the scope and range of his leniency measures towards the Communists, and the less radical elements in the Government holding back on this delicate and emotionally explosive issue. Frustrated in his desires, Plastiras now began openly to criticize his colleagues. The situation had clearly become intolerable, and on 17 August the Liberals announced their withdrawal from the Government.

Early the following morning Plastiras saw the American Chargé d'Affaires to ascertain what the American attitude was going to be in the situation as it was now developing. If he hoped for support he was disappointed: Mr Minor told him plainly that this was a matter for the Greeks themselves to decide and the Americans had no intention of interfering. All he was prepared to do was express the hope that the crisis would be resolved quickly, that the solution would be within the parliamentary framework, and that the new Government should enjoy the confidence of the Chamber.

Plastiras was left with no choice: the same afternoon he saw the King and submitted his resignation.

In view of the various defections and transfers of party allegiance that had taken place in the Chamber since the elections, the King asked the Speaker to advise on the present state of the parties before he began his consultations. The list which the Speaker prepared showed that on 18 August 1950 the position was as follows:

Populist Party (Tsaldaris)	63
Liberal Party (Venizelos)	63
EPEK (Plastiras-Tsouderos)	46
Democratic Socialist Party (Papandreou)	34
Left-wing coalition	12
National Unionist Party (Kanellopoulos)	6
Others	26
	250

Since it was the action of the Liberal Party in withdrawing its support that had precipitated the fall of the Plastiras Government, the King gave the mandate to Venizelos, whose party shared first place in Parliament with the Populists.

Venizelos's efforts to secure the collaboration of the other parties proved abortive at first, and two days after receiving the royal mandate he had still made no progress. At this point the King considered the moment had come to make the necessary preparations for putting the 'Papagos emergency plan' into effect, and Metaxas called on the Field-Marshal to inform him that it now seemed likely that Venizelos would fail, in which case Papagos could expect to be asked by the King to form a government on the lines previously agreed. To Metaxas's surprise and consternation, Papagos now announced that he was no longer prepared to accept the mandate, and that further efforts should be made to find some other solution. He gave no specific reason for his change of attitude, but the answer could probably be found in his relationship with Markezinis, the leader of the minuscule New Party who had hitched his star to Papagos, a soldier by training and by mentality who felt rather out of his depth in the world of Greek politics. In the brilliant lawyer who had devoted his spare time to a life-long study of Machiavelli the Field-Marshal had found a shrewd and sophisticated political adviser on whose counsel he was becoming increasingly dependent, and when he had first been approached in mid-July in the matter of forming an emergency cabinet, Papagos had indicated that he would like to include Markezinis in any government he was going to be called upon to lead. This suggestion had been rejected on the grounds that Markezinis was too controversial a figure, and it was reasonable to suppose that this fact was not unconnected with the Field-Marshal's refusal now to implement the original understanding.

Rather than prolong the crisis Venizelos had himself sworn in as Premier on 21 August with an exclusively Liberal skeleton Cabinet of seven ministers who shared between them all the twenty-odd portfolios, with Venizelos assuming the Ministries of Foreign Affairs, Interior and National Defence in addition to the premiership.

A few days later agreement was reached with the Democratic Socialists, five of whose members, including their leader George Papandreou, entered the Government. As for EPEK, the most that could be secured from them was an assurance of their parliamentary support, but not their participation in the Government; on 4 September, however – two days before Venizelos was due to appear before Parliament to ask for a vote of confidence – EPEK suddenly reversed their decision and announced that they would not support the Government, with the result that when the vote was finally taken on 9 September the Government was defeated by 124 votes to 106.

Venizelos duly resigned, advising the King to dissolve Parliament and proclaim new elections. The King was not satisfied that all the possibilities of the present Chamber had been exhausted, and decided to make another effort by asking the Populist leader Tsaldaris to form a broadly-based government. After fruitless negotiations with the other parties, however, Tsaldaris abandoned the attempt, but to facilitate a solution to the deadlock he promised his support to any coalition formed under Venizelos. Similar assurances being forthcoming from Papandreou, inter-party nego-tiations were resumed and on 13 September a new three-party coalition Government consisting of Liberals, Populists and Democratic Socialists was sworn in, with Venizelos holding the premiership as well as the Ministry of Foreign Affairs and with the leaders of the other two parties, Tsaldaris and Papandreou, as Vice-Premiers. On 16 September the new Government received a vote of confidence in the Chamber by 153 votes to 43, with 54 abstentions. So ended four weeks of acute political crisis.

Having been largely instrumental in ousting Venizelos from the premiership in March 1950 with his 'open letter', Mr Henry Grady could scarcely remain as American Ambassador in Athens now that Venizelos was Prime Minister again. He was consequently trans-ferred to Teheran and his place in Athens was taken on 25 September 1950 by Mr John Peurifoy, a younger man who had had a meteoric rise in the United States service from lift-boy to Under-Secretary of State.

On 2 November the Populist element withdrew from the three-party coalition following allegations in the press of implication in charges of embezzlement relating to the Piraeus Port Authority. Next day Venizelos formed a new Government comprising only the Liberals and the Democratic Socialists, with himself retaining the premier-ship and Papandreou the vice-premiership. The new administration received a vote of confidence on 16 November by 164 votes to 54, the Populists supporting the Government despite their withdrawal from it.

Part Five

1950-1957

Part Two

⇒ 28 ⇐

The new year had not long begun when a new crisis developed, this time in the relations between Field-Marshal Papagos and the King.

Papagos had complained that certain members of the Royal Household were manifesting hostile sentiments towards him in a manner that could be interpreted as reflecting unfriendly feelings towards the Field-Marshal on the part of the King and Queen as well. Papagos had been personally reassured by the King on more than one occasion that these allegations were completely unfounded insofar as they related to himself and the Queen, who had always cherished the warmest feelings towards him and held him in high esteem not only as the honoured First Soldier of Greece but also as a personal family friend. Papagos appeared mollified by these reassurances but later reverted to the subject, his remonstrances being finally narrowed down to one person – the King's Private Secretary and friend of many years, 'Bouly' Metaxas. The King did not accept these charges – though the ebullient 'Bouly' was well known for his extrovert sense of humour and could on occasions be liable to verbal indiscretions – but at the same time he could scarcely ignore the Supreme Commander's feelings. He did not wish to condemn Metaxas by dismissing him out of hand, nor could he afford to offend the Field-Marshal by ignoring his complaints. A way of circumventing the dilemma was finally found: the institution of 'the King's Civil Cabinet' was abolished, and with it also went the Chief of the King's Civil Cabinet, Metaxas, who happened to be abroad at the time. In its place, a 'General Secretariat of the King' was set up and the legal adviser to the Crown, Mr Michael Pesmazoglou, a distinguished lawyer, was temporarily put in charge of the new office.

Papagos did not appear to be completely satisfied by this gesture, however, and on 30 May announced his resignation as Supreme

Commander of the Armed Forces. Although the Field-Marshal said in his official statement that he was giving up this post for reasons of health, it was widely assumed that his resignation was merely a preliminary step to his entering the political arena – so much so that the Prime Minister, Venizelos, announced at a press conference next day that the Field-Marshal had authorized him to deny that he was going into politics, while Papagos himself in an impeccable Order of the Day announcing his resignation to the Armed Forces reiterated that he was relinquishing the Supreme Command for reasons of health and called on all troops to 'carry on quietly with their duties under their capable chiefs, with strict discipline and devotion to country, King and Government'.

The King, to whom Papagos had announced his resignation in private audience on 30 May, tried to dissuade the Field-Marshal but without success. Later the same day he wrote the following letter to him:

30 May 1951

My dear Field-Marshal,

It is with deep sorrow that I address this letter to you following our discussion this morning concerning your resignation from the Supreme Command of the Armed Forces for reasons of health which you submitted yesterday to the Minister of National Defence.

During our conversation I tried to make you change your mind and, in addition to my own views and sentiments in the matter, I expounded to you all the other compelling reasons why you should remain at the head of our Land, Sea and Air forces.

To my regret you insisted that your decision was irrevocable because, as you explained to me, your state of health does not allow you for the present to exercise your onerous duties.

I am therefore obliged to deprive myself of your invaluable services, and wish to express to you my great satisfaction and the gratitude of the nation for all you have done for our country.

Without forgetting your participation in the wars of liberation of 1912–22, I have particularly in mind your contribution in the preparation of the armed forces during the critical years before the Second World War, your glorious Command of the Albanian campaign and your equally successful termination of the difficult and highly perilous guerrilla war.

These incomparable services place you among the outstanding personalities who have worked for the independence and the glory of the Hellenic nation.

I desire you to know that, despite your relinquishing of the Supreme

Command, I shall always regard you as my first Adviser in military matters affecting the country.

To this letter Papagos duly replied the following day:

Athens, 31 May 1951

Your Majesty,

On relinquishing the Supreme Command of the Armed Forces I have an easy conscience that I have done my duty both towards the country and towards the Crown.

Today more than at any other time I feel deep gratitude towards Your Majesty for providing me with the opportunity to serve my country once again at a time of grave peril.

I beg Your Majesty to be graciously pleased to accept my heartfelt thanks for the letter you have done me the honour to address to me, and I avail myself of this opportunity to assure Your Majesty once again of my great and sincere devotion to your person and to the Dynasty.

I pray that the Almighty may always grant glory, good health and long life to Your Majesty, for the good of the nation.

The resignation of the Field-Marshal came as a big shock to the Americans, who were anxious to avoid any organizational upheavals in the Greek armed forces at a time when unity was of paramount importance. The new American Ambassador, Mr John Peurifoy, who was in the United States on leave when these dramatic developments took place, flew back to Athens immediately and tried to persuade Papagos to reconsider the matter.

As the press was also playing up the story that the Field-Marshal had resigned because of the hostile attitude of the Court, the Royal Household decided to make the King's position easier by resigning *en masse*. On 4 June the following announcement was issued from the Palace:

The Grand Chamberlain announces that he has submitted the following petition to The King:

Your Majesty,

In view of reports circulating to the effect that the resignation of Field-Marshal Papagos is due not to reasons of health but to the hostile attitude of the Court, and in order to assist Your Majesty's great and patriotic task, the Grand Chamberlain begs respectfully to place the resignation of the entire Royal Household at the disposal of Your Majesty.

Your Majesty's most obedient humble servants,

There followed thirty signatures, ranging from the Grand Chamberlain himself to the Secretary of the Privy Purse and including the Equerries, the Ladies in Waiting, the Royal Physicians, the King's dentist and the Veterinary Surgeon of the Royal Stables.

But Papagos remained adamant, and on 4 June the Prime Minister, Venizelos, issued a statement saying that all efforts to persuade Field-Marshal Papagos to resume his post as Supreme Commander had been unavailing.

The Supreme Command was now taken over by the King himself, who issued the following proclamation as his first Order of the Day:

I have assumed the Supreme Command of the Armed Forces to fill the vacancy created by the resignation of Field-Marshal Papagos for reasons of health. I have taken this decision on the recommendation of my Government, and I shall retain the Supreme Command for the duration of the special conditions which make necessary the post of Supreme Commander.

I express my complete satisfaction to Field-Marshal Papagos and emphasize my regret that the country should be deprived of his invaluable services.

The Armed Forces of the country are today in an enviable state. They are all that the country holds most precious, and by their indisputable quality and combatant spirit give to Greece an advantageous position among the countries of the civilized world.

I have full confidence and faith in the Chiefs of the Armed Forces. I expect from one and all to continue with devotion the work that has been achieved up to the present, and I shall expect a concentrated effort in the training and continuous improvement of cooperation and performance of the Services.

The country needs its soldiers today more than ever, and it is imperative that bravery and sacrifice should be accompanied by battleworthiness.

The sacrifices of our heroic dead have bequeathed to us a heritage that allows no limits to the amount and extent of our efforts.

Let no one forget, from the most senior officer to the simple soldier, that the Armed Forces of the country are the most sacred instrument of the nation and of the nation only; and that the soldier is a soldier and nothing else.

Officers, non-commissioned officers and men of the Armed Forces, you are the personification of the heroic and glorious history and tradition of the Hellenic nation. The honour and security of the country is in your hands. I know that at all moments of crisis you will honour the sacred arms of Greece of which you should always be proud, as I and the whole country are proud of you.

PAUL R
Supreme Commander

The excitement over Papagos's resignation had scarcely subsided when another crisis broke out in the Venizelos-Papandreou partnership: the Vice-Premier had proposed an increased wheat subsidy for the farmers, which Venizelos had rejected on the grounds that the budget could not bear the additional burden. The Democratic Socialist Ministers promptly withdrew from the coalition on 30 June, and Venizelos inevitably submitted his resignation. The King refused to accept it, and on 2 July sent the following written appeal which he asked the Prime Minister to communicate to all the political leaders:

Thirteen Governments have succeeded one another during the short duration of my reign.

These frequent changes are due mainly to the parties' conviction that each one of them will be in a position to give better leadership to the country than the government which preceded it.

It must be admitted by all, however, that these frequent changes, despite the good will of those who bring them about, do not contribute to the progress of this country. The programmes planned for all sectors are delayed in their execution and are often finally cancelled. This is because other governments intervene between the formulation and the execution of these plans, and before these governments have had a chance to become well versed in the matter they have had to cede their place to their successors. Thereby a great part of the valuable help of our Allies and the efforts of the people is being wasted.

In seeking the perfect we sacrifice the good, whereas the people only demand that they be assured of a good and energetic administration . . .

I believe in the patriotism and the good will of you all and I also believe that your controversies and criticisms of each other are not based on any personal interests but are aimed at serving the well-being of the Greek people. Taking this for granted I address to you on behalf of the Greek people not a request, but a demand, to present to me as soon as possible a Government representing either all or as many parties as possible. This Government appearing before Parliament must be able to obtain a vote of confidence. If elections are indispensable then this Government can prepare for elections, but until that day the country cannot remain ungoverned and torn by arguments and criticisms.

Our country demands unreserved cooperation from you all so that by common struggles, common efforts, unity of thought and the abilities of every one of us we shall overcome the difficulties which I believe are purely temporary.

If, in spite of this appeal, you cannot achieve the necessary cooperation and you do not succeed in forming such a Government then I, inspired by the fundamental principles of our Constitution and also by the vital interests of the Greek people, shall be obliged to find a solution myself. In that case, however, the political world of this country will be burdened with the responsibility that it did not help me in my present effort to achieve a National Rally.

But the King's appeal fell on deaf ears. An all-party conference ended in deadlock, and on 3 July Venizelos formed an all-Liberal Government which managed to obtain a vote of confidence by 125 votes to 74. The Premier then announced that his Government would resign as soon as the Chamber had approved a new electoral law and fixed the date for general elections.

The new Electoral Bill was introduced in Parliament without further delay. It was a modified form of the proportional representation system recently adopted in France and provided that only parties obtaining at least seventeen per cent of the total votes cast in the first count (twenty per cent in the case of party coalitions) would participate in the second and third counts, the aim being to facilitate the formation of stable governments by strengthening the representation of the larger parties at the expense of the smaller groups.

Events now developed more rapidly. On 25 July the Electoral Bill was passed with the support of all three major parties – the Liberals, the Populists and EPEK. True to his word, Venizelos resigned three days later but was requested by the King – after a conference of party leaders held under Paul's own chairmanship – to form a 'caretaker' government with the stipulation that in order to avoid any suspicion of partiality the ministries directly involved in organizing the elections – Interior, Justice and National Defence – should be entrusted to non-political personalities. The new Venizelos Government thus formed was sworn in on 30 July, and on the same day Parliament was dissolved and general elections proclaimed for 9 September.

On the same day also Papagos dropped his bombshell. To the political correspondents of the Athens newspapers whom he summoned to his villa at Ekali that afternoon he announced that he had decided to enter politics and that he would be taking part in the forthcoming elections. 'I invite my fellow-countrymen to give me their confidence so that Greece may obtain the stable government she needs,' he said, adding that 'with the King and Queen as our symbols, we can all unite for the cause of Greece.'* He was not just forming another party, he said, but heading a new movement. Nor was he going to cooperate with any existing political group: all who wanted to join him should come as individuals united under his banner, with no other party affiliations or loyalties.

On 11 August Papagos outlined the programme of his movement, which he called the 'Greek Rally'. After warning that the country should not be completely dependent on American aid and that Greece's economic recovery should be undertaken by the Greeks themselves, he pledged his movement to a programme of reforms in the economic, social and political spheres with the aim of expanding productivity, keeping down prices, improving the standards of living, achieving economic stability and decentralizing the administration. 'You followed me faithfully on the battlefield,' he said. 'Now I call on you to join me in the battle for peaceful recovery and reconstruction.'

Papagos's decision to enter politics, or rather the manner and the circumstances of its announcement, came as something of a shock to the King, who was in principle averse to professional soldiers becoming politicians – especially men of the rare prestige and immense authority of Papagos, to whom the nation looked up as the embodiment of its military glory and the guardian of its security. There was another aspect of the matter, however, which troubled the King: until the very eve of his announcement the Field-Marshal had been categorically denying, both to the King personally and to others, that he intended going into politics. Indeed, some of the party leaders, including the Prime Minister, Venizelos, had agreed to the dissolution of Parliament and the proclamation of new elections very largely on the strength of the conviction – a conviction reinforced by assurances to that effect from the King himself – that Papagos would not be participating in the elections; Paul now felt that he had misled these people.

---

* This particular remark evoked a statement from the Palace Secretariat warning politicians against involving the Crown in their political campaigns, and emphasizing that the King stood above parties and maintained an absolute impartiality towards all candidates.

There was also the formal aspect of the matter. Papagos was still a serving soldier and as such it was surely incumbent upon him, the King felt, to advise the Sovereign in advance of his intention to enter politics and to seek permission to resign his appointments; instead of which the King had learned of his decision from the newspapers.

The elections took place without incident on 8 September. The Greek Rally under Papagos emerged as the leading party with 114 seats, EPEK (Plastiras) coming second with 74 seats and the Liberals (Venizelos) third with 57. The pro-Communist E.D.A. won 10 seats, while the Populists were reduced to 2 seats (their leader Tsaldaris and a Turk representing a constituency in Thrace) and the Democratic Socialists were completely annihilated, polling just over 37,000 votes altogether and not winning a single seat.

With hopes frustrated that one party with an overall majority might at last be able to form a strong government, Paul began once more the familiar weary round of consultations.

He was now assisted in his task by a new political adviser in the person of George Ventiris, one of the closest collaborators of the great Eleftherios Venizelos, who had until recently been living in Switzerland for reasons of health. To people who asked him why he did not go back to Greece he would reply that as he did not have long to live he would prefer to spend what little time was left to him in peace and quiet. It was the time of the trouble over 'Bouly' Metaxas and Paul was in sore need of someone to turn to for assistance and advice in political matters; who better than Ventiris, whose past links with Venizelos had inevitably endowed him with some of the charisma of the great Cretan and automatically rendered him a respected figure among politicians of all shades. Ventiris was approached and finally agreed to come to Greece. For a few weeks after his arrival the King consulted him in an unofficial and private capacity, but when the position of Secretary-General became vacant in August with the resignation of Michael Pesmazoglou it was offered to Ventiris, who immediately accepted.

The King saw the political leaders separately one after the other, in the order of their parliamentary strength. His meeting with Papagos was not without drama. It was the first time the two men had seen each other since their estrangement, and Papagos began the conversation with protestations of his devotion towards the monarchy and the King personally. Feeling that some explanation for his past actions would also not come amiss, he told the King

that his original intention to abstain from politics had been shaken
by reports quoting the King as saying that 'Papagos should consider
carefully the consequences if he goes into politics' and that 'If
Papagos goes into politics and becomes Prime Minister I shall pack
my bags and leave with my family.' These alleged remarks had
sounded very much like threats, said Papagos, and had caused him
to change his mind and go into politics after all.

After assuring Papagos that the sentiments attributed to the King
were quite untrue and that his esteem and affection for the Field-
Marshal remained unchanged, Paul urged that what was important
now was to give the country a viable and strong government, which
in the circumstances could only be achieved by a coalition. Papagos
found himself unable to agree: his own view was that the mandate
should be entrusted to him as leader of the relatively largest party,
with authority to dissolve Parliament if necessary and hold elections
on the majority system. He precluded any cooperation with the
other parties, which he regarded as serving narrow party interests,
whereas his own Greek Rally was above such party considerations.

'Do you not fear that elections on the majority system might
divide the country?' asked the King.

'The country is already divided, Your Majesty,' was Papagos's reply.

After similarly ascertaining the views of the other politicians the
King convened a conference on the morning of 27 September at the
Palace of the leaders of the three major parties – Field-Marshal
Alexander Papagos (Greek Rally), General Nicholas Plastiras
(EPEK) and Sophocles Venizelos (Liberal) – at which he himself
presided.

The King opened the proceedings by appealing to the three men
to work together in the service of their country. The vote of the
Greek people, he said, clearly showed that what was required was
the cooperation of the three parties. The problems to be faced
rendered a united front imperative, and mutual concessions were
necessary to achieve this. Let the conflicts and recriminations of the
election period be now forgotten. 'The fact that all three of you
come from the Army,' concluded the King,* 'is a happy augury.
The Army is a good training ground for discipline and self-sacrifice.
I am confident that as soldiers all three of you will hearken to the
call of the nation.'

* Venizelos too had begun his career as a regular Army officer and had reached the
rank of Colonel when he resigned his commission to go into politics.

Papagos then spoke. Past experience, he said, had proved that coalitions were not the answer; an administration that was not self-sufficient lacked stability and freedom of action, even when it enjoyed the confidence of other parties. Elections were the only solution: the people must be given the opportunity to choose a homogeneous and stable government. He could not share responsibility for experiments in which he had no faith, and he therefore recommended new elections with the majority system.

Plastiras was the next to speak, and said that he unreservedly accepted the King's appeal. To have new elections when the final results of the last one had not yet been declared would be a waste of valuable time. A tripartite government was not an ideal solution either, but it was the best possible in the circumstances. He proposed that the premiership of such a coalition should go to Papagos as leader of the biggest party; but for his part, he was quite prepared to support even a government of the other two parties only, if that were considered more practicable than a three-party coalition.

Venizelos agreed with Plastiras, and said that the problems that had to be faced – including the probable reduction of American aid by $70 million – rendered imperative a temporary political truce and the formation of a coalition government. If in the event the three parties found it impossible to cooperate, new elections could always be held on the majority system later on. He therefore accepted the King's appeal, and like Plastiras he too would also support a government of the other two parties if necessary.

Having heard what the other two leaders had to say, Papagos reiterated that he was in principle still opposed to any government that was not homogeneous.

On that note the conference ended.

Later that day Paul decided to make one final attempt to obtain Papagos's cooperation by writing a personal letter to him. He did not underestimate the weight of the reasons on which the Field-Marshal based his refusal to cooperate, he wrote, but the circumstances were abnormal, and even if Parliament could give a homogeneous government it would still be preferable to have a coalition. New elections so soon after the last ones would lead to new divisions and conflicts; was it right that the unity of the nation should be jeopardized for the theoretical principle of the advantages of single-party government? The leaders of the other two parties had responded to the King's appeal and had proposed the Field-

Marshal as Premier, accepting him as the national leader. The King could not believe that a soldier and a statesman who had rendered such services to the country would now refuse to place himself at the head of the national effort.

But Papagos was not to be persuaded. He did not want the King to think that his attitude was the result of hasty considerations, he wrote in his letter of reply; his decision had already been made before the elections. His aim in participating in the elections had been to give the country the homogeneous and stable administration it so badly needed. Compromises and experiments were luxuries permissible in normal conditions, not in the present critical times. Elections on the majority system would provide a strong government and a healthy opposition. Taking all things into consideration, he was unable to change his attitude nor was he prepared to share in the responsibility of a solution in which he had no faith.

With a three-party coalition definitely frustrated by Papagos's non-cooperation, Plastiras and Venizelos now proposed a government of their two parties only, which between them mustered 131 out of the 258 seats in the Chamber. The new administration, with Plastiras as Premier and Venizelos as Deputy Premier and Minister of Foreign Affairs, took the oath on 27 October 1951 and five days later was given a vote of confidence in Parliament by 131 to 115.

One of the first acts of the new Chamber was to approve certain amendments to the current Constitution of 1911. This revision, which was approved on 22 December 1951 by 132 votes to 8 (the left opposed it and the Greek Rally deputies walked out of the Chamber before the vote was taken), granted women the vote and the right to stand for Parliament; empowered the Government to expropriate large estates for re-distribution among landless farmers; made provision for the Queen to act as Regent in the King's absence abroad during the minority of the heir to the throne; and clarified the provisions relating to the order of succession to the throne, concerning which there had been some ambiguity in the relevant article in the original constitution. This stated simply that 'The Greek Crown and its constitutional rights are hereditary and pass to the legitimate and lawful descendants of King George I by order of primogeniture, preference being given to the males.' What was obviously meant – and this was the interpretation given whenever the occasion had arisen in the past – was that the Crown passed to the descendants of the reigning King by order of primogeniture, males taking precedence over females; and, failing such heirs, to the direct lineal descendants of the founder of the dynasty King George I in the same order. It had been argued by some legal pedants, however, that the phraseology of the original article could be construed as meaning that the succession would pass absolutely to the eldest male descendant of King George I. This (in 1951) would have made Paul's eighty-two-year old-uncle Prince George, and not Paul's own eleven-year-old son Constantine, heir to the throne; or alternatively would have meant that while Constantine was the heir apparent, old Prince George and not Paul's daughters Sophie and Irene was next in line after Constantine. The revision of this article therefore made it clear that the reigning Sovereign's own offspring, female as well as male, had priority over all others in the order of succession, as is the case with the British Crown. The new revised Constitution was ratified by King Paul on 1 January 1952.

Despite its precarious majority, the EPEK-Liberal Coalition Government remained in office for almost exactly a year. Throughout this period it enjoyed the full support and willing cooperation of the King, who was anxious that another electoral contest, with all its concomitant rousing of passions, should not be inflicted on the country until and unless it became unavoidable.

During this period also the energetic role played by George Ventiris as liaison between Paul and the Government earned the King's Secretary-General a status of authority which he did not hesitate to use in all directions whenever the circumstances required it. Having been totally converted from a republican into a constitutional monarchist, he saw himself as the defender and interpreter of the institution of 'crowned democracy' to his friends and devotees – most of them erstwhile republicans – who were now the Government of the country. The fervour of his sincerity and the patent honesty of his intentions had a profound influence on the people with whom he came into contact, especially Plastiras, on whom the cumulative burden of advancing years, failing health and the responsibilities of office, coupled with the mesmerizing impact of the advice and guidance of Ventiris in his messianic role of reconciler of monarchist and republican, had a deeply mellowing effect. The wolf-lean 'black horseman', the leader of innumerable insurrections, the executioner of Cabinet

Ministers, the firebrand rebel who had ousted two Kings, had now gradually been transformed into a gently-spoken, white-moustachioed patriarch radiating benevolence and good-will to all and sundry, and especially towards Paul and Frederica, for whom the old warrior had now developed the affectionate sentiments of an indulgent father towards his children. Towards individuals whose political convictions differed from his own he now showed a tolerance and a sympathetic understanding that would have seemed incredible only a few months before. When Greece joined NATO, Plastiras offered Pipinelis – whose political philosophy was the complete antithesis of his own – the vital post of Greek representative to that organization. 'I know you are no friend of mine,' said Plastiras, 'but you are the right man for the job and I know you will do your duty.' Pipinelis was very touched by this demonstration of faith and told Plastiras that although indeed he was not, and never would be, among his political friends, he would do his best to live up to the trust placed in him. 'God be with you, my boy,' said Plastiras (Pipinelis was sixty-three at the time), embracing him with tears in his eyes. 'What does it matter if you support me or somebody else, we are all Greeks and we all love our country.'

On 29 January 1952 the Deputy Premier and Minister of Foreign Affairs, Sophocles Venizelos, left on an official visit to Turkey as a first step towards improving Graeco-Turkish relations. Both before his departure and after his return Venizelos had urged the advisability of a State visit to Turkey by Paul, and despite the unfavourable reaction of Ventiris, who argued that a Turkish State visit to Greece should come first since the Turkish President had only assumed office a month ago whereas Paul had occupied the throne for five years, the King agreed in principle. Venizelos's visit was returned by the Turkish Premier and the Foreign Minister, who arrived in Athens on 26 April, and at a press conference in Athens just before their departure for home on 2 May the Turkish Premier, Mr Adnan Menderes, announced that King Paul and Queen Frederica had accepted an invitation to pay a State visit to Turkey the following month.

⇒ 29 ⇐

In February 1952 Paul travelled to England to attend the funeral of King George VI, whose daughter Elizabeth, now Queen, was married to Paul's first cousin Prince Philip. While in London Paul saw Mr Dean Acheson, the U.S. Secretary of State, who was also in London at the time. The King was constrained to seek this meeting in view of the fact that the Americans, in their earnest and constant desire to have a strong administration in Athens that could provide the necessary cooperation for their economic aid programme and the wider defence arrangements of NATO, were now becoming disenchanted with the precarious Plastiras-Venizelos coalition and were not disguising their view that elections, which would probably bring the Greek Rally to power with a healthy clear majority, might be a better solution after all. The American Embassy in Athens had been manifesting these tendencies more openly lately, and had also shown an inclination occasionally to intervene in purely domestic military matters which the Greek General Staff regarded as its own exclusive concern.

The King began by expressing to Acheson the gratitude of the Greek people for all that the U.S.A. had done for Greece. But these sentiments, he continued, could be affected by unwarranted intervention on the part of American officials in domestic matters of detail, which showed lack of understanding of the Greek mentality and could create complications and misunderstandings that would cause irreparable harm. The Greeks were highly sensitive to such things, and too blatant a manifestation of hostility towards Plastiras, for example, would merely have the opposite effect and enhance his popularity among the people. The King elaborated on this theme, citing various instances in support of his argument, and Acheson finally promised to look into the matter and give suitable instructions if necessary.

246

While in London the King also saw the British Permanent Under-Secretary for Foreign Affairs with whom he raised the question of Cyprus. The rigid attitude of the Foreign Office was not only unreasonable, said Paul, but was also creating embarrassing problems for the Crown in Greece. What Greece was asking at this stage was not the immediate satisfaction of Enosis (the union of Cyprus with Greece) but only the recognition of the fact that the question did exist and that a solution would be found in due course. The Under-Secretary, however, could offer little comfort to the King: the situation in the Middle East was creating great problems for Britain, and any discussion of the Cyprus question should be ruled out for the present.

On 9 March 1952 Plastiras collapsed after a cerebral thrombosis. Though still able to see people and conduct a conversation with only occasional lapses, he was clearly no longer able to carry out the duties of Premier and Venizelos was appointed Acting Premier. Paul and Frederica visited Plastiras at his house, and Ventiris went to see him frequently. Reporting to the King on one of these visits on 22 March, Ventiris said that Plastiras had been in a reminiscent mood that day, recalling his stormy past and his violent conflicts with the Crown.

'After all I have done to them,' he said, 'how could I expect them to believe in me?' But the way things had turned out, he was now devoted to the King and Queen with all his heart. 'Tell them that when Plastiras loves someone, it is for ever. Whatever happens I shall never let them down. If God grants me another year or two on this earth, I shall defend the King and Queen with my very life.'

Four days before the King's departure for Turkey Ventiris wrote him a highly emotional letter. He had been induced to take this step by a visit from the Archbishop of Athens and also by his own feelings in a matter which his traditionalist upbringing and his long association with Eleftherios Venizelos had brought very close to his heart:

Athens, 4 June 1952

Your Majesty,

I am informed that the programme of the State visit to Turkey includes a tour of the Cathedral of St Sophia.

May I be permitted to submit, with the most profound respect, that Your Majesty should decline any such proposal.

I do not speak as the King's Secretary-General. I speak as a Greek and as a member of the Orthodox Church addressing himself to the First among all Greeks and to the most devout Orthodox of us all. It is inconceivable that the son of Constantine, the remote but worthy successor of the Emperor Palaiologue who fell on the walls of Constantinople, should set foot in the Sacred Ark of the Hellenic Nation now that it has become a Turkish Museum. If the King cannot enter the most sacred of our National Shrines in circumstances dreamed of by generations, both enslaved and free, then let him not enter at all.

Do not, Your Majesty, I beseech you, place a tombstone on the most cherished tradition of our nation.

I beg Your Majesty to forgive me and to believe that my plea is not the voice of duty but the anguished cry of love.

Although the Ministry of Foreign Affairs did not share Ventiris's view and was of the opinion that the wider political aims of the royal visit would be helped by a call at St Sophia, the matter was finally left to the personal discretion of the King. In the event, the Turks were discreet enough not to press the point, and the King found an excuse not to visit the Cathedral after all.

On 8 June 1952 Paul and Frederica set off on their State visit to Turkey, travelling to Istanbul by sea on board the Greek flagship *Elli*. Besides being King Paul's first State visit since his accession to the throne, this was also the first time a Greek Sovereign had set foot in Constantinople since the days of Byzantium. From Istanbul the King and Queen proceeded by train to Ankara, where Paul's first act was to lay a wreath on the tomb of Kemal Ataturk, the founder of modern Turkey.

While the King and Queen were still in Turkey the condition of the Prime Minister, General Plastiras, took a sudden turn for the worse. The ailing man was finally persuaded to go abroad for special medical treatment and on 11 June he left for France, Venizelos being appointed Acting Premier during his absence, which lasted two months.

From his sick-bed in Paris Plastiras wrote to the King:

23 June 1952

Your Majesties' highly successful visit to Turkey and the invaluable political and national benefits which the country has derived from it compel me to write these words.

Your Majesty,

The services which you have rendered to the country by the democratic manner of your appearance with the Queen among the Turkish people have exceeded all expectations and will soon bear precious fruit for the country. You have given wings to the Government's foreign policy that will enable it to soar boldly towards the realization of our national dreams and aspirations, which the country was unable to achieve in the recent past despite many efforts, the wasteful shedding of blood and incalculable material sacrifices.

I pray Your Majesty to be graciously pleased to convey to the Queen also my deep respects and my most heartfelt congratulations on the highly successful and democratic manner of her appearance among our friends the Turkish people.

Your Majesty's faithful and devoted subject,

N. P. Plastiras

⇒ 30 ⇐

The question of Cyprus with its repercussions on Anglo-Greek relations was now becoming a subject of increasing concern to the King. Paul had always felt that a dispute of this kind, with its broad popular appeal and its inevitable emotional overtones, was by its very nature a matter in which the Crown, because of its national basis and its aloofness from party political considerations, could play a significant role. His own close personal and family links with Britain enabled him to a certain extent to remove the Cyprus dispute from the political to the national plane. He allowed no opportunity to pass, private or public, without utilizing it to emphasize the spontaneous and permanent nature of the special relationship between the Greek and the British people. When on 25 April 1952 he unveiled a memorial in Athens to the British and Commonwealth troops who had fallen in Greece in the last war, he seized the occasion once again to speak in this vein:

I believe in friendship. I believe that where this can be given to individuals it can also be given to nations, especially when both sides share the same qualities of soul.

Your own land was in flames, and yet you sent us your sons to fight by our side. And when the end came and those who were still alive had to leave our country, we gave flowers to our friends knowing they would return. Our faith in you was justified because you did return. May it be to the eternal glory of our British friends that at the darkest hour of our fight against Communism also, Greek freedom was unhesitatingly paid for with British lives.

Surely there is no greater love than that one friend should lay down his life for another. As long as Greek and Briton lie in the same grave on Greek soil, so long shall their friendship be treasured by us from generation to generation.

Although the principal motive of the Greek State visit to Turkey had been the need to create a friendly atmosphere for joint defence arrangements following the entry of the two countries into NATO, Cyprus had also been an important consideration for the King. The Foreign Under-Secretary Evangelos Averoff, who had accompanied the King on the journey as Minister in Attendance, had discussions with the Turkish Premier and Foreign Minister whom he was able to reassure concerning the treatment of the Turkish minority in Cyprus. The Turks had actually promised to support Greece's efforts with Britain, and had implemented this undertaking shortly afterwards by speaking in that spirit to the British Ambassador in Ankara; but the only result of their action had been the abrupt postponement of the proposed visit of the Turkish Premier and Foreign Minister to London, which was put off by the British until the following October.

The Greek Government also tried to follow up the matter after the King's return from Turkey, and on 7 July 1952 the Acting Premier, Venizelos, raised the question with the British Ambassador in Athens, Sir Charles Peake. Greece was very worried about the effects of the Cyprus dispute on Anglo-Greek relations, said Venizelos, and might be obliged by sheer force of public opinion to take the matter to the United Nations if no other way of dealing with the problem could be found. The British Ambassador replied that Cyprus was indispensable to Britain as a military base for the defence of the Empire, and no British Government would be disposed to make any concessions. To Venizelos's argument that Britain could have any bases she wanted anywhere in Greece including Cyprus after Enosis, the Ambassador replied that this was not the same thing, and cited Britain's unfortunate experience in Egypt where similar agreements had proved useless. Venizelos said that Greece would be content with a simple British declaration to the effect that when the present troubled international situation had settled the Cyprus question would be re-examined; such a declaration would enable Greece to ask the Cypriots not to disturb Anglo-Greek relations in the meantime. But the Ambassador could offer no hope of even the smallest gesture, and presumably as a mark of Britain's displeasure that the matter should have been brought up at all, the Ambassador pointedly omitted to invite Venizelos to a dinner at the Embassy a few days later which the King had been asked to attend.

These rebuffs did not discourage Paul from his efforts to do all he could to avert anything that might exacerbate Anglo-Greek relations. To this end he was prepared to stretch his constitutional privileges to their fullest extent, and in this attitude he had the full sympathy and cooperation of Ventiris.

An example of this was the question of Greece's diplomatic relations with Egypt, which had been interrupted following the insistence of the Egyptian Government that foreign envoys should be accredited to King Farouk as King of Egypt and of the Sudan. In deference to Britain's susceptibilities in the matter and in common with other NATO countries, Greece had recalled her Ambassador some months previously because the Egyptian authorities had refused to accept his credentials, which were addressed to Farouk as King of Egypt only. But Greece had to consider the interests of the large Greek communities established in Egypt, and on 23 June 1952 the Greek Government announced its decision to normalize diplomatic relations with Egypt by accrediting a Greek Ambassador in the manner demanded by the Egyptians. This initiative inevitably provoked a vigorous reaction from the British Government deprecating Greece's decision; it also came as a complete surprise to King Paul, whose Secretary-General complained to Venizelos that the King had not been consulted. Venizelos replied that he considered such matters did not require prior consultation, but if the King disapproved he could always withhold the Ambassador's *exequatur*. A matter of fundamental constitutional principle had been raised, however, and Ventiris thought it proper to clarify the position in writing.

Royal Palace, 28 June 1952

My dear Minister,

You will permit me to outline the King's views on the matter of the Ambassador to Cairo.

The relations between this country and foreign States are naturally the competence of the Government. But the country's foreign policy generally is carried out with the knowledge and approval of the Crown, which is entitled to be informed in advance of the Government's views since the Sovereign will be called upon to ratify with his signature or his approval the negotiations or actions of the competent Minister. In this specific case the King does not disagree with the appointment of an Ambassador to Egypt. He has simply expressed the view that this was not the most suitable moment and that sufficient preparation had not been made on the British side. Had the matter, therefore, been put to His Majesty he would have expressed this view and after the Government had expounded its arguments a solution would have been reached.

I wish to repeat that there is no question of a disagreement nor of criticism after the event, especially since the King had approved the nomination of the Ambassador. But the King avails himself of this opportunity to renew his recommendation that he be kept informed of the Government's ideas on major aspects of foreign policy before decisions are made.

Three weeks later Ventiris found occasion again to draw Venizelos's attention to the continuing deterioration of Anglo-Greek relations. The Acting Premier agreed and confessed that he had been much disappointed and offended by the hostile reaction of the British Foreign Office to all the approaches that had been made on the Cyprus question.

By mid-July incipient signs of disintegration in the Government coalition were becoming evident. For some time the opposition deputies had been boycotting Parliament, while its press was waging a persistent campaign for new elections on the majority system; contemplating the monolithic solidarity of the Greek Rally from their own sadly divided ranks, several Government supporters were reportedly considering a transfer of loyalties.

At the same time the U.S. Ambassador, Mr Peurifoy, was discreetly allowing it to be understood that the Americans were disillusioned and unhappy about the Government's lack of vigour, and that perhaps a good interim solution would be to have a government for a few months under Papagos with the collaboration of Venizelos's Liberals, which would give it a much healthier parliamentary basis than the razor-edge majority of the present EPEK/Liberal coalition. Within the Cabinet, the sick Premier's prolonged absence abroad and the unlikelihood of his being able effectively to resume his duties for some time, if at all, was creating mutual suspicions and uncertainty about the future; Venizelos was known to be increasingly apprehensive about the way the situation was developing and was reported to be turning a willing ear to the Americans' suggestions of collaboration with Papagos.

On 10 August 1952 Plastiras suddenly returned to Athens. Though obviously still a sick man with not long to live he insisted on resuming his duties immediately, confidently assuring his friends and colleagues that his health was now fully restored and that he would lead his party to victory at the next elections, whatever the system of voting. In his first audience with the King after his return he seemed unable to concentrate on what was being discussed, and after a while the King was obliged to call in Ventiris to help steer the conversation.

A tense atmosphere was developing, people were becoming impatient and irritable; even Ventiris began to show signs of strain. On 17 September a pro-Greek Rally newspaper disclosed that a series of violently anti-American articles which had been appearing anonymously in another Athenian newspaper were written by Ventiris's journalist brother Nicholas. Ventiris immediately submitted his resignation to the King on the grounds that there should be no shadow of suspicion concerning the sentiments of those who served the Crown. The King rejected the resignation, but as news of it had been made public – Ventiris himself had made no secret of it – a statement was issued from the Palace saying that members of the Court could not be considered responsible for the actions of their relatives and the resignation had therefore not been accepted.

The matter could have ended there, but Ventiris was not prepared to let it rest: it was necessary, he insisted, for the American Ambassador – to whom there were disparaging references in the offending articles – publicly to disclaim any reservations concerning the King's Secretary-General. The King saw Mr Peurifoy, who assured him that he had never doubted Ventiris's sentiments, and that he would be happy to appear in public with Ventiris to demonstrate the harmony between them. But Ventiris was adamant: only a public statement by the Ambassador would meet the situation adequately. The Foreign Under-Secretary Averoff and Peurifoy together produced a draft to the effect that the Ambassador was completely satisfied with the King's assurances concerning the Secretary-General. Ventiris angrily rejected this out of hand: he was not going to have the Sovereign appear anxious to reassure any foreign Ambassador about the integrity of any member of his Household.

By this time the King had had enough. He summoned Ventiris and told him firmly that the matter was now closed. Ventiris pleaded that all he was trying to do was safeguard the prestige and authority of the Crown, and his sole concern was that the

Americans should not entertain any suspicions regarding the King's servants and, by implication, the King himself; he therefore insisted on going, and handed the King a draft announcing the King's acceptance of his resignation. Paul tore it up, and handed Ventiris another draft which he had himself prepared:

The King has confirmed to his complete satisfaction that the reasons which led the Secretary-General to submit his resignation are not valid, and has commanded Mr George Ventiris to remain at his post.

11 November 1952

Constitutionally impeccable to the last, Ventiris protested weakly that the use of the term 'commanded' might be misconstrued, but the King was not to be deflected.

'They can say what they like, you are staying,' was his final word.

It was now September. From his frequent contacts with Cabinet Ministers and others Ventiris was able to confirm for himself that the reports of confusion and disagreement within the coalition were all too true and that the fall of the Government was now merely a matter of time.

There were two ways of dealing with this eventuality: another coalition or the dissolution of Parliament and new elections.

Any coalition that did not include the Greek Rally was doomed to the same fate as the present one, in view of the Rally's massive parliamentary strength. Preliminary soundings of the opposition leaders had elicited a lukewarm response at first, but when more specific approaches were made the Rally drew back and rejected all offers.

There remained only the second alternative, but a new problem now arose. The King was anxious that the elections should be held under a non-party 'service' government to ensure that there would be no subsequent accusations of gerrymandering. All the political leaders were in agreement on this, and when the matter had been broached with Venizelos while Plastiras was still absent abroad the Acting Premier had agreed that when the moment came the Government would resign so that the King could appoint a 'service' administration to organize the elections. On 9 September, however, a harassed Venizelos informed Ventiris that during a Cabinet meeting that day he had found himself in direct disagreement with Plastiras, who had blandly announced that after Parliament passed the new electoral law – which would be the signal to go ahead with the elections – he would be receiving the King's mandate to dissolve Parliament and organize the new elections. Plastiras was so categorical about this statement as to give the impression that he had the King's authority to make it, and Venizelos wanted to know if there had been any changes in the King's attitude in the matter. Ventiris reassured him on this very important point, but to clarify the situation the King summoned Plastiras and Venizelos to a joint audience the following day – at which Ventiris was also present – and made it clear that while he personally had no views on the system of voting, which was a matter for Parliament to decide, he had definitely decided that the elections would be held under a 'service' government to be appointed in due course. Plastiras plaintively asked why the dissolution of Parliament was not to be entrusted to him as leader of the Government majority. Ventiris explained that this argument would be valid only if Plastiras were leader of a homogeneous majority, which was not now the case, and that if the dissolution was to be entrusted to the biggest party then by rights it should go to Field-Marshal Papagos. Plastiras seemed convinced and promised to abide by the King's decisions.

On 3 October Parliament passed the Electoral Bill adopting the simple majority system of voting, dividing the country into 99 constituencies and increasing the number of Deputies from 258 to 300. Three days later the King received Plastiras and Venizelos together to hear the Government's recommendations in accordance with constitutional procedure. Plastiras was of the opinion that Parliament should not be dissolved just yet, but left the final decision to the discretion of the King. Venizelos thought the Government would be unable to remain in office even if its present parliamentary strength were increased by a few votes.

The following day the King received the Greek Rally leader Field-Marshal Papagos and the Populist leader Constantine Tsaldaris, from among whose followers the Rally derived most of its support. Papagos repeated his oft-expressed view that Parliament should be dissolved forthwith and elections held under a service government. The King sounded him concerning the choice of person to lead the service government, and was pleased to ascertain that the Field-Marshal had no objection to Mr Demetrius Kioussopoulos, a senior official in the Supreme Court of Justice,

14 Villa Mon Repos, Corfu.
15 Tatoi.

16 Formal occasion.

17 Inspecting troops in the North.

18 Frederica, amateur artist, painting in Corfu.

19 Paul the gardener.

20 Greece wins an Olympic Gold Medal! The proud parents congratulating their son after his yachting victory, Naples 1960.

whom the King already had in mind. Tsaldaris was totally opposed to new elections, and proposed that a last attempt should be made by himself for the formation of another coalition under Plastiras, with which he felt sure some Greek Rally followers would finally collaborate.

It now remained for the King to ascertain the Government's final views before reaching a decision. Paul was particularly anxious that no pressure should be brought on Plastiras and that whatever steps were now taken by the Sovereign should have the Government's support – better still, that they should be recommended by the Premier himself. His hopes were realized, and on 8 October a communiqué announced that the Prime Minister had advised the King to dissolve the Chamber and hold elections under a service government. On 9 October the King dissolved Parliament and proclaimed general elections for 16 November 1952.

On 10 October Plastiras was received in audience by the King to submit his resignation. He bowed respectfully and said: 'Let there be done whatever Your Majesty wishes. There is no need for speeches.' The King expressed gratitude to Plastiras for his services to the country, and the old General wept as he replied: 'It is I who am grateful to Your Majesty for your confidence and your many kindnesses. It was more than I expected and perhaps more than I deserved.' He kissed the King's hand and withdrew.

Immediately afterwards Mr Kioussopoulos was introduced into the royal presence and received the mandate to form a 'service' government, which was sworn in the following day.

The elections of 16 November 1952 were contested by three main groups: the Greek Rally led by Field-Marshal Alexander Papagos, the EPEK-Liberal coalition jointly led by General Nicholas Plastiras and Sophocles Venizelos, and EDA, a combination of left-wing groupings supported by the outlawed Greek Communist Party. Immediately after the dissolution of Parliament several prominent EPEK-Liberals had defected to the ranks of the Greek Rally, which had also been joined for electoral purposes by the Democratic Socialist leader George Papandreou.

The elections gave the Greek Rally a landslide victory with 239 out of the 300 seats in the new Chamber. The EPEK-Liberals won the remaining 61 seats and EDA failed to return a single member. Plastiras himself was defeated in his Athenian constituency but

Venizelos managed to survive by standing in a constituency in Crete where the charisma of the name of Venizelos could not fail.

Five days before the elections Ventiris wrote the following letter to the King:

Your Majesty,

In the event of the Greek Rally securing an absolute majority in the elections next Sunday and its leader becoming Prime Minister, I would like Your Majesty to have at your disposal my resignation as Secretary-General should the new Premier require it.

As I have already explained to Your Majesty, I firmly believe that according to our constitutional practice the leader of the parliamentary majority has the right to make it a condition of his cooperation with the Crown that there should be relations of mutual confidence between himself and the King's political adviser. Should Field-Marshal Papagos consider that such relations do not exist with me, I would be the first to wish not to be a cause of friction between Your Majesty and Your Majesty's responsible First Minister, in addition to which I am conscious of my own inability to collaborate with the Field Marshal. The majority leader, elected as such by the free vote of the people, is entitled to count on the unreserved cooperation of the Crown in the discharge of his mission, especially during the early days of his mandate.

With the most profound respect and boundless devotion,

G. Ventiris

On 16 November the resignation of George Ventiris was formally announced and John Koutsalexis, a senior diplomatist, was appointed in his place.

On 23 November 1952 a new Government headed by Field-Marshal Papagos was sworn in by the King. It was the first administration formed by the Greek Rally, which was to remain in power in one form or another for the next ten years.

⇉ 31 ⇇

In January 1953, immediately after the official visit of the Italian Prime Minister Signor de Gasperi – the first visit to Greece by an Italian Premier since the end of the war – Paul went abroad for a change of scene and a rest, leaving Frederica to act as Regent during his absence. He was in Germany visiting Frederica's parents when the condition of the Duke of Brunswick, who had been ill for some time, suddenly took a turn for the worse. On 30 January 1953 the Duke died, excusing himself to the end for taking so long about it.

A few days later Paul arrived in London, where he stayed for nearly a fortnight. His visit was strictly unofficial, but while in London he was appointed an Honorary Admiral in the British Navy, a distinction also held by his grandfather King George I. He also had discreet contacts with the Foreign Office: on 18 February the Permanent Under-Secretary, Sir William Strang, called on him at his hotel and the following day the King went to the Foreign Office to return the visit. His conversations were mainly concerned with Cyprus, though it could not be said that any progress had been made by the time he left for Athens, the British having remained adamant in their refusal even to discuss the matter.

With a professional soldier of international repute as head of government it was natural that the new Greek administration should concentrate its efforts first on problems of security and defence. The indispensable pre-requisite for any defence arrangement in the eastern Mediterranean clearly being close cooperation between Greece, Turkey and Yugoslavia, the successful rapprochement between Greece and Turkey sealed by Paul's State Visit to Turkey was now followed up by an intensification of similar approaches to Yugoslavia which had already been initiated by the previous government. The culmination of these efforts was the signature of a

Tripartite Treaty of Friendship and Cooperation at Ankara on 28 February 1953, the treaty being speedily ratified by Greece and Yugoslavia on 23 March and by Turkey on 18 May of the same year.

Similar success could not unhappily be claimed in the sphere of Anglo-Greek relations, which were being increasingly bedevilled by the Cyprus question. In March 1953 the Archbishop of Cyprus* came on a visit to Greece, his arrival being the signal for pro-Enosis demonstrations and clashes with the police in the streets of Athens.

On hearing that Queen Frederica as Regent during the King's absence was going to receive Archbishop Makarios in audience, the British Ambassador in Athens, Sir Charles Peake, wrote to the Grand Chamberlain advising against it. In a letter to the Greek Foreign Minister on 6 March 1953 explaining his action, Sir Charles wrote:

It is my considered opinion that for Archbishop Makarios to be received by Her Majesty will have a harmful effect on Anglo-Greek relations. I must maintain that view, and I should certainly have been failing in my duty as Her Britannic Majesty's Ambassador in Greece if I had not presented it in the proper quarter. I would interpose here that no thought of criticism of Her Majesty is in my mind. Her Majesty is Regent and She Can Do No Wrong. My Government will, however, find it difficult to understand that my advice on this question was not asked, and that when proffered it was not taken. . . . It will be hard for my Government to understand how it comes about that Archbishop Makarios, a British subject whose name has been so much mentioned in connexion with events which caused injuries to some seventy Greek citizens, should receive this mark of consideration from Her Majesty the Queen of the Hellenes.

To expect a Greek Sovereign not to receive the elected leader of a community that was Greek by race, language and religion, though politically still the colony of a foreign Power, showed a lamentable

* Makarios III, at thirty-seven the youngest prelate ever to occupy the Archiepiscopal throne of the Church of Cyprus, which was founded by St Barnabas in A.D. 45 and comes next in seniority only to the four Patriarchates in the Eastern Orthodox Church. By tradition the Archbishop of Cyprus is elected by the people both as Primate and as 'Ethnarch' or National Leader. Among other privileges granted by the Byzantine Emperors and retained to this day, the Archbishop of Cyprus wears Imperial Purple, carries a crozier tipped by the Imperial Orb and not by the customary twin serpents of other Orthodox prelates, and signs his name in red ink.

lack of appreciation of public feeling in the matter. The Ambassador was advised that his intervention was most unwise, and Archbishop Makarios was duly received in audience by the Queen-Regent.

In the summer of 1953 the British Foreign Secretary, Mr Anthony Eden, who had undergone a series of major operations earlier in the year for an internal complaint, went on a six weeks' convalescence cruise in the Mediterranean. In the course of his travels Mr Eden visited Greece, and on 22 September the Prime Minister, Field-Marshal Papagos, called on him at the British Embassy in Athens.

After the usual exchange of courtesies Papagos expressed concern over the way Anglo-Greek relations were developing as a result of the Cyprus dispute. Before the Premier could go any further Eden interrupted sharply to say he was on holiday and was not prepared to discuss the matter. Papagos ignored the interruption and continued that this was an ideal opportunity for an informal talk but Eden abruptly rose to his feet and walked to the window, ostentatiously paying no further attention to what Papagos was saying. The Field-Marshal now also got up and with a sharp edge in his voice said that the Prime Minister of Greece preferred to speak to people face to face and not to address their backs. Eden replied wearily that he absolutely refused to discuss Cyprus. Papagos insisted that the future of half a million Greeks could not be dismissed just like that, to which Eden retorted irritably that there were hundreds of thousands of Greeks living in the United States and in Egypt: was Greece asking to annex those countries too? The Field-Marshal apparently failed to see any humour in this remark, and after wishing Eden a pleasant journey took his leave.*

Soon after the accession of Queen Elizabeth II to the British throne, preliminary soundings had been made by the Foreign Office for a State visit to England by King Paul.† These approaches had reached a stage where a formal invitation was about to be issued, but Papagos now intervened and indicated that the matter should not be pursued any further as the climate created by the Cyprus dispute precluded any such visit on the part of the Greek Sovereign.

* I searched in vain for Lord Avon's own version of this dramatic meeting in the volume of his Memoirs covering that period.[24]

† It was understood at the time that after King George VI died a note was found in his desk to the effect that Paul should be the first foreign Head of State that the young Queen should invite to England.

In May 1953 Mr John Foster Dulles, who had succeeded Mr Dean Acheson as U.S. Secretary of State following General Eisenhower's election to the presidency on 4 November 1952, set out on a fact-finding mission to the Middle East and Southern Asia. On his way back he stopped in Athens on 27/8 May for a review of defence and economic problems with the new Greek leaders. During his stay Mr Dulles was received by the King and Queen, to whom he conveyed an invitation from President Eisenhower to visit the United States later in the year. The President was anxious that Paul and Frederica should see as much of the United States as possible, and suggested a stay of four to five weeks.

Meanwhile, a national calamity struck Greece: on 10 August 1953 a violent earthquake shook the Ionian Islands, devastating Cephallonia, Ithaka and Zakynthos.* The casualties were heavy: 455 killed, nearly 1,000 injured, over 25,000 houses destroyed, 100,000 people rendered homeless.

Paul and Frederica hastened to the scene of the disaster and toured the whole area, comforting the stricken and helping with the relief and rescue work. It was on this occasion that Paul became really aware, in an immediate and vivid sense, of the extent to which the mere presence of the King and the manifestation of his personal interest and concern for the misfortunes of humble people could completely eliminate all barriers or reservations and could impart spiritual comfort and moral encouragement. Everything was still in chaos, with the authorities striving hard to cope with a situation far beyond their capabilities at that early stage. People were squatting about on the ground near the ruins of their homes, still stunned and unable to grasp fully the extent of the catastrophe that had descended upon them, listlessly waiting for somebody to come to their help and tell them what to do. As Paul and Frederica walked among them they would get up and follow them silently, trying to come close enough to touch them. A priest who had collapsed from his efforts looked up as the King passed and beckoned him to approach. When Paul reached him and put his arm round his shoulder, the old man looked up at him. 'I can do no more,' he muttered piteously, 'I can do no more,' and stroked the King's face

* Admiral Earl Mountbatten, Commander-in-Chief of the British Mediterranean Fleet, who flew over the devastated areas said in a broadcast on 14 August that 'it seemed as though a giant hand had been put on the roofs of the buildings and pressed down hard until they collapsed'.

like a child. Another man, an elderly peasant with one arm in an improvised sling, walked in step alongside the King and after a while put his head on the King's breast, still keeping pace with him, just weeping in uncontrollable grief.

Perhaps for the first time in his life Paul felt himself completely at one with the people, and the fact that they obviously felt the same way about him, the fact that even old people looked upon him as a father, filled him with gratitude and humility. In the midst of this nightmare scene of elemental tragedy, a great happiness suffused his soul and made all the bitterness and the sorrows of the past sink into oblivion.

The visit to the United States was a lengthy affair and a judicious mixture of official ceremonies and informal functions. Paul and Frederica arrived in New York on 28 October 1953 on the liner *United States*, and their tour took them to Washington, Boston, Detroit, Chicago, San Francisco, Los Angeles, Houston and other cities where Paul made several speeches, some of them formal and dealing with matters of policy and affairs of state, others on a less formal note on more mundane subjects.

Over the years since Paul's accession to the throne a system of joint labour in speechwriting had been evolved between Paul and Frederica. One of them would walk about the room throwing out ideas and phrases which the other would jot down, then the roles would be reversed, and finally a rough draft would be worked out and then put away for a while. Then the draft would be gone through again and marginal notes made first by the one and then by the other, and after that a final draft would be prepared. Except for very informal occasions, the draft would invariably be sent to the Prime Minister for information or comment.

On 3 November Paul addressed the eighth General Assembly of the United Nations.

I stand before you with deep respect. For me, no building encloses this Congress: I see no individuals separated from each other by language, race or religion. In my mind, as I gaze upon you from my Greek platform, I see before me the spirit of Man emanating from the heart and soul of each one of you. It is to this spirit that I bow my head ...

The same emotions, such as suffering, pity and hope, link us within one great experience and prove the oneness of our inner lives. The people in Russia suffer as much as the people in Greece. The young boy who bravely goes to war to defend his country makes the same sacrifice in leaving his family whether he comes from America or Europe, from Asia or Africa or Australia. The tears of one mother are the tears of all.

Exhausted but happy, Paul and Frederica boarded the S.S. *Independence* on 3 December for the journey home. By universal consent the tour had been an unqualified success. In a farewell message thanking the American people for their hospitality and kindness, Paul said:

Truly you are a great people. Your greatness lies not only in the power of your armed forces but far more in the fundamental goodness of your heart.

I have always believed that deep human sentiments such as friendship, generosity, unselfishness, understanding and love must balance, if not outweigh, material means if we want to build a better world.

I leave you with a deep sense of optimism because I know that you possess all these qualities in abundance.

In their private moments together, at the bungalow in Petali or on their long walks in the woods of Tatoi among the foothills of Mount Parnes, Paul and Frederica would seek mental relaxation by putting out of their minds for a while the mundane preoccupations of their life, finding some measure of spiritual escape in discussions of a metaphysical nature. The meaning and interpretation of terms like Matter, Energy, Power, fascinated them – Frederica in a scientific sense, Paul in a philosophical context and in relation to religion.

Shortly after his return from the visit to the United States, Paul was informed that the University of Athens wished to confer on him an Honorary Degree of Doctor of Philosophy. The ceremony took place on 25 February 1954, and his speech of acceptance provided Paul with an opportunity of expounding some of the ideas that had been occupying his mind:

What the world was up against, he said, was not a social or political or economic crisis, but essentially a spiritual crisis. The old moral and spiritual values were no longer capable of kindling the heart of humanity. The spirit of man should again be stirred into making western civilization a spiritual driving force. Man's material progress should be matched with new courageous thought, and the right explanations for this world of Matter had to be found within the newly discovered world of Power.

For many centuries past Religion had revealed through faith that this Power was the Divine Power. Science for its part had offered convincing proof of the existence of a Supreme Power and at the same time the existence of Unity, of the oneness of Matter and Power. Science had thus rendered the greatest service and support both to religious sentiments and to philosophic thought. This new concept of the world embraced the material and the abstract within a single whole and a single Unity.

It was a significant and encouraging thing that Science always found its culmination in the principles of Christian religion. The concept of Unity and of Creation were indissolubly bound with the concept of Love and Humility.

Predictably, Paul's speech provoked widespread and controversial discussion; Father Ieronymos Kotsonis, the King's erudite and progressive Chaplain,* reported that the Hierarchy of the Greek Church was puzzled and disturbed by Paul's incursion into what they regarded as their own exclusive sphere of thought, and suggested that perhaps an explanatory statement might be advisable to dispel these fears. Feeling that the true meaning of what he had said had not been fully understood and reluctant to modify his remarks in any way, Paul had to wait until a later occasion – the conferment of a Degree of Doctor of Theology by the University of Thessaloniki the following year – provided him with the opportunity of clarifying his views.

In February 1954 Archbishop Makarios arrived in Athens on a five-week visit during which he was received in audience by the King and had talks with the Greek Government, which assured him that Greece would raise the question of Cyprus at the United Nations if Britain did not agree to bilateral talks on the matter. Any hopes of such talks, however, were brusquely dispelled by the British Foreign Secretary, Mr Anthony Eden, who on 15 March 1954 stated in the House of Commons that 'as has been made clear to the Greek Government, Her Majesty's Government cannot agree to discuss the status of Cyprus'.

With further progress effectively deadlocked by Eden's intransigent attitude, Paul suggested to the Prime Minister that a direct approach to the British Premier, Winston Churchill, might be a useful course of action – after all, it was Churchill who on his first visit to Cyprus as Colonial Under-Secretary in 1907 had said: 'I think it is only natural that the Cypriot people, who are of Greek

---

* Later Archbishop of Athens and Primate of all Greece.

descent, should regard their incorporation with what may be called their mother country as an ideal to be earnestly, devoutly and fervently cherished. Such a feeling is an example of the patriotic devotion which so nobly characterizes the Greek Nation.' Papagos welcomed the idea; the King, however, as Head of State was precluded by international usage from corresponding on political matters direct with the Prime Minister of a foreign country. In the end it was decided that the letter should come from Frederica, who had met Churchill on her last visit to England and had got on very well with him. The text was drafted by Paul and Frederica after a lengthy preliminary discussion with Papagos, and the draft was duly sent to the Field-Marshal for comment. The Prime Minister made one or two changes which he explained in a covering letter to Frederica, in which he also said that he felt sure the approach to Churchill would contribute towards 'keeping the door open' with Britain.

The letter, which was sent to England by hand of the Earl of Leicester – an old friend of the Greek Royal Family who happened to be visiting Greece at the time – was calculated to appeal to the emotional side of Churchill's character. Greece and Britain, it said, had been united in friendship for many years: they shared the same noble ideals, and when Britain stood alone during one of the most critical moments in her history in the last war the Greeks had fought by her side. The Greek people had a great love for England and what England stood for; it was a love made possible by a total lack of any sense of inferiority; but now a small island called Cyprus was causing an estrangement between the two countries. The Greeks, who were a proud people, were puzzled and hurt by Britain's refusal even to discuss the future of a people who were European and Christian and resented the fact that they were expected to remain colonials in these enlightened times when less developed people in other parts of the world were being given their independence. All Greece was asking for was that the door should remain open for discussions to determine a gradual evolution of the Cyprus question to the satisfaction of both countries.

Churchill's reply was not long in coming:

10, Downing Street,
Whitehall.

April 7, 1954.

Madam,

Lord Leicester brought me Your Majesty's letter.
I shall show it to the Foreign Secretary, but while we
fully share your feelings on the subject of Anglo-Greek
friendship it would not be right for me to leave Your
Majesty in doubt of our conviction that this is not the
time, in the interests either of Greece, Great Britain,
or, wider still, of NATO, for discussion about changes in
the government of Cyprus.

The island is of vital importance to the defence
of the Middle East and of the Mediterranean.   While
that remains the case, disturbance of the present
regime could do nothing but harm to us all.   I remember
with emotion the friendly feelings shown by the Greek
people in the war to the British armies who came to help
defend them, first from Nazi invasion and later from
Communist revolution.   If a third world war should come
it might well be that British blood would once again be
shed to save Greece from invasion.   I can assure
Your Majesty that withdrawal from Cyprus would
certainly not help to that end and might, indeed,
fatally weaken the combination on which the safety
of us all depends.

I beg you to convey my respectful good wishes
to the King and remain

Your Majesty's obedient servant,

Winston S. Churchill

Her Majesty The Queen of The Hellenes.

On 28 July 1954 in the course of a lengthy debate on the Cyprus question in the House of Commons, the Minister of State for Colonial Affairs, Mr Henry Hopkinson,* stated that 'there can be no question of any change of sovereignty in Cyprus'. Later in the same debate he went even further:

It has always been understood and agreed that there are certain territories in the Commonwealth which, owing to their particular circumstances, can never hope to be fully independent.... There are some territories which cannot expect to be that.... I have said that the question of the abrogation of British sovereignty cannot arise – that British sovereignty will remain.

Adding insult to injury, the Secretary of State for the Colonies, Mr Oliver Lyttelton,† said during the debate:

I can imagine no more disastrous policy for Cyprus than to hand it over to an unstable though friendly Power.

– a remark scarcely calculated to contribute towards improving Anglo-Greek relations.

At the same time the British Government offered Cyprus a new constitution – the constitution proposed in May 1948 had been rejected by the Cypriots on the grounds that it specifically precluded any discussion of the status of the island. The new constitution provided for an Executive Council of nominated and elected members, the former being in a permanent majority. In the Legislature also the Executive was assured of a built-in majority – as the Governor of Cyprus somewhat naïvely put it in an explanatory broadcast to the people of Cyprus on 6 August 1954, 'how best can the Executive Council obtain both a full and frank discussion of its policy in the Legislature and at the same time be certain of getting reasonable support for those policies?'

On 3 May 1954 Field-Marshal Papagos had given formal notice that if the British Government persisted in its negative attitude towards the Cyprus question, Greece would be left with no alternative but to appeal to the United Nations. He said he would leave the final decision to the last minute, which he did, but on 20 August 1954, five weeks before the General Assembly was due to begin its

Application, under the auspices of the United Nations, of the principle of equal rights and self-determination of peoples in the case of the population of the island of Cyprus.

* Later Lord Colyton.
† Later Viscount Chandos.

labours, the Greek Government formally requested that the following item should be inscribed on the Agenda:

Cyprus now ceased to be an Anglo-Greek dispute and automatically became an international issue.

The Cyprus question had not yet cast its shadow over Graeco-Turkish relations, however, and the atmosphere between Greece and Yugoslavia also was now sufficiently favourable to permit a State Visit to Greece by President Tito. This took place on 2–6 June 1954, and the outcome of the talks between the Yugoslav leader and Field-Marshal Papagos was a decision to transform the Tripartite Balkan Pact into a full military alliance, which was duly signed at Bled on 9 August, linking three well-trained armies with a total potential of some seventy divisions in a highly sensitive area of the Western defence system.

Meanwhile, Greece's efforts in the United Nations did not bear much fruit, the final outcome being the adoption of a resolution by the General Assembly on 17 December 1954 to the effect that 'for the time being it does not appear appropriate to adopt a resolution on Cyprus'. The failure of Greece's appeal was the signal for the outbreak of serious disturbances in Cyprus and in Greece, where the demonstrations were not only against Britain but now also assumed an anti-American character because of the refusal of the United States to support the Greek case in the United Nations.

On 20 December 1954 King Paul made a broadcast over Athens Radio:

Our Cypriot brothers demand their freedom through the right of self-determination, for which two great wars have been fought. Greece, faced with Britain's refusal to discuss the subject directly, was compelled to bring the issue before the United Nations. As long as the Cypriots proclaim their indomitable will to decide their own destiny, no power on earth can thwart the natural evolution of this desire. But let us not forget that our friends who have disappointed us in the Cyprus affair are the same who today, in the past, and in the future, guarantee our security and that of the free world. I call upon all Greeks to remain objective and calm, and not to forget that our traditions impose good sense in our emotions and clarity in our judgement. I appeal to my people at this difficult time to remain worthy of our high traditions, and with Hellenic nobility and pride to remain faithful to our friends.

Early in 1955 an underground militant organization, EOKA ('National Organization of Cypriot Fighters') made its appearance in Cyprus, its activities against the British steadily mounting until they eventually reached the proportions of full-scale guerrilla war against the British forces. It was led by Colonel George Grivas, a Cypriot-born former Greek Army officer who had led a resistance organization in Greece during the occupation and who now assumed the name 'Digenis Akritas', a legendary Greek warrior, in his crusade for the liberation of the Cypriot people.

During this time the Greek Government was also facing a domestic crisis. On 2 April 1954 Spyros Markezinis, the party's organizer and political brain, resigned as Minister of Coordination as a result of growing differences with the Prime Minister, Field-Marshal Papagos. This estrangement increased with the passing months, and on 11 November 1954 Markezinis announced his formal secession from the Greek Rally altogether. He was followed by some thirty members of the Rally, with whom he now formed his own party, the Progressives.

For a year a vague uneasiness at the back of his mind had been troubling Paul over the misgivings to which his speech at Athens University on 25 February 1954 had given rise among the conservative elements of the Greek Orthodox Church. He knew perfectly well that his analysis of the inter-relation between Matter and Energy had been erroneously interpreted as an expression of materialistic philosophy, whereas on the contrary what he had tried to show was that there was really no contradiction between the scientific approach and religious faith.

On 28 May 1955 he was at last provided with an opportunity of dispelling this misunderstanding. The occasion was highly appropriate: the conferment upon him of a Degree of Doctor of Theology by the University of Thessaloniki, the great city where St Paul preached and wrote his two Epistles, the historic Macedonian capital which Paul's warrior father had liberated from the Ottoman yoke and where his gentle grandfather had died at the hands of an assassin.

Paul put all his religious philosophy into this speech, which he wrote himself from beginning to end without any assistance from anyone:

I have always felt that the mission to be King in our Orthodox country is intimately connected with the mission of our Orthodox Church. Our mission is through love to try, live and express the message of Christ within ourselves and our People, and for all of us together to become real Apostles of our Christian faith.

To be a true Christian means to recognize that the spirit of God – and God is Love – lives in all of us. It means that we should respect and serve this spirit within each other, and so help to bring it into full consciousness. In this way we shall learn to understand that the Spirit of God is that Oneness, that Unity, that Love, which includes all things seen and unseen. It is the Divine spark in our soul, which when brought into full consciousness is kindled to a flame linking us with the only true light, the light that is God.

At the University of Athens I spoke about the Oneness of all things as it is being revealed to us by science. The discovery of the Atom, the splitting of the Atom, the reducing of the smallest particle to a mere wave has destroyed all philosophies whose foundations lie in materialism. We have to learn to accept the fact that Matter and Mind are different in appearance but one in essence. By this I mean that Matter has lost its reality and in the end there is only Mind, Divine Mind.

In the same way as the doubting Thomas was allowed to use his hands to strengthen his wavering faith, so have the Sciences been given to man by the Grace of God, in order to discover and touch the truth which his weakening faith was unable to grasp . . .

I believe that the time has come for a tremendous spiritual awakening. Within our lives we must learn to overcome all feelings of separation from our one and only source, God, or as I called it before, Divine Mind.

Christ, through his life, showed us the way towards unity with God, and he has asked us to follow His example, not any more by word of mouth, but with our spirit and with our heart. He gave us a simple method, a method that lies within the very experience of our life: it is Love. Each one of us loves someone. It may be mother, father, husband, wife, child or friend. It is the one experience we have which lifts us from self-love to the love of another. If we can keep this as an unselfish emotion alive in our consciousness we are already lifting our spirit towards a higher plane, towards a higher Love. When we know others to be as much part of Divine Mind as we are ourselves then we can also love them as ourselves and so fulfil Christ's great command, 'Love thy neighbour as thyself.'

Christ's example and prayer demands for us all to become more conscious of our unity with God.

God created a beautiful universe, as well as men and women in His own image. We must not make the mistake of creating God in our own image and then attributing to Him all the mistakes that are of our own making.

The responsibility to make our world a better place, to bring happiness and love to others, is a purely individual responsibility. The solution to man's problems and his longing to live in peace with his neighbours cannot be left as the lone responsibility of politicians, priests and Kings.

We often complain about politicians, that they cannot achieve political unity. The time has come for us to help them. A man stable within himself will be a first-class citizen; and that nation, whose citizens have found their intellectual and spiritual unity, will contribute more to human civilization and world harmony than any other who alone depends upon its political slogans, armed forces and atom bombs.

We often blame our priests for not giving us a solution to our spiritual and moral problems. We must remember that not even Christ could live our life for us. He could show us the way, but we have to do the walking ourselves.

No words can ever express the gratitude I feel for the love and confidence that my people have given me during these terribly difficult years. It is because of this love and my boundless confidence and love for my people that an unseen unity has been established between us, which nothing and no one can ever destroy. I pray to God that my son and his heirs will also learn from you, as I have learned, that true majesty and love lies in your heart and soul. I am fully conscious that my service to my People is also part of my service to God.

With the situation in Cyprus steadily deteriorating as a result of the intensification of the activities of EOKA, the British Government found itself no longer able to maintain the position that the Cyprus question was an exclusively domestic problem. On 29 June 1955 Sir Anthony Eden – who had succeeded Sir Winston Churchill as Prime Minister on 6 April 1955, after being appointed a Knight of the Garter the previous year – invited Greece and Turkey to a tripartite conference in London 'on political and defence questions which affect the Eastern Mediterranean, including Cyprus'. The conference, which was at Foreign Minister level, began on 29 August with Mr Harold Macmillan – now Foreign Secretary – in the chair; it broke up a week later having achieved nothing beyond the reiteration of their countries' positions by the three Foreign Ministers. This was scarcely surprising, and was indeed no more than Britain was expecting from the conference, the principal aim of which so far as Britain was concerned was not so much to find a solution to the problem – this was too much to hope for at the time – but to make Britain's international position easier and perhaps make more palatable the new constitutional proposals that had been prepared for Cyprus.* As regards Britain's attitude

---

* This is frankly admitted by Eden, who writes in his *Memoirs*:[25] 'By securing a precise definition of these differences we hoped to show the true nature of the problem. The exact terms of our proposals for the future could then be presented.'

towards the whole Cyprus question, this was succintly re-affirmed at the conference by Mr Macmillan. 'The British Government regard it as essential,' he said, 'that the United Kingdom should continue to remain in possession of Cyprus in order to enable her to carry out her obligations in the Eastern Mediterranean and the Middle East. Nothing has since occurred in any way to modify that view, and I am bound to say that there is no prospect of any change in the foreseeable future.'

The repercussions of the failure of the tripartite conference were swift in coming. On 6 September, while the delegates were still in London, violent anti-Greek riots broke out in Constantinople and Smyrna, the two Turkish cities where substantial Greek communities still remain; hundreds of Greek-owned shops and premises were wrecked and looted, many Greek churches were desecrated and destroyed, houses occupied by Greek officers attached to the NATO Southern Command were set on fire – all under the indifferent eyes of the Turkish police who remained passive spectators throughout the orgy of destruction.* The extent of the anti-Greek riots was effectively hushed up in Britain. Only one newspaper gave it any prominent publicity; a factual summary of this newspaper's story in the B.B.C. Greek news bulletin was deleted on instructions at the last moment, and a Greek announcer who read it out nonetheless was instantly dismissed.†

---

* 'The Turkish riots . . . were undoubtedly connived at, if not promoted by the Government.'[26]

† Eden at least could scarcely plead surprise at the Turkish reaction. The contention that he actively encouraged the Turks to manifest more vigorously their opposition to Enosis is supported by a characteristic comment in his *Memoirs*:[27] 'The Turkish newspapers had hitherto been more outspoken than the Turkish Government, which had behaved with restraint. It was as well, I wrote on a telegram at the time, that they should speak out, because it was the truth that the Turks would never let the Greeks have Cyprus.' It is not clear whether this was meant as a directive to the British Ambassador in Ankara or whether Eden was merely making a marginal note for the sake of posterity. Be that as it may, one can surely detect a suggestion of self-justification when he notes shortly afterwards: 'The conference dispersed. As it did so, riots broke out in Istanbul and Izmir, directed against the Greeks. The strength of the Turkish feeling was beginning to declare itself.' Nor does Eden hesitate in apportioning responsibility. When the U.S. Government made representations to the Turks on the subject of the anti-Greek riots while at the same time expressing to the Greek Government their gratification at the calmness of the Greeks, Eden feels constrained to write: 'We pointed out that it was the Greeks who had started the trouble and that it would go on until their agitation stopped.' Eden was able to prevail on the U.S. Government to vote against the Greek Government's proposal that the Cyprus question should again be inscribed on the Agenda of the U.N. General Assembly, thus ensuring its rejection.

⇒ 32 ⇐

The new crisis in Graeco-Turkish relations following the collapse of the London Tripartite conference found Paul and Frederica in Yugoslavia, where they arrived on 8 September 1955 to return the visit President Tito had paid to Greece the year before. During their six-day stay in Yugoslavia they toured the country – Belgrade, Zagreb, Ljubljana, Bled, Split, Dubrovnik – and spent the last two days informally with Tito and his wife at their summer retreat on the island of Brioni.

If Graeco-Turkish relations were at their nadir, there was at least the consolation that relations with Yugoslavia could not be better. Tito also made it quite plain where his sympathies lay on the Cyprus question: Yugoslavia, he told newspaper correspondents on 15 September, fully supported the right of self-determination for the Cypriot people.

On a personal level also the visit was a complete success. Though Paul and Tito represented opposite poles of political thought, they were both sincere men dedicated to their different missions, and a mutual understanding which soon matured to friendship developed between the two men. Just before the departure of his royal guests Tito asked, almost shyly, whether he and his wife might spend a few days privately in Greece; Paul and Frederica said they would be delighted to have them as their guests the following June.

For some months now the ageing Prime Minister, Field-Marshal Papagos, had been ailing. His condition was becoming steadily worse and by the middle of 1955 he was permanently confined to his bed, no longer able actively to participate in government. The two deputy Premiers, Stephanos Stephonopoulos and Panayotis Kanellopoulos, would visit him from time to time to report, for the Field-Marshal still insisted on retaining the premiership; but the

274

lack of a firm hand at the helm was making itself felt among the ranks of the Greek Rally, where disintegrating tendencies had already been set in motion by the defection of Spyros Markezinis and his supporters. Inevitably, there was also a growing rivalry between the two Deputy Premiers as to which one of them would eventually take over from the Field-Marshal, both as leader of the party and as premier – an uncertainty made no easier by the Field-Marshal's disinclination to nominate either of them as his successor while he was still able, even nominally, to hold the premiership himself.

For Paul the situation was becoming particularly difficult. His regular working sessions with the Prime Minister had been interrupted for several months and the expedient of using the two Deputy Premiers as virtual couriers between the Palace and Papagos's sickbed was proving most unreliable and unsatisfactory, especially at a time when the Cyprus crisis demanded frequent consultations between the Sovereign and his First Minister.

The parliamentary opposition was no less concerned about the situation. A few days before the King's departure for Belgrade, Venizelos wrote him a letter drawing attention to 'the highly irregular exercise of authority by a government that is virtually headless as a result of the prolonged illness of the Prime Minister'. This was a constitutional anomaly contrary to the essential meaning of governmental responsibility, said the Liberal leader, since the person who carried that responsibility was unable to exercise his functions; this state of affairs was having a stultifying effect on the whole machinery of government and should be terminated as soon as possible by the formation of a service government, the dissolution of Parliament and new elections. Soon after the King's return from Yugoslavia Venizelos returned to the attack: on 27 September he saw the King's Private Secretary and asked him to convey to the Sovereign that in view of the continuing illness of the Prime Minister, the Government should be called upon to resign without delay and new elections should be proclaimed.

Already, before leaving for Yugoslavia, Paul had been persuaded that this situation could not be allowed to continue, but had finally decided to postpone action for a while longer. His resolve was temporarily shaken after his return by the two Deputy Premiers' bland assurances that the Premier's health was showing signs of improvement, but an unannounced visit by the King had quickly dispelled any lingering doubts that Paul may have had: Papagos had barely recognized him and was scarcely able to carry on a conversation.

Convinced that action could no longer be deferred, the King sent Papagos the following letter, which was drafted with the assistance of the legal adviser to the Crown:

Royal Palace, 1 October 1955

My dear Prime Minister,

Your protracted illness has unhappily deprived me for some months now of the possibility of personal collaboration with you, which is not only necessary but is also prescribed by the constitution, according to which you are my principal adviser.

This lack has been more evident for some time in view of the prevailing difficult conditions, in the handling of which I have not had the benefit of the views and counsels of my Prime Minister, which are indispensable to me. I now feel that this situation should not be allowed to continue.

The government of which you are the head enjoys the confidence of parliament, being the outcome of the will of the majority of the people; it is therefore my wish that any solution envisaged should be within the framework of the present government, while at the same time rendering it possible for me to collaborate personally and constantly with the Head of Government.

The members of your administration have been and continue to be my devoted advisers, as you also, Mr Prime Minister, have been my invaluable counsellor. I deeply regret that your continuing illness prevents my actual contact with yourself who as Prime Minister not only coordinate the various sectors of the civil and political life of the country and the State machinery, but are also the person regarded as my particular adviser. Thus one of the most fundamental bases on which the exercise of the Royal Authority rests, the Premier's function of responsibility, is lacking, to the detriment of the wider interests of the country.

In these circumstances I feel obliged to ask you to advise me, in writing since it cannot be done otherwise, as to how you envisage the solution of the problem.

The country is passing through difficult times, and it is my desire that both you, as leader of the majority party, and the other political elements of the country should afford me your assistance in dealing with them.

I avail myself of this opportunity, Mr Prime Minister, to express to you my boundless esteem and gratitude for the invaluable services you have rendered at various times both to the country and to my own person, and to assure you that these will always remain alive and unalterable.

To this letter, which was typewritten, Paul added a final sentence in his own hand:

I pray to Almighty God for the speedy and complete recovery of your health.

PAUL R.

The meaning and purpose of the King's letter were perfectly clear: if the Field-Marshal could no longer discharge his functions as Prime Minister, he should make room for someone else.

But if Papagos's illness was disrupting the machinery of government, it was still preferable – in the estimation of influential elements in the Greek Rally – to his resignation and all the consequent upheavals. The Greek Rally was not a party but a conglomeration of political groups which had found it politically expedient to collaborate at the elections under the Field-Marshal's banner. Their sole common factor was their readiness to accept Papagos as their leader; with the cohesive force of the Field-Marshal's prestigious name removed, there would be nothing to prevent the disintegration of the Rally into its numerous constituent parts.

The view of these elements evidently prevailed: in the reply which Paul received two days later Papagos agreed that his prolonged illness prevented him from discharging his duties properly and promised to nominate a deputy soon. 'I have spent my life in the service of the country and of your Royal House,' concluded the Field-Marshal, 'and I pray that the Almighty will give me strength to resume my collaboration with Your Majesty.'

This was not at all what the King had expected, and he immediately wrote a second letter to Papagos:

Royal Palace, 3 October 1955

My dear Prime Minister,

I have received your letter of today in reply to mine of the 1st instant, for which I thank you.

The solution which you recommend as my constitutional adviser does not fully respond to the contents of my letter. Your substitution in the exercise of your duties and functions as Premier by a member of your government does not remove the irregularity in the exercise of my own duties to which my letter referred.

It is only natural that your substitute should feel constrained to keep you constantly informed and to seek your guidance on the grave matters affecting the country, and as a result the person exercising the duties of

277

Prime Minister will lack the necessary sense of prime-ministerial responsibility. At the same time, I also will continue to be unable to collaborate personally and constantly with the Head of my Government. Finally, you also will be deprived of the necessary peace and quiet so necessary for the restoration of your health, which is so valuable to the nation.

Nevertheless, I accept as a temporary expedient the solution which you have responsibly proposed after weighing all the factors involved, in view of the fact that these recommendations come from my responsible adviser and the leader of the majority party in parliament.

The temporary expedient proved to be very temporary indeed, for a few hours after the letter was sent Papagos was dead: at 11.30 p.m. on Tuesday, 4 October 1955, the Field-Marshal succumbed from an internal haemorrhage. As soon as they heard the news, Paul and Frederica drove to the Field-Marshal's house at Ekali at 2.15 a.m. on Wednesday morning to offer their condolences to his widow and family.

Earlier in the evening and some two hours before the Prime Minister's death, Athens Radio broadcast a report that Papagos had nominated Stephanopoulos as his substitute for the duration of his incapacitation. Kanellopoulos, the other Deputy Premier, took great offence on hearing this news of which he had been told nothing before. Evidently considering that Papagos's decision had been obtained when the dying man could not be considered fully responsible for his actions, he immediately resigned from the Government, taking with him those members of it who acknowledged him as their leader.

The demise of the Prime Minister automatically entails the demise of the Government. On the afternoon of 5 October Stephanopoulos and Kanellopoulos requested an audience of the King and formally submitted the resignation of the Government.

The problem of finding a suitable successor to Papagos had been occupying Paul's mind ever since it had become obvious that the Field-Marshal did not have long to live. It might normally have been supposed that the King's choice would have rested on one of the two Deputy Premiers, but Paul had already decided against such a course. Both Stephanopoulos and Kanellopoulos had their own following in the Cabinet and among the rank and file of the Greek Rally, but neither of them could hope to command the undisputed loyalty and authority which the Field-Marshal had enjoyed in his prime as leader of the Rally. To appoint one of them would automatically alienate the other, as indeed Kanellopoulos's reaction to Papagos's nomination of Stephanopoulos had already proved. On the other hand, the Greek Rally was still indisputably the majority party in Parliament, and whoever was selected as the next Head of Government would have to be acceptable to it.

For some time now a new name had been making itself heard in Greek politics: Constantine Karamanlis, a Macedonian lawyer, who at the time of Papagos's death was Minister of Public Works in the Government. He had entered politics in 1935, when he was elected Populist Party Deputy for his native town of Serres, which he continued to represent uninterruptedly at all subsequent elections. He had left the Populist Party in 1951 to join the Greek Rally, and had held office in various administrations as Minister of Labour, Transport and Social Security, culminating in his appointment to the Ministry of Communications and Public Works in the Papagos Government in which he was rapidly making a name for himself as an incorruptible politician of great drive and imagination. In his periodic working sessions with the King he had impressed Paul by his obvious talents and his conscientious application to the tasks of his Department, especially the planning and implementation of an ambitious programme of road-works which the country badly needed but had somehow never managed to acquire, due largely to conflicting local interests and rival claims for priority. Paul had also made it his business to inform himself on the standing of Karamanlis within the Greek Rally and his reputation in the country at large; the reports he had received had been uniformly favourable.

At 8.30 p.m. on 5 October 1955 the King summoned Constantine Karamanlis to the Palace and entrusted him with the mandate to form a Government. The new Cabinet, which was sworn in the following day, was drawn entirely from the Greek Rally and included nine of the outgoing Ministers, though both Stephanopoulos and Kanellopoulos were dropped. On 12 October Karamanlis duly appeared before Parliament and obtained the mandatory vote of confidence by a majority of 200 votes to 77 after announcing that new elections would be held in six months' time.*

---

* King Paul's selection of Karamanlis has been questioned on the grounds that the new Premier was not at the time the chosen and accepted leader of the majority party, whereas both Stephanopoulos and Kanellopoulos as Deputy Premiers could at least be regarded as having a prior claim. It is indisputably the King's constitutional right,

After that the situation developed swiftly. In December the Chamber approved a new electoral law abolishing the former method of election by simple majority which had ensured Papagos's landslide victory in 1952, and replacing it by a mixed system combining the majority vote and the proportional systems in the smaller constituencies, with straightforward proportional representation in constituencies with over ten seats. On 4 January 1956 Karamanlis announced the formation of the National Radical Union (E.R.E.) as the successor to the Greek Rally, which he maintained could not survive its founder in its original form, and most of whose members now flocked to the new leader. On 10 January Parliament was dissolved and on 19 February general elections were held.

The election was contested by two main political groups: the newly-formed E.R.E. under Karamanlis, and a conglomeration of parties ranging from the right-wing Populists to the pro-Communist E.D.A., collaborating as the 'Democratic Union' under the nominal leadership of Mr George Papandreou in order to benefit from the provisions of the new electoral law, which strongly favoured large parties and was indeed designed to promote a two-party system of government on the western model.

Though E.R.E. secured only some forty-five per cent of the vote as against nearly fifty per cent by the 'Democratic Union', the vagaries of the new electoral system gave Karamanlis 165 out of the 300 seats in the new Chamber. The King entrusted the mandate to him and on 26 February the new Government was sworn in.

On the domestic front prospects were set fair. Collaboration between the King and his new Prime Minister were smooth and harmonious, and though the combined opposition was becoming daily more vociferous in its attacks in Parliament, it was too divided within itself to offer any serious impediment to the Government's programmes and policies.

---

however, to nominate any person he chooses for the premiership, provided the appointment is confirmed, as it was in this instance, by a vote of confidence in Parliament. In this connexion it is interesting to note that a similar situation in England was dealt with in an identical manner. When Mr Harold Macmillan resigned as Prime Minister on 19 October 1963 because of ill-health, Mr R. A. Butler, the Deputy Premier, was generally expected to succeed him. In the event, however, the premiership went to the Earl of Home, who was not elected leader of the Conservative Party until 11 November, three weeks after his appointment as Prime Minister and after he had renounced his Earldom and successfully contested a by-election so that he could enter Parliament.

⇒ 33 ⇐

By this time dramatic developments were taking place in the Cyprus
dispute. Shortly after the disastrous London Conference in
September 1955 Field-Marshal Sir John Harding, Chief of the
Imperial General Staff, was appointed Governor of Cyprus. He
arrived in Nicosia on 3 October, and during the next few days had
repeated and lengthy consultations with Archbishop Makarios, who
remained adamant on the fundamental issue that the right of self-
determination was an indispensable basis for any settlement of the
Cyprus problem: after the recognition of that principle, and only
then, was he prepared to cooperate with the British authorities.
The British were equally unyielding on their position as defined by
Macmillan at the tripartite conference. The new Governor's talks
with the Archbishop were eventually suspended with an agreed
announcement that the two parties 'had stated their separate views
without being able to reach agreement'. EOKA now stepped up its
activities, and on 27 November 1955 the Governor proclaimed a
state of emergency throughout Cyprus, making the carrying of arms
and ammunition an offence punishable by death. At the same time
the 10,000 British troops on the island were placed on a war footing,
their numbers being augmented by further reinforcements from
Britain.

After visiting Athens for discussions with the new Greek Premier
Karamanlis and other Greek leaders, Archbishop Makarios returned
to Cyprus and resumed his contacts with the Governor. On
26 February 1956 the British Colonial Secretary, Mr Alan Lennox-
Boyd, also arrived in Cyprus and joined in the discussions, but the
differences could still not be bridged, and on 5 March the talks were
broken off again, Archbishop Makarios issuing a statement calling
on the Cypriots to 'continue the struggle for self-determination
until the British Government shows respect for our national

aspirations'. Faced with this deadlock, the British took drastic action: on 9 March 1956 Makarios was arrested at Nicosia airport as he was about to board a plane for Athens and deported to the remote Seychelle Islands in the Indian Ocean.

Reaction in Greece was swift and violent. Anti-British demonstrations broke out throughout the country, the Greek Ambassador in London was recalled and the British Institute in Athens was closed. For their part the British authorities intensified military operations against EOKA and began jamming Athens Radio broadcasts. On 13 March the Greek Government formally asked for the Cyprus question to be placed once more on the Agenda of the next session of the General Assembly of the United Nations.

Opinion in Britain, too, was divided on the deportation of Makarios: both the Leader of the Opposition, Mr Hugh Gaitskell, and the Leader of the Liberal Party, Mr Clement Davies, were highly critical of this action and condemned it as 'an act of folly' and 'an act of madness'. The U.S. Government also expressed its strong disapproval.

As for the Greek Government, Prime Minister Karamanlis denounced the deportation as 'an unprecedented and despicable act', and declared that Greece would continue to give unconditional support to the Archbishop. The Greek parliamentary opposition was even more violent in its attitude, accusing the Greek Government of not taking a sufficiently strong line – a charge which the Foreign Minister, Spyro Theotokis, took so much to heart that he resigned, being replaced by Mr Evangelos Averoff.

It was at this critical and highly delicate juncture that the British Premier, Anthony Eden, saw fit in a speech at Norwich, on 1 June to refer to Cyprus in terms to which the Greeks could not fail to take grave offence.

The United Kingdom's vital interest in Cyprus is not confined to its NATO aspect. Our country's industrial life and that of Western Europe depends today, and must depend for many years to come, on oil supplies from the Middle East. If ever our oil resources were in peril, we should be compelled to defend them. The facilities we need in Cyprus are part of that defence. We cannot, therefore, accept any doubt about their availability. . . . No Cyprus, no certain facilities to protect our supply of oil. No oil, unemployment and hunger in Britain. It is as simple as that.

It may have been very simple to Mr Eden, but what the Greeks read in his remarks was that British interests of a crude mercenary nature were preventing a proud people from achieving their independence. 'The whole civilized world,' proclaimed Mr Karamanlis, 'will refuse to accept that oil interests – which are in no way threatened by Greece anyhow – can prevail over moral principles, liberty and justice.'

In the midst of this highly charged atmosphere the King could scarcely remain passive. In his Speech from the Throne at the ceremonial opening of the new Parliament on 2 April, Paul declared that the entire Greek people and the Orthodox Church were united as one single soul in their support of the Cypriot demand for self-determination and would pursue with unswerving will their efforts for the satisfaction of the Cypriot national struggle. At the same time he deplored the deterioration in Anglo-Greek relations, and declared that 'Greece is deeply grieved by events which have disturbed her friendly feelings towards a people with whom she had been linked by bonds of traditional friendship'.

In the summer of 1956 Paul and Frederica paid two State visits abroad – to France on 5–7 June and to Western Germany on 17–21 September. In between they were host to Marshal Tito and his wife.

After Tito proposed an unofficial visit to Greece, Paul and Frederica had set about trying to devise some way of satisfying the Yugoslav leader's desire for privacy and informality that would at the same time allow for the necessary security measures. Athens was much too hot in July, which ruled out Tatoi. As for Petali, where the Royal Family usually spent their informal leisure time, the accommodation there consisted of one ramshackle bungalow just large enough for Paul and Frederica on their own; in any case, the owner of the little island had intimated some time ago that he now wanted it for his own use, so for the last two years Paul and Frederica had spent the summer in Corfu instead.

When the Ionian Islands were ceded to Greece in 1864 as a good-will gesture by Britain on the elevation of King George I to the Greek throne, Queen Victoria had also made a personal gift to the young King of the Hellenes of the villa of Mon Repos on the Island of Corfu. This elegant little Regency house, which was originally built for his Greek-born wife in 1828 by a former British Governor of the Ionian Islands, Sir Frederick Adam, stands in its own grounds on a small promontory just outside the town of Corfu commanding a magnificent view over the sea and surrounded by an almost tropical luxuriance of trees and flowers which thrive in the temperate humidity of the climate. King George I had left Mon Repos in his will to his youngest son Prince Andrew – father of Prince Philip, Duke of Edinburgh, who was actually born there – from whom King George II had bought it in 1937. It had been requisitioned by the Italians during the occupation, and had later been used to accommodate refugees; though the building itself had suffered little damage other than the ravages of neglect, all the furniture had disappeared.

Just about the time that Paul and Frederica seriously began to think about making Mon Repos habitable as an alternative to Petali, the British-owned Lake Copais Company was expropriated following a generous compensation agreement with the Greek Government. The company's property in Central Greece included a manager's residence consisting of a house situated in four acres of attractively landscaped grounds, and as a farewell gesture the company made a gift of this house to King Paul for use as a shooting lodge. The King had never had occasion to use the house, which remained in his possession as something of a white elephant; it now transpired that the Government could make good use of it for the administration of the newly-expropriated property. An amicable arrangement was finally reached whereby the State took over the Copais house and its grounds, and in exchange Mon Repos was re-decorated and a small guest-house consisting of two bedrooms and a sitting-room, with bathroom and kitchen, was built among the trees behind the villa itself.

Life at Mon Repos settled into a pattern of informality that became an established way of life for the two summer months that the Royal Family now spent there each year. Paul would get up at sunrise and do some gardening. At first he had only the gardener to help him, but the grounds were in such a bad state that he soon realized more hands were needed. The gardener recruited a couple of local lads who were interested in gardening; they told their friends about their early morning work at 'the King's house up on the hill', and very soon there were nine more volunteers, in addition to three sons of members of the staff at Mon Repos. Paul named the little group 'the King's Own Volunteer Regiment' and appointed himself their colonel. The boys would muster every morning in the garden where the King would join them punctually at seven o'clock.

They would all have a glass of milk, and after an hour or so weeding the garden, pruning the trees, cutting flowers for the house and looking after the grounds generally, the boys would be taken to the kitchen for a good breakfast before going home. After shaving and taking his bath Paul would have his own breakfast: coffee, an egg and toast with honey; meanwhile, the rest of the family would have come down and they would all go to the beach for their morning swim. They would stay there for an hour or an hour and a half, swimming or lying in the sun, after which Paul would have a gin and tonic and smoke his first cigarette. Smoking was a vice in which he had indulged heavily from his early youth, using a plain cigarette holder to keep the smoke away from his over-sensitive eyes. Frederica had also been a fairly heavy smoker but gave it up soon after she married. She tried hard to persuade Paul to do the same, but without success. 'Who is stronger, you or that piece of dried cabbage?' she said to him in exasperation on one occasion after another unsuccessful attempt. He took the cigarette holder out of his mouth, carefully inserted a fresh cigarette, lit it, puffed luxuriously at it, and then replied very deliberately: 'That piece of dried cabbage is stronger, and you had better get used to the idea.' She had never raised the matter again.

After their swim they would return to the house, where they would each go about their various occupations until it was time for lunch, to be followed by a rest and a nap. Later in the afternoon they would usually go for a drive, Paul at the steering wheel of his open jeep with Frederica by his side and the children sitting behind. They would drive out to various places on the island – to Pelekas, where the whole of Corfu can be seen from the iron belvedere built there by the Kaiser, or to Palaiocastritsa to the north-west, where they would sit for a drink in the local café. At sunset they would return to Mon Repos for dinner, after which they would see a film on the improvised open-air cinema on the roof at the back of the house or listen to music, which now played a very important part in Paul's life.

He had always loved the piano – while living in exile with his sisters in Florence he had taken lessons regularly – but it was not until the war that his interest had really been aroused, through his acquaintance in Alexandria with Gina Bachauer, then a little-known artist driven from her home in Greece by the occupation and giving recitals and concerts in aid of various Greek charities. She would play regularly for Paul and his family at their house and Paul would often join her at the piano. 'I can think of no greater happiness than to be able to play a concerto by Beethoven or Bach or Rachmaninov,' he once said to her; 'that really would be the greatest day of my life.' He never achieved this dream, but constant practice and lessons from Gina Bachauer whenever she was in Greece improved his proficiency to a degree that he could play Bach and Chopin preludes and Beethoven sonatas with almost professional skill. After dinner at Tatoi or at Mon Repos in Corfu in the summer, whenever Gina was present, the whole family would gather to hear her play, Paul moving his armchair close to the piano. Occasionally Gina would play a concerto – Rachmaninov or Tchaikovsky or Grieg – with Paul 'singing' the orchestral parts in his deep bass voice. The evenings would usually finish on a gay note with Gina playing Viennese waltzes and Paul and Frederica dancing and the children singing.

It was to this happy family atmosphere that Tito and his wife came as Paul and Frederica's personal guests on 24 July 1956, staying for five days in the recently completed little guest-house behind the villa at Mon Repos. Tito much enjoyed this vacation in Corfu, where he was able to relax as he seldom could in his own country, and in his turn invited Paul and Frederica to his private retreat on the island of Brioni. They went the very next summer. The emphasis again was on informality, though this was variously interpreted. On one occasion Tito arranged to take his royal guests on a trip in his motor-boat and warned them to wear informal clothes. With his lackadaisical Corfu habits in mind, Paul put on a khaki pair of shorts and nothing else, carrying a T-shirt over his arm; Tito appeared immaculately dressed in white duck, with collar and tie, and a hat. After a moment of embarrassed silence Tito gave a roar of laughter and started peeling off his clothes; everybody relaxed again with the two men both stripped to the waist.

The cordial relationship established between Paul and Tito on a personal basis was followed up by friendly contacts at government level also, and on 4 December 1956 the Prime Minister Karamanlis and the Foreign Minister Evangelos Averoff visited Belgrade for talks with the Yugoslav leaders. The Tripartitie Balkan Pact may have become dormant as a result of the widening gulf between Greece and Turkey over Cyprus, but cooperation between Greece and Yugoslavia was going from strength to strength, and the Yugoslavs made no secret where their sympathies lay on the Cyprus question. 'The Yugoslav Government,' said the communiqué issued at the end of the Graeco-Yugoslav talks in Belgrade on 7 December 1956, 'basing its views on the principle of the right of peoples to self-determination, expresses sincere sympathy with the population of Cyprus, as well as its readiness to lend moral and political support to all constructive efforts aimed at a just settlement of this question.'

On the domestic scene, however, party strife was becoming increasingly bitter, the frustrations of the Cyprus problem providing ready ammunition for opposition attacks on the Government. On 18 May 1956 George Papandreou and Sophocles Venizelos wrote a joint letter to the King warning him of 'the risks to which the country was being exposed' as a result of the Government's policies, and charging Karamanlis with lack of vigour in the prosecution of the national cause of Enosis; the Government, they claimed, had lost the confidence of the people and lacked the necessary authority to deal with the issues confronting the nation. 'We consider it our sacred duty,' concluded the two opposition leaders, 'to submit to Your Majesty as Head of State the thoughts and anxieties induced by the present situation, preferring that they should be brought to Your Majesty's attention now rather than that our fears should be proved right by History tomorrow.'

All this was of course part and parcel of the time-honoured Greek political tradition of opposing the Government in office on every point and on all fronts; one such controversy, however, which developed into a major cause of friction related to an issue affecting the King personally.

The King's Civil List, which is voted annually by Parliament, had by common consent become inadequate to meet the needs of the Crown. Out of this annual allowance all expenses of the Royal Household had to be met, and these included the salaries of Court officials; wages, food and clothing of all domestic staff; all travelling expenses of the Royal Family; maintenance and running costs of all the royal residences; entertaining; purchase and maintenance of cars, etc.

The Greek Crown has no private means. Only the Villa Mon Repos in Corfu is the absolute property of the King; Tatoi, which automatically becomes the property of each reigning monarch by right of succession, is entailed and cannot be disposed of partially or in whole. The Royal Palace in Athens and other official residences in Thessaloniki and elsewhere are the property of the State.

The approval of the Civil List is normally a non-party matter, the Government and the opposition usually agreeing on the details in advance to ensure a non-controversial vote. In this instance, however, the customary prior understanding had not materialized, and already before the question was raised in the Chamber the Civil List and the King's finances generally had become the subject of heated public discussion, spreading to other aspects of the matter, such as whether senior officials of the Royal Household should also be allowed to hold remunerative positions in private industry. Despite this lack of prior agreement the Government decided to ask Parliament to approve an increase in the Civil List from 635,000 to 960,000 drachmas per month, but after a heated debate the opposition walked out of the Chamber just before the vote was taken, leaving the measure to be approved by the votes of the Government's supporters alone.

This was the first time such an issue had arisen during his reign, and Paul found himself in a dilemma. There was no doubt at all that the Royal Household could not make both ends meet. At the same time he was resolved that there should always be unanimity among the elected representatives of the people, irrespective of party, in matters relating to the basic non-political aspects of the monarchy. To ignore the Government's majority vote on the subject, however, would imply disagreement between the Sovereign and his Government, which would automatically entail the resignation of the latter.

After carefully considering the matter, he decided to compromise. He signed the Legislative Decree providing for an increase in the Civil List. At the same time he wrote to the Prime Minister pointing out that the Civil List was voted by Parliament not so much for the King's personal comfort but for the dignified appearance of the constitutional Head of State. As this was linked with the obligations of the Sovereign both at home and abroad, he would wish that the procedural formalities should be observed without unseemly disputation: this had clearly not been the case in the present instance and for this reason he had decided to forgo the increase, which should therefore not be inscribed in the Budget. As, however, it was impossible to meet the expenses of the Royal Household out of the existing Civil List, he had decided to institute fundamental changes in Court so as to restrict expenditure to a minimum.

With regard to the question whether individuals in honorary

positions in Court should be allowed to hold directorships or other positions for which they received remuneration, the King pointed out that this had been the custom for many years now with the full knowledge and acquiescence of all post-war governments. If the Government was now laying down the principle that the two were incompatible, the individuals concerned would of course immediately conform.

The action which Paul took to cut down expenses was swift and drastic: he closed down the Palace in Athens. He had never really regarded the building in Herod Atticus Street as anything other than an official residence for use on formal occasions, and had always preferred Tatoi as a home. The cost of maintaining the Palace accounted for a substantial portion of the Civil List which in the circumstances he felt he could ill afford. Henceforth consultations with his Ministers took place at Tatoi – a forty-five-minutes' drive from Athens – and official entertaining on a modest scale was also done at Tatoi. As for the big reception on New Year's Day, the main event of the year held annually in the Throne Room at the Palace with something like one thousand dignitaries filing past the King to offer their respects, in the year 1957 the reception did not take place at all: it could only be held in the Palace, and the Palace was closed.

This state of affairs continued for six months until on 31 March 1957 the Prime Minister wrote to the King informing him that the Government and the opposition were no longer in conflict concerning the Civil List and requesting the Sovereign to accept the increased amount already approved by Parliament, which he did.

➡ 34 ⬅

Throughout this period Paul and Frederica made a point of finding time uninterruptedly to continue their programme – now established by practice as a characteristic and essential feature of their reign – of regularly touring various parts of the country. In addition to annual visits linked with local events, like the liberation of Janina on 21 February, the liberation of Thessaloniki on 26 October and the feast of St Andrew, patron saint of Patras, on 30 November, there were also tours for Paul to inspect provincial garrisons and frontier posts, and for Frederica to inaugurate welfare projects or to inspect Paidoupolis and other institutions within the all-embracing sphere of activity of the Royal Welfare Fund.* Though emotionally highly satisfying, these tours were arduous and exhausting: on one of them lasting six weeks in June–July 1955 in northern Greece Frederica visited 118 children's homes, over and above numerous other engagements in between. Any local disaster, such as the Volos earthquake on 21 April 1955 which made nearly 100,000 people homeless, and the earthquake in Santorini on 9 July 1956 which destroyed or rendered unusable more than half the houses on the island, would also bring Paul or Frederica or both on the scene in a matter of hours.

On the subject of Cyprus there was little or no progress. On 12 July 1956 the British Government appointed Lord Radcliffe, an eminent jurist, as 'constitutional Commissioner for Cyprus' with the task of formulating recommendations for a new constitution, but as Lord Radcliffe's terms of reference specifically excluded self-determination, his efforts were doomed to failure and when the 'Radcliffe constitution' was published on 19 December 1956 it was promptly rejected by the Greek Government.

* In 1956 and 1957 alone there were seventeen such tours to various parts of the country.

At the United Nations the question of Cyprus again came up for discussion, Greece having submitted another appeal to the General Assembly. Greece's recourse had been countered by a British complaint on the same subject, and on 14 November 1956 the General Assembly decided to combine the two complaints as one item on the Agenda:

Question of Cyprus: (a) Application, under the auspices of the United Nations, of the principle of equal rights and self-determination of peoples in the case of the population of the Island of Cyprus; (b) Complaint by the United Kingdom of support from Greece for terrorism in Cyprus.

In the end and after lengthy debate, the General Assembly approved a compromise resolution on 26 February 1957 stating that any settlement of the Cyprus problem required an atmosphere of peace and freedom of expression, and re-affirming 'the earnest desire that a peaceful, democratic and just solution will be found in accordance with the purposes and principles of the U.N. Charter, and the hope that negotiations will be resumed and continued to this end'.

Shortly afterwards the Secretary-General of NATO, Lord Ismay, sent letters to all three Governments involved offering his good offices for conciliation, but the offer was rejected by the Greek Government on the grounds that no binding decisions could be reached in the absence of the Cypriot people themselves. The Greek reply also insisted that the release of Archbishop Makarios was an essential pre-requisite for any constructive negotiations on Cyprus.

Meanwhile, on the British side Mr Harold Macmillan had succeeded Sir Anthony Eden as Prime Minister. With the growing threat that the Cyprus dispute might bring about a collapse of defence arrangements in the south-eastern flank of the NATO security system, and with Eden's inhibiting influence removed from the scene, the new British Government at last embarked on a more conciliatory and realistic policy: on 28 March Archbishop Makarios was released.

Shortly before this development Mr Macmillan met President Eisenhower in Bermuda. On his return to London the British Premier denied allegations that some sort of compromise arrangement involving the Archbishop's release had been made at the Bermuda Conference, though his denial was somewhat equivocal: the strategic importance of Cyprus had indeed been discussed, he admitted, but neither he nor the President had made any reference to 'a decision which must rest wholly within the responsibility of the British Government and of no one else'.

The point is a fine one. The fact remains that, with the Government's willing agreement, King Paul had written to President Eisenhower shortly before the Bermuda conference asking for his support:

10 March 1957

Dear President Eisenhower,

Now that Mr Macmillan's visit to the United States is imminent, I would ask you to be so kind as to discuss with him the solution of the Cyprus problem.

The recent unanimous resolution of the United Nations proposed negotiations between the parties concerned.

The only personality who could negotiate with the British on behalf of the Cyprus people is Archbishop Makarios of Cyprus, who is exiled in the Seychelles Islands in the Indian Ocean. His release would be a definite step towards a possible solution of this thorny situation.

No matter what outsiders may say, Makarios is the elected spiritual head of the population of Cyprus. Any decision that he would take, I am sure, the Cypriot people will support.

According to the Greek mentality, there is no other personality or authority that could be found in Cyprus or Greece, under present circumstances, to take any decision that would be accepted by all concerned.

In ending this letter, Mr President, I want to express to you my people's and my own admiration for your courageous contribution to the peace and tranquillity in this part of the world.

My wife joins me in sending you and Mrs Eisenhower our best wishes.

PAUL R.

The release of Archbishop Makarios was welcomed in Athens as a positive step towards a settlement of the Cyprus problem. The Prime Minister, Mr Karamanlis, expressed the hope that the Cypriot leader's release was 'an indication of the British Government's desire to seek a peaceful and just solution which would lead to the restoration of the old friendship between our two nations'; and the Greek Ambassador to London, who had been recalled in protest against the Archbishop's arrest, now returned to his post.

Soon after his arrival in Athens, the Archbishop himself addressed a letter to the British Prime Minister in which 'as the spiritual and elected national leader of the Greek people of Cyprus' he reaffirmed his willingness to take part in bilateral talks (with Britain) 'on a basis of the application of self-determination in accordance with the United Nations Charter'. Mr Macmillan's reply, after expressing the British Government's readiness 'to consider the views of any individuals or communities in Cyprus, including the Archbishop, on the proposals for self-government' repeated that Britain's position on the question of self-determination remained unchanged.

Greece once again raised the question of Cyprus at the 12th session of the United Nations General Assembly, but a resolution expressing the 'earnest hope that further negotiations and discussions will be undertaken with a view to having the right of self-determination applied in the case of the people of Cyprus', though adopted by 30 votes to 20 in the Political Committee, failed to secure the mandatory two-thirds majority in the General Assembly required to make it an authoritative recommendation. The only ray of hope was the replacement of Field-Marshal Harding as Governor of Cyprus by the more liberal-minded Sir Hugh Foot, who arrived in Nicosia on 3 December 1957 with the mission of drawing up a plan for an interim period of self-government leading to a possible change of status.

Part Six

1957-1964

⇒ 35 ⇐

Paul had now been ten years on the throne. His reign had begun inauspiciously with the country in the throes of the 'bandit war', and had passed through a difficult period of transition from internal conflict to peace and rehabilitation. During this time he had had to deal with a variety of crises, always seeking to reconcile opposing viewpoints, intervening whenever circumstances made it necessary but confining his initiatives within the generally accepted area of his constitutional authority. Unlike his brother George, who had suffered frustration and disillusionment all his life because people did not live up to his high expectations of them, Paul had learned to accept people for what they were and to try instead to bring out what was best in them, recognizing that they all, each in his own different way, were no less concerned for the interests of the country than he was and were therefore equally entitled to his consideration and respect. It was this approach that had made possible a harmonious and fruitful collaboration with individuals as varied as Sophoulis, Plastiras, Ventiris, Papagos and Karamanlis. It was this tolerance and sympathetic understanding, this acceptance of the other person's philosophy as equally valid and sincerely held though sometimes diametrically opposed to one's own, that made it possible for a man of his background and character to achieve a genuine personal friendship with someone like Tito, who was the complete antithesis to himself in every respect except in his devotion to the interests of his people.

Ideas and attitudes of which Paul had hitherto been conscious only in a nebulous way had gradually formulated into more definite shape, moulded and strengthened by the weight of experience gained in the exercise of the duties of his position. His family history and his upbringing, his experience of the problems of life at first-hand as an exile, his war-time activities, all combined to instil in him an earnest and imaginative approach in the interpretation of his functions as monarch.

Kingship, as he understood it and tried to practise it, was the outer manifestation of a whole inner process. The King had to learn to sanctify within his own soul the trust and devotion of his people. He should be the ever-present mirror of all that was best in others, and should therefore seek always to improve his own character and learn to reach out to God with his soul, thus raising not only himself but his people also to a spiritually higher level. The people themselves might be oblivious of this process, but he himself should never cease to be aware of it. So long as he was conscious of this mission he would be immune to flattery or reproach, he would accept both success and failure with equanimity: the plaudits of the people were simply a recognition of his efforts on their behalf, a tribute from the best in them to the best in him. Kingship was a sacred mission that had to be expressed at all levels, because fundamentally it was the task of all human beings to learn to express God and to seek Him in others. Being born to the Crown simply made him personally more conscious of this mission.

These principles underlying his conception of the role he was called upon to play in life would frequently find expression in private conversation with people close to him; occasionally a hint of these inner thoughts would appear in his public speeches, especially if the occasion were propitious as in the case of his orations to the Universities of Athens and Thessaloniki.

Early in 1958 a split occurred in the E.R.E. (Government) Party: a group of its supporters, including prominent ministers like Panayotis Papaligouras and George Rallis, found themselves in disagreement with the basic provisions of their party's new electoral law which provided for a 'reinforced' system of proportional representation favouring the two major parties – the E.R.E. under Constantine Karamanlis and the Liberal Party, now reunited under the joint leadership of George Papandreou and Sophocles Venizelos – by awarding them a premium of seats if they polled over twenty-five per cent of the total national vote. The dissidents felt so strongly in this matter that on 2 March 1958 the two ministers resigned, and together with thirteen other deputies withdrew their support from the Government. Thus deprived of its parliamentary majority the Government had no choice but to resign, and Karamanlis advised the King to dissolve Parliament and proclaim general elections as soon as possible.

After the usual consultations with the political leaders the King appointed on 5 March a non-party caretaker administration under Mr Constantine Georgacopoulos, the President of the Greek Red Cross, and Parliament was dissolved on 2 April after it had passed the new electoral law by the mandatory two-thirds majority. General elections on the new system were held on 11 May, the outcome being once again a victory for E.R.E. which was returned to power by an even larger majority, with 173 out of the 300 seats and 41 per cent of the total votes cast. Thanks to the new electoral system none of the other parties qualified for bonus seats, having failed to secure the requisite minimum of 25 per cent. A further surprise was that in the new Chamber the extreme left-wing E.D.A. with 78 seats (24·3 per cent of the votes) now became the leading opposition party, the Liberals having secured only 36 seats and 20·7 per cent of the vote. On 17 May 1958 another E.R.E. Government under Karamanlis was sworn in, most of its ministers being the same as in his previous Cabinet.

On 2 June 1958 Paul's only son, the Crown Prince Constantine, celebrated his eighteenth birthday and thus attained his majority, according to Article 42 of the Constitution.

A perfect relationship existed between father and son. Paul had suffered greatly from the disadvantage that while heir to the throne when his brother was King he had taken virtually no part in affairs of State. There had been affection and mutual respect between the two brothers all their lives, but King George II was by nature a man to whom the sharing of responsibility did not come easily; Paul had often felt he could have been of assistance to his lonely and over-worked brother, but King George's rigid sense of obligation to duty would not allow him to pass on to others, not even to his heir, any of the tasks which he insisted on regarding as the King's exclusive burden. The result was that when Paul had unexpectedly been called to the succession on the premature death of his brother, he had suddenly found himself in the seat of supreme authority with virtually no previous experience and with only a slight conception of the nature and magnitude of the task that confronted him; that he had made a reasonable success of it was simply evidence of his aptitude and common sense. He was determined that his own son should be spared the unnecessary disadvantages under which he himself had laboured, and he took early and effective steps to this end.

First of all, he had ensured that his son's primary and secondary education should not be private and exclusive, as had been the custom for all members of the royal family. It had begun in a small school at Psychico, where Constantine shared a class with nine local boys of his own age drawn from all walks of life, and had continued at Anavryta, the boarding school run on the system propounded at Salem and Gordonstoun by Dr Kurt Hahn, which Constantine joined in 1949. He had also done his full military service in all three branches of the services, including a tough commando course in which he had shown particular aptitude.*

One aspect of his son's education, however – his preparation for the royal duties that would one day devolve on him – King Paul undertook himself. From about 1951, when Constantine was only eleven, Paul had instituted a custom that his young son should be present in his father's audience room while the King was conducting business of State or having a working session with one of his ministers. The boy would sit quietly behind his father, listening to all that was being said but saying nothing himself. As his son grew older, the King would occasionally interrupt the audience to explain some point to him, and perhaps discuss the matter with him later in greater detail when they were alone.

The culmination of this methodical and sustained system of practical training was reached when Constantine became eighteen. He was now encouraged to comment and join in the discussion at audiences at which he was present, and would occasionally be asked by his father to deputize for him in some official duty. He would also frequently accompany his parents on their tours of the provinces.

On 28 June 1958, at a ceremony held in the Trophy Room of the Parliament building to celebrate his majority, Crown Prince Constantine was commissioned an officer, being appointed to the most junior rank in all three Services. Immediately after he had given the prescribed oath to the King as Commander-in-Chief of the Greek Armed Forces, Constantine was addressed by his father in the following words, which it had taken Paul many hours of meditation and labour and emotional effort to draft:

* King Constantine holds a Fourth Degree Black Belt in *karate*.

Constantine,

God has graciously destined you to reign over this glorious, gallant and noble nation of ours.

This Divine favour granted to you is an outstanding mark of honour and a legacy of great responsibility.

As from this day you shall be my helper in the endeavour to further the progress and well-being of my people.

I am confident that your love of the Greek people, equal as it is to my own deep affection, will bring you as much happiness as it brings to me.

In paying the price of their glorious history and in enduring the consequences of their age-long struggles, even to this day, in defence of mankind, the Greek people have not as yet been able to develop their capabilities to the full and to achieve the standard of well-being to which they are justly entitled. For this very reason they deserve every mark of affection and regard and every act of sacrifice on your part.

Be a just, kind and indefatigable worker for the advancement and glory of Greece.

Uphold steadfastly the democratic principles of our institutions and the constitutional liberties of our people.

Devote your life to the happiness of the country; there is no task more noble nor more important than this.

Remember always that it is preferable that the King should suffer than that the suffering should fall on the nation and the country.

Endeavour to show yourself worthy of the Greek Soldier, whose leader you will be in the future. When the time comes, you will take your place at the head of the Greek Armed Forces, the bearers of a heroic and glorious tradition. Keep them devoted to duty and battleworthy, the guardians of our traditions, respected by our friends and feared by our enemies, the priceless jewel of a proud nation. May they never be forced to strike.

Be the protector and guardian of our Holy Church. Draw your strength from the love between you and your people.

Redress offence by pardon,
Discord by unity,
Error by truth,
Doubt by faith.

I pray that you and my people may know days of glory in the noble struggle for progress and civilization.

May God Almighty make you an instrument of peace, and always keep guard over Greece and over you, Constantine my son.

⇒ 36 ⇐

The Cyprus crisis was building up to a climax. Tension between
Greek and Turk on the island was mounting following the formulation of a new Turkish policy as a counter to the Greek demand for
Enosis: *Taksim*, partition of Cyprus between Greece and Turkey.
The activities of EOKA now ranged over virtually the whole of the
island, with violence no longer confined to Cypriot against Briton
but spreading to Greek Cypriot against Turkish Cypriot.

On 19 June 1958 Britain announced a new plan for Cyprus.
Hopefully named 'an adventure in partnership' by the British Prime
Minister Mr Harold Macmillan, its basic provisions consisted of a
continuation of British sovereignty for seven years, the setting up of
separate Greek and Turkish Houses of Representatives during this
period, with Greek-Cypriots and Turkish-Cypriots enjoying dual
nationality, i.e. British as well as Greek or Turkish respectively,
and the promise that after seven years Britain would be prepared to
share sovereignty of the island with Greece and Turkey subject to
retention of bases and facilities. The plan was rejected by Makarios
the very next day – it ran counter to the fundamental and inalienable
right of the people of Cyprus to self-determination, he said, and the
proposed partnership in fact amounted to a triple condominium
over the island; the Cyprus question, insisted Makarios, was a matter
that concerned Britain and Cyprus alone. Minor modifications of the
plan after visits by Mr Macmillan to Athens, Ankara and Nicosia
had no effect on Makarios or the Greek Government, both of whom
still rejected the proposals as being tantamount to partition and
therefore totally unacceptable.

On 10 September 1958 Paul and Frederica paid a State visit to
Switzerland. On arrival the King made an official speech in which he
said, *inter alia*: 'I see oppression falling on Greeks who wish to be
free, who are entitled to be free, and who will become free one day,'

and also referred to 'the demand of 430,000 Greek-Cypriots for their freedom and the right of self-determination'. Statements such as these would often be interpolated into the King's speeches both at home and abroad – the Sovereign's public utterances are normally drafted by his Government, whose policy it now was to keep the Cyprus issue at the forefront of international attention at all levels.

The most elementary knowledge of the function of a constitutional monarch should have made it obvious – especially in Britain, where even the most controversial programmes of the government in power are enunciated by the Sovereign as 'my policy' at the opening of Parliament – that such statements were the voice of the Government speaking through the mouth of the King. But by this time the bitterness between Britain and Greece had reached such proportions that considerations like these were brushed aside and Paul's remarks would be seized upon by the press and presented as manifestations of King Paul's personal feelings towards Britain. 'The right-wing terrorists in Cyprus are men of the same stamp as the left-wing terrorists in Greece who tried to topple King Paul from his throne' claimed a leading article in a London newspaper. 'Common sense if not gratitude should warn him now against endorsing their actions.'[28] In an editorial entitled 'The Silent King' another London newspaper castigated Paul and Frederica for not condemning the killings. 'Is King Paul dumb?' demanded the newspaper indignantly. 'Has Queen Frederica suddenly lost her tongue? Why have they never said a single syllable of regret for the murdered, the maimed in Cyprus? . . . If they dislike what is happening in Cyprus, if they resent the justifiably tough reaction of British troops, they should know that a word from them could stop it all tomorrow. And if that word doesn't come? Clearly they must be stripped of all British honours and be told never to expect a welcome again in this country which has helped them both so much.'[29]

Items like these, filed away in newspaper offices and resuscitated in later years as and when required, were mainly responsible for gradually creating a legend that Paul and Frederica were 'anti-British'. One such report, to the effect that King Paul had requested the German authorities to exclude British officers from a reception in his honour in Hanover[30] was categorically denied at the time by all concerned as being completely untrue, yet this did not prevent the *Sunday Express* from commenting five years later: 'When visiting

West Germany, King Paul asked that Britons should be excluded from the functions, saying he would lose popularity if he was in any way associated with British uniforms.' Such comments wounded Paul to the heart. He loved Britain next only to his own country; he had spent some of the best years of his life there, his closest friends were British, his family had the most intimate ties with the British Royal Family. As a Greek he deplored the official British policy towards Cyprus and fully shared his countrymen's feelings in the matter – he made no secret of that, least of all to his British friends. But to suggest that this automatically made him anti-British was a process of thought which he failed to understand and which he rejected utterly.

At the end of August 1958 the truce called by EOKA while the Macmillan plan was being studied came to an end. The armed bands resumed their activities with increased violence, inter-communal strife reaching a scale verging on civil war. Meanwhile, the British Government announced that the Macmillan plan would be implemented anyhow, with or without Cypriot cooperation.

On 22 September 1958 a new and significant development took place: in an interview with Mrs Barbara Castle, then Vice-Chairman of the Labour Party, who was in Athens on a private visit, Arch-bishop Makarios indicated that after a fixed period of self-government Cyprus could become an independent State linked neither with Greece nor with Turkey, but guaranteed by the United Nations. This represented an important shift in the attitude of the Archbishop, whose policy hitherto had been inflexible on the demand for self-determination progressing inevitably to ultimate Enosis. An emergency meeting of the Greek Cabinet on 29 August endorsed the Archbishop's new approach, but the British Government was still unresponsive: in a letter to the Greek Premier, Mr Macmillan said that the Makarios proposal was not within the scope of the immediate problem.

On 1 October 1958, despite all opposition, the Macmillan plan was put into operation in Cyprus; Makarios's response was to exhort the Cypriots to resist any implementation of the plan. Meanwhile, Graeco-Turkish dissensions were also infiltrating NATO, where Greece now announced the withdrawal of all Greek officers and their families from the NATO South-Eastern European Headquarters in Smyrna.

21 Royal guests on the grand staircase at the Palace in Athens after the wedding of Princess Sophie with Don Juan Carlos of Spain. The group includes Queen Juliana and Prince Bernhard of the Netherlands, King Olav of Norway, Queen Ingrid of Denmark, Queen Ena of Spain, the Count and Countess of Barcelona, King Michael and Queen Anne of Roumania, Queen Helen of Roumania, Prince Rainier and Princess Grace of Monaco, The Grand Duke and Grand Duchess of Luxembourg, Marina Duchess of Kent, Princess Olga of Yugoslavia, the Duchess of Aosta and Earl Mountbatten.

22 Paul returning to harbour after a yachting expedition.

23 State opening of Parliament. King Paul reading the Speech from the Throne, with the Queen and the Crown Prince beside him. The Government benches are on the left; above the rostrum is the Diplomatic Gallery.

Domestic politics in Athens were also becoming somewhat exacerbated. After three years in power the Karamanlis administration was
beginning to show the wear and tear of the responsibilities of office;
some of the frustrations of the opposition were also being vented on
the King, whose initiative in choosing Karamanlis in the first place
as a successor to Papagos was now being assailed as a partisan action
which in its long-term consequences had favoured one particular
party. The King's subsequent support of Karamanlis – a support
which Paul invariably gave to all his Prime Ministers irrespective of
political orientation, on the principle that, so long as it enjoyed the
confidence of King and Parliament, the government in power was
entitled to the support of the Sovereign – was also resented by the
other politicians, who saw their own prospects of power diminishing
conversely in proportion to the strengthening of Karamanlis's
position.

These sentiments found expression in a letter which Venizelos
wrote to the King on 1 July 1958. The Liberal leader began by
recalling that he had been the first of the old republican guard to
accept the monarchy without reservations after the plebiscite of 1946
– an example, he emphasized, which had proved decisive in in-
fluencing others to follow suit. He had also been at the forefront of the
struggle against Communism – 'it was I who gave the order to
suppress by force the insurrection in the Greek Armed Forces in
the Middle East during the war' – and he had participated in every
post-war coalition government that had opposed foreign-inspired
Communism.

Venizelos then proceeded to castigate the Government for its
ambivalent attitude towards the Communists. The Communist
Party itself was proscribed; yet the E.D.A., which was simply the
Communist Party under another name, was allowed to function
freely, though this did not prevent the leaders of E.D.A. from being
excluded from consultations in which other party leaders
participated.

'I tell you in all sincerity,' continued Venizelos in his letter to the
King, 'that you have no right to make distinctions between one party
leader and another. E.D.A. is a recognized political organization and
its elected Deputies have given the prescribed oath of loyalty to
Your Majesty. By what logic is the Head of State making distinctions between party leaders?' The time had come, he said, for
the Communist Party to be made legal so that it could come out

in the open as in other countries. 'You will permit me to say this, me, whose hatred of Communism you are in a position to know well.'

But this was not the main reason for the letter, as the next sentence showed:

'I must admit that until the death of Field-Marshal Papagos the attitude of the Crown was impeccable – indeed, I may say that if anything the Crown showed greater sympathy towards the old republican camp.... Unfortunately things began to change after the Field-Marshal's death. Your partiality for the Karamanlis Government has poisoned the political atmosphere. I say to you once again, Your Majesty, that you acted wisely in entrusting the mandate to the man of your choice because you considered him to be the one best able to hold the right together. But what was a fatal mistake on your part was your obvious desire for Karamanlis to win the elections of 1956 and your help to this end by entrusting the conduct of the elections to him despite the objections of the other political parties. You should have been more careful, especially in view of the fact that it was thanks to your action that he had imposed himself as leader of his party instead of E.R.E. being allowed to choose their leader for themselves. Since then the international situation has deteriorated, national disasters have followed one another, yet you have still not seen fit to intervene, as you might well have done, although the country was heading for national disaster, as the recent Cyprus developments have shown.'

The letter went on to reproach the King for authorizing the elections of May 1958, from which Karamanlis had emerged greatly strengthened with E.D.A. as the next largest party. The Liberal Party, he warned, could not survive electoral laws designed to ensure the return of the party already in power – though he admitted that, through force of circumstances, he had himself voted for the electoral law of which he now complained.

'I know that your intentions are good,' he went on, 'and I am sure that you are doing all you can for the good of the country. But you must prove to us in an unmistakable manner that it is your intention – as I am sure it is – to reign without favour or distinction over all the Greeks and not only some of them.'

Venizelos concluded his letter with protestations of his loyalty and renewed assurances of his sentiments towards the person of the King. 'I have no other concern or ambition than to serve my country and the Crown, which I regard as identified with the best interests of Greece.'

On reading the letter Paul asked his old friend 'Babbi' Potamianos – who was now one of the King's Honorary Aides-de-Camp General and whom Paul often used on private and confidential missions – to see Venizelos, with whom Potamianos was also on very friendly terms, and explain to him that the letter would have to be shown to the Prime Minister. Venizelos had no objection. He repeated to Potamianos more or less what he had said in the letter, adding that a solution had to be found to the Cyprus problem. Such a solution would of necessity be onerous for Greece, since it was bound to fall short of Greece's publicly-proclaimed aspirations, and would clearly be more palatable if negotiated by a coalition government comprising all the non-Communist elements in Greek politics.

Potamianos expressed surprise at some of the expressions used in the letter, saying that the same point could have been made in less objectionable language. 'I wrote that letter as from one friend to another,' replied Venizelos. 'I am sure the King will not misunderstand.'

Karamanlis was understandably furious on being shown the letter and asked that no reply should be sent. This was contrary to the intention of the King, who fully appreciated Venizelos's motives in writing and did not wish to offend someone who was not only a distinguished political leader but also a personal friend; at the same time, he could scarcely ignore the wishes of the Prime Minister, who after all had a personal interest in the matter. It was finally agreed that the King's Private Secretary should answer in the following terms:

Royal Palace, 9 July 1958

I am commanded by The King to inform you that he has received and read your letter of the 1st instant.

His Majesty also desires me to say he has formed the impression that in the drafting of your letter insufficient consideration was given to the fact that, in all his actions during his reign, the King has always shown a scrupulous regard for the spirit and the letter of the Constitution.

⇒ 37 ⇐

The year 1959 saw the end of the Cyprus crisis, which had dominated the Greek political scene, as well as Paul's own life, for five years now. On 5 December 1958 the United Nations General Assembly, after a protracted and heated debate, unanimously adopted a resolution expressing confidence that the parties to the Cyprus dispute would continue their efforts 'to reach a peaceful, democratic and just solution in accordance with the United Nations Charter'. In the spirit of this recommendation, a series of contacts in Paris between the Greek and Turkish Foreign Ministers prepared the ground for a summit meeting held on 5 February 1959 in Zurich where the Premiers and Foreign Ministers of Greece and Turkey made a thorough reappraisal of Graeco-Turkish relations. Announcing at the end of the six-day talks that the question of Cyprus had been discussed at length in a spirit of mutual under-standing, the official communiqué said that a compromise agreement had been finally reached and proposed that a tripartite conference should be held so that Britain might also be brought into the agreement – an invitation which the British Government accepted with alacrity. Back in Athens, Mr Karamanlis said that this was the happiest day of his life, and Archbishop Makarios also welcomed the agreement as laying the foundations for the solution of the Cyprus problem.

The conference, which opened in London on 17 February, began in an atmosphere of drama and tragedy. Archbishop Makarios, the Greek-Cypriot delegation consisting of leaders of the Ethnarchy Council (the Archbishop's Advisory Council) with the mayors of the six principal towns in Cyprus, and a Turkish-Cypriot delegation, all arrived in London on 15 February in three separate flights. The Greek Premier Karamanlis and the Foreign Minister Averoff accom-

308

panied by their advisers arrived two days later. Because of poor visibility at London Airport, the Turkish Airlines Viscount bringing the Turkish Premier Adnan Menderes and his colleagues from Ankara that same evening was diverted at the last moment to Gatwick airport; approaching the runway, the aircraft suddenly went off course and crashed in a wood near by, bursting into flames. Of the twenty-five passengers only ten survived. These included Mr Menderes, who was taken to a London hospital suffering from severe shock and injuries which prevented him from participating in the subsequent discussions.

Although all went well on the first day of the conference, it became apparent the following day that difficulties had arisen in the Greek camp. Archbishop Makarios had had time to make a more careful appraisal of what had been agreed upon between the Greek and Turkish Governments at the Zurich meetings, and on mature reflexion was reluctant to commit himself irrevocably in what was clearly to be the most important decision in his whole life. Lengthy consultations with his advisers – who were themselves divided on the issue – failed to dispel his misgivings, and the combined persuasive efforts of Mr Karamanlis and Mr Averoff also proved of no avail.

In Athens the Deputy Premier Kanellopoulos,* who was keeping the Palace informed of developments in London, reported to the King on the Archbishop's reluctance to sign. It required no elaboration of the implications to bring home to the King that a breakdown of the London conference, after all the hopes that were being placed on it, would be an anti-climax which no Greek government could hope to survive, and that the elections that would follow would inevitably be fought on the Cyprus issue alone. After carefully weighing the situation Paul decided that this was an occasion on which his Government could reasonably expect some manifestation of active support on his part. He appreciated that the responsibility resting on the Archbishop's shoulders was as heavy as any man had ever had to bear; at the same time the sufferings of the Cypriot people, whom he regarded as no less Greek than the inhabitants of Greece itself, could not be prolonged indefinitely,

---

* Panayotis Kanellopoulos, who had become co-leader of the Populist Party in March 1958 and had been returned as a Deputy for that party in the elections of 11 May 1958, was appointed Deputy Prime Minister in the Karamanlis Government on 5 January 1959, a few days after formally joining the E.R.E. Party.

nor could the Cyprus problem be allowed to continue poisoning relations between Greece and her Western allies. In a personal message Paul conveyed these considerations to Archbishop Makarios in London.

Early next morning Makarios announced that 'after a night of prayer and meditation' he had decided to accept the Zurich Agreement, and in his speech at the final session of the London Conference that day he said:

Yesterday I had certain reservations. In overcoming them I have done so in a spirit of trust and good-will towards the Turkish community and its leaders. It is my firm belief that with sincere understanding and mutual confidence we can work together in a way that will leave no room for dissensions about any written provisions and guarantees. It is the spirit in the hearts of men that counts most.

The Cyprus dispute formally ended on the evening of 19 February 1959 when the Prime Ministers of Britain, Greece and Turkey initialled the agreement in the hospital room where Mr Menderes was still recovering from his air accident. The details of the agreement were announced four days later. It consisted of a number of documents comprising the following:

A Declaration to the effect that Cyprus would become an independent Republic with a Greek-Cypriot President and a Turkish-Cypriot Vice-President, and detailing the basic structure of the new State;
A Treaty of Guarantee of the Republic of Cyprus by Britain, Greece and Turkey;
A Treaty of Alliance between Britain, Greece and Turkey to defend Cyprus against any aggression;
A British Declaration that Britain would relinquish sovereignty over Cyprus to the new Republic, with the exception of two areas to be retained as British military bases;
A Declaration by all parties concerned accepting the above provisions as the agreed basis for the final settlement of the Cyprus problem;
A statement on agreed measures to implement the new arrangements for Cyprus.

On 1 March 1959 Archbishop Makarios returned in triumph to his native Cyprus after an absence of three years. A week later Colonel George Grivas, leader of EOKA, issued a statement proclaiming his full support for the London Agreement, calling on all Cypriots to rally round Archbishop Makarios, and abjuring all

political or public activities in Cyprus or Greece in the future.*
On 17 March the guerrilla leader, whose *nomme de guerre* of Digenis
had become a legend in Cyprus, arrived in Athens where he was
acclaimed as a national hero by the vast crowds lining the streets
through which the diminutive, black-moustachioed, trim little
figure in rough plain khaki pullover and beret, field-glasses slung
round his neck and holstered pistol at his belt, drove in triumphal
procession in an open car. The following day he was promoted
Lieutenant-General – the highest rank in the Greek Army – and
proclaimed 'worthy of the Nation', the highest honour which the
Vouli, the Greek Parliament, can bestow. On 19 March he was
received in private audience by King Paul who conferred on
him the Medal of Valour and the Grand Cross of the Order of
George I.

On 13 December 1959 Archbishop Makarios was elected President
of Cyprus, with Dr Kutchuk, leader of the Turkish-Cypriot community, as Vice-President; and on 16 August 1960 Cyprus was
proclaimed and internationally recognized as an independent
Republic, attaining at last the dignity of Statehood after many
centuries of alien occupation.

In 1959 Paul and Frederica paid two State visits abroad: to
Ethiopia in March and to Italy on 19 May to mark the restoration
of friendly relations between Greece and Italy after the unhappy
interlude of the war. On the conclusion of the official visit on
22 May, Paul and Frederica travelled by railway to Florence to
stay with his sisters, Queen Helen of Roumania and the Duchess
of Aosta, at the Villa Sparta. Three days later Paul inaugurated the
new Institute of Byzantine Studies in Venice, and from there the
whole family – their children had joined them in Florence –
proceeded to Zurich.

Like most of the members of his family, Paul suffered from bad
eyesight. Both his brothers were victims of the same affliction, and
all three had worn a monocle from their early youth – King George

---

* These declarations did not inhibit General Grivas from vigorous dispute with
Archbishop Makarios over some of the provisions of the London Agreement very
shortly afterwards, nor from launching a new party, the National Regeneration Movement, in Greece eighteen months later. The General's incursion into politics proved
disastrous – a few politicians rallied to him at first, but the party disintegrated shortly
before the elections of 29 October 1961, in which Grivas finally did not participate at
all.

because ordinary spectacles were not allowed in the crack Garde-regiment zu Fuss at Potsdam where he had received his military training, King Alexander because he thought a monocle looked more dashing than glasses, and King Paul because he hated being cluttered up with spectacles but had to have a lens for his very weak right eye.* With the passing of the years – he was now approaching sixty – Paul's eyesight had been steadily deteriorating. He had already taken to wearing contact lenses. Frederica, whose own eyesight was none too good, had been induced to try them on one of her visits to Munich by an assistant in a bookshop who noticed she was screwing up her eyes when she was looking at a book. He had inquired whether perhaps she was short-sighted, and when she admitted she was and did not like wearing spectacles, he told her that he also was very short-sighted but wore contact lenses. She had never seen them before, and when the shop-assistant mentioned that there was an optician a few doors away who stocked them she immediately went there and had herself fitted. It had taken her nearly two weeks to become accustomed to them, but after that there was no difficulty, and she subsequently persuaded Paul to be fitted also.

Although contact lenses were a great relief to him, Paul knew that sooner or later he would have to undergo an operation for cataract, and arrangements had been made for him to have this done immediately after the State visit to Italy. The operation was performed on 30 May 1959 by Professor Marc Amsler in his clinic in Zurich, and was completely successful. Paul left the clinic on 11 June, and returned to Athens with Frederica and the children on 20 June. With the contact lenses he now wore constantly his vision was almost perfect – 'I can see the bees on top of Hymettus,' he would reply to people who inquired after his eyesight. The rest of his life he never ceased to give thanks for not losing the gift of sight – 'Only a short time ago,' he said gratefully when inaugurating an Ophthalmological Congress in Athens on 18 April 1960, 'my eyesight was saved thanks to your science and to the sympathy that gives wings to your knowledge and healing to your patients.'

* If bad eyesight is indeed hereditary, its prevalence among members of the Greek Royal Family can probably be traced to Queen Olga, who was extremely short-sighted from a very early age. Several of her children were myopic – especially Prince Christopher and Prince Andrew, who had to wear glasses from the age of twelve. Queen Helen of Roumania suffers from cataract in its most acute form and Paul's son, King Constantine II, has worn contact lenses since the age of fifteen.

Just before the close of 1959, a ceremony of a purely dynastic
nature took place in the throne room of the Palace in Athens.

When King Otho abdicated the throne and left Greece in 1862,
he took with him the crown and other regalia which he had brought
from his native country when he had come to Greece. The
dynasty that succeeded Otho had no regalia – 'the Ionian Islands
are the only jewels I bring with me,' was the proud boast of young
King George I when someone asked him where his crown was – and
these were scarcely missed since there is no coronation ceremony in
Greece but simply a solemn proclamation and a swearing-in before
Parliament when a new King ascends the throne. Otho's regalia
had duly joined other family treasures of the House of Wittelsbach
in Munich, but in 1959 the Head of the House, Duke Albrecht of
Bavaria, intimated that he wished to present them to the Royal
House of Greece, and on 20 December 1959 the Duke's son came
to Greece and handed the Crown, the Orb and the Sword of State
to King Paul at a private ceremony in the Palace in Athens.

Accepting the regalia as Head of the reigning House of Greece,
King Paul paid handsome tribute to the unhappy Otho. During the
flush of their early years of independence the Greeks had been
highly sensitive to any foreign influence and had become irritated
and impatient with the hordes of counsellors and advisers from his
native Bavaria with whom Otho, in his anxiety to give Greece the
benefits of European expertise, had insisted on surrounding himself.
Thanks largely to the autocratic manner of many of these advisers,
with whom his name had inevitably been associated in retrospect,
Otho had not left a very happy memory behind him, but the passing
of time had made possible a more dispassionate assessment of him as
an individual on his own merits, and later generations now recognized that a deep love for Greece and a genuine desire to help his
new country had been the fundamental motivation of most of the
actions of the first King of independent Greece.

It was in this vein that Paul now spoke. Addressing Duke Albrecht's son, who had just handed the regalia to him, Paul said that the
repatriation of the emblems of King Otho of Greece provided a link
between his own family and the dawn of history of Modern Greece:

Hellenism is a spiritual expression [he said]. That is why to the title of
Philhellene which history has bestowed on your ancestor King Ludwig I
of Bavaria I wish to add the title of Hellene. His son, King Otho of
Greece, was already a Hellene before he arrived in Greece. He came here

imbued with the Hellenic spirit. It was he who laid the foundations of the Greek State.

In the same way that your compatriots gaze each day upon the public buildings which King Ludwig I erected in Munich in the classical style, so we here in Greece can also admire the handsome classical buildings with which King Otho and the Bavarian architects who came with him have enriched the City of Athens.

These royal emblems which now come into the possession of my House shall also belong to the House of Wittelsbach for all time.

From the age of six when he had first sailed a boat with his father in Alexandria, Paul's only son Constantine had been attracted by sailing. This interest had steadily grown into a deep love for that sport, for which Paul himself had always cherished an abiding passion,* and by the time Constantine was eighteen it was evident to the expert eye that the young prince had in him the qualities of that rare phenomenon, a truly classic sailor. He began to take part in major races, frequently competing against his father and mother, both of whom raced their own boats.

In 1958 Constantine was given a Lightning-class racer as a Christmas present, and he now spent most of his spare time sailing this craft, usually in the very early hours of the morning. He had found himself two sailing companions to crew for him regularly, and with steady practice the trio trained themselves into a perfectly coordinated team. A bold idea now began to germinate in Constantine's mind: to compete in the Olympic Games due to be held in Italy in the summer of 1960. The Greek Navy had recently presented him with a Danish-built Dragon racing yacht which the Prince found ideally suited to him, and any hesitations he may have entertained now disappeared: he decided to enter for the Olympics in that class.

A period of intensive training now began, with Paul and Frederica – who had in the meantime themselves acquired Dragons – frequently pacing their son on his practice runs in Phaleron Bay. In due course the Crown Prince and his team left for Naples, where the sailing Olympics were to be held, and not long afterwards the converted minesweeper *Polemistis*, with Paul

* Competitive sailing in Greece was virtually threatened with extinction in 1947 by a government measure classifying racing yachts as 'luxury pleasure craft' for tax purposes, and it was largely thanks to the energetic efforts of Paul as Commodore of the Royal Hellenic Yacht Club that the Government was finally persuaded to exempt racing yachts from this category.

and Frederica and their two daughters on board, dropped anchor in the Bay of Naples among the other vessels that had come to watch the races. The *Polemistis*, which normally served as a royal yacht, was not a large vessel as ships go, and being on the active strength of the Royal Hellenic Navy as a fighting unit it had undergone only a minor refit a few years earlier for its additional duties of conveying the King on his travels by sea; it now had to provide accommodation for several more persons than originally intended, and also became a floating headquarters for the Greek team, which would assemble on board at the end of the day for lengthy discussions on strategy and tactics in which Paul and Frederica, both expert sailors, usually joined.

The Dragon races began on 29 August, the contest consisting of seven runs over a triangular course of some twelve miles, with twenty-seven entrants from different countries competing. In the first heat Constantine did badly, coming in tenth, but he did much better in the next three heats, gaining third place in the second and third races and coming in first on the fourth. There was a break for three days, the runs being resumed on 5 September, when Constantine came in fourth; in the sixth run he gained second place, and in the seventh and final race on 7 September he came fourth. Discarding his worst performance in accordance with scoring rules for Olympic sailing, Constantine showed a consistently good performance, being among the first four in all his runs: *Nirefs*, with Crown Prince Constantine at the helm and Zaimis and Eskietsoglou crewing, had won.

For the first time in fifty years and only for the second time since the revival of the Olympic Games in 1896, Greece had won a Gold Medal. It was an event to which the Greek people insisted on giving suitable recognition, and on his return home the young Olympic victor – the adjective 'Olympionikis' was to precede Constantine's name or title from now on – was given a civic welcome, driving through the streets of Athens in an open car, with his proud parents seated behind him, amid scenes of proud enthusiasm reminiscent of the victory of the Greek marathon runner sixty-four years earlier.*

* When Louis, an illiterate shepherd lad who spent the eve of the race in prayer, trotted barefoot into the newly built marble stadium in Athens at the end of the gruelling run from Marathon itself in 1896, the sons of King George I left their seats in the royal stand and hurried down to the arena to provide an escort for the victor, trotting behind him in line abreast in their full dress uniforms, swords clanking and spurs jingling, all the way round the track to the winning post.

Although he had made no particular study, in the academic sense, of the legal and constitutional aspects of the institution of the monarchy, Paul had an inborn sense of what the role of the Sovereign should be. If challenged he would probably have admitted that he had never heard of Bagehot's classic definition of the duties of the Crown as being to advise, to encourage and to warn, but it was precisely on these principles that his reign was modelled. He insisted on the first requirement and expected to be kept fully informed and constantly briefed by his ministers on all developments both on the home front and in the international field; he observed the second by according to every one of his Premiers his full cooperation and support, even when human factors and historical considerations might have been expected to induce reservations in his attitude; and he never hesitated to apply the third, firmly and persuasively, whenever he felt the circumstances warranted his intervention.

Politicians of all shades of opinion had come to appreciate the King's scrupulous impartiality, and their personal relations with the Sovereign both when in office and while in opposition were animated by sincere respect and frank admiration for the way he exercised his constitutional functions – though the very nature of politics, and more particularly Greek politics, made it necessary for the same politicians who enjoyed the King's support while in power to complain bitterly in public when the same support was given to their opponents when in office. For his part Paul was content, as his grandfather had been before him, to promote and encourage a continuous process of development and renewal in the field of politics so that as many people as possible might be offered opportunities of exercising their talents.

In the interpretation of his duties Paul also felt that his 'right to warn' should not be restricted to the political field. On the same day – 17 January 1961 – that he wrote to the Prime Minister drawing his attention to various manifestations of Communist activity within the State machinery, he also felt it incumbent upon himself to send a memorandum to the Government advising against the construction of a funicular railway on Mt Lycabettus in the heart of Athens on the grounds that it would spoil the aesthetic beauty of the scene.* In the same memorandum he deplored certain tourist

* His advice was not heeded and a funicular was duly built, but it was sited so discreetly as to be virtually invisible.

projects in Corfu which he felt would vulgarize the amenities of that lovely island, and also drew attention to the unattractive design and incongruous appearance of some of the hotels being put up in various parts of the country. 'Would it not be more useful,' he asked, 'if some of the money spent on luxury hotels could be allocated instead for the construction of poor people's homes?' – in a certain district which he named, the Communist vote had dropped by twenty per cent only six months after the Royal Welfare Fund had built a housing estate there, he pointed out significantly.

⇒ 38 ⇐

The Government had announced its intention of enacting a new electoral law in anticipation of the next elections: this was duly laid before Parliament on 6 May 1961 and was passed after lengthy debate on 27 June. It adopted a complex system of 'reinforced proportional representation' similar to the previous law except that single parties were now required to poll at least 15 per cent (instead of 25 per cent) of the total votes cast throughout the country in order to qualify for the second allocation of seats, two-party coalitions required 25 per cent (instead of 35 per cent) and coalitions of three or more parties 30 per cent (instead of 40 per cent). The new law also allowed civil servants and members of the armed forces to vote – they had been denied this right in the previous elections.

On 20 September 1961 Parliament was dissolved and the Karamanlis Government resigned, being replaced by a service government headed by Lt-General Constantine Dovas, Chief of the King's Military Household, and consisting of senior civil servants, professors, lawyers and retired officers.

The elections were held on 29 October 1961 and were once again won by E.R.E. which polled just over 50 per cent of the total votes, securing 176 out of the 300 seats – three more than it had held in the previous Chamber. Six weeks before the elections Papandreou, Venizelos and a number of other politicians had formed a new party, the 'Centre Union', to fight the elections as a united bloc, and this party came second with 33·7 per cent of the poll and 100 seats. The Pan-Democratic Agrarian Front, a combination of the pro-Communist E.D.A. and other like-minded groups, came third with 14·6 per cent of the poll and 24 seats – a big drop from the 78 seats previously held by the extreme left. On 4 November 1961 the new Karamanlis Government was sworn in – the fourth consecutive

318

administration formed by the Macedonian politician who had now held the premiership continuously since Papagos's death in 1955.

But the clouds were not slow in appearing. Instead of a fragmented opposition consisting of several uncoordinated parties under mutually-distrustful leaders, the Government was now confronted by a compact party of one hundred Deputies led by the redoubtable 'grand old man' of Greek politics George Papandreou – the veteran who regarded himself as the man on whom the mantle of the great Venizelos had fallen, the frustrated politician who had held office in numerous administrations since his first ministerial appointment in 1923 but whom the ultimate prize of the premiership had always eluded (with the exception of a few hectic and tragic months in 1944), the seventy-three-year-old orator with the gifts of a Demosthenes and the mercurial temperament of a prima donna whose burning and inexorable ambition it had become in his advancing years to occupy the Premier's seat before his days were ended.

Already, on the morrow of the announcement of the election results Papandreou had issued a violent statement denouncing them as 'the product of violence and fraud' and declaring that the Centre Union would not recognize the new Government. These charges were indignantly repudiated by General Dovas who pointed out that every single protest that had been made by the Centre Union right up to the day of the elections had been fully satisfied, that by common admission complete order and freedom had prevailed at the elections and that abstentions had been the lowest for fifteen years. Karamanlis also rejected the Centre Union's accusations, pointing out that Papandreou had a long tradition of denouncing the results of elections he did not win – even the 1951 elections, which had been organized by his present partner Sophocles Venizelos.

When the King drove to the Chamber on 2 December 1961 for the State opening of Parliament the Centre Union Deputies were conspicuous by their absence, in which they were joined by the Deputies of the extreme left who could scarcely be expected to ignore this split in the anti-Communist camp. * On 7 December the new Government was given a vote of confidence by 174 votes to 21, the opposition Deputies again being absent, though by that date they

---

* Nine Centre Union Deputies who defied their leader and attended Parliament were expelled from the party.

had all taken the statutory oath of allegiance in order to be able to draw their salaries.

Thus began a virulent and sustained campaign by the Centre Union – 'the unrelenting struggle' as Papandreou called it – against the Government. It was waged in the Chamber (to which the Deputies duly returned after a few days), it was waged in the press and it was waged at public meetings throughout the country, reaching such a pitch of hysteria that at one point the Centre Union was demanding that General Dovas and the principal Ministers in his caretaker Government should be impeached for high treason.

The Government's comfortable majority in the Chamber enabled it to weather Papandreou's 'unrelenting struggle' without much difficulty, but the continuous attacks inevitably drew sharp retorts which all added to the heat of the atmosphere.

Papandreou now also began to aim his shafts at the Crown. With his masterly command of the Greek language he coined a new slogan which in the Greek original has an epigrammatic alliterative quality which quickly turned it into a catch-phrase: 'The King reigns but the Government governs.' It was never made quite clear to what particular action this imputation of royal interference was supposed to refer, unless it was the King's disinclination to hearken to Papandreou's exhortations to dismiss Karamanlis out of hand and hold new elections.

The next step in Papandreou's campaign was a boycott of all official functions to which as leader of the opposition and as a Knight Grand Cross of the Order of George I he was automatically invited. This extended to the Palace itself: an invitation to a Court Ball on 14 December 1961 in celebration of King Paul's sixtieth birthday elicited the laconic reply that 'Mr George Papandreou will not be attending', though Sophocles Venizelos and Spyros Markezinis found it more courteous to excuse themselves on the grounds of absence abroad.

On 13 September 1961 the engagement was announced of Princess Sophie, King Paul's elder daughter, to the Infante Juan Carlos, Prince of the Asturias, only son of the Count of Barcelona.* The two young people had first met on the cruise organized by Frederica on the S.S. *Agamemnon*, when they were both about

* On 22 July 1969 Don Juan Carlos was formally nominated future King of Spain and was given the title 'the Prince of Spain'.

fourteen, but it was not until the summer of 1961 when they had
met again in London for the wedding of the Duke of Kent that they
had become romantically attached to each other – the first Frederica
knew of it was when the Crown Prince who was in London with his
sister at the time telephoned his mother one night to tell her that
there was 'something funny going on between Sophie and Juanito'.
After the Kent wedding Juan Carlos joined the Greek Royal
Family at Mon Repos in Corfu, and it was there that he actually
proposed to Sophie.

The wedding took place in Athens on 14 May 1962. Don Juan
Carlos being Catholic and Sophie Greek Orthodox, it was necessary
to have two wedding ceremonies – one in the Roman Catholic
Cathedral of St Denis and another in the Greek Orthodox
Cathedral. It was a splendid occasion, with over one hundred
members of other European royal families attending the wedding,
the old State landau which had served as a bridal coach for Paul
and Frederica at their own wedding being pressed into service once
again.

According to the Greek constitution only the King and the
Diadoch or heir to the throne are entitled to a Civil List, which is
voted annually by Parliament: no other member of the Royal
Family receives an allowance of any kind from the State. Out of this
Civil List the King has to meet not only the personal expenditure of
himself and his family but also all the running expenses of the Royal
Household. Having no private means (except the Tatoi estate and
the villa Mon Repos in Corfu) the Crown had always found considerable difficulty in making both ends meet. When his brother
King George II died intestate in 1947, Paul as next of kin duly
inherited Tatoi, Mon Repos and the small house in Chester Square
in London which King George had bought a few months earlier
and which Paul now gave to his youngest sister Katherine.* Since
Paul's accession to the throne there had been three increases in the
Civil List, which in 1961 stood at some $400,000 per annum, but
these adjustments had lagged well behind the continuous rise in the
cost of living and had very inadequately compensated for the

* Princess Katherine married a British army officer, Major Richard Brandram, in
Athens on 21 April 1941 and subsequently made her home in England. By special
dispensation of the King of England she was granted the status of a Duke's daughter and
is styled the Lady Katherine Brandram.

reduction in the purchasing power of the drachma following two devaluations.

Faced suddenly with all the additional expenses connected with his daughter's wedding, Paul found himself unable to meet his financial obligations as a father. For a while he contemplated selling a parcel of land from the Tatoi estate, but the legal complications involved in breaking the entail obliged him to abandon the idea. After much hesitation he asked the Government, through his Keeper of the Privy Purse, for an advance of 4 million drachmas (about £50,000) repayable in regular monthly instalments to be deducted from the Civil List. This was the period of the 'caretaker' Government of General Dovas, and as the question of an increase in the Civil List had been under consideration anyhow the Government immediately acceded to the King's request.

Not long afterwards it became evident that news of this loan had come to the knowledge of the parliamentary opposition which, for reasons best known to itself, chose to see something reprehensible in the transaction. Meanwhile, the new Government under Karamanlis had come into power and the Foreign Minister, Evangelos Averoff, who happened to be on terms of personal friendship with King Paul, took it upon himself to help the Palace extricate itself from what he considered to be a potentially embarrassing situation: he advanced the sum in question out of his own pocket to the Keeper of the Privy Purse so that the loan from the State could be repaid immediately.

On hearing of this two days later the King immediately summoned Averoff to whom – after expressing deep appreciation for his motives in intervening in the matter – he handed a cheque in settlement of the full amount, which Paul had borrowed from a bank on the usual commercial terms.[31]

The incident of the royal loan was instrumental in injecting a note of urgency into the related subject of financial provision for Princess Sophie. It has been traditionally the custom in Greece for Parliament to vote a sum of money as a dowry for the King's daughters when they marry. Usually this vote is a formality divorced from political considerations, with all sides in the Chamber joining in manifestations of good-will towards the bride. But on this occasion it was not to be. The whole atmosphere in Parliament had by now become so exacerbated that the question of Princess Sophie's dowry soon deteriorated into a controversial issue and it was only after a stormy three-day debate that the Dowry Bill was finally approved.

A close and harmonious relationship had developed between King and Premier over the years that Karamanlis had now been in office. Paul had a very high regard for the Macedonian politician's many qualities, especially his personal integrity and his ability to inspire loyalty and maximum effort in others, which had been the virtues that had induced the King to select him in the first place as the most suitable successor to Papagos on the Field-Marshal's death in 1955; and Karamanlis had always found the King unfailingly cooperative and ready at all times to give support whenever the weight of his prestige was required by the Government, both on the domestic front and in matters of foreign policy as in the case of the Cyprus question.

But inevitably misunderstandings had arisen, and the blame for this probably lay with both sides. In his indignant reaction to the opposition's continuous barrage of vituperation, Karamanlis was becoming perceptively aggressive and short-tempered, especially with the colleagues who were closest to him, with whom for that very reason he felt least inhibited; and this lack of restraint would occasionally manifest itself even in his contacts with the King and Queen. For his part Paul was also beginning to be irritated by the constant sniping against him and the Queen and by the insidious manner in which a campaign of denigration was being conducted by a section of the press against the Crown. Exasperated by his constitutional inability to reply to these attacks, Paul felt that the Government should require no prompting from him to defend the Crown against unjust accusations, particularly since it was patently clear that these tactics of the opposition were attributable exclusively to party political motives. In the acutely sensitive atmosphere engendered by the continuous harassment of Papandreou's 'unrelenting struggle', minor differences now had a tendency of swelling into major disputes, and incidents that would normally have been ignored or dismissed as trivial developed a habit of assuming a significance out of all proportion to the issues involved. Both the King and the Premier were becoming increasingly aware of this atmosphere and of the intangible estrangement that seemed to be building up between them, and with his usual directness Paul suggested that it might help to clear the air if the points on which there appeared to be differences between them were put down on paper.

In a personal letter he wrote to Karamanlis on 5 October 1962 – in reply to one he had received from the Premier two days earlier – Paul dealt with these points frankly and without evasion. He began by referring to the campaign against the King and Queen by certain politicians and some newspapers of the left and centre. Paul felt that his position precluded him from becoming personally involved, but the Government, whose duty it was always to protect the Crown and the regime, should be doing more in this respect.

Paul went on to the controversy that had arisen over the Civil List. There had been unseemly argument over Princess Sophie's dowry, and the Government had shown a singularly inept sense of timing in choosing that particular moment to introduce the Bill increasing the Civil List instead of handling this delicate matter by agreement with the other political parties as had been the custom in the past. Public opinion should also have been suitably enlightened on the subject instead of being left a prey to the mendacious propaganda of scandal-mongering mischief makers.

There had been allegations of luxury and extravagance at Court, yet no Royal Household was more unpretentious than the Greek Court. He was the first King of Greece not to have his residence in the Palace but in a simple country house built by his grandfather at his own expense. During his fifteen years on the throne he had toured the length and breadth of the country in 'campaign' conditions so as not to incur any expense to the State.

There had been critical references to 'frequent absences abroad'. His father and his grandfather had been in the habit of spending two or three months each year on foreign visits without anyone raising any objections; he himself usually went to England for two weeks and occasionally visited his wife's relatives in Austria for another fortnight. In any case, modern methods of transport enabled him to return to Greece if required in a matter of hours, much more quickly than he could reach Athens from some places inside Greece. In the matter of travelling he was making do with jeeps and a very uncomfortable converted mine-sweeper. Furthermore, the King was being criticized as being the owner of palaces and other residences which in actual fact did not belong to him, were not used by him, and in some cases had been built without his knowledge or consent. He felt the Government should make it its business to enlighten the public on all these matters instead of allowing false impressions to go unchallenged.

He agreed that the Royal Welfare Fund had perhaps outlived its original purpose and should now be re-organized on a different basis.

Paul concluded his letter on a personal note:

'These are private thoughts addressed to you in all friendship and which I want you to regard as further evidence of the confidence and high esteem which I cherish for you.'

This frank exchange seemed to have a cathartic effect on the relations between the two men, and in his traditional New Year message shortly afterwards Paul also availed himself of the opportunity to emphasize that the Crown stood above politics. 'It is of no importance to me whether you belong to this or to that political party,' he said. 'My love goes out to each and every one of you, and my faith in you is as unflinching as your brave hearts.'

It was not very long, however, before Paul and Karamanlis found themselves irreconcilably divided over another issue – an issue that would normally have been expected to prove the happiest of occasions instead of becoming the cause of the final break between them: the State visit to England.

⇒ 39 ⇐

The Cyprus settlement had removed the sole remaining obstacle to the restoration of Anglo-Greek relations to their former state of harmony and warmth. On 20 September 1960 Cyprus was admitted to full membership of the United Nations, and on 16 February 1961 the newly elected House of Representatives in Nicosia voted to join the British Commonwealth, to which Cyprus was duly admitted on 14 March 1961 when Archbishop Makarios took his place among the other Commonwealth Premiers at the London Conference – indeed, taking precedence over them all as the only Head of State among Heads of Government. Travelling eastward to India and Pakistan early the same year Queen Elizabeth stopped at the British base at Akrotiri – the first reigning British Monarch to visit Cyprus since Richard I in 1191 – for a friendly meeting with Archbishop Makarios. And on 28 September 1962 the Archbishop-President himself arrived in Athens on an official visit, being received by King Paul with all the honours due to a Head of State including the blue sash of the Order of the Redeemer.

Only one thing now remained to put the seal on this painstaking process of healing the rift between Greece and Britain: a State visit to London by the King and Queen of the Hellenes. Preliminary soundings in Athens in December 1961 had met with a very favourable response, and it had been agreed then that the middle of 1963 would be a suitable time for the visit. On 20 February 1963 it was announced simultaneously in London and Athens that King Paul and Queen Frederica had accepted an invitation from Queen Elizabeth to stay at Buckingham Palace from 9 to 12 July 1963.*

Meanwhile, the 'unrelenting struggle' was working itself up to

---

* Although both Paul and his brother King George II had visited London many times, there had been no State visit to England by a Greek monarch since 1905, when King George I paid an official visit to his brother-in-law, King Edward VII.

fever pitch, the main stream of its venom now being directed at the Palace. In December 1962 a left-wing journalist who had just returned from a visit to the Dowager Duchess of Brunswick in Germany published a scurrilous article about Queen Frederica in an Athens newspaper castigating her and her brothers, the Princes of Hanover, for 'stripping their mother of her possessions and abandoning her to the streets'. This proved a little too much for the Director of Public Prosecutions who now decided that the State could no longer tolerate such affronts to the person of the Queen:* copies of the newspaper with the offending article were confiscated by the police, and the publisher and editor were arrested and charged, the author of the article himself as a Member of Parliament being immune. The trial lasted three days and was mostly taken up by a procession of prominent politicians of the Centre who came forward as character witnesses for the defence; the accused were duly found guilty and sentenced to fifteen months' imprisonment.

On 2 February 1963 Paul and Frederica left on a State visit to India and Thailand. It was the time of the Chinese invasion of India in the north, and Paul found occasion in his speeches to express Greece's admiration for the resistance of the Indian people 'whose very credo, as our own, is peace'. He also paid lavish tribute to India as the cradle of human thought and as the source of many philosophies and cultures: 'Even the very principles of our Christian faith have roots in the rich soil of the goodness and love of the Indian soul.'†

Shortly after the King's return to Athens invitations were sent out by the Palace for the centenary of the Greek Dynasty, which coincided with a State visit to Greece by the King and Queen of Denmark. It was at the official banquet in honour of his Danish cousins that Paul formally announced the betrothal of his son and heir Constantine to the youngest of King Frederick's three daughters, the sixteen-year-old Princess Anne-Marie, which was to link the Royal House of Greece yet again with the House from which it had originally stemmed one hundred years earlier.

* Article 14 of the Greek Constitution makes specific provision for legal action to be taken against publications deemed to be insulting to the Sovereign or the immediate members of his family.

† This last remark was interpolated in a speech at the last moment by Paul, who was subsequently called upon by the ultra-conservative Synod of the Greek Church to explain exactly what he meant.

George Papandreou, who was naturally among those invited, declined the invitation in a ten-page letter to the King. The decision of the Centre Union to boycott the centenary celebrations, he wrote, did not have a personal character; it was a political gesture and was intended as a protest against 'the existence of a fraudulent majority in the Chamber and an illegal government in office'. Papandreou then expounded the ingenious argument that 'since at least one E.R.E. Deputy in each constituency has been returned by fraudulent means' and since there were fifty-five constituencies in the country, it followed that E.R.E. was not entitled to 172 Deputies but at most to 120, which meant it did not enjoy a majority at all and therefore had no right to call itself the Government of the country.

After explaining at length the reasons why the Centre Union had decided to challenge this state of affairs and after refuting allegations against the Centre Union's motives in launching the 'unrelenting struggle', Papandreou turned to the role of the King, whose intervention as Moderator of the Constitution he invoked.

The constitutional functions of the Sovereign, he said, were threefold:

Firstly, the King was himself the national adviser of his own official Counsellors;

Secondly, the King appointed and dismissed his Ministers, but the Government had to have the support of Parliament, whose vote of confidence it was obliged to obtain;

Thirdly, if Parliament refused its confidence to the Government, the King had the right to dissolve Parliament and proclaim elections within forty-five days.

The King was therefore entitled before dissolving Parliament to advise his Counsellors; if his advice were not heeded and if the King considered that the wider interests of the country so demanded, he had the right to appoint a new government which should then seek a vote of confidence from Parliament.

Having made clear that what he was demanding was the dismissal of Karamanlis and the holding of fresh elections under another government, Papandreou wound up his letter on an ominous note: if the King did not have the will or the courage to impose a democratic solution as indicated, a new national division was inevitable, and the people would then know how to do their duty with all the means at their disposal.

After vainly waiting a few days for a reply Papandreou released the text of his letter to the press, issuing at the same time a statement to the effect that 'the Sovereign has identified himself with the illegitimate E.R.E. Government' and that 'a critical situation has thus arisen'. For his part Karamanlis announced that Papandreou's letter did not require an answer and that the Government still enjoyed the confidence of the King and the people and would continue with its task.

Papandreou's retort to this snub was even more ominous: 'The citizens of democracy,' he proclaimed, 'will now become the soldiers of democracy.' But such extravagant fulminations against the Crown were finding little support among the more responsible members of Papandreou's own party – the joint leader of the Centre Union, Sophocles Venizelos, went out of his way at this time to seek an audience of the King, declaring immediately afterwards at the Palace gates that 'the King is entirely impartial towards the political parties'.

On 20 April 1963 Queen Frederica arrived in London with her younger daughter Princess Irene to attend the wedding of Princess Alexandra of Kent to Mr Angus Ogilvie. They were greeted at London Airport by the bride's mother, the Greek-born Princess Marina, Duchess of Kent, and drove to Claridge's Hotel where they were to stay.

Shortly after Frederica's arrival at the hotel a group of demonstrators, mostly Greek Cypriots carrying placards with Communist slogans, gathered outside. Among them was Mrs Betty Ambatielos, the British-born wife of a Greek Communist seamen's leader serving a long prison sentence in Greece for subversive activities.* Mrs Ambatielos – herself a very active Communist and a one-time Athens correspondent of the Communist mouthpiece, the *Daily Worker* – entered the hotel and demanded to see Queen Frederica, who declined to receive her. Mrs Ambatielos remained in the

---

* Anthony Ambatielos and nine others were sentenced to death in 1948 for aiding the Communist guerrillas in their armed rebellion against the State. Trade union protests against these sentences were effectively scotched by the British Foreign Secretary, Mr Ernest Bevin, who declared in February 1949: 'The allegations that these men are being prosecuted because they are trade unionists is quite unfounded. They have been brought to trial on specific charges of treason in aiding the rebels. Ambatielos, for example, was sentenced to death for recruiting and collecting for the bandits, not for trade union activities. He is, of course, a well-known and active Communist.' These death sentences were subsequently commuted to life imprisonment, and Ambatielos was released some years later.

foyer and while she was still there Frederica and Princess Irene came down the stairs and went out by the side door in Davies Street with the intention of walking the short distance to Grosvenor Square to visit some friends. As soon as she perceived the Queen leaving the hotel Mrs Ambatielos dashed out into the street after her and coming up from behind pushed Princess Irene to one side and seized the Queen by the shoulder, twisting her round and shouting for the release of her husband. In the meantime the demonstrators in front of the hotel in Brook Street had become aware that something was happening at the side entrance and came running round the corner. Frederica managed to shake herself free from Mrs Ambatielos's grasp – the security officer who belatedly came to her assistance was grabbed by the demonstrators and dragged to the ground – and hurried down Davies Street with her daughter, taking the first turning she came to in the direction of Grosvenor Square. It was not until she had reached the bottom of this street, Three Kings Yard, that she realized it was a cul-de-sac. She turned to go back, only to see some of the demonstrators coming towards her. She rang the first door-bell she could find. The door was opened by an attractive young woman in a dressing-gown – it turned out to be an American actress called Marti Stevens staying in a rented flat – to whom the situation was hurriedly explained; Frederica and her daughter were invited in and the door was slammed shut. Fortified by a stiff brandy Frederica telephoned the hotel and shortly afterwards the security officer arrived and escorted her to Grosvenor Square.

This incident took place on 20 April, which was a Saturday. The London correspondent of the leading Athenian afternoon newspaper, *Mesimvrini*, got hold of the story and cabled it to his paper after checking the facts with Queen Frederica herself, which he was able to do as he happened to be personally known to her. No morning newspapers are published in Greece on Monday, so the first the Greek public knew of the incident was when the *Mesimvrini* appeared with the story on Monday afternoon.

Reaction in Greece was swift and predictable. The Foreign Minister, Evangelos Averoff, who had already received a report of the incident from the Greek Embassy in London,* summoned the

---

* M.Michel Melas, appointed Ambassador in London only five months earlier, was so shaken by the incident that he suffered a heart attack and had to be rushed by ambulance to the London Clinic.

British Chargé d'Affaires and expressed 'deep concern' – in diplomatic parlance one degree short of a formal protest – over the incident and at the inadequate protection afforded by the British authorities to the Queen. For its part the Greek press, in a rare manifestation of unanimity induced no doubt by an affront to Greek national pride, accused the British Government of failing to take proper measures 'to avert the deplorable, inhospitable and outrageous behaviour of British citizens, albeit Communists, towards a lady who is a guest of their country and the Queen of a friendly and allied nation', as one newspaper indignantly put it.

On 26 April 1963 the British Foreign Secretary, Lord Home, conveyed his Government's formal apologies to Queen Frederica in writing:

> Your Majesty will know with what deep distress I have learned of the two incidents which occurred on the 20th and 22nd of April* to mar Your Majesty's visit to this country. In my own name and that of the Home Secretary I should like to express our sincere apologies. We greatly regret that Your Majesty should have been subjected to such an experience.

Feelings in Greece were running so high by this time that it was thought advisable to publish the text of this letter, together with a Greek Government statement to the effect that with the British apology the incident could now be regarded as closed. But fresh complications were coming from another quarter; although the Greek newspapers had given much publicity to the dramatic events at Claridge's, the British press had published little or nothing about the incident with the result that the terms of Lord Home's apology came as something of a shock to most people who naturally assumed that the apology referred to the vociferous but otherwise orderly protests outside Claridge's – it was not until 30 April that the British newspapers were able at last to give the full story on the basis of a statement issued by the Greek Embassy, supplemented by Miss Marti Stevens's own graphic account of what had happened.

Meanwhile, a spate of questions by Labour M.P.s had appeared on the Order Paper in the House of Commons. Why was it considered necessary to apologize at all, one Hon. Member wanted to know, 'in view of the fact that the apology covered only the exercise by certain citizens of the normal British democratic right

---

* On the Monday following the main incident Frederica had to be smuggled out of Claridge's to avoid demonstrators outside.

of making representations by peaceful demonstration'? The Prime
Minister's somewhat evasive replies to this and other questions on
the subject did not improve matters: Queen Frederica had been the
subject of certain unfortunate incidents, he said, and courtesy
required that an apology should be made. Should not the apology
have referred to the incompetence of the Government's arrangements and not to the right of peaceful demonstration in Britain? the
questioner insisted. No, said Mr Macmillan, the normal arrangements had been made but a hitch had occurred. Would the Prime
Minister give details? No, said Mr Macmillan, he did not think it
necessary to go into the precise character of the incidents, which
should be neither exaggerated nor under-estimated. Another M.P.
pointed out that there seemed to be some conflict over the facts of
the case: would not the Prime Minister arrange for an impartial
inquiry to establish what exactly had taken place? That was a
different matter, said Mr Macmillan without answering the question.
The demand for an inquiry was repeated by the leader of the
opposition, Mr Harold Wilson, and Mr Macmillan could no longer
evade the issue: an inquiry was unnecessary, he said, since he
regarded the matter as closed. 'A certain incident took place which
led to a disturbance and the Queen having to take refuge in a house
nearby. That was unfortunate, and I think it right that an apology
should be made.'

All this was highly unsatisfactory, as the British press soon made
clear. 'The grovelling apology which the Foreign Secretary Lord
Home has made to Queen Frederica of Greece is unnecessary and
will be seriously misunderstood,' protested the Labour mouthpiece
the *Daily Herald*. At the other end of the scale the Conservative
Sunday Express also professed indignation: 'Lord Home has made
a grovelling apology to this foreign queen. . . . Is he ashamed that
people in Britain are still allowed to demonstrate against despotism?
Let the Greek Queen know that the British people do not join in
Lord Home's apology.'

Sentiments such as these were scarcely calculated to smooth
ruffled feelings in Greece, where the incident had by now assumed
a political complexion. The blame for the events at Claridge's could
hardly be laid at the door of the Karamanlis Government, but this
did not mean that political capital could not be made out of it all
the same. Already, the day after the story of the incident appeared
in print the leading opposition newspaper had come out with a

suggestion that the Greek State visit to England, now just ten weeks off, should be cancelled or at least postponed, and in one of those swift changes of mood that had earned him the nickname of 'weather-vane' the opposition leader Mr George Papandreou suddenly forgot his vendetta against the Palace and put himself forward in the new role of champion of the Crown. The Greeks, he said, initiating a censure motion against the Government, were deeply embittered by what had happened to Queen Frederica in London and by the discussions in the British press and the House of Commons: 'We give no one the right to treat Greece as a satellite or as a protectorate, and in this we stand united as one nation.' The Greek Government had become vulnerable to foreign criticism because it had turned Greece into a police and party State, he declared, and fresh elections were the only means of putting an end to the defamation of Greece abroad.

Immediately after the Claridge's incident the Greek Government had indicated that the arrangements for the State visit remained unchanged. With public feeling being worked up, however, the Government now found it expedient to allow it vaguely to be understood that the visit was 'under consideration', and correspondents' despatches from Athens to that effect began to appear in London, where a certain amount of concern was also being manifested about the way Anglo-Greek relations seemed to be going. 'In view of the publicity concerning the recent incident involving the Queen of the Hellenes, will Her Majesty's Government make it clear that in their opinion this should not be allowed to disturb the existing good relations between Britain and Greece?' asked Lord Swinton in the House of Lords, thus providing the Foreign Secretary with the opportunity to declare that

Her Majesty's Government attach the greatest value to our ancient and traditional friendship with Greece. . . . We value Greece as an ally in NATO and as a co-signatory of the Cyprus agreement and we trust that this incident for which I have expressed my regrets will not be allowed to damage relations between our two countries.

The Prime Minister was even more explicit on this point. Replying to questions in the House of Commons, Mr Macmillan made it very clear that the British Government attached the greatest importance to this matter:

I hope very much that this visit will take place as planned. There is a long tradition of friendship between Greece and Britain dating now over 100 years and cemented by our alliance through two long and terrible wars. It is true that this friendship came under strain at the time of the troubles in Cyprus but these have now happily been settled. The proposed visit will, therefore, mark the restoration to their traditional vigour of the friendly relations between our two countries. . . . It is hoped that this visit will be of the greatest value to our ancient and traditional friendship with Greece, and it is the outward and visible sign of that fact.

At the same time, at the meeting of the NATO Council in Ottawa in May, Lord Home assured the Greek Foreign Minister, Evangelos Averoff, that the British Government was most anxious that the Greek royal visit should take place as planned, and reiterated that the British authorities would take all necessary measures to ensure that no demonstrations should be allowed to mar the visit.

There was by now reliable evidence that the anti-Greek manifestations in London were not quite as spontaneous as they had been made out to be. The Claridge's incidents, said a Foreign Office spokesman, 'were Communist inspired to upset relations between the British and Greek Governments, but it would not seem that the well-prepared and highly organized campaign to worsen relations between our two countries has achieved the result it aimed at.' Foreign Office experts who had made extensive research into the organization behind the demonstrations outside Claridge's had come to the conclusion that the affair had been deliberately staged to bring about the embarrassment of the British Government in the eyes of the Greek Government and the Greek Royal Family.

It was against this background that the Premier Constantine Karamanlis asked to see the King and recommended that in the prevailing circumstances it might be advisable for the State visit to be postponed until a more propitious time.

The Premier's advice did not come as a surprise to Paul, who had been following developments with a growing sense of anxiety and frustration. He had already considered the question in his own mind and had come to the conclusion that to postpone the visit would be wrong. Such a visit had already been cancelled once in 1953 when the Cyprus crisis had compelled Papagos to advise the King to decline Queen Elizabeth's invitation; to refuse it a second time would be an act of discourtesy towards the Queen of England of which he was temperamentally incapable. It would also be tantamount to spurning the hand of friendship that was being extended by Britain: the British Government had gone out of its way to emphasize the importance attached to the visit, and to cancel it at the last moment would not only be an affront to a great and friendly power but would also show Greece as bowing to pressure from a clamorous but irresponsible minority.

Paul explained his point of view to Karamanlis and asked him to consider yet again the grave issues involved. Meanwhile, the whole Royal Family left on a tour of the Peloponnese in the course of which, not surprisingly, Frederica was singled out for a particularly warm welcome. Immediately afterwards General de Gaulle arrived on a State visit, in the middle of which Paul was struck down with appendicitis and had to be rushed off to the Evangelismos hospital for an emergency operation.

As soon as the King was well again Karamanlis reverted to the question of the State visit. He had considered all aspects of the matter but was still of the same opinion, and his advice as the King's responsible First Minister was that the visit should be postponed. The King had also thought much on the subject and had been reinforced in his own conviction that the visit should take place as planned. After a two-hour discussion on 10 June the two men were no nearer agreement. In the end Paul asked Karamanlis to give the matter some more thought and come back the following day with his final answer.

The position was now clear. According to Greek constitutional practice, when the Prime Minister finds himself in disagreement with the Sovereign he resigns. On 11 June 1963 Karamanlis saw the King and submitted his resignation.

In view of the opposition's past clamour that Karamanlis should go, the King was anxious that there should be no misconception as to the true reason for the resignation of the Government, if only in fairness to Karamanlis himself, whom Paul held in the greatest esteem. At their final meeting Paul offered the outgoing Premier the Order of the Redeemer but Karamanlis respectfully declined it, probably because acceptance might have been interpreted as signifying his retirement from politics. At the same time Paul decided to issue a proclamation explaining his own position in the crisis:

Our democratic form of Government requires that the people should be kept fully informed of what happens in the country. It is in this spirit that I desire to communicate direct with my people and to give the reasons which have caused the Government to resign, as well as my own feelings in this matter.

I have accepted with great regret the resignation of the Prime Minister, Mr Constantine Karamanlis. We have collaborated harmoniously for a long time while I followed the successful efforts of the Government under him for the development and progress of our country. I express to Mr Constantine Karamanlis my complete satisfaction with his services to the country.

The resignation of the Government is due to a difference of opinion which has arisen as a result of my non-acceptance of the Prime Minister's recommendation that the State visit to Great Britain fixed for 9 July 1963 should not take place.

After due consideration I believe that in the present circumstances the interests of the country require that the State visit should take place. I consider that this matter is of a wider national importance and I deem it to be my duty not to agree to a course of action that would, in my opinion, be detrimental to the country before I avail myself of the means provided by the constitution in order to enable a new responsible advice to be tendered on the subject.

My considered opinion that the realization of the State visit is necessary is based on the fact that its postponement or cancellation would serve the aims of those who wish to undermine the security of Greece, and it is neither right nor proper that the Greek people should submit to the pressure of a small number of people who are consciously or unconsciously serving Communist aims directed against the State and who do not represent the views or sentiments of our allies and traditional friends, the British people.

The refusal of the invitation of the Queen of England, after it had been officially accepted, would be a blow to the friendship and mutual confidence which exist within the NATO alliance and which constitute the indispensable pre-requisites for the successful pursuit of the defensive struggle for existence being waged by our country.

All Greeks, myself first of all, were distressed and grieved by the unfortunate incidents in London last April. But we should not ignore the fact that these feelings were shared by the vast majority of British people whose Government officially expressed regrets and apologies and has in subsequent assurances and messages asked that the visit should take place as planned.

In view of these considerations I feel that the threat of insignificant and irresponsible demonstrations, which would in no way reflect the true

24 State Visit to England, July 1963. King Paul drives in state with Queen Elizabeth from Victoria Station to Buckingham Palace.

25 King Paul, wearing the Order of the Garter and the uniform of an Admiral in the British Navy, replies to the City's official welcome at the Guildhall, London.

26 Crown Prince Constantine taking the miraculous ikon of the Virgin of
Tinos to his dying father at Tatoi.

sentiments of the British people and which could not affect the King and Queen of the Hellenes, should not mislead us into withdrawing our acceptance of the invitation.

The grave crisis and the bitterness through which Anglo-Greek relations passed in recent years are now happily things of the past. The gallant British people have always come to our side in times of peril. We have experienced their bravery at close quarters. We are proud to give hospitality to their dead who fell on Greek soil in common struggles with ourselves. Today the British people, through their Queen and in my person, have extended an invitation to the Greek nation.

The brave honour the brave.

The King's first step after acceptance of the resignation of Karamanlis was the usual preliminary formality of ascertaining the state of the parties in the Chamber. The Speaker supplied the figures, which showed that E.R.E. still commanded a clear majority with 180 out of the 300 seats, the Centre Union coming a good way behind in second place with 79 seats, the pro-Communist E.D.A. third with 22 seats and Mr Markezinis's Progressives last with 16 seats.

Paul already knew what Karamanlis's views were: the outgoing Premier's parting recommendations had been that a caretaker administration should be appointed to dissolve Parliament immediately and hold new elections. This was advice that the King found himself unable to accept. The constitution stipulated that elections must be held within forty-five days from dissolution of Parliament, which meant that the State visit would have to be cancelled since the King could scarcely absent himself from the country in the middle of an election. Paul summoned the leader of the opposition, George Papandreou, whose advice to the Sovereign was very different: a political government enjoying the confidence of Parliament should be appointed to assume responsibility for the State visit and also to prepare the ground for elections. The Centre Union, he said, would support such a government but would be against having elections right away, as a purge of the State machinery and changes in the electoral law were indispensable pre-requisites. Meanwhile, he declared in a burst of magnanimity, all disagreements between the Centre Union and the Sovereign were wiped out.

For his part, Mr Markezinis, who was summoned next, was also in favour of a political government to take responsibility for the State visit, which he firmly believed should still take place.

Consultations and soundings in all directions continued for five days, at the end of which the problem seemed no nearer solution. In the final analysis the hard fact remained that E.R.E. still enjoyed a healthy overall majority in the Chamber and any proposal that could not secure its support was doomed to failure from the start. The key to the problem was clearly Karamanlis, who during this time had repeatedly manifested his willingness to be helpful to the King in his endeavours and who now went even further by indicating that he was prepared to accept without reservation any proposal the King might put forward.

On 17 June the King saw Karamanlis, who suggested that the premiership of a 'service' government should be entrusted to Panayotis Pipinelis, a member of the outgoing Cabinet.

A diplomatist by profession, 'Taki' Pipinelis had entered politics in 1953 after a meteoric rise in the Greek diplomatic service. A dedicated supporter of the monarchy, he had given loyal service to the Crown throughout his life, especially during the war years when he had been seconded to the Household of King George II and had played a very important role in securing the King's eventual return to Greece. His career as a politician had not been very successful: when he stood for Parliament in the elections of 1958 he had been defeated, but this had not deterred Karamanlis from appointing him extra-parliamentary Minister of Commerce three years later.

Though highly respected for his integrity and his undoubted abilities, Pipinelis had no personal following among the rank and file of E.R.E.; the mere fact that he had been nominated by Karamanlis himself, however, would go a long way towards ensuring the party's support. To make Pipinelis's task easier, Karamanlis also announced publicly that he had recommended to his party to support the King in his efforts to settle the political crisis, and in a final gesture of self-immolation he also announced that he was going abroad and would return only when the date of the next elections was officially announced.

On 17 June the King summoned Pipinelis and asked him to form a 'service' government. Two days later the new Cabinet, consisting of non-party personalities, was sworn in. Besides the premiership, Pipinelis also kept the Ministry of Foreign Affairs for himself, thus ensuring that he personally would accompany the King on the State visit to England.

An administration headed by a former E.R.E. cabinet minister was not what Papandreou had bargained for, and the very next day he denounced the new Government as 'inspiring no confidence in its ability to hold fair elections'. Venizelos on the other hand was more accommodating and secretly promised to give the Government his support if three of its members, who had served as Secretaries-General in the outgoing government and could therefore be regarded as having political affiliations, were replaced. The three offending ministers were duly dropped, and on 26 June the Pipinelis Government appeared before Parliament for the customary statement of policy. In the vote of confidence that followed E.R.E. voted in favour and the Markezinis Progressives voted against, giving the Government a majority of 172 to 14.

In the Greek Parliament voting is by nominal roll: as each Deputy's name is called out he answers Yes or No from his seat. Before voting began, all the Centre Union Deputies rose and left the Chamber – all except Venizelos, who casually strolled over to the teller and told him that he was giving the Government a 'vote of tolerance'. Then he too stalked out.

⟫ 40 ⟪

On Tuesday, 9 July 1963, King Paul and Queen Frederica, attended by the Prime Minister, Pipinelis, arrived in England for the State visit. When the Comet aircraft touched down at Gatwick Airport the Duke of Edinburgh, himself a Prince of Greece by birth and a first cousin to Paul, was there to greet them. Travelling by special train with a large replica of the Greek Coat of Arms on the engine, the royal party arrived at Victoria Station in London where Queen Elizabeth and the other members of the British Royal Family were waiting to welcome them. After the presentations on both sides had been made, Paul inspected a guard of honour of the Grenadier Guards in the station courtyard while a forty-one-gun salute was fired from Hyde Park and the Tower of London. The party then boarded open horse-drawn carriages and drove the short distance to Buckingham Palace, Paul in naval uniform riding in the first carriage with Queen Elizabeth, and Frederica in the second with Prince Philip.

Outside Victoria Station and along the route to the Palace thousands of people had gathered to cheer the procession. As the first carriage turned into Victoria Street, Mrs Ambatielos – the woman responsible for the 'Claridge's incident' the previous April – dashed into the road shouting for the release of her husband but was quickly hustled away by the police.

On arrival at the Palace Queen Elizabeth conferred the Order of the Garter on King Paul, who in his turn presented Queen Elizabeth with the Order of the Redeemer.

In the afternoon Paul and Frederica drove to Westminster Abbey to lay a wreath on the grave of the Unknown Warrior and visit the shrine of Edward the Confessor. Mrs Ambatielos also arrived with a wreath of her own but was removed by the police until after Paul and Frederica had gone.

At the end of the first day of the visit Paul and Frederica were entertained by Queen Elizabeth at a banquet at Buckingham Palace at which warm words were exchanged between the two monarchs. Proposing the toast of her guests, Queen Elizabeth said that Greece's heroic resistance against the invaders in the last war had been 'a source of pride and inspiration to us all. . . . Perhaps the greatest courage and kindness were shown by countless hundreds of villagers in all parts of your country who risked everything to hide and protect Allied servicemen trapped in Greece and Crete.' After the war, said Queen Elizabeth, the Greek people refused to succumb to the tyranny which had already engulfed their neighbours. 'Today we are proud to have such a valiant people as our allies in NATO and in the ranks of the free peoples of the world.' These things alone made the royal visit most welcome, but it also marked the strength of the long-standing and traditional friendship between the two countries. It was a friendship which could survive temporary disagreements and a friendship which she was confident would be enduring.

In his reply King Paul said that modern Greece and British civilization were heirs to the same ancient Greek classical spirit; during the modern history of the two nations this affinity had been the inspired source of strength in overcoming the forces of darkness. From the moment they rose to fight for their independence the Greeks had always found at their side an ally and a friend in the British nation and its leaders. 'There have been moments of uncertainty for sincere supporters of Anglo-Hellenic good understanding such as are bound to occur at one time or another between the firmest of friends. However, these moments were only transient, precisely because the sincere feelings of traditional Graeco-British friendship prevailed in the end.'

While the banquet was going on at Buckingham Palace a crowd of demonstrators, mostly supporters of the pacifist 'Committee of 100', gathered in Trafalgar Square nearby to march on the Palace. A week earlier the Commissioner of Police of London had issued regulations forbidding street processions during the royal visit, but the 'Committee of 100' ignored the ban. The police closed the Admiralty Arch gates which give access to the Palace and diverted the demonstrators to Whitehall, where several scuffles took place and some arrests were made. Meanwhile the nonagenarian Lord (Bertrand) Russell presented himself at the gates of Buckingham Palace and handed in a letter protesting against the royal visit.

Earlier in the day an attempt by a left-wing Labour Member of Parliament to provoke an emergency debate on the action of the Commissioner of Police in forbidding demonstrations proved unsuccessful: the measures, ruled Mr Speaker, were an instance of the ordinary administration of the law and as such did not qualify for emergency debate under standing orders.

Minor incidents also occurred on the second day of the visit. In the morning, when Paul and Frederica drove to Westminster for a trip by barge up the Thames, the ubiquitous Mrs Ambatielos again tried to approach the royal visitors but was restrained by the police and removed to Scotland Yard nearby where she was detained until after the royal party had embarked.

For Paul and Frederica, the highlight of the visit was undoubtedly the luncheon given in their honour by the Lord Mayor of London in the historic Guildhall in the City. When Paul stood up to reply to the toast all the guests present, some six hundred people, spontaneously rose to their feet and gave him a standing ovation 'the like of which I have not seen in my whole life' as one veteran Alderman put it. Paul was obviously taken aback, flushing with pleasure and looking about him with an embarrassed smile on his face. The message that was being conveyed to him by this cross-section of the population of the capital was unmistakable, and he immediately responded to it. 'Our heartfelt thanks go out to the people of London for the magnificent reception they gave us yesterday and today,' he said in a voice trembling with emotion. 'It was an impressive display which brushed aside every trivial attempt by irresponsible persons to create misunderstanding between our two peoples.'

Paul's remarks, obviously spoken extempore, were drowned by renewed applause, at the end of which he reverted to the speech he had personally prepared and which was on the same basic theme, that Anglo-Hellenic friendship was strong enough to survive the strains imposed on it.

When we were challenged by the vastly superior Axis powers we looked at Great Britain and saw ourselves. . . . I am proud that at a time when Great Britain was alone, when the whole of Europe lay defeated, when the United States and Russia were not yet in the war, we stood by you as you stood by us. While here in London you were winning the first victories in the air, we in Greece were winning the first victories by land. During those months, inspired by each other's superhuman heroism, Britain and Greece formed an unseen union which spelled hope and freedom to a despairing world.

I firmly believe that no shadow of past unhappy events nor the confused thinking of a few individuals can ever tear apart what was forged during the war. It is to this unseen union with our common ideals of freedom and democracy that I pledge my people and my faith.

That evening there was a special performance of *A Midsummer Night's Dream* at the Aldwych Theatre, and once again there were demonstrations outside. By this time it had become obvious that these protests were the work of an organized group of left-wing extremists. 'A Communist stunt,' was how the former Labour Premier Earl Attlee contemptuously put it, and the Home Secretary, Mr Henry Brooke, was even more explicit. 'This is the work of a handful of Communists and anarchists,' he said. 'I think the people of London have become ashamed of the way 500 people or so have made stupid demonstrations and they are thoroughly fed up with it.'

The third and final day of the State visit began with a tour by King Paul of the naval base at Portsmouth, while Frederica inspected a school for handicapped children in Hampshire and a radio research station in Berkshire. In the evening Paul and Frederica gave a farewell banquet in honour of Queen Elizabeth and Prince Philip at Claridge's Hotel at which the gold dinner service brought from Athens specially for the occasion was much admired.

On 12 July Paul and Frederica returned to Athens. In a proclamation to the Greek people the King said that the success of the State visit marked the beginning of a new happy era in Anglo-Greek relations.

In the aircraft flying back to Athens the Major Domo asked if he might have a word with Queen Frederica. With some considerable embarrassment he informed the Queen that after the banquet eleven pieces of cutlery and three menu holders from the gold dinner service were found to be missing.

⇉ 41 ⇇

With the State visit safely behind, Pipinelis now demanded and obtained another vote of confidence and then announced that general elections would be held on 3 November 1963. A new Bill was introduced providing for a 'reinforced' proportional representation system of voting as a compromise between the Centre Union's demand for simple proportional representation and E.R.E.'s preference for the majority system, but this still proved unacceptable to Papandreou, with the result that the Centre Union abstained from the final vote in the Chamber, the Bill being passed through its final stages by the E.R.E. vote alone.

Papandreou now raised a new objection: the Pipinelis Government, he said, could not be regarded as a truly 'service' government inasmuch as the Premier himself belonged to E.R.E. A completely non-party administration should be in office during the election period, otherwise the Centre Union would adopt a policy of 'dynamic abstention' and boycott the elections.

On 25 September Paul summoned a conference of parliamentary party leaders at the Palace under his chairmanship. Papandreou and Markezinis were there as chiefs of the Centre Union and the Progressive Party respectively, and E.R.E. was represented by the triumvirate who were now conducting the affairs of the party in Karamanlis's absence abroad. Pipinelis, as Prime Minister, also attended, and the twenty-three-year-old Crown Prince Constantine sat by his father's side.

The outcome of the conference, which lasted several hours, was simply a reiteration of the attitudes already adopted. The majority party (E.R.E.) reaffirmed its confidence in the Pipinelis Government; Papandreou expressed personal esteem for Pipinelis but insisted that a service government could not possibly have as its premier someone who was a leading member of a political party;

344

and Markezinis also asked for a change of government. Pipinelis himself pointed out that by accepting the premiership he had in effect sacrificed his political ambitions since he was excluding himself from participation in the elections; if his presence in the Government was creating difficulties, however, his resignation was always at the King's disposal.

From his self-imposed temporary exile in Paris Karamanlis also sent messages to the effect that he was strongly in favour of the Pipinelis Government remaining in office, but perhaps some members of the Government might be dropped as a concession to the Centre Union if that were considered necessary. As a last resort Pipinelis might also be allowed to go, but this should be delayed until it had become clear beyond any doubt that Papandreou's boycott threat was not a bluff.

The King now found himself in an invidious position. On the one hand the parliamentary majority was asserting its undoubted right that the government in office should be acceptable to it; on the other the opposition was threatening to frustrate the elections unless they were conducted by a government acceptable to the Centre Union. To keep Pipinelis in the premier's chair until the last moment would place the whole burden of responsibility squarely on the King since by that time it would be too late for the Centre Union to change its plans and the King would inevitably be blamed for not invoking his constitutional prerogative and changing the government sufficiently early to make it possible for the Centre Union to participate in the election.

Pipinelis personally was convinced that Papandreou would not go through with his boycott threat: even if he did, argued the Premier, the party would split from top to bottom over this issue and the Centre Union would thus cease to be a factor of any significance in the political scene for some time to come.

Paul, to whom Pipinelis confided these thoughts, was frankly shocked. Having no political axe to grind himself he could find no joy in the prospect of the disintegration of one of the two major political forces in the country and its fragmentation into a state of frustrated impotence that would enable the thinly disguised Communist E.D.A. to arrogate to itself the role of His Majesty's principal parliamentary opposition.

On 26 September the King summoned Pipinelis and handed him the Royal Decree dissolving Parliament and ordering elections for

3 November 1963. Next day he accepted Pipinelis's resignation and invited Mr Stelio Mavromichales, President of the Supreme Court, to form a non-party caretaker administration to organize the election.

Papandreou immediately sent an enthusiastic message to the King. The country was now back on the road of normality, he said, and the Centre Union would take part in the elections.

On the same day Karamanlis returned to Athens and resumed the leadership of the E.R.E. party for the forthcoming battle at the polls.

The results of the general elections of 3 November 1963, though inconclusive, showed a clear swing to the Centre Union which emerged as the largest party with 138 out of the 300 seats in the Chamber. E.R.E. came next with 132 and then the pro-Communist E.D.A. with 28 seats, four more than it had held in the previous Parliament. The Progressives were annihilated, losing 14 out of their 16 seats, including that of their leader Spyros Markezinis.

His task completed, the caretaker Premier Mr Mavromichales duly resigned. Meanwhile Paul received Papandreou, who asserted his claim to the premiership as leader of the largest party in Parliament. Karamanlis, whom the King saw next, was very pessimistic: the indecisive nature of the election results had greatly complicated the situation, he warned, and those who were trying to over-simplify it were the victims of miscalculations.

If Paul had any hopes that the two major national parties might cooperate in a coalition government, they were dispelled after his interviews with the two leaders. On 6 November he asked Papandreou to form a government, which was sworn in two days later.

His self-confidence restored now that the premiership was finally his, Papandreou announced that he did not intend to seek cooperation or support from any quarter but would only accept the adherence of individual Deputies who defected from their own party; he felt sure, he predicted, that a sufficient number would do so by the time he faced Parliament the following month.

He was wrong. When the roll was called on 24 December at the end of a four-day debate, E.R.E. voted solidly against. Papandreou still had a majority, but the 167 Deputies who supported him consisted of his own party and E.D.A.: if he chose to remain in power now, he could only do so by the grace of the Communists.

Less than eight weeks after becoming Premier, Papandreou

resigned. After ascertaining that the existing Chamber was incapable of providing an alternative government, the King dissolved Parliament and ordered new elections for 16 February 1964 after appointing a caretaker government under Mr John Paraskevopoulos, a veteran banker.

Meanwhile, a dramatic event had intervened: on 9 December Constantine Karamanlis announced that he was retiring from politics. Long before the elections, he said, he had made the decision to put an end to his political career if he found it impossible to put his programme for a radical reform of Greek political life into effect; he also felt that his withdrawal from the political scene at that particular moment might facilitate a way out of the deadlock.

While a startled Greek public was still reading this announcement Karamanlis boarded an aeroplane with his wife and left for Paris on an 'extended visit'. Seven years later he had still not returned.*

* From its independence in 1821 to the resignation of the Karamanlis Government in 1963, Greece had 171 governments in all under seventy-eight different Prime Ministers. Eleftherios Venizelos served as Premier intermittently for a total of over twelve years but Constantine Karamanlis holds the record for the longest unbroken spell of nearly eight years, allowing for two election 'caretaker' governments. The shortest premiership of all was that of Anastasios Charalambis who was appointed on 16 September 1922 and resigned the following day.

⇒ 42 ⇐

Towards the end of 1963 Paul complained of pains in his leg. The Queen was in Madrid at the time for the birth of her daughter Sophie's first child, and during one of his frequent telephone calls the King had mentioned he was feeling rather depressed, for no particular reason; also his leg hurt when he moved it. The Royal Family's physician, Dr Thomas Doxiadis, who was also in Madrid, had a word with the King on the telephone and advised him to be careful not to take more antibiotics than were actually prescribed – a thing he was sometimes inclined to do – as this could be the cause of his depression.

Two days before Christmas the Queen returned from Spain – her first grandchild Princess Elena having been born in the meantime – and Doxiadis immediately went to Tatoi. He found that in addition to a bad attack of influenza the King had a painful swelling of the veins of the right leg. Next day he examined the King again, this time with Alexander Manos, head surgeon at the Evangelismos Hospital. Strong anti-rheumatic drugs were prescribed: the pain and the swelling subsided, but similar symptoms now began to appear in the other leg.

All this time the King had been carrying on with his normal routine. On New Year's Eve he went with his family as usual to the party which Dimitri Levidis, Grand Marshal of the Court, gave every year at his hill-top house at Pallini, near Athens, but he did not feel very well and left soon after midnight.*

Frederica had a long-standing engagement in the United States to receive an honorary degree from Columbia University, but now

---

* It was Levidis's last party. He died a few days later at the age of seventy-three having served three Kings in exile and in Greece and having been rewarded for his faithful services with the Grand Cross of the Order of the Redeemer a few months before his death.

she was in two minds about going. Doxiadis, however, insisted that no useful purpose would be served by her remaining in Athens, so with her daughter Irene she left by air for Paris on 15 January *en route* for New York.

As soon as she arrived in Paris she telephoned Athens. The King sounded quite cheerful and passed off his 'creaky old bones' as nothing to worry about, so on 16 January the Queen sailed from Le Havre for New York.

The same day at Tatoi the King was put through a medical check-up by Doxiadis, Manos and an orthopaedic specialist, the spine and pelvis being X-rayed with portable apparatus brought from the hospital. The photographs showed some minor displacement of the lower vertebrae of the spine which could reasonably be assumed to be the cause of the pain in the leg, and the mattress on the King's bed was replaced by a flat wooden board on which he was obliged to lie for the next few days.

By this time the doctors were becoming suspicious as to the root cause of the trouble, and a thorough radiological examination was begun. To avoid speculation in the press, which had so far merely reported that the King was suffering from a bout of lumbago, Paul was taken to Evangelismos Hospital in an ambulance late at night – in the middle of a sudden snowstorm, a rare phenomenon in Athens which lies inside the horseshoe of the plain of Attica sheltered on three sides by mountains and facing the sea on the other. Cortisone was being prescribed at this stage to ease the pain, but although this had the desired effect the King now began to complain of pains in his stomach.

Meanwhile the Queen had arrived in the United States. Not to be outdone by London, some left-wing groups in New York had called out their members to demonstrate at the docks and seven pickets – six men and one woman – carrying a banner, FASCIST GO HOME – PLENTY HERE WITHOUT YOU, took up positions half an hour before the ship was due to dock. They had not reckoned with the elements, however. For some days past Manhattan Island had been in the grip of arctic weather. Huge slabs of ice were floating about in the dock basin, and as the liner moved slowly sideways towards Pier 86 on the Hudson River, the captive ice piled up higher and higher between the ship and the pier until a massive jagged wall of it prevented the ship from coming any closer. The gangway could not stretch out far enough from the pier to the ship, so hot steam was blown on to the ice to melt it. Inch by inch the ship edged closer until at last a gangway could bridge the gulf. Over a hundred reporters, photographers and television cameramen who had been waiting impatiently on the quayside all this time swarmed on board, and for the next hour the Queen sat in the ship's saloon answering questions fired at her from all directions while bulbs flashed and photographers begged her to 'look this way, Your Queenship' and 'smile, baby, smile'. These unscheduled delays had been a little too much for the shivering demonstrators waiting on shore, however, and long before the Queen disembarked they had packed up and gone home.

The next day was the seventy-fifth anniversary of the foundation of Barnard, the women's undergraduate college of Columbia University, and this was the occasion chosen to confer a degree of Doctor of Laws on Queen Frederica. Some Columbia students had already announced that they were going to stage a 'silent demonstration' in protest against 'the oppressive nature of the Greek regime', and about two dozen of them duly appeared; but when the Queen drove across the campus to the steps of the Low Memorial Library where the reception committee was waiting, the only demonstrators to be seen were some Greek students carrying banners of WELCOME YOUR MAJESTY TO THE HEARTH OF CIVILIZATION. The hostile pickets had apparently gone to the wrong place on the other side of the campus, at 116th Street and Broadway, where after waiting in vain for someone to demonstrate against they had folded up their banners and called it a day.*

Later that evening Frederica felt like talking to her husband. Her lady-in-waiting had gone to bed, so she picked up the telephone herself and asked to be put through to Athens.

'Athens Georgia or Athens Ohio?' the night telephonist wanted to know.

'Athens Greece.'

'But that's in Europe. I'll give you international.'

A new voice came on the line, and Frederica again asked to be put through to Athens Greece. 'And I want to speak to the King,' she added.

---

* A Greek journalist pointed out to one of the pickets that the Greek slogan he was carrying was upside down. 'Look, bud, I get a dollar fifty an hour to carry this thing, not to read it,' was the reply.

'Which King?'

'There's only one King in Athens Greece, and his name is Paul. I would like to speak to him personally please.'

'Who is calling?'

'The Queen. The Queen of the Hellenes.'

'That's a ship, isn't it?'

On 2 February the Crown Prince telephoned his mother in New York. It was a Sunday, and the Queen had invited a number of people to lunch in her suite at the Waldorf Towers. The call from Athens came through just as they were about to sit down, and the Queen excused herself to take the call from her bedroom. She was away for over half an hour, and as soon as lunch was over and the guests had all gone she announced that she was returning to Athens immediately. She volunteered no explanation for this sudden change of plan and it was generally assumed that the Cyprus crisis, which had been building up all that week bringing Greece and Turkey to the verge of open hostilities, had made her immediate return to Athens advisable.

In actual fact the Crown Prince had chatted to his mother about various family matters and then suddenly, in the middle of conversation, he had said to the Queen: 'Mama, why don't you come home right away? Papa is getting bored with us children's conversation.' It was enough. The Queen knew her family well enough to sense that her son would not have dropped a hint like that unless there was good reason for it, especially as she was due back in four days' time anyhow.

What the Crown Prince had not told his mother was that on 31 January, after a radiological investigation of the King's lungs, spine and other areas had proved negative, X-rays of the stomach had revealed definite signs of cancer.

The King was still up and about at Tatoi, though in constant pain. The two doctors, Doxiadis and Manos, had a discussion with the Crown Prince as to what should now be done. One suggestion was that the King should be flown to the United States while the Queen was still there; he could then have more tests and if an operation were necessary he could have it there. But it was felt that such a journey at such short notice would make the King suspicious – he was not told, either at this stage or indeed at any time during his illness, that he was suffering from cancer, though it is virtually certain he guessed before the end; he had a habit of weighing himself first thing every morning and must have noticed that for some time he had been steadily losing weight for no apparent reason, and he knew enough about cancer to recognize this sign of the disease.

It was at this stage that the Crown Prince telephoned New York, and as the Queen had intimated that she was coming home at once it was decided to wait until she returned. Meanwhile, Manos flew secretly to London with the X-rays to consult two eminent specialists, Sir Stanford Cade of Westminster Hospital and Mr Edward Muir, Surgeon to the British Royal Family.

The Queen arrived in Athens on Monday morning, 3 February, and was met at the airport by the Crown Prince. In the car as they drove out to Tatoi she suddenly turned to him and said in anguish: 'Papa mustn't die! He mustn't die!' The Crown Prince was completely taken aback. 'Of course he won't die. Why should he?' But she was not listening. At Tatoi the car went past the saluting Evzone sentry in his dark-blue winter cape and wound along the drive under the snow-covered pine trees to the front of the house where the King stood waiting at the door to welcome his wife back home.

After dinner that evening the family saw a film in the small private cinema in the basement, after which the King went to bed. Climbing the stairs was too much of an effort for him now – there is no lift at Tatoi – and for some days he had been sleeping in the ground-floor study he normally used for his afternoon nap. The Queen then sent for Manos and Doxiadis, who was now living-in at Tatoi, and heard from them for the first time what she had already suspected from her son's telephone call.

The King had to have an operation urgently, but where? There was a man in Sweden who had developed a new surgical technique; a clinic in Switzerland had a reputation for remarkable results with radiotherapy; in England and in Germany there were several eminent specialists of international repute. But taking the King abroad would make the nature of his illness obvious both to himself and to the public, with incalculable effects on the political mood of the country, now in the throes of the election campaign. Suggestions that specialists should be summoned from abroad and that more Greek doctors should be called in were also abandoned when the Queen asked bluntly if that would be of any practical use and Doxiadis was obliged to admit that it could make very little difference one way or the other.

The Queen turned to Manos: 'Can you operate here at Tatoi?' He looked up in surprise. 'Am I to do it, then? Don't you want to ask one of the English specialists?' The Queen was quite emphatic. 'This is a very serious operation – as I understand it, my husband may not live through it. You are a Greek. I know you love my husband; you have always been our surgeon; we have complete confidence in you and I know you will do your best. I want you to do it because my husband trusts you and because you will do it with love and not just as a doctor.'

But could the operation be performed at Tatoi, where there would be privacy and the King would be among the familiar surroundings he loved so much? Manos said that all the necessary arrangements could certainly be made at Tatoi – in fact, he would prefer it to the hospital.

The Queen then took it on herself to prepare the King psychologically. She told him that the doctors had located a scar in his stomach from an old ulcer and that the strong drugs he had been taking for his lumbago had aggravated the lesion, which now had to be removed. She showed him the fatal X-rays and pointed out the ominous shadow of the 'scar'. She even made a drawing of the stomach on a piece of paper and explained to him where the surgeon would make the incision and how he would remove that part there, and then stitch the two ends together here and here, and how in time the stomach would expand and be able to function again quite normally.

The elections were scheduled for 16 February – elections in Greece are always held on a Sunday – and naturally the operation could not take place before then. Meanwhile, the King was being given massive doses of cortisone to relieve the pain, and medical bulletins issued to the press spoke of 'a steady improvement' in his condition.

On 13 February Paul said he felt well enough to go for a drive. They all got into the car, the Queen and Princess Irene in the back and the Crown Prince in the driver's seat, but the King motioned his son to move over and took the wheel himself. A broad smile spread over his face as he pressed the starter and the big car moved slowly down the drive and out on to the road through the forest. Since childhood driving a car had been one of the great joys of his life and he had never grown out of it. He had learned all he knew about cars from his brother Alexander, who had taught him to drive at the age of fourteen in a weird vehicle that had only two seats, one behind the other just like the cockpit of an aeroplane. Paul would sit in front with Alexander behind holding a stick which he would bring down across his brother's shoulders with a whack whenever the pupil did something wrong. When the children were still young Paul would always drive his family himself on their vacations in Europe, but when his son was old enough to have his own car the family would travel in two vehicles, changing places from one car to the other on the road and talking to each other over the radio telephone. Paul had always enjoyed driving fast, and even today, as soon as the car had left the winding country road through the Tatoi estate, he pressed his foot on the accelerator and the car roared down the fine arterial road towards Athens. Just before the road enters the centre of the city he forked left past the marble Olympic Stadium and into the dead-straight Syngros Avenue to the sea, turning right at the bottom and heading for the hump of the Kastella along the wide sweep of Phaleron Bay. Soon he was on the narrow road overlooking the yacht harbour at Tourkolimano. He stopped the car and they all gazed down at the anchorage below with the white schooners and the powerful cabin cruisers riding at anchor and the racing yachts under their canvas shrouds resting on their cradles in front of the boathouses. This was where he used to come early in the morning on those lovely hot summer days, barefoot and stripped to the waist, sailing out into the bay in his Dragon, sometimes alone, sometimes with his wife crewing for him, more recently with every member of his family each in their own racers, his son in the craft that had won him his Olympic gold medal. A wave of nostalgia, a premonition of doom, came over them all. The Crown Prince took the wheel and they drove back home.

On Sunday, 16 February 1964, four and a half million Greek men and women went to the polling booths and cast their votes for the second time in fifteen weeks. By Monday morning it was clear that Papandreou had won a landslide victory. The caretaker Premier went to Tatoi at noon on Monday to report the election results to the King – Centre Union 174, E.R.E. 104, E.D.A. 22 – and to submit his resignation. The King immediately entrusted the mandate to the seventy-six-year-old leader of the victorious party.

Papandreou had been expecting this summons and had his list of ministers ready by Tuesday morning; but since that Tuesday in 1453 when Constantinople fell to the Turks and the Byzantine Empire disappeared from the face of the earth, no Greek will ever undertake anything of importance on a Tuesday if he can possibly help it. He will not marry, he will not baptize his children, he will not launch a ship on a Tuesday; and no Greek politician would dream of tempting providence by taking the oath of office on a Tuesday. So it was not until Wednesday that George Papandreou and his Cabinet, in frock coats and top hats, arrived at Tatoi to receive from the King's own hands their formal appointment as His Majesty's Government.

The King had always attached particular importance to the ceremony of swearing in a new Government. He felt that this was the summit of every politician's career and that it was only right and proper that it should be accorded the significance which the occasion merited. He invariably insisted on strict observance of the prescribed ceremonial, and this was going to be no exception even though because of his illness the ritual was taking place at Tatoi and not in the throne room at the Palace at Athens.

The new Premier and his Ministers were shown into the drawing-room, and a few minutes before the appointed time the King came into the adjoining room where all his family were assembled. He was in the full-dress uniform of a Field-Marshal of the Greek Army – a rank traditionally held by the Sovereign alone – the high gold-encrusted collar thrusting up his chin, the glittering epaulettes making his broad shoulders even broader, the jewelled stars of the four Greek Orders on his left breast, the oval commemorative medallion he had himself designed for the centenary of his Dynasty on his right breast, the Chain of the Family Order of St George and St Constantine round his neck. He had always been a fine figure of a man, with his great height and powerful build, and today he looked truly magnificent. There was about him an air of quiet dignity, of rigid devotion to duty, that made everybody in the room stand up in silence; only the grim look of suppressed pain on his face gave an atmosphere of tragedy to the scene. He walked with difficulty. His son went up to him and put his arm round his waist to support him, but the King gently disengaged himself, placed his hand instead on his son's shoulder and walked leaning on him to the door. He nodded to the footman to open the door and then pushed his son firmly away: this was the King's task, his alone. He drew himself up and walked briskly into the room where the Ministers were waiting.

The oath was administered by the aged Archbishop, and the Premier made a short speech thanking the King for his confidence and wishing him a speedy recovery. All this time the King was on his feet leaning against the piano, his hands behind his back gripping the top. Now he moved away from his support and walked round the room, greeting each Minister in turn and congratulating him on his appointment. Champagne was brought in and the King drank the health of his new Government, and the new Government drank the health of the King. Then he moved towards the door. 'If you need me, you know where to find me,' he said looking back, smiling and nodding gently. He opened the door and went through to the next room. He had performed the role his position demanded of him, he had discharged his duty this last time as he had done all his life. Now his huge arms slumped heavily round the shoulders of his son on one side and his wife on the other. Slowly, painfully, they half-carried him to bed.

He never walked again.

That evening an official announcement was issued saying that the King's lumbago had subsided but X-rays and laboratory tests had revealed an inflammation of an old ulcer in the stomach. The King had expressed the wish, the announcement continued, that this should not be made public in order not to cause alarm, but pathological treatment had not eliminated the trouble and other steps, i.e. surgery, were now being considered. Until that moment nobody outside the King's immediate entourage had been told the details of his illness; even among the family only the Queen and the Crown Prince knew all there was to know. Rumours had been circulating, of course, and the day before the elections the 'caretaker' Premier had found it necessary to issue a reassuring statement denying that the King was gravely ill but was simply suffering from 'an attack of lumbago, from which he was on the road to recovery'. The Prime Minister was telling the truth as he knew it, and he had considered it his duty to issue the denial because any uncertainty concerning the King's health – completely unjustified, as he honestly believed –

would have injected an element of anxiety and doubt into the atmosphere of the impending elections. Only twelve days earlier Sophocles Venizelos, the Liberal leader who had for many years exerted a sobering influence on the more obstreperous elements of the Centre, had died of heart failure on board ship on his way to Athens after addressing a political meeting in his native Crete. Coming on top of this, and with the electoral tempo rising to fever pitch as polling day approached, any possibility of the King's death would have meant the removal from the scene of what to many people constituted the sole symbol of stability and the natural rallying point of nationalist sentiment. Another possible repercussion might well have been the postponement of the elections, which at that particular moment would have been regarded as a 'political act' in view of the special circumstances that had led up to the elections. After the polling had finished and a new Government had been sworn in, it was a different matter. Now there was an elected Head of Government, and the Crown Prince lost no time in informing Papandreou of the King's true condition.

All this time the press had been clamouring for news, and criticism of the Government and the Palace for not giving out sufficient information had been mounting. Outside Tatoi a small army of reporters had gathered at Varibobi, a popular resort to which the Athenians flock for dinner in the summer evenings when the heat in the capital becomes too oppressive. All the open-air restaurants and clubs were closed for the winter now and the whole district was completely deserted, with several inches of snow on the ground and the temperature below freezing point. Only one roadside café remained open and there the newspapermen had encamped, to the delight of the proprietor who suddenly found himself inundated with unexpected customers. To avoid undue hardship the reporters had worked out a rota system: look-outs were posted along the road about two hundred yards in each direction so that any car coming from Athens towards Tatoi or leaving Tatoi for Athens could be spotted in time for a signal to be transmitted to the café. The others would then rush out and stand in the middle of the road, forcing the car to a standstill. Anybody entering or leaving the royal estate would thus find himself besieged by a swarm of pleading news-hungry newsmen who would then rush back to the café and scramble for the one and only telephone, usually to report that there was no further news.

On 20 February the King signed a decree appointing his son Regent for the duration of his incapacitation through illness. On the same day the two British specialists arrived from London. After examining the patient and conferring with their Greek colleagues they agreed that an immediate operation was advisable.

A room at Tatoi had already been turned into an operating theatre; all the necessary equipment had been brought from the Evangelismos Hospital and had been installed under Manos's personal supervision.

The whole of Thursday the King lay resting before the operation. The Queen sat with him all day and through the night. He dozed for short periods but did not seem able to sleep properly, so the Queen put on some records of the *Messiah*. Some of the choruses he asked for again, and when the nurse entered the room next morning they were still listening to the music, holding hands. The anaesthetist gave the injection and the King drifted into unconsciousness as the 'Hallelujah' filled the room.

The operation took nearly five hours and was performed by Manos, with the two British specialists and the other Greek doctors in attendance. When the cavity of the stomach was exposed it was seen that the infection had spread profusely over most of the surface, but after consultation it was decided to proceed with the operation. An extensive gastrectomy was made, nearly three-quarters of the stomach being removed and a new opening made from the stomach to the bowel below. The growth cut away was the main area affected, but patches of infection were clearly visible in the remaining part of the stomach. During the operation a blood transfusion became necessary and plasma already donated by the King's two daughters – both of the same blood group as himself – was given.

The bulletin issued after the operation was signed by all five doctors present and said simply that the King had undergone an operation 'for stomach ulcers', which was true as far as it went. A second bulletin issued later that night said that the King's post-operational condition was satisfactory and his temperature and pulse were normal, all of which was perfectly true.

When the King came round from the anaesthetic his family were by his bed. He motioned them to come closer and kissed them all one after the other. Then he dropped off to sleep again.

The critical forty-eight hours after the operation passed and the patient's condition steadily improved. He could now take liquid food, sit up in bed and read the newspapers.*

Meanwhile the Queen fell ill herself. Since some days before the operation she had not moved from the King's side, giving him his drugs, feeding him, making conversation, playing records of his favourite music. All night long she would sit in an armchair near him, arranging his pillows and straightening the bedclothes whenever he stirred. Sooner or later the strain was bound to tell. She began to feel feverish. Thinking she was sickening for a cold – an influenza epidemic was sweeping Athens at the time – she dosed herself with aspirin and told nobody, but her temperature still went up and she began to have fits of shivering. She confessed to Doxiadis, who found she had pneumonia and ordered her to bed. She refused to go, so he gave her a big dose of antibiotics, but she still did not seem to respond; so he examined her again more thoroughly and discovered that she was also suffering from a kidney complaint. By this time she was frantic with anxiety and semi-delirious with pain, and it was only when Doxiadis had a brainwave and protested that her coughing was disturbing the King that she agreed to go to her own room. It was the only night she spent away from her husband the whole of that fortnight. Next day she was back at his side, which she never left again.

The King could now get up for short periods and sit in an armchair listening to gramophone records. He began to shave himself again instead of letting his valet, Thomas, do it for him. His daughter Sophie had arrived from Spain with her family and the King would often ask for his granddaughter, now three months old, to be brought to him. She would sit gurgling in his lap in the armchair, or when he was in bed she would sprawl across his vast chest playing with the three little gold crosses he always wore on a chain round his neck.

Hopes began to rise. After all, there are hundreds of people with cancer leading more or less normal lives as useful members of society despite the knowledge that their days are literally numbered: Foster Dulles carried on as Secretary of State for years after revealing he had cancer. Tentative plans began to be discussed about a

* One of the reasons why the medical bulletins consistently referred to 'stomach ulcers' and nothing more was the fear that the King might learn the truth from the papers, of which he had always been an avid reader. When the press mentioned that the two visiting British doctors were cancer specialists, the Queen saw to it that the newspapers conveniently disappeared at Tatoi that day.

period of convalescence abroad, with the Crown Prince carrying on as Regent in the meantime.

Even the weather changed. A bright spring sunshine now spread over the plain of Attica and the last snows of winter melted away.

On Sunday afternoon, 1 March, as he was sitting up in bed reading a letter, the King suddenly gave a gasp of pain and fell back. Frederica, who had been sitting on the bed by his pillow, threw herself behind him to break his fall and cushioned his back with her body while the hurriedly summoned doctors applied emergency treatment. When she tried to release herself after a while the grimace of pain on Paul's face made her keep absolutely still. She stayed like that until the King could be eased back into the bed without risk. By that time she had been lying in the same position for nearly six hours, unable to move and with the full weight of the King's body on top of her. Semi-conscious, rigid with cramp and her legs swollen grotesquely, she had to be carried out. An hour later she was back by her husband's bedside.*

The King had suffered a pulmonary embolism, a blood clot in the left lung. As he lay in agony the Crown Prince whispered in his ear: 'Papa, every Greek is thinking of you with love and hope.' His father smiled: 'To be the object of love like that ... It is wonderful!' The words came painfully. 'Tell them I thank them. Tell them Goodbye from me.'

Nearly fifty years before, when the King's father King Constantine lay gravely ill with typhoid, the Ikon of Tinos had been brought to his bedside. Constantine, to whom the last rites had actually been administered, had just enough strength to kiss the ikon before losing consciousness. A few hours later he woke up feeling better, and within a week he had fully recovered.

This Ikon of 'the Holy, the Merciful, the Joy-bringing Virgin' was discovered in 1822 by a humble village priest who was told in a dream to dig at a certain spot in the island of Tinos. It has always been credited with miraculous powers, and every year on the Feast

---

* It may be recalled that a very similar incident occurred when Queen Victoria lay dying at Osborne in 1901, the same year that Paul was born. The Kaiser (Frederica's grandfather) was among those present in the room. 'Victoria's doctor, assisted by the Kaiser, supported her on her pillow, one on each side. Not until she died two and a half hours later did the Kaiser withdraw his arm; nor could he ease the strain by changing sides with the doctor, for his left arm was withered.'[32]

of the Assumption on 15 August thousands of pilgrims go to Tinos where the ikon is kept in a church built over the spot where it was found and where on that day it is taken in procession through the streets. Sick people who have despaired of a medical cure lie on the ground along the processional route so that the healing shadow of the Virgin may pass over them, and the precious offerings festooned round the ikon, including a magnificent sapphire given by Constantine's wife, are palpable evidence of the gratitude of those whose faith in its healing powers had brought them relief.*

The custodian of the ikon now offered to send it 'to visit and cure the ailing King' – since that day in 1915 when it was taken to another ailing King it had never left the island of Tinos – and the fast destroyer *Sfendoni* was immediately despatched to fetch it. The octogenarian Primate of All Greece, surrounded by the Metropolitans of the Holy Synod in their crowns and vestments, stood at the quayside at Piraeus to receive the sacred picture. Near them in sombre black stood the Cabinet. Just as the destroyer was drawing alongside shortly after midnight the Crown Prince arrived alone, driving his own car; he went on board at once and was taken straight to the cabin where the ikon had been placed. He crossed himself and kissed the glass-covered picture, then took it firmly in both hands and walked with it down the gangway while a guard of honour paraded on deck. At the foot of the gangway the Prince transferred the ikon gingerly into the old Archbishop's trembling hands. Then the Metropolitans and the Ministers began to file past the Primate who held up the ikon for them to kiss. But the ceremonial was dragging on too long for the impatient young man whose father lay dying twenty miles away. With a respectful word of apology to the white-bearded prelate, he snatched the ikon from his hands, walked quickly with it to his car and roared off to Tatoi, where he took it straight into his father's room.

The King raised himself up in bed, made the sign of the cross three times and reverently kissed the ikon. The Prince held up the ikon for all present to come forward and kiss and then placed it on a table where a kandili, its flickering wick floating in oil, was already burning.

* It was on such a day in 1940 that Mussolini sent one of his submarines to sink a Greek warship lying at anchor in the harbour of Tinos at a time when Greece and Italy were still at peace, and there are many people in Greece today who will tell you that Mussolini's shattering defeat at the hands of the Greek Army not long afterwards was merely another token of the powers of the miraculous ikon.

The whole of Wednesday afternoon and late into the evening Paul and Frederica listened in silence to 'St Matthew's Passion'. He scarcely slept during the night, and when Thursday dawned he was wide awake. Later that day Father Ieronymos, the Chaplain, entered the room with the Sacraments. 'Kali Ygeia,' he said. The King laughed. 'Health! That doesn't come into it any more.' He closed his eyes while the Chaplain murmured absolution, then took Holy Communion with his whole family.

The Crown Prince and his two sisters were standing silently by the bed. Frederica had cradled the King's head on her breast, her arms around him holding him close to her. He looked up at her and smiled.

'A thousand thanks for everything,' he said.

'I thank you for having chosen me,' she said, humbly.

There was absolute stillness in the room in the presence of God.

Genealogical Table

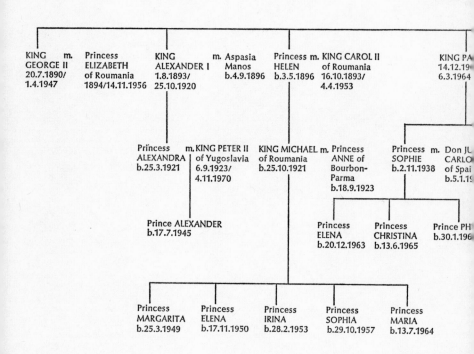

KING GEORGE I
24.12.1845/18.3.191.

KING CONSTANTIN
21.7.1868/11.1.1923

KING m. GEORGE II 20.7.1890/ 1.4.1947	Princess ELIZABETH of Roumania 1894/14.11.1956	KING ALEXANDER I 1.8.1893/ 25.10.1920	m. Aspasia Manos b.4.9.1896	Princess m. HELEN b.3.5.1896	KING CAROL II of Roumania 16.10.1893/ 4.4.1953	KING PA 14.12.19 6.3.1964

Princess m. KING PETER II
ALEXANDRA of Yugoslavia
b.25.3.1921 6.9.1923/
4.11.1970

KING MICHAEL m. Princess
of Roumania ANNE of
b.25.10.1921 Bourbon-
Parma
b.18.9.1923

Princess m. Don JU
SOPHIE CARLO
b.2.11.1938 of Spai
b.5.1.19

Prince ALEXANDER
b.17.7.1945

Princess
ELENA
b.20.12.1963

Princess
CHRISTINA
b.13.6.1965

Prince PH
b.30.1.196

Princess MARGARITA b.25.3.1949	Princess ELENA b.17.11.1950	Princess IRINA b.28.2.1953	Princess SOPHIA b.29.10.1957	Princess MARIA b.13.7.1964

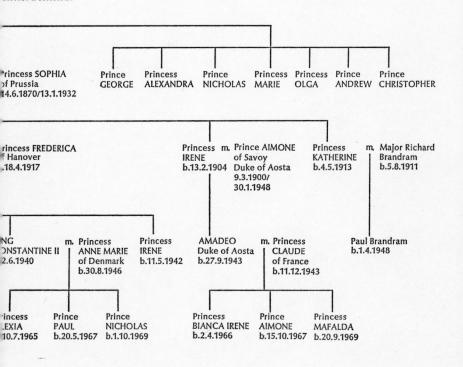

Grand Duchess
OLGA of Russia
3.9.1851/18.6.1926

Princess SOPHIA
of Prussia
14.6.1870/13.1.1932

Prince
GEORGE

Princess
ALEXANDRA

Prince
NICHOLAS

Princess
MARIE

Princess
OLGA

Prince
ANDREW

Prince
CHRISTOPHER

Princess FREDERICA
of Hanover
b.18.4.1917

Princess
IRENE
b.13.2.1904

m. Prince AIMONE
of Savoy
Duke of Aosta
9.3.1900/
30.1.1948

Princess
KATHERINE
b.4.5.1913

m. Major Richard
Brandram
b.5.8.1911

KING
CONSTANTINE II
b.2.6.1940

m. Princess
ANNE MARIE
of Denmark
b.30.8.1946

Princess
IRENE
b.11.5.1942

AMADEO
Duke of Aosta
b.27.9.1943

m. Princess
CLAUDE
of France
b.11.12.1943

Paul Brandram
b.1.4.1948

Princess
ALEXIA
b.10.7.1965

Prince
PAUL
b.20.5.1967

Prince
NICHOLAS
b.1.10.1969

Princess
BIANCA IRENE
b.2.4.1966

Prince
AIMONE
b.15.10.1967

Princess
MAFALDA
b.20.9.1969

Bibliographical Notes

1 During the years between her marriage in 1889 and her mother's death in 1901 Sophie received from the Empress Frederick over two thousand letters, totalling about a million words. They were edited by Arthur A. Gould Lee under the title *The Empress Frederick Writes to Sophie*, London, 1955.
2 Published by The Right Book Club, London, 1938.
3 Captain Walter Christmas, *The Life of King George I of Greece*, London, 1914.
4 *The World Crisis – The Aftermath*, London, 1929.
5 Harold Nicolson, *Curzon: the Last Phase*, London, 1934.
6 Published by Ikaros, Athens, 1964.
7 Edited by Demetrius Caclamanos, Oxford, 1937. Venizelos's voluminous notes and annotations, consisting of historical, geographical, and etymological comments on the original, taking up eleven hand-written volumes, remain unpublished.
8 Sir Reginald Leeper (British Ambassador to Greece, 1943–6), *When Greek Meets Greek*, London, 1950.
9 *Ciano's Diary*, edited by Malcolm Muggeridge, London, 1947.
10 General A. Papagos, *The Battle of Greece*, Athens, 1949.
11 Winston S. Churchill, *The Second World War*, vol. II.
12 Anthony Eden, *The Eden Memoirs: The Reckoning*, London, 1965.
13 Sir Reginald Leeper, op. cit.
14 ibid.
15 ibid.
16 ibid.
17 ibid., p. 72.
18 Harold Macmillan, *The Blast of War*, London, 1967.
19 ibid.
20 Anthony Eden, op. cit., p. 500.
21 Harold Macmillan, op. cit., p. 612.
22 Winston S. Churchill, *The Second World War*.
23 Report of the British Parliamentary Delegation which visited Greece in August 1946.

24 Anthony Eden, *Full Circle*, London, 1960.
25 ibid., p. 400.
26 Harold Macmillan, *The Tides of Fortune*, London, 1969.
27 Anthony Eden, *Full Circle*, pp. 400–401.
28 *Evening Standard*, 11 September 1958.
29 *Sunday Express*, 5 October 1958.
30 *Daily Telegraph*, 19 September 1956.
31 The essential details as set out here were disclosed by Mr Averoff himself in a letter published in the newspaper *Eleftheros Kosmos* on 6 September 1969.
32 Elizabeth Longford, *Victoria R.I.*, London, 1964.

Index

Index

EOKA, 269, 272, 281–2, 302, 304, 310
E.O.N., 81–3, 107
EPEK, 219, 221, 223, 227–8, 238, 240–1, 244, 253, 257
Erbach, Prince, 117, 119
E.R.E., 280, 298–9, 306, 309, 318, 328–9, 337–9, 344, 346, 354
Ernst Augustus, 1st Duke of Cumberland, King of Hanover, 90
Ernest August, 3rd Duke of Cumberland, 10, 90, 91
Ernst August, 4th Duke of Cumberland, Duke of Brunswick (father of Queen Frederica), 90–1, 93, 96, 100, 117–8, 210, 259
Evening Standard, 370

Farida, Queen of Egypt, 127
Farouk, King of Egypt, 127–30, 252
Fleet, General James van, 199, 225
Foot, Sir Hugh, 293
'Fourth of August', 77–82, 103, 113
Francoise, Princess (wife of Prince Christopher), 57
Frederica, Queen of the Hellenes (wife of King Paul). Ancestry and family background, 89–91; early years, 91–2; engagement and marriage to Paul, 94–101; organises comforts for Greek troops, 116–7; evacuated to Crete and Egypt, 122–7; incident with King Farouk, 127–8; refugee in South Africa, 130; friendship with General Smuts, 135–6, 144; moves to Egypt, 149; return to Greece, 177–9; launches Northern Provinces Welfare Fund, 181; meeting with General Marshall, 189–92; visits beleaguered Konitsa, 192–3; awarded Greek Military Cross, 193; establishes children's refugee settlements, 197–198; interest in nuclear physics, 210; appeals for abducted children, 223–5; writes to Churchill on Cyprus question, 266–7; incident with Mrs Ambatielos in London, 329–33; visit to U.S.A. to receive

Columbia University Degree, 348–351; at husband's bedside during his last moments, 352–62
Frederick III, Emperor of Germany, 18, 68
Frederick VII, King of Denmark, 10, 11
Frederick VIII, King of Denmark, 10, 18, 91
Frederick the Great, 33
Frefrada (yacht), 62–7
Freyburg, General Lord, 123

Gaitskell, Hugh, 282
Gasperi, Alcide de, 259
Gaulle, General Charles de, 335
Georgacopoulos, Constantine, 299
George V, King of England, 28, 30, 33, 52
George VI, King of England, 83, 131, 246, 261
George v, King of Hanover, 2nd Duke of Cumberland, 90
George I, King of the Hellenes, 9–19, 21, 25–6, 32, 35, 40, 43, 55, 90, 93, 129, 130, 243–4, 259, 283–4, 313, 315, 326
George II, King of the Hellenes, 18, 20, 33, 35, 40, 42–5, 51–6, 58–9, 61, 68, 72–4, 76–80, 82, 93–107, 112–4, 116, 118–23, 127–31, 135–53, 156–164, 166–73, 177–81, 183–6, 195, 284, 297, 299, 311–2, 321, 326, 338
George, Prince (son of King George I), 15, 19, 23, 32, 57, 244
George, Prince of Hanover (brother of Queen Frederica), 216
Gonatas, General Stylianos, 51, 53–4, 205
Gounaris, D., 52, 137
Grady, Henry, 222, 229
Grazzi, Signor, 114
Greek Rally, 239–41, 243, 246, 253–8, 270, 275, 277–80
Gregory v, Oecumenical Patriarch, 3
Grivas, General George, 270, 310–1
Guelph, House of, 89–91

371

Index

373

Index

374